Mathematical applications
in accounting

John M Ferran
477-4607

D1575216

Fundamentals of OPERATIONS RESEARCH

Fundamentals of
OPERATIONS RESEARCH

RUSSELL L. ACKOFF
Professor, Statistics and Operations Research
University of Pennsylvania

MAURICE W. SASIENI
Marketing Division
Unilever Ltd.
London

JOHN WILEY & SONS, INC., NEW YORK · LONDON · SYDNEY

Copyright © 1968 by John Wiley & Sons, Inc.

All Rights Reserved
This book or any part thereof must not
be reproduced in any form without the
written permission of the publisher.

Library of Congress Catalog Card Number: 67-27271
Printed in the United States of America

To WILLIS J. WINN *from R. L. A.*

To the late FRANK SOUTHAM *from M. W. S.*

Preface

The activity called *Operations Research* (OR) developed during World War II, but its origins can be traced back much further. Throughout the war, its practitioners were far too busy with current problems to devote themselves either to a conscious analysis of methodology or to the writing of books that would pave the way for their successors. Texts did not begin to appear until the 1950s, when OR achieved recognition as a subject worthy of academic study in universities. Since then, not only have a large number of schools provided courses leading to advanced degrees in OR but the subject has been recognized as becoming more and more important to students of economics, management, public administration, behavioral science, social work, mathematics and statistics, and the many branches of engineering. This is not surprising, because OR attempts to provide a systematic and rational approach to the fundamental problems involved in the control of systems by making decisions which, in some sense, achieve the best results in light of all the information that is profitable for use.

Since the mid-1950s, a great many OR texts have appeared, ranging from reviews for the benefit of business men (who need to know the type of assistance that they can expect from OR) to rigorous mathematical analysis of specific problems, suitable for both the specialist and the academician.

Subsequently, there have been books that deal with the analysis of a wide range of problems but, for the most part, writers have devoted themselves to analysis of mathematical models rather than to analysis of problems. This has had two consequences. First, the reader is usually required to make a translation between the necessarily simplified models, presented in the texts, and the real world in which few problems are simple and in which there are a host of practical difficulties. Second, emphasis on the analytical approach requires a level of mathematical expertise, which is not possessed by many students.

In this text, we have tried to reconcile a rigid mathematical treatment of the subject with a conceptually oriented qualitative treatment. For those who intend to practice OR, we hope this book will provide a better comprehension of the real world than most texts offer. For those who want to understand OR without practicing it, we hope this book will provide a better grasp of its methods, techniques, and tools than do most texts.

In the first four chapters, we discuss general aspects of formulating problems and the manner in which to select appropriate criteria for choosing between alternatives. Chapters 5 to 14 deal with a particular types of problem. In these chapters, we have tried to avoid mathematical derivations and, consequently, we have relied primarily on mathematical intuition. Nevertheless, a comprehension of these chapters requires some acquaintance with differential and integral calculus and some knowledge of probability theory. A one-semester course in each subject probably will be sufficient. With less than this amount of mathematics, we could only have produced a "cookbook" with unexplained rules for numerical computation. In many cases we have stressed computational rules rather than algebraic abstractions but, although few rigorous proofs are given, we have tried to give enough of the reasoning behind the techniques to make them appear plausible.

In Chapters 15 and 16 we return to general methodological problems and consider how the results obtained by the techniques developed in Chapters 5 to 14 can be evaluated, implemented, and controlled. In the final chapter we discuss the problem of planning and, here, we touch on some complex and difficult matters that are at the frontier of OR. We believe that there are few limits to the potential areas of application of OR, and it is our hope that this chapter will stimulate future producers and consumers of OR to push beyond its current limits.

We have been greatly helped in the preparation of this book by discussions with Dr. Julius Aronofsky, Professors Patrick Rivett, Samuel Litwin, Sankar Sengupta, and Roger Sisson. We thank our secretaries, Pat Taylor and Hermine Otruba, for work on the manuscript, and our wives, Alexandra Ackoff and Amelia Sasieni, for suffering with us (or, perhaps, without us) during the period in which this book was written.

RUSSELL L. ACKOFF
MAURICE W. SASIENI

Philadelphia and London
March 1967

Contents

Fundamentals of OPERATIONS RESEARCH

CHAPTER 1

Introduction: The Nature of Operations Research

PREVIEW

In this chapter we attempt to do four things: (1) to give an account of the development of operations research (abbreviated to OR); (2) to define it, and to identify and illustrate its essential characteristics; (3) to discuss its relationship to other fields, and (4) to explain the organization of this book.

In this and subsequent chapters the illustrations are drawn largely from industrial applications of OR. It should be borne in mind, however, that OR has been used extensively in governmental (federal, state, and local), military, and nonprofit organizations (e.g., schools, labor unions, hospitals, and libraries). It is being used increasingly in such diverse areas as fire fighting in forests, water conservation, agricultural and mining operations, dental and medical services, and national, state, regional, and city planning.

THE DEVELOPMENT OF OR

The term "OR" seems to have been first used about 1939, but as is true of other scientific developments, once OR had been individuated and named, its roots could be traced back far into the history of science and society. Even the oldest scientific disciplines—the natural sciences—were individuated and named only about a century ago, but once they were identified, scholars went back through history and applied the new names to much earlier work. Newton, for example, was known as a natural philosopher in his own day, not as a physicist.

Although the roots of OR may extend back before the First Industrial Revolution, it was certainly during this revolution that the need which OR was to fill began to develop. Until the middle of the last century most industrial enterprises employed only a handful of men. The advent of machine

1

tools—the replacement of man by machine as a source of power—and the development of national transportation and communication systems fertilized industry, which began to grow into the mature form that it now has. As companies expanded, it became less and less possible for one man to manage them; therefore, the owner[1] divided his job into parts, which he assigned to others. For example, managers of production, finance, personnel, marketing, and research and development began to appear. With further industrial growth even these functions were subdivided; for example, production was sometimes divided into procurement or purchasing, maintenance, traffic, quality control, and production scheduling. As populations grew and spread, new markets were formed and new sources of raw material were discovered. Consequently, industrial operations were dispersed geographically. Multiple production facilities and sales offices became commonplace and each required its own management. Thus the functional and geographic segmentation of management that we know today was a natural consequence of the industrial growth brought about by the First Industrial Revolution.

New types of applied science developed to provide assistance to each new type of management as it appeared. For example, the application of physics and chemistry to problems of production gave rise to mechanical and chemical engineering. Later, with the introduction of techniques and substantive knowledge supplied by statistics and psychology, industrial engineering also developed. Market research, industrial (micro) economics, and industrial psychology and sociology were among the many other management-oriented applied-scientific disciplines that appeared. As more specialized forms of management emerged, so did more specialized applications of science, such as materials handling engineering, statistical quality control, maintenance and reliability engineering, and advertising research.

An important aspect of this development lies in something that did not happen: science was not applied to the emerging executive function of management. To understand the nature and significance of this fact let us first make clear the nature of the executive function. Each time that a managerial function is broken down into a set of different subfunctions, a new task is created—that of *integrating* the diverse subfunctions so that they serve efficiently the interests of the whole. The integrating task is the executive function of management.

To carry out the executive function it is necessary to establish objectives for, and measures of, the performance of the subunits reporting to it. For example, company executives normally establish the following objectives for the main functions of business.

[1] The nature of the owner also changed. The advent of joint stock companies had a profound effect on the rise of the professional manager.

Production. To maximize the amount of goods (or service) produced and to minimize the unit cost of production.

Marketing. To maximize the amount sold and to minimize the unit cost of sales.

Finance. To minimize the capital required to maintain any level of business.

Personnel. To maintain morale and high productivity among the employees.

Such objectives are hard to disagree with in principle but, because they are inconsistent, they are even harder to pursue in practice. Consequently, their pursuit sets up conflicts between the units reporting to the executive. To illustrate this point, let us consider the attitude toward inventory policy that develops in each of the four managerial functions cited above.

The production department wants to produce as much as possible for as low a cost as possible. This can be attained only by producing one product continuously. If more than one product is required, the least expensive procedure is to produce as much at one time (per production run) as possible. Such a policy minimizes the time lost in changing equipment to produce something else (setup) and obtains the efficiencies that the practice of long production runs provides. If the production department were to manufacture relatively few products in as long and continuous production runs as possible, a large inventory spread over relatively few products would occur. Hence the production department generally prefers a policy that permits a large inventory and requires a small product line.

The marketing department also wants large inventories so that a customer could be supplied today with anything that he may want tomorrow. But because the marketing department desires to sell as much per sale as possible, it must be able to provide the widest possible range of products. Hence the production and marketing departments normally come into conflict over the extent of the product line, marketing urging the inclusion of many low-volume and even unprofitable items and production urging their exclusion.

The financial department, in pursuit of its objective of minimizing the capital that is required to run the business, wishes to reduce the amount of money that is "tied up" in it. One of the easiest ways of doing this is to reduce inventories, hence the capital "tied up" in them. The financial department normally believes that inventories should rise and fall in proportion to the rise and fall of the company's sales.

When sales are low, however, the personnel (and the production) department does not want to reduce production and lay off workers because such an action lowers morale, reduces available skills, and involves the costs of firing and subsequent hiring and training of new workers. Hence the personnel department is interested in maintaining production at as constant a level as possible. This requires producing up to the level of the inventory when sales are low and depleting inventories when sales are high. Hence the financial and personnel departments have different ideas about what the company's inventory policy should be.

Now, it is the executive's responsibility to set an inventory policy that in some sense best serves the interests of the company as a whole, not the interests of any one function reporting to him. This integrating task requires that the whole system be taken into account; this is the essence of the executive's job.

The executive function, in industry, developed gradually, as did organizations themselves. The executive was not subjected to violent stimuli from new technology as was, for example, the production manager. The executive grew into his problems, and their solution appeared to require nothing but good judgment based on relevant experience. The executive, therefore, felt no need for a more rigorous scientific way of looking at his problems. However, increasingly heavy demands were made on his time and he sought aid from those who had more time for, and experience with, the problems at hand. It was this need which gave rise to management consultants, but their activity was not initially based on the use of science or scientific research. Because what we call OR is in fact the use of scientific research to aid the executive, OR was late in developing in industrial management. The lack of growth of OR might have continued indefinitely, had it not been for the developments within military organizations at the outbreak of World War II.

Military organizations had gone through the same type of organizational evolution as had industry, and for the same reasons. The development of new technologies and growth required increased division and specialization of managerial skills. Four major managerial functions appeared in the military establishment: administration (G1), intelligence (G2), operations and training (G3), and supply and logistics (G4). Each of these were in turn divided into various types of subfunctions (e.g., G4 was divided into ordnance, signal, transportation, engineering, and so on). These were further subdivided and, as in the industrial case, more and more widely dispersed geographically.

The major difference between the evolutionary development of military executives and that of their industrial counterparts was to be found in the twenty year gap between the end of World War I and the beginning of World War II. During this period military technology was being developed more rapidly than it could be absorbed effectively into military tactics and strategy. Little wonder, then, that the British military executives and managers turned to scientists for aid when the German air attack on Britain began. Specifically, they sought aid in incorporating the then new radar into the tactics and strategies of air defense. Small teams of scientists, drawn from any discipline from which they were willing to come, worked on such problems with considerable success in 1939 and 1940. Their success bred further demand for such services, and the use of scientific teams spread to the Western Allies—the United States, Canada, and France. These teams of scientists were usually assigned to the executive in charge of operations—to the "line"; hence their work came to be known as *operational research* in the United Kingdom and by a variety of names in the United States: operational analysis, operations evaluation, operations research, systems analysis, systems evaluation, systems research, and management science. The name operations research was and is the most widely used, and we use it here.

At the end of the war different things happened to Operations Research in the United Kingdom and in the United States. In the United Kingdom expenditures on defense research were reduced; this led to the release of many OR workers from the military at a time when industrial managers were confronted with the need to reconstruct much of Britain's manufacturing facilities[2] that had been damaged by bombs. In addition, after the Labour Party came to power the nationalization of several major and basic industries was begun. Executives in the nationalized basic industries, in particular, sought assistance from the OR men leaving the military organization and received it. Coal, iron and steel, transport, utilities, and many other types of industries began to create industrial OR.

In contrast to the situation in Great Britain, defense research in the United States was increased and OR was expanded at the end of the war. Most of the war-experienced OR workers remained in the service of the military. Industrial executives did not call for help, because they were returning to a familiar peacetime pattern that did not involve either major reconstruction of plant or nationalization.

The eventual involvement of science in industrial problems of the executive type in the United States is due to the advent of the Second Industrial Revolution. World War II had spurred scientific advances in the study of communication, control, and computation, which produced the technological basis for *automation:* the replacement of man by machine as a source of control. In the late 1940s the new revolution began when electronic computers became commercially available. The potentialities of these electronic brains as a new tool for management were broadcast far and wide, and nontechnically trained executives began to look for help in the selection and utilization of computers. The emerging search for assistance was accelerated by the outbreak of the Korean conflict, which placed increased demands for greater

---

[2] The reasons for the need for reconstruction were many. One reason was war damage; the practice of retaining obsolete equipment so long as it was still working also added to the need for reconstruction.

productivity on a large part of American industry. Therefore, in the early 1950s industry began to absorb some of the OR men who trickled out of the military; a few consulting firms, universities, research institutes, and governmental agencies absorbed others. Thus OR began to spread and expand in the United States.

Within a decade there were at least as many OR workers in academic, governmental, and industrial organizations as there were in the military. (There are about 4000 in the United States.) Today more than one half of the largest companies in the United States have or are using OR. A national society was formed in 1953—The Operations Research Society of America. Other countries rapidly followed suit, and in 1957 the International Federation of Operational Research Societies was established. Journals began to appear—three in the United States, one in Britain, followed by others in a wide variety of languages. Courses and curricula in OR began to proliferate in the United States, and to develop more slowly in other countries.

In short, after one decade of vigorous growth in military organizations, OR continued its growth in the military and developed very rapidly in industrial, academic, and governmental organizations.

We have described briefly why and how OR came into existence and grew. We have characterized it, however, only in a very general way and have said little about what it is and how it operates. It is in this direction that we now turn.

THE MEANING AND NATURE OF OR

Many definitions of OR have been offered, as well as many arguments as to why it cannot be defined. In examining the definitions that have been offered we should remember that neither the old and well-established sciences nor science itself has ever been defined in a way that is acceptable to most practitioners. Nevertheless, the following definition provides a useful basis for an initial understanding of the nature of OR, especially when related to the historical background just covered: OR can be considered as being:

(1) The application of scientific method

(2) by interdisciplinary teams

(3) to problems involving the control of organized (man-machine) systems so as to provide solutions which best serve the purposes of the organization as a whole.

The essential characteristics of OR, identified in this definition, are (*a*) its system (or executive) orientation, (*b*) the use of interdisciplinary teams, and (*c*) the application of scientific method to problems of control. We now consider each of these in more detail.

The Systems (*or Executive*) Orientation of OR

This orientation is based on the observation that in organized systems the behavior of any part ultimately has some effect on every other part. Not all these effects are significant or even capable of detection. Therefore, the essence of this orientation lies in the systematic search for significant interactions in evaluating actions or policies of any part of the organization.

This approach to organizational problems is dramatically opposed to that involved in "cutting a problem down to size." OR workers almost always enlarge the initial concept of a problem presented to them to include interactions that are not incorporated in its formulation by management. To deal with the enlarged, hence more complicated, problems, new research methods have had to be developed.

Let us return for a moment to the inventory problem that was discussed earlier. If we considered production control and inventory only from the production department's point of view, we would fail to perceive the effects of any policy, so derived, on the volume and cost of sales, and on the financial and personnel requirements of the business. In OR an attempt is made to take account of all the significant effects, to make them commensurate, and to evaluate them as a whole.

The Interdisciplinary Team

The division of the domain of knowledge into specific disciplines is a relatively recent phenomenon. It is a product of the nineteenth century. Until about the end of the seventeenth century it was possible for one man to learn and retain most, if not all, of the "scientific" knowledge that mankind had accumulated. Hence there was no need for specialization, and all pursuits of knowledge were called *philosophy*. But as the stock of knowledge began to exceed the storage capacity of the human brain, specialization took place. Natural philosophy came to be distinguished from traditional, nonempirically oriented philosophy. Later it came to be known as natural *science*. Starting in the middle of the last century, natural science was divided into physics and chemistry. A short time later biology began to be individuated, and just before the end of the century psychology as well. The social sciences came into their own early in this century. Each of these have been further divided and subdivided. Today we have more than one hundred scientific disciplines.

We have become so accustomed to classifying scientific knowledge in a way that corresponds to the departmental structure of universities that we act as though nature were also so structured. Nothing could be further from the truth. There are no such things as physical problems, biological problems, psychological problems, economic problems, and so on. There are only problems; *the disciplines of science represent different ways of looking at them.* Any problem may be looked at through the eyes of every discipline. But, of course, it is not always fruitful to do so. This is the same point made earlier but in a different guise: there is no such thing as a production, marketing, or financial problem in an organization; these are only different ways of considering organizational problems.

We could explain an automobile's being struck by a locomotive at a grade crossing, for example, either in terms of the laws of motion, or the engineering failure of warning devices, or the state of health of the driver, or his mental state, or the social use of automobiles as instruments of suicide. Which way we look at the event depends on our reasons for considering it. If, for example, we wanted to prevent the reoccurrence of such an event, we would consider the problem in such a way as to obtain an effective solution in the shortest time or at the least cost.

From experience we extract fruitful ways of examining most of the familiar and recurring problems. For unfamiliar and complicated situations we tend to use that approach to problems which is the most familiar to us. It is not surprising, therefore, that when confronted with the problem, say, of increasing the productivity of a manufacturing facility, the personnel psychologist will try to select better workers or improve the training that they are given. The mechanical engineer will try to improve the machines. The industrial engineer will try to improve the plant layout, simplify the operations performed by the workers, or offer them more attractive incentives. The systems and procedures analyst will try to improve the flow of information into and through the plant, and so on. All may produce improvements, but which one of them or which combination of them is the best? For complicated problems, we seldom know in advance. Hence it is desirable to consider and evaluate as wide a range of approaches to the problem as possible. This is the reason for interdisciplinary research teams.

Because more than one hundred pure and applied scientific disciplines have been identified, it is clearly not possible to incorporate each into every research project. But it is desirable to have representation on a team of as many disciplines as possible and to subject the team's work to critical review from the widest variety of these disciplines that are not represented on the team.

The Method of OR

In most discussions of the scientific method, *experimentation* is cited as being essential. Unfortunately, however, experimentation in the narrow sense—that is, physical manipulation of variables—is often not possible or practical when governmental, military, or industrial organizations are involved. In industry, for example, a company cannot risk failure in order to conduct a successful experiment. Of course, experimentation is sometimes possible, particularly on subsystems, and can and does play an important role in OR; nevertheless more likely than not, the total system under study cannot be subjected to it. Therefore, a research approach that does not involve experimentation (in the narrow sense, entailing physical manipulation of the subject under study) on the total system must be used in the majority of cases.

A suggestion can be found in the method used by astronomers who are in much the same situation as is the operations researcher (although this may change in the near future). The astronomer can observe the system that he studies, but cannot manipulate it. Therefore he constructs *representations* of the system and its operations (*models*) on which he conducts his research. The OR worker must usually do the same.

Models in OR take the form of equations, which—although they may be complicated from a mathematical point of view—have a very simple underlying structure:

$$U = f(X_i, Y_j)$$

where U is the utility or value of the system's performance.

X_i are the variables that can be controlled.

Y_j are variables (and constants) that are not controlled but do affect U.

f is the relationship between U and X_i and Y_j.

In addition, one or more equations or "inequations" are frequently required to express the fact that some or all of the controlled variables can only be manipulated within limits. For example, the amount of machine time allocated to products cannot be less than zero or greater than the total time available; and the sum of the amounts of money budgeted to different departments of a company cannot exceed the total amount available. The performance equation and the constraints together constitute a model of the system and of the problem that we want to solve. Hence it is a *decision*, as well as a *system*, model.

Once the model is constructed, it can be used to find, exactly or approximately, the optimal values of the controlled variables—values that produce the best performance of the system for specified values of the uncontrolled variables; that is, we can *derive a solution* to the problem from the model. How this can be done depends on the nature of the model.

A solution may be extracted from a model either by conducting experiments on it (i.e., by *simulation*) or by mathematical analysis. In some cases mathematical analysis can be conducted without any knowledge of the values of the variables (i.e., abstractly or symbolically), but in others the values of the variables must be known (i.e., concretely or numerically).

For certain types of function, f (e.g., elementary algebraic relationships), if the constraints are not too numerous, classical mathematics provides powerful tools for finding the best values of the controlled variables. In recent years many new mathematical techniques have been developed to handle problems in which the constraints are numerous enough to make computations prohibitive by classical methods. Some of these techniques are discussed in this book.

On the other hand, the function, f, may consist of a set of computational rules (an *algorithm*) that permits us to compute utility (U) of performance for any specified set of values of the controlled and uncontrolled variables, but does not permit the finding of optimal values of the controlled variables directly. Usually we can also specify a procedure for selecting successive trial values of the controlled variables so that they converge on the optimal solution. For some algorithms the cost of finding the best solution may be excessive when compared with its improvement over a good solution that can sometimes be found with relative ease. Each time we compute U from a new set of X_i for specified values of Y_j, we learn something about how the system works. From this information we may conclude that another set of X_i-values will yield an improvement. If we can estimate the size of the improvement in advance of the detailed computations, we can compare it with the cost of calculation and decide if further trials are justified.

The system may be such that all the Y_j cannot be known in advance of the decisions about X_i. For example, if one of the Y_j is next month's sales and one of the X_i is this month's production level, we may have to make our decision knowing only the probability distribution of sales. In such cases, if f is simple enough, we can sometimes average over the unknown variables and select decisions that result in the best average value. However, the averaging process is frequently so involved that this is not feasible. Instead we are forced to conduct experiments on the model (i.e., simulations) in which we select values of the uncontrolled variables with the relative frequencies dictated by their probability distributions. This allows us to compute the corresponding values of U, and ultimately its distribution. Sometimes such experiments are performed entirely within a computer.

In some cases the role of the human decision maker in the system may not be understood well enough for explicit representation in the model. Then the simulation may involve humans in a role-playing capacity. Such simulation is called *operational gaming*.

Whatever procedure is used, an optimal or near-optimal solution is sought. An optimal solution is one that minimizes or maximizes (as appropriate) the performance measure *in a model*, subject to the conditions and constraints represented *in that model*. Optimization therefore yields the best solution to the problem *that is modeled*. But because a model is never a perfect representation of the problem, the optimal solution is never *the* best solution *to the problem*. Hopefully, the model is a "good" representation of the problem, hence the optimal or near-optimal solution derived from it is a "good" approximation of the optimal solution to the problem and is at least significantly *better* than the policy or procedure that it is meant to replace.

Because the optimizing values of the solution improve the system's performance only if the model is a good representation of the system, the correspondence of the model to reality must be *tested* and the solution must be *evaluated*. That is, its performance must be compared with the policy or procedure that it is meant to replace.

Finally, because the objective of OR is not merely to produce reports but to improve the performance of systems, the results of the research must be *implemented* (if they are accepted by the decision makers). Here the ultimate test and evaluation of the research is made; hence it is in this phase of the inquiry that the operations researcher has the greatest opportunity for learning.

If the decision under study is one that will be made more than once, it is very likely—considering the nature of the systems studied in OR—that the values of the uncontrolled variables and even the structure of the system will change between decisions. Therefore, significant changes in the system and its environment must be detected and the solution must be adjusted as required by them. That is, solutions that are rules for repetitive decisions or decisions that extend over time must be *maintained* or *controlled*.

To summarize, we have identified five stages of an OR project:

1. Formulating the problem
2. Constructing the model
3. Deriving a solution
4. Testing the model and evaluating the solution
5. Implementing and maintaining the solution

Chapters 2, 3, 4, 15, and 16 are devoted to these methodological stages of an OR project.

Although these phases of an OR project are normally initiated in the order listed, they usually do not terminate in this order. In fact, each phase usually continues until the project is completed and continuously interacts with the others. For example, the successful formulation of the problem depends on having at least tentatively considered each of the other steps, and especially the implementability of a solution to it. Although we must discuss these phases of OR separately, it should be borne in mind that they are likely to overlap in time and to interact.

PROTOTYPE PROBLEMS

Since its inception OR has been applied to a wide variety of problems. Most of these, however, have been *tactical* rather than *strategic* in nature.

The distinction between tactical and strategic problems is not a simple one, because it is based on at least three characteristics of problems, each of which involves a matter of degree.

First, one problem is more tactical than another if the effect of its solution has a shorter duration or, what is essentially the same, if its solution can be modified or reversed easily. The longer the duration of the effect of a solution to a problem, the more strategic it is. Hence a problem involving what to produce tomorrow is more tactical than that of where to build an additional plant. OR has been applied more often to short-run than to long-run problems. We might refer to this characteristic of a problem as its *range*.

Second, one problem is the more strategic the larger the portion of the organization that is directly affected by its solution. Therefore, a problem involving selection of an accounting convention is likely to be more tactical than, say, corporate budgeting. This characteristic of a problem can be referred to as its *scope*.

Finally, one problem is the more strategic the more it involves the determination of ends, goals, or objectives. All problems involve the selection of means to accomplish desired outcomes, but many take the desired outcomes as given or provided. To the extent that they do, they are tactical. Hence corporate planning, which must establish organizational goals and objectives, is more strategic than is a problem involving the minimization of transportation costs in which such minimization is taken as being a desirable outcome. This characteristic of a problem can be referred to as its *ends-orientation*.

There are no clear cutoff points on the scales representing these three characteristics that distinguish tactical from strategic problems. Hence at best we can only say of one problem that it is more or less tactical or strategic than another with respect to each of these characteristics.

As mentioned above, most, but by no means all, of OR has been occupied with problems that are tactical rather than strategic in nature. Therefore, most of this book is concerned with applications of OR to tactical problems. In the last chapter, however, we look at strategic problems in some detail and discuss the role that OR has and can play in their solution.

In one sense, no two tactical problems are ever exactly the same. In another sense, tactical problems tend to cluster into a few well-defined types. The sense in which no two tactical problems are exactly the same is one that refers to their *content*. The sense in which they tend to fall into clusters is one that refers to their *form*. Every problem has both form and content. These are like the head and tail of a coin; we can look at and discuss them separately, but we cannot "have" them separately. *Form* refers to the way in which the properties of a problem (variables and constants) are *related* to each other. *Content* refers to the nature (meaning) of these properties. For example, many different pairs of variables can be related to each other in a way that can be represented graphically by a straight line. Thus pairs of variables that are linearly related have the same form but not the same content.

We separate the form of a problem from its content by the process of *abstraction.* The language in which we express the form of experience abstracted from its content is that of mathematics. Hence a mathematical decision model is a representation of the form of a problem.

Abstraction of the form of a problem from its content requires knowledge of its content. Managers of operations and those involved in them tend to know their content better than do researchers. In general, researchers cannot afford the time and effort required to become as well acquainted with a problem's content as are those who are involved with it. Therefore, operations researchers must exploit the contextual knowledge of problems that managers and others have. It is for this reason that OR is best performed when there is active collaboration and involvement of managers and operating personnel.

As already indicated, an important consequence of the application of OR to a wide variety of tactical problems is that a small set of problem types has been identified which accounts for most of these problems. Because of the frequent reoccurrence of these problems, techniques have been developed for modeling them and for deriving solutions from these models. These *prototype* problems are the following:

1. Allocation
2. Inventory
3. Replacement
4. Queuing
5. Sequencing and coordination
6. Routing
7. Competitive
8. Search

In Chapters 5 to 14 each prototype problem is considered in some detail. The order in which they are considered derives from expository considerations. In real situations they frequently "emerge" from each other, not necessarily in the order listed, as the conception of the system being dealt with is enlarged. For example, many operations researches begin with inventory problems because (1) they are generally the simplest conceptually, (2) the techniques for handling them are highly developed, (3) the data required by these techniques are usually believed to be available (but seldom are), and (4) managers responsible for inventories are frequently quantitatively oriented, hence do not usually feel as threatened by OR as do less technically oriented managers.

As we shall see, inventories involve what is apparently the simplest operation that can be conceived—holding or storing resources. The decisions required generally entail the determination of how much of a resource to acquire or when to acquire it. A large number of resources may be involved— for example, in determining how many of each of a large number of parts to purchase or produce, and when to do so. Once such a multi-item inventory problem is solved, it may become apparent there are not enough facilities to produce all the items specified in the solution. It then becomes necessary to *allocate* the available production facilities to the jobs to be done in such a way as to minimize the losses that result from not being able to carry out the solution to the inventory problem originally considered in isolation

The solution to the allocation problem is usually based on a model in which facilities are assumed to be available without interruption. In reality, of course, interruptions occur: facilities break down and require repair, power failures occur, workers or needed material do not show up where and when expected. Consequently, it may become apparent that the allocation of facilities should take these possible delays into account. To do so requires solving a *queuing* problem.

Queuing models generally assume a rule for selecting the next among the things (jobs) waiting for service (e.g., repair) on which work will be done. In some cases the order in which these jobs are carried out has a significant effect on the total time required to do all of them or on the distribution of completed times around the dates on which they are due. Where this is so, research may be required to find that *sequence* in which the jobs should be done so that some objective expressed in terms of total time or completion times is met.

If equipment or men must be prepared (set up) for doing each job of a set and if the amount of preparation depends on the order in which the jobs are done, setup costs as well as time considerations may have to be taken into account. To do so involves solving a *routing* problem for reasons that are not apparent now but will become clear when this type of problem is discussed in detail.

If this illustrative problem were considered over an extended period of time, it would be necessary to consider the *replacement* of equipment that is wearing out or is worn out.

Up to this stage in the development of the problem we have been concerned almost exclusively with the behavior of the system under study, not with the behavior of outside parties who affect the organization's performance, such as suppliers, customers, or competitors. If their behavior is taken into account in attempting to purchase materials at a lower price, for example, or to sell more or at a better price, a *competitive* problem is involved. Such problems are generally considered to be very complex and difficult to solve. Hence they are usually tackled by an OR team only after sufficient confidence in the team has been built up for the management to permit "risky" research. It should be noted, however, that in general the more difficult and risky the research, the greater is the payoff that a solution will yield.

Finally, the larger the scope of problems undertaken by OR and the range of solutions that are implemented, the greater is the need for generating, collecting, and treating the information required to implement and maintain this effort. Frequently this results in a study of the information and communication support system. Problems that involve the determination of how much and what information to acquire, how to acquire it, and how to treat it once it has been acquired, are *search* problems.

It should be apparent from this discussion that management problems can seldom be isolated from one another. Hence, although OR can be organized on a problem or project basis, it is most effectively utilized when the research is permitted to enlarge its scope as it proceeds and to incorporate, simultaneously or sequentially, as wide a range of interacting problems as possible.

Most executive problems cannot be effectively contained in a model of any one type Although we can construct models that incorporate several of these types, in general we cannot derive solutions from them. The prototype models are the largest that can usually be solved in one piece. But because real problems involve several prototypes, we must frequently "decompose" the problem into solvable parts and use the solution obtained from one part as an input to a second part, and so on. We may then have to use the output of the last part to re-evaluate one or all of the partial solutions previously obtained. In effect, when dealing with multiple models, a solution is often sought by proceeding sequentially from one model to another and repeating the cycle until a satisfactory solution to the total problem is obtained.

There is nothing sacred or permanent in the eightfold classification of problem types. In time new ones will appear and old ones will be combined as we develop the capability of solving them jointly. The boundaries between them are fuzzy and become more and more so as they are generalized and overlaps are revealed. Some of the mathematical techniques that are used in deriving solutions from models—for example, linear and dynamic programming—are applicable to models of different types. For this reason models are sometimes classified by the kind of mathematics required for their solution. We have chosen here to classify them by their managerial rather than mathematical characteristics in order to emphasize the problem orientation of OR. It is only too easy to think of OR as applied mathematics rather than as applied interdisciplinary science, and to become so engrossed in the techniques that it employs as to lose sight of the end sought.

It should also be noted that a number of problems that are the most interesting from the research point-of-view may not fit any of the model types. Such problems present a particularly exciting challenge and pave the way for eventual identification of new problem types.

Subsequent discussions of prototype problems and their models and solutions is not intended to imply that the models presented are tools to be placed in a kit from which they are to be drawn as needed. Ready-made models seldom fit real problems. Models usually have to be custom-made. But if the exposition of these theories is treated as an exercise in building models and deriving solutions, it will provide a foundation on which models suited to particular problems can be constructed.

MODES OF MANAGEMENT AND CONTROL

It is as important to be aware of what OR cannot do or cannot do well as it is to be aware of what it can do. One useful way of obtaining such a perspective is to classify and analyze what managers can do to improve organizational performance and the sources of science-based assistance that are available to them.

Managers manage *organizations*. Organizations are a type of *system*. A system is a set of interrelated entities. The entities may be abstract, as in the number system, or concrete, as in the solar system. Organizations are clearly concrete systems, but not all concrete systems are organizations. Organizations are distinguished by four essential characteristics, each of which is subject to managerial manipulation. Hence these characteristics also define what we shall call the "modes of management." The characteristics are as follows.

1. *Content*. An organization must consist of at least two purposeful entities, which are capable of selecting objectives and the means by which to pursue them. This is the minimal content requirement. In the types of organization with which we are concerned in this book, the purposeful entities are men. Such organizations also usually involve three other types of resource: *machines* (in which we include plant, equipment, and facilities), *materials*, and *money*.

2. *Structure*. The purposeful entities of which the system is composed are divided into at least two subgroups, which are responsible for different kinds of activity. That is, there is a functional division of labor within the system: not all the components of the system do the same thing, but most (or a significant portion) of what they do is intended to serve some overall objectives of the system. An industrial organization is characteristically divided into at least production, marketing, finance, personnel, and research or engineering functions. Military organizations are similarly divided, for example, into administrative, intelligence, operations and training, and supply and logistics functions.

3. *Communications*. The purposeful entities of the system must be capable of responding to (interacting with) each other and the system's environment. This requires the ability to obtain information either directly by observation

or indirectly by communication. Communication is the cement that holds the elements of an organization together.

4. *Control.* The system must be capable of at least partial self-control, that is, of setting its own objectives, evaluating its performance relative to these objectives, and initiating or modifying behavior directed toward improving performance. It must also be capable of modifying its own content, structure, communications, and even its own control system. An organization must therefore be *adaptive* and *self-organizing*.

Now let us consider each of these characteristics from the point of view of what managers can do about them and what science can do in helping management do it better.

Content

1. *Men*

1.1. *Selection and training* is directed toward increasing the capabilities of members of the organization and hopefully thereby improving their performance and that of the organization. Management can obtain aid from *personnel psychologists* in the design and operation of such procedures.

1.2. *Work study* is directed toward improving the behavior of men by instructing them about what to do and how to do it without necessarily changing their capabilities. Aid can be obtained from *industrial engineers* through time and motion studies.

1.3. *Motivation* is directed toward inducing men to do better by manipulating their environment (physical and social) or by providing appropriate incentives. *Industrial* and *social psychologists*, *sociologists*, and *industrial engineers* can and have assisted managers in this way.

2. *Machines* (and plant): *design*, *construction*, and *maintenance* of equipment and facilities directed toward the following:

2.1. *Improving the performance of individual machines.* This has been the function of what might be called "traditional" *engineering:* mechanical, chemical, civil, and so on.

2.2. *Improving the performance of men operating the machines in the facilities.* The use of *physiology*, *psychology*, and *engineering* in designing equipment and facilities in which men can operate effectively is known as *human engineering* or *human factor analysis*. (Chapanis, 1961.)

2.3. *Improving the performance of the overall man-machine system.* Here the concern is with the way machines interact with one another and the way men interact with the machines. Such an approach is characteristic of *systems engineering*. (Goode and Machol, 1957; Chestnut, 1965.)

3. *Materials*

   3.1. *Improving quality of the following:*

      3.1.1. *Basic or raw materials.* In this area *physicists chemists, metallurgists* and other emerging types of materials specialists can provide aid.

      3.1.2. *Components or finished products.* Aid in product or component design can be obtained from a wide variety of *engineers. Value analysis* is a procedure that engineers have recently found useful.

   3.2. *Maintaining quality* of basic or raw materials and component or finished products. Here the manager can receive assistance from practitioners of *statistical quality control.*

  4. *Money.* Improvement in the acquisition, retention, and use of financial resources has been the concern of those in *accounting, finance,* and *economics.* (These fields have been coming together more and more, so that separation of their functions is no longer possible, particularly in industrial organizations.)

Structure

The manipulation of organizational structure is still largely a matter of intuition and art. Only recently has any scientific competence begun to develop in this area. Organization theory (for example, Haire, 1959) is energing but is not yet sufficiently developed to be applied in any systematic way to most organizational problems. Our understanding of organizational structure, particularly as it relates to the effectiveness with which an organization can control itself, is growing as a result of two recent developments: (1) the application of *cybernetic* concepts to the design of organizational structure (Beer, 1959) and (2) the use of social psychology to induce members of an organization to modify its structure or overcome the limitations imposed by it (Bennis, 1966). We shall return to this topic shortly.

Communication

The capacity of improving organizational communication by use of scientific methods and scientifically derived knowledge is only beginning to emerge. The mathematical theory of communication associated with Shannon (Shannon and Weaver, 1949) is not applicable here, only to the design of physical systems for processing messages. The growing body of potentially relevant knowledge and research procedures can be found in such works as Miller (1951), Cherry (1958), Pierce (1961) and Smith (1966).

Practical studies of communication systems in an organization are therefore largely judgmental and experimental. They are performed primarily by *systems* and *procedures analysts* (called *organization and methods analysts* in the United Kingdom). Because of the growing role of electronic computers in communication systems, more and more use is being made of science and technology in the design of the physical aspects of communication systems, which should not be confused with the organizational aspects of such systems which to a large extent still evade modern technology. We return to this topic in Chapter 17.

Control

It will be recalled that control involves setting objectives, evaluating performance, and initiating or modifying behavior and/or content, structure, and communications of the organization. This, or at least part of it, is the preoccupation of OR. OR has been primarily concerned with the initiation or modification of organizational behavior; that is, it is interested in what an organization does with its content, structure, and communications rather than in what these aspects of an organization are. The reason is that OR has not had the capability of effectively modeling these aspects of an organization taken separately, and therefore of relating them to each other and to organizational behavior. Recent researches by some experts in these modes and by some operations researchers have been closing the gaps between the modes. As a result it is becoming increasingly difficult to classify by mode some of the work done by behavioral scientists, industrial, human, communications and systems engineers, economists, and operations researchers. This foreshadows the emergence of an ability to deal simultaneously with organizational problems in a multimodal way. In Chapter 17 we examine this development.

The multimodal scientific approach to organizational problems must be even more system-oriented and interdisciplinary than OR has been. Because OR has embodied these characteristics more than any other type of scientific activity, and because much of the impetus for this enlargement of scope has come from OR, these new developments are being absorbed by OR. As a result OR is growing conceptually, methodologically, and technically. This will undoubtedly increase its ability to serve those responsible for organized human activity. It is important, therefore, for those entering the practice of OR not only to know what that practice *is*, but also what it *is becoming* and what they might help make it.

DISCUSSION TOPICS

1. Take some familiar problem, such as automobile accidents or overpopulation and consider which scientific disciplines can contribute to its solution and how.
2. (*a*) Consider how a decision by a marketing department to add or delete a product from its product line may affect the performance of each function of a

business. Do the same for a decision to add a new plant. (*b*) How might a decision to expand mass transit in a city affect its performance in health, education, welfare, and other public services?

3. (*a*) What problems usually identified with different disciplines have the same form? (*b*) How does the concept of an *analogue* relate to that of the *form* of problems, and that of an *analogy* to the *content* of a problem?

4. Compare the pricing decisions of a company and its decision to add a new product line with respect to each of the three characteristics that distinguish tactical from strategic decisions.

5. Is OR a discipline, a profession, a field of study, a methodology, a set of techniques, a philosophy, or a new name for an old thing?

Suggested Readings

In the Bibliography that follows are listed selected general articles and books that provide insight to, and understanding of, the nature and use of OR. Exposure to a number of apparently different ways of characterizing OR and to a variety of its applications is the best way to uncover the common core of meaning that individuates the field.

Attention is also called to the Proceedings of the three international Conferences on Operational Research (1957, 1960, and 1963) published by the English Universities Press (London).

The flavor of OR can also be captured by browsing through the principal English-language journals: *Management Science* (Series A and B), *Naval Research Logistics Quarterly*, *Operational Research Quarterly*, and *Operations Research*. The last two are particularly good for this purpose.

A number of general and specialized bibliographies are available. Among the general ones are the following:

> *Operations Research: An Annotated Bibliography*, by James H. Batchelor, Vol. I (1959), Vol. II (1962), Vol. III (1963), and Vol. IV (1964), St. Louis University Press, St. Louis, Mo.
>
> *A Comprehensive Bibliography on Operations Research*, (two volumes), by the Operations Research Group, Case Institute of Technology, John Wiley and Sons, New York, 1958 and 1963.

The recently initiated *International Abstracts in Operations Research* is also a useful source of information on, and summary of, current literature.

Bibliography

Ackoff, R. L., "The Meaning, Scope, and Methods of Operations Research," in *Progress in Operations Research*, Vol. I, R. L. Ackoff (ed.), John Wiley and Sons, New York, 1961, pp. 1–34.

————, and P. Rivett, *A Managers' Guide to Operations Research*, John Wiley and Sons, New York, 1963.

Beer, Stafford, "Cybernetics and Operations Research," *Operational Research Quarterly*, **10** (1959), 1–21.

————, *Cybernetics and Management*, The English Universities Press, London, 1959.

————, *Decision and Control*, John Wiley and Sons, New York, 1966.

Bennis, W. G., "Theory and Method in Applying Behavioral Science to Planned Organizational Change," in *Proceedings of International Conference on Operational Research and the Social Sciences*, J. R. Lawrence (ed.), Tavistock Publications, London, 1966.

Bevan, R. W., "Trends in Operational Research," *Operations Research*, **6** (1958), 441–447.

Camp, G. D., "Operations Research: The Science of Generalized Strategies and Tactics," *Textile Research Journal*, **25** (1955), 629–634.

Chapanis, A., "On Some Relations between Human Engineering, Operations Research, and Systems Engineering," in *Systems: Research and Design*, D. P. Eckman (ed.), John Wiley and Sons, New York, 1961.

Cherry, Colin, *On Human Communication*, John Wiley and Sons, New York, 1965.

Churchman, C. W., R. L. Ackoff, and E. L. Arnoff, *Introduction to Operations Research*, John Wiley and Sons, New York, 1957.

Crowther, J. G., and R. Whiddington, *Science at War*, His Majesty's Stationery Office, London, 1947.

Dorfman, Robert, "Operations Research," *American Economic Review*, **50** (1960), 575–623.

Duckworth, W. E., *A Guide to Operational Research*, Methuen, London, 1962.

Eddison, R. T., K. Pennycuick, and B. H. P. Rivett (eds.), *Operational Research in Management*, The English Universities Press, London, 1962.

Goode, H. H., and R. E. Machol, *Systems Engineering*, McGraw-Hill Book Co., New York, 1957.

Goodeve, C. F., "Operational Research as a Science," *Operations Research*, **1** (1953), 166–180.

————, and G. R. Ridley, "A Survey of O. R. in Great Britain," *Operational Research Quarterly*, **4** (1953), 21–24.

Haire, Mason (ed.), *Modern Organization Theory*, John Wiley and Sons, New York, 1959.

Hertz, D. B., "Progress in Industrial Operations Research in the United States," in *Proceedings of the First International Conference on Operational Research*, Operations Research Society of America, Baltimore, 1957, pp. 455–467.

————, and Eddison, R. T. (eds.), *Progress in Operations Research*, Vol. II, John Wiley and Sons, New York, 1964.

Jessop, W. N., "Operational Research Methods; What Are They?" *Operational Research Quarterly*, **7** (1956), 49–58.

Johnson, Ellis, "A Survey of Operations Research in the U.S.A.," *Operational Research Quarterly*, **5** (1954), 43–48.

Kaufmann, Arnold, *Methods and Models of Operations Research*, Prentice-Hall, Englewood Cliffs, N.J., 1963.

Kendall, M. G., "The Teaching of Operational Research," *Operational Research Quarterly*, **9** (1958), 265–278.

McCloskey, J. G., and F. N. Trefethen (eds.)., *Operations Research for Management*, Vol. I, The Johns Hopkins Press, Baltimore, 1954.

——, and J. M. Coppinger (eds.), *Operations Research for Management*, Vol. II, The Johns Hopkins Press, Baltimore, 1956.

Miller, D. W., and M. K. Starr, *Executive Decisions and Operations Research*, Prentice-Hall, Englewood Cliffs, N.J., 1960.

Miller, G. A., *Language and Communication*, McGraw-Hill Book Co., New York, 1951.

Morse, P. M., "Operations Research Is Also Research," in *Proceedings of the First International Conference on Operational Research*, Operations Research Society of America, Baltimore, 1957, pp. 1–8.

——, and G. E. Kimball, *Methods of Operations Research*, The Technology Press, Massachusetts Institute of Technology and John Wiley and Sons, New York, 1951.

Page, Thornton, "Operations Research as Defined in this Journal," *Operations Research*, **2** (1954), 86–88.

Pierce, J. R., *Symbols, Signals, and Noise*, Harper and Brothers, New York, 1961.

Rivett, B. H. P., "A Survey of Operational Research in British Industry," *Operational Research Quarterly*, **10** (1959), 189–205.

Shannon, C. E., and W. Weaver, *The Mathematical Theory of Communication*, University of Illinois Press, Urbana, 1949.

Smith, A. G. (ed.), *Communication and Culture*, Holt, Rinehart and Winston, New York, 1966.

Solow, Herbert, "Operations Research," *Fortune*, **43** (April 1951), 105f.

——, "Operations Research Is a Business," *Fortune*, **53** (February 1956), 128f.

Williams, E. C., "Reflections in Operational Research," *Operational Research Quarterly*, **5** (1954), 39–42.

CHAPTER 2

Problem Formulation

THE NATURE OF A PROBLEM

To find the solution to a problem, we must first be able to find the problem and formulate it so that it is susceptible to research. The operations research worker, like the medical doctor, is usually presented with symptoms, rather than a diagnosis. Ordinarily he must look for additional symptoms before he can diagnose correctly. To find and formulate a problem correctly, he must know what a problem is.

Let us begin by considering the conditions that are necessary for the existence of the simplest possible problem situation.

1. There must be an individual (I) to whom the problem can be attributed. He occupies an environment (N).

2. He must have at least two courses of action (C_1 and C_2) that he can pursue; that is, he must be able to make a choice of behavior.[1]

3. There must be at least two possible outcomes (O_1 and O_2) of his choice, one of which he prefers to the other; that is, there must be at least one outcome that he wants—an objective.

4. The courses of action available to him must provide some chance of obtaining his objective (say, O_1), but they cannot provide the same chance. Otherwise his choice would not matter. Thus if $P(O_j \mid I, C_i, N)$ represents the probability that an outcome O_j will occur if I selects C_i in N,[2] then $P(O_1 \mid I, C_1, N) \neq P(O_1 \mid I, C_2, N)$. Hence the choices must have unequal efficiencies for the desired outcomes.

If these four conditions are satisfied, a problem can be said to exist, but the individual (I) can be said *to have* the problem only if he does not know

---

[1] A course of action is defined by either one or more (qualitative or quantitative) values of controlled variables, for example, the number of items purchased at a specified time or the number purchased at one time and the frequency of purchase.

[2] The environment, N, is defined by values of the uncontrolled variables, Y_j.

what course of action is "best" and if he wants to know this. That is, he
must be in doubt about the solution.

In brief, then, an individual can be said to have a problem if he wants
something, has alternative ways of pursuing it which have some, but unequal,
efficiency for obtaining what he wants, and he is in doubt about which course
of action to select.

Problem situations can be considerably more complicated than this
"minimal" type, and the kind of problem with which operations research is
usually involved generally is. Complexity can arise from any one or a combination of the following conditions:

1. A group rather than an individual has the problem.

2. The environment (N) changes in ways that affect the efficiencies of the
courses of action or the values of the outcomes.

3. The number of alternative courses of action may be very large.

4. The number of objectives may also be very large and these objectives
may not be completely consistent; that is, the decision maker may want his
cake and to eat it too.

5. The courses of action selected by the decision maker(s) may be carried
out by others (the operators), whose willingness and ability to act are therefore relevant.

6. Persons not involved in making or carrying out the decision may be
affected by it and react to it favorably or unfavorably; for example, in
business, the outcome of a decision may be affected by customers, competitors,
the public, and the government.

To formulate a problem, then, we must have the following information:

1. Who will make the decision?

2. What are his (or their) objectives?

(From these and other data we derive a measure of performance, U, for
evaluating the alternative courses of action.)

3. Which aspects of the situation are subject to the decision maker's
control (the controllable variables, X_i) and over what ranges these variables
can be controlled (the restrictions or constraints).

4. What other aspects of the environment, involving humans or not, can
affect the outcomes of the available choices (the uncontrolled variables, Y_j).

It will be recognized that we must know the components of the decision
model referred to in Chapter 1. Hence formulating a problem for research
consists in identifying, defining, and specifying the measures of the components of a decision model. Determination of the relationship between
these components (the function, f) is the objective of the model-construction
phase of the research.

DIAGNOSIS

Problems are normally brought to the operations researcher by those who control all or part of an organized man-machine system. Initial conversations are largely taken up with uncovering symptoms, documenting them, and describing them as precisely as possible. These initial conversations should extend beyond the managers in charge of the operations to those members of their staff and operating personnel who are involved in them. During this process of uncovering symptoms, progress can be made toward the formulation of the organizational objectives.

Formulating Objectives

The objectives of an organization, whatever its character, are of two types—*retentive* and *acquisitive*. Retentive objectives are those directed toward retaining or preserving either resources of value (e.g., money, time, energy, equipment, and skills) or states (e.g., comfort of individuals, safety, and stability of employment). These objectives are concerned with what is consumed by courses of action; hence they can be referred to as *inputs*.

Acquisitive objectives are concerned with acquiring resources or attaining states that the organization or its managers do not have. These are the *outputs* of the decision. Organizational objectives, then, can always be translated into maximizing outputs and minimizing inputs, or maximizing the difference between output and input (i.e., profit in the generalized, not necessarily monetary, sense).

Retentive objectives can usually be uncovered by presenting the decision makers, their staff, and operating personnel with possible solutions to the problem and by determining whether or not they would accept each solution if it were the ultimate recommendation based on the research. When the answer is "No," an analysis of the reasons usually reveals constraints and inputs that are relevant to the problem. For example, the managers of one company rejected one of a set of possible locations of a new factory because operating there would involve negotiating with a union official with whom they had had some undesirable experiences. In another case, probing the possibility of home delivery of a consumer product revealed laws that prevent such delivery in some states.

Presenting alternative potential solutions, finding preferences, and probing the reasons reveal output—as well as input—objectives. For example, one company's manager preferred diversification in one direction rather than another because it required him to learn a new technology and he wanted an intellectual challenge as well as a profitable expansion.

Examination of the measures used by management to evaluate total organizational performance, and the performance of units within the organization, also reveals relevant objectives. Finally, one can analyze the reasons for previous decisions in the relevant area. In effect, one can try to find out why the organization thinks it did what it did in the past. The reasons uncovered provide insight into organizational objectives.

Objectives generally need to be continually reformulated during the course of the research, but an early tentative formulation of them provides a valuable criterion that can be used to select pertinent information from the unlimited amount of information that exists in most organizations.

System Analysis

To determine (1) who actually makes the decisions, rather than who is authorized to make them or who has the responsibility for making them, and (2) what the controllable and uncontrollable variables are, detailed knowledge of the system involved in the problem and its environment is essential. Experience has shown that such knowledge can seldom be obtained by merely questioning those involved in operating or managing the system. Therefore, the researchers must frequently "start from scratch" and build up a complete and accurate description of the system's operations. Such a description is needed both to formulate the problem precisely and to design the implementation and control of the solution that is eventually obtained. Furthermore, a detailed knowledge of how the system operates is necessary for the researchers to communicate effectively with the system's managers about their problems.

The most efficient way of learning how the system actually operates is to perform a *system analysis*, which is a process analogous to the physical examination that a doctor performs on his patient after initial discussion of symptoms. Clearly, what one looks for and how one looks are largely determined by the information obtained during the initial discussions in which symptoms and objectives were probed.

An analysis of the system can be performed in the following way:

1. Determine whose needs or desires external to the organization it tries to satisfy. For a business this usually involves identifying the customers and the type of goods or service that they want and the company can provide. For a governmental agency, it may be the need of a portion of the population (e.g., the aged or the farmers) for a service. For a military unit, it may be the need of another unit for the maintenance of its equipment or for supplies.

2. Determine how this need or desire is communicated to the organization. In a business, for example, the need may be communicated in the form of an order given to a salesman. Then, depending on what appears to be relevant, one might determine how many salesmen and accounts there are, how many orders are received per unit time, the distribution of the sizes or orders, the distribution of orders over the product line, and so on. The amount of detail that one seeks at this and succeeding points depends on how relevant the details appear to be in formulating the problem. As the researcher's conception of the problem changes, he may have to return for information that he did not obtain the first time.

3. Determine how the information on needs is recorded and transmitted to others in the organization. For example, an order or requisition is usually prepared in multiple copies. Each of these copies should be followed to its ultimate disposition: destruction or permanent file. At each point at which the information is received, a determination should be made of what happens to it. In general, two kinds of things can happen to it.

First, the information can be transformed in some way. It may be translated into coded form, condensed, expanded, consolidated, and so on. The result is usually the preparation of a new form, which also is usually prepared in multiple copies. These should also be traced to their ultimate destinations, and so on.

Second, at some points in the system the information may be used to reach a decision and issue instructions. At such points instructions should be followed to their consummation. In most systems one form of instruction results in the ordering and eventual receipt of resources in the system (e.g., raw material or money). The flow of resources should then be followed through its processing, noting at each point, as in the case of information handling, the rate of each process, the capacity at the point, and other relevant information. Instruction emanating from the flow of information will meet the resource processing at key points, which should be noted. Ultimately the finished product or service will be delivered to the customer.

The information about the system obtained in the steps described is usually best recorded on a series of flow diagrams, which are liberally sprinkled with notes and appended with copies of the forms used in transmitting information and instruction.

Once this information has been collected, it can be subjected to analysis. First, all transmissions of information that do not produce action—so-called "information copies"—can be eliminated from the diagram. Operations on resources that occur between control points can be condensed into one composite operation. By geometrical manipulation of the resulting flow diagram, crossing lines can be minimized and frequently eliminated. The fewer the crossings, the easier it is to perceive the nature of the flow. Understanding of the flow can be facilitated by the use of different symbols for information-transformation points, decision-making points, and files. Color can be used to distinguish between the flow of information, instruction, and resources, and even different documents or products. Figure 2.1 shows a typical initial

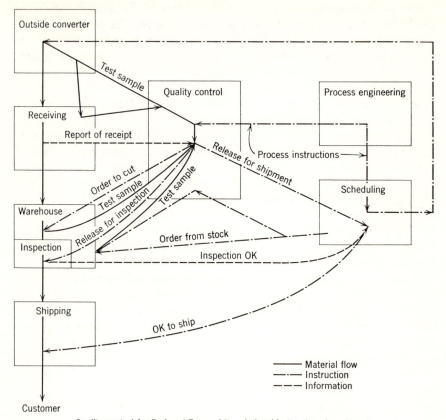

Quality control for Rod and Bar and its relationship to other departments

Figure 2.1 Example of initial notes in a system analysis.

recording of information; Figure 2.2 is a finished diagram of a production process.

The finished diagram is a descriptive model of the organization's operations. Preparation of such a flow diagram usually reveals many symptoms that are not likely to be revealed in conversation. It also helps in identifying the controllable and uncontrollable but relevant variables, those who make decisions, and the information that is available to them when they make decisions.

In a system analysis of one production process it was found that many parts that had not been originally scheduled for production were being processed on an emergency basis because lack of them was delaying assembly of finished products The analysis also revealed the cause of the shortages: independent control of withdrawal of parts from stock by both the production-control and replacement-part departments. An organizational change removed this cause of shortage and prepared the way for a comprehensive production and inventory control system.

In another case in which a shortage of parts was delaying assembly of finished products, it was found that most of the time period between receipt of an order and shipment of the finished product was consumed by paper work. Eleven of the thirty days normally available were consumed by delays at one paper operation that involved checking orders for appropriate identification of the finished product. This operation was shown to be redundant by the system analysis; hence it was possible to increase the time available for producing parts and thus reduce the number and duration of delays in the assembly process.

These examples illustrate how courses of action that can alleviate, if not solve, a problem can be uncovered by a system analysis.

The descriptive model of the system can also reveal points at which control can be, but is not being, exercised. For example, in the system analysis of another parts-production process it was found that parts were classified into those to be made by the company and those to be bought from others on the basis of a study that had been made many years before, although the product-mix and production facilities had changed considerably since that time. It was possible to develop a process by which the decision could be continually reviewed in light of the changing load on the shop and the cost of purchase. This produced significant reductions in costs.

In brief, then, a system analysis can provide the background information needed in formulating the problem and the model required to solve it. Development of the model usually raises further questions about the objectives, courses of action, and uncontrolled variables. Thus system analysis and model construction frequently interact to produce a more nearly complete understanding of the system and the problem to be solved than can be obtained by other means.

The system analysis and the resulting diagram have other important uses. They provide a basis for estimating the time, cost, and amount of research effort required to solve the problem that is eventually formulated, and indicate the potential advantages in so doing. Furthermore, the diagram is almost always a useful tool for management, because it reveals how the organization actually operates rather than how it is supposed to work.

TYPES OF PROBLEMS

Once the decision makers, their objectives, the courses of action, and the uncontrolled variables have been identified and defined, it is necessary to construct a measure of performance that can be used to determine which alternative is best and what function of this measure (the "objective function")

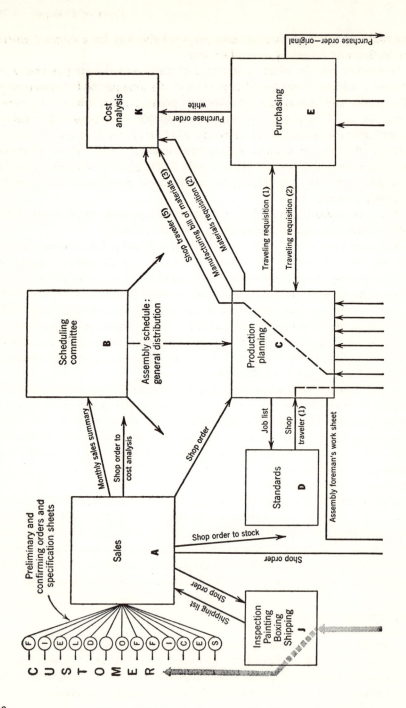

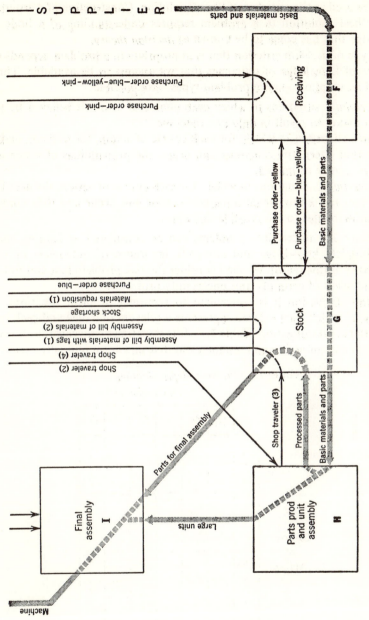

Figure 2.2 Control and materials flow chart.

should be used as the criterion of "best" solution. Construction of a criterion of the "best" solution to a problem requires understanding of a body of knowledge that has come to be known as *decision theory*.

The type of decision criterion that is appropriate to a problem depends on the state of knowledge of outcomes that we assume to be available. Three types of assumption—hence problem types—are possible:

1. *Certainty:* situations in which each course of action is believed by the decision maker to result in only one outcome.

2. *Risk:* situations in which, for each course of action, the decision maker believes that alternative outcomes can occur, the probabilities of which are known or can be estimated.

3. *Uncertainty:* situations in which, for each course of action, the decision maker does not know which outcomes can or will occur and thus connot assign probabilities to the possible outcomes.

Certainty and uncertainty problems can be considered as limiting cases (e.g., complete knowledge and complete ignorance of outcomes) of risk problems. For this reason we shall consider the risk problem first and follow it by discussion of certainty and uncertainty problems.

For this discussion it is convenient to represent problem situations by matrices, in which each column represents a relevant outcome and each row a potential course of action (Table 2.1). It is sometimes convenient to formulate the courses of action and outcomes so that they form mutually exclusive

TABLE 2.1   *Problem Representation*

Outcomes

	O_1	O_2	$\cdots$	O_j	$\cdots$	O_n
C_1						
C_2						
.						
.						
.						
C_i						
.						
.						
.						
C_m						

Courses of Action

and exhaustive sets (i.e., only one can be selected or can occur, and one must be selected or must occur). This can always be done by performing a "Boolean expansion" on any set of elements (courses of action or outcomes). For example, if we have two outcomes o_1 and o_2 that are not exclusive and exhaustive, we can form four composite outcomes that have these properties:

O_1: o_1 and o_2 occur
O_2: o_1 occurs but not o_2
O_3: o_2 occurs but not o_1
O_4: neither o_1 nor o_2 occurs

In general, if there are n "elementary" outcomes, the Boolean expansion will yield 2^n composite outcomes. When n is large, it may be more convenient to deal with the smaller number of elementary outcomes and only "compose" those sets of elementary outcomes that must be evaluated.

Risk Problem Situations

Consider the simple choice situation represented in Table 2.2, where the entries in the cells represent the utilities of the outcomes to the decision maker. Such a table is called a *payoff matrix*.

TABLE 2.2 *A Simple Payoff Matrix*

	O_1	O_2
C_1	1	5
C_2	2	3

The payoff for each C_i-O_j pair is the utility of the difference between the output (O_j) and the input associated with C_i. Hence, if C_1 and C_2 in Table 2.2 required the same input, their payoffs in each column would be the same. The fact that the payoffs in the columns are different indicates that the courses of action involve different "costs" in achieving the same outcome.

If, in the situation represented in Table 2.2, we know or can estimate the probability of each outcome given each course of action, $P(O_j \mid C_i)$, we can proceed as follows:

Suppose that $P(O_1 \mid C_1) = 0.7$ $P(O_1 \mid C_2) = 0.4$
$P(O_2 \mid C_1) = 0.3$ $P(O_2 \mid C_2) = 0.6$

We can then compute the *expected utility* of each course of action, $EU(C_i)$:

$$EU(C_1) = 0.7(1) + 0.3(5) = 2.2$$
$$EU(C_2) = 0.4(2) + 0.6(3) = 2.6$$

It would seem reasonable, then, to select C_2 because it *maximizes expected utility*. This is the criterion that is generally accepted as the most appropriate in risk problem situations.

The criterion can be stated more generally as follows:

$$\max_{C_i} [EU(C_i) = \sum_{j=1}^{n} P(O_j \mid C_i) U(O_j, C_i)] \tag{2.1}$$

This criterion can be used in a relatively straightforward way as long as the outcomes are formulated so as to be exclusive and exhaustive. But, as indicated above, this is not always feasible.

For example, suppose that an organization wants to minimize cost and to minimize service time to customers. An objective of the form—to minimize (or maximize) V—involves a set of outcomes. V is a variable that can assume values on a scale S_V. In any situation involving such a scale there are either

TABLE 2.3   *A Two Quantitative-Objectives Problem*

	O_1 = to minimize V				O_2 = to minimize W			
	v_1	v_2	$\cdots$	v_m	w_1	w_2	$\cdots$	w_n
C_1								
C_2								
$\cdot$								
$\cdot$								
$\cdot$								

smallest units that we can measure or units such that smaller quantities are of no practical significance. For example, in measuring the cost of operating a factory, units of a hundred, thousand, or ten thousand dollars may be the smallest of interest or the smallest that we can measure. Therefore, if V is cost in, say, thousands of dollars, we can let $v_0 = \$000$, $v_1 = \$1000$, $v_2 = \$2000$, and so on. Similarly, if we let W = service time, which is to be measured in days, we can let $w_0 = 0$ days, $w_1 = 1$ day, $w_2 = 2$ days, and so on. There might be a prohibitively large number of possible combinations of values of V and W. If there are m possible values of V and n of W, there would be mn possible combinations in an exclusive and exhaustive set of outcomes. We can, however, represent the problem situation as shown in Table 2.3. In this representation each use of each course of action would result in two outcomes, one value of V and one of W, $v_j w_k$. If the utility of both outcomes taken together is equal to the sum of their separate utilities, we do not have to determine the utilities of each combination in advance. But if the utility of the combination is not equal to the sum of the utilities of the components, that is, if

$$U(v_j, w_k) \neq U(v_j) + U(w_k), \tag{2.2}$$

it appears that we must determine the utility of each combination of outcomes that has any chance of being produced by any course of action. However, there is another (and usually easier) way of handling such a situation. Suppose that we can transform units on the V-scale into values on the W-scale. That is, suppose that we can find the *tradeoff function* that transforms

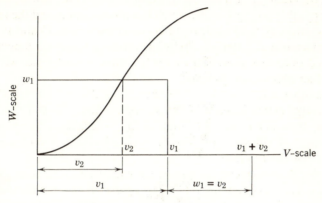

Figure 2.3   A tradeoff function.

values on one scale onto the other (for example, see Figure 2.3). By use of such a function we can convert a combination of outcomes (v_1, w_1) to one outcome $(v_3 = v_1 + v_2$, where v_2 is the transformed value of $w_1)$ and express all combinations of outcomes on one "standard" scale. This procedure can be applied to any number of outcome scales.

Therefore, to maximize expected utility in a risk problem we may require not only measures of efficiency (probabilities of outcomes) and utility of outcomes, but also tradeoff functions. The latter may not be necessary in principle, but they may be essential from a practical point of view. Later in this chapter we shall consider how the measures of efficiency and utility, as well as tradeoff functions, can be obtained in practice. But let us first consider criteria of performance other than maximum expected utility which are sometimes used in risk problem situations. We shall examine them in an order that reflects the strength of the utility assumptions made by them, from the weakest to the strongest.

If we were to examine completed OR studies, we would find that few of them had employed expected utility as a measure of performance. Other simpler types of measure are generally used. These are equivalent to expected utility under certain utility conditions. Hence in using any of the simpler measures it is important to be aware of the assumptions about utility that are required to make the results of using such measures equivalent to maximizing utility. We shall consider three types of simplification: maximizing effectiveness, satisficing, and maximizing efficiency.

Maximizing Effectiveness. If we have two objectives—for example, to maximize V and minimize W—a complete description of an outcome requires specifying a point in the V-W space (v_j, w_k). As already discussed, if points on the W-scale can be transformed into points of equivalent utility on the V-scale by means of a trade-off function, the outcome can be expressed as a single number on the V-scale, which is a function of v_j and the transformed w_k. Now values on the V-scale represent combinations of V- and W-outcomes. If for any course of action we obtain the probability density function of these combined outcomes expressed as single values on one scale, we have what is called an *effectiveness function*.

Put another way, if we have the probability density (efficiency) functions of a course of action on each of two outcome scales, V and W, and a tradeoff function $W = \phi(V)$, we can combine the V-efficiency function and the transformed W-efficiency function into an effectiveness function expressed on the V (or the W)-scale.

Courses of action can be compared with respect to their effectiveness functions. This is commonly done. The course of action with the maximum expected effectiveness is frequently taken as the "best," but maximization of expected effectiveness is not always equivalent to maximization of expected utility, as, to take an extreme case, when utility is a monotonically decreasing function of values on the effectiveness scale.

The point is that in using "maximum expected effectiveness" as a criterion of choice, one should be certain that some utility assumption holds that makes this criterion equivalent to maximizing expected utility. Unfortunately, in most OR studies such assumptions are usually made implicitly rather than explicitly; hence they are seldom justified in any self-conscious or explicit way. Fortunately, closer examination frequently shows that the assumptions are justified.

A common practice in situations in which the researcher wants to avoid transforming a W-scale into a V-scale is the following. For each of the specified set of W-values, that course of action is found which has an expected W-outcome equal to the specified W-value and which minimizes (or maximizes, whichever is appropriate) the expected value of the V-outcome.[3] The results can then be displayed graphically as shown in Figure 2.4. For each point there is a corresponding "V-minimizing" course of action. Such a display is presented to the decision maker and he selects that point at which

[3] This procedure can be applied to more than two scales. See Feeney (1955).

he wants to operate. The corresponding course of action is then selected. In such a case the decision maker implicitly makes utility judgments about combined *V-* and *W*-outcomes. It should be noted, however, that he is presented only with expected outcomes and not with the distribution (hence variability) of outcomes associated with various courses of action. He may select a point whose expected effectiveness has maximum utility to him, but the associated course of action may not yield maximum expected utility. For example, the course of action may have a greater probability of yielding a

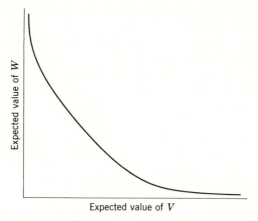

Figure 2.4   Mimimum expected value of *V* for specified expected values of *W*.

disastrous outcome than another course of action whose expected effectiveness has less utility. Hence utility assumptions are involved that justify dealing only with expected values of effectiveness functions.[4]

Satisficing.   If one has a particular level of performance for which he strives, and for which he is willing to settle, he is said to be satisficing. Hence if there are two or more objectives measured on different outcome scales, the need to transform these into one effectiveness scale is sometimes avoided by optimizing with respect to one and satisficing with respect to the other. For example:

> To maximize (or minimize) the average efficiency (or inefficiency) relative to the *V*-outcome, and to attain a level of performance on the *W*-outcome scale equal to or exceeding a specified value, w_a.

This combines maximization with respect to *V* and *satisficing* with respect to *W*. Attainment of a value no less than w_a is imposed as a requirement on

[4] A common example of this occurs when the *V*-scale represents the cost of holding inventory and the *W*-scale is the probability of shortages that arise.

the acceptability of any solution. Satisficing is usually used when it is very costly to evaluate all alternative courses of action.

This criterion involves the following utility assumptions. First, it assumes that an outcome on the W-scale of less than w_a has no utility, and that all other outcomes have equal utility. Second, it assumes that the utility of any possible outcome on the V-scale has less utility than an outcome on the W-scale of w_a or greater. Finally, it makes some utility assumption (such as were previously cited) that justifies ignoring the dispersion of the V-outcomes around the expected V-outcome.

Maximizing Efficiency.   If there are two or more objectives measured on different outcome scales and all but one is ignored, the efficiency relative to only this one may be maximized. The utilities of all values on the scales of the neglected objectives are essentially assumed to be zero. This is equivalent to assuming that there is only one objective. This is about as strong an assumption as one can make. Little wonder that it is seldom justified.

Certainty Problem Situations

The certainty problem can be considered as a limiting case of the risk problem—the probability of each outcome is known or believed to be equal to one or zero. Consequently, the criterion used for such problems is the limiting case of maximizing expected utility. By substituting values of one and zero for $P(O_j \mid C_i)$ in (2.1) we obtain

$$\max_{C_i} [U(C_i) = U(O_j, C_i)] \tag{2.3}$$

where

$$P(O_j \mid C_i) = 1.0$$

which is the *maximization of utility*.

For example, consider the simplest problem situation, in which there are two alternative courses of action, C_1 and C_2, and two outcomes, O_1 and O_2. If C_1 is known always to produce O_1 and C_2 always to produce O_2, we only need to know which outcome has the greater utility to determine which course of action is the better of the two. The same is true for any number of courses of action and outcomes, if the outcomes form an exclusive and exhaustive set.

If the outcomes are not mutually exclusive and if the utility of any combination of outcomes is equal to the sum of the utilities of the elementary outcomes, we need only add the utilities of the outcomes associated with each course of action. If the utilities are not additive, we must determine the utility of the combined outcomes. If a large number of such combinations can occur, it may be desirable to use tradeoff functions to transform combined outcomes to single values on a common scale and determine the utility function of this scale.

Because there is no variability associated with outcomes, the justification for the use of maximum effectiveness as a criterion of decision instead of maximum utility is not complex as it is in risk-type problems. All that one needs to know is whether or not the utility function is monotonically increasing. If it is, the course of action with maximum effectiveness yields as much or more utility than any other course of action.

Because certainty problems do not involve probabilities as do risk problems, models of them are deterministic; hence they usually are easier to construct and solve. Such models often are so much easier to handle than are their probabilistic counterparts that they are used even when the situation is known to be probabilistic. In some cases the probabilistic version of the problem may yield models that are not capable of exact solution. Hence the researcher is frequently confronted with a choice between an exact solution to an approximate (deterministic) model and an approximate solution to a more exact (probabilistic) model. Evaluation of the alternatives often favors the former. This is particularly true in allocation and inventory problems. The techniques for solving deterministic models of such problems are so powerful that they are often applied to models in which average values of probabilistic variables are used as if they were unique values of deterministic variables. Considerable testing of such practice, particularly by its application to simulated probabilistic systems, has shown that the solutions derived are often as good as, or almost as good as, those derived from probabilistic models.

Uncertainty Problem Situations

In real problem situations that initially appear to offer no knowledge of outcome probabilities, the researcher can and generally does seek information about these probabilities by research. Some of the techniques will be discussed later. Nevertheless, it is conceivable that the researcher or decision maker has little confidence in his estimates of outcome probabilities, and that he has no opportunity to improve these estimates. He may therefore prefer to act as though he had no knowledge of these probabilities. For this reason, and because the operations researcher should be aware of what has been done on uncertainty problems, we shall consider criteria of choice that have been proposed for such problems.

Three criteria have been suggested for selecting a course of action in uncertainty problem situations: *maximum* (and *minimax*), the *generalized maximun*, and the *minimax regret*. We shall consider each in turn.

Maximin. A decision maker who is confronted with the problem represented in Table 2.2 can reason as follows:

1. If I select C_1, the minimum gain that I can obtain is 1.
2. If I select C_2, the minimum gain that I can obtain is 2.
3. There, I will select C_2 because it maximizes the minimum gain.

The criterion employed in this argument is called *maximin*. It is generally attributed to von Neumann. This criterion is defined precisely as

$$\max_{C_i} \min_{O_j} [U(O_j, C_i)] \qquad (2.4)$$

where $U(O_j, C_i)$ is the utility obtained by the decision maker if O_j is obtained by use of C_i in the relevant environment.

The "solution" in this case has several interesting properties. Suppose that the outcome were selected by an opposing decision maker who had to pay for the utilities achieved by the first decision maker. The opponent might reason as follows:

1. If I select O_1, the maximum loss that I can incur is 2.
2. If I select O_2, the maximum loss that I can incur is 3.
3. Therefore, I will select O_1 because it minimizes the maximum loss.

This criterion is *minimax:*

$$\min_{O_j} \max_{C} [U(O_j, C_i)]. \qquad (2.5)$$

Now, in this problem

$$\max_{C_j} \min_{O_j} [U(O_j, C_i)] = \min_{O_j} \max_{C_i} [U(O_j, C_i)] = 2.$$

If this equality holds, the problem is said to be solved. The solution that has a value of 2 in the illustration occurs at (C_2, O_1), which is called a *saddle point*: there is no higher value in its column and no lower value in its row. A payoff matrix with more than two outcomes may have several saddle points, but they will always be equivalent.

The essential property of a saddle point is that the two corresponding strategies are "best" for each decision maker in the sense that each knows the worst that can happen to him and that the worst is as good as possible. If either departs from the saddle point, his opponent may take advantage of the situation. For example, if C_1 (in Table 2.2) is chosen in the hope of gaining 5, it is possible that O_1 will occur and yield only 1.

Now consider a payoff matrix that has no saddle point, such as that in Table 2.4. In this case

$$\max_{C_j} \min_{O_i} [U(O_j, C_i)] = (C_1, O_1) = 2$$

and

$$\min_{O_j} \max_{C_j} [U(O_j, C_i)] = (C_2, O_1) = 3.$$

The minimax and maximin solutions are not equivalent. Therefore, it is possible for the decision maker to assure himself of more than a minimum gain of 2 by employing what is called a *mixed strategy*. Such a strategy consists of selecting C_1 with a probability P_1, and C_2 with probability P_2 such that

$$P_1(2) + P_2(3) = P_1(5) + P_2(1),$$

TABLE 2.4   *A Payoff Matrix
with no Saddle Point*

	O_1	O_2
C_1	2	5
C_2	3	1

and more generally, so that

$$P_1 U(O_1, C_1) + P_2 U(O_1, C_2) + \cdots + P_m U(O_1, C_m)$$
$$= P_1 U(O_2, C_1) + P_2 U(O_2, C_2) + \cdots + P_m U(O_2, C_m). \quad (2.6)$$

Perhaps the easiest way to understand how a mixed strategy is chosen is to imagine that a consultant (whose services are free!) approaches the decision maker and offers him a plan that is guaranteed to provide him with an average gain of G. How would such a plan work? Suppose that C_1 is chosen with probability P_1 and C_2 with probability $P_2 = 1 - P_1$. Then, if the outcome is O_1, the expected gain is $2P_1 + 3P_2$ and if the outcome is O_2, the gain is $5P_1 + P_2$. Because G was guaranteed, we must have

$$(1) \quad 2P_1 + 3P_2 \geq G$$

and

$$(2) \quad 5P_1 + P_2 \geq G,$$

so that no matter what the outcome, the gain is at least G. Now suppose that another consultant offers a second plan which guarantees G'. Clearly the second plan will be accepted if $G' > G$. In fact, the best possible plan would be the one with the largest guarantee. It is not hard to show that with only two outcomes, two courses of action, and no saddle point, the largest G occurs when both (1) and (2) are strict equalities; that is, when

$$G = 2P_1 + 3(1 - P_1) = 5P_1 + (1 - P_1)$$

from which we obtain

$$P_1 = \tfrac{2}{5} \quad \text{and} \quad G = 2\tfrac{3}{5}.$$

Similar reasoning will show that if O_1 occurs with probability Q_1 and O_2 with probability $Q_2 = 1 - Q_1$, the decision maker who chooses the outcome will lose on the average an amount L and L may be made as small as possible with suitable choice of Q_1. It may be shown that the smallest value of L is equal to $-2\tfrac{3}{5}$. In fact, if $Q_1 = \tfrac{4}{5}$, the gain to the first decision maker is $2\tfrac{3}{5}$ no matter which decision he makes.

This kind of reasoning may be generalized to any situation with a finite number of decisions and outcomes.

The weakness of the reasoning lies in the assumption that the outcomes are chosen by a rational being whose interests are directly opposed to our own.

We must assume, therefore, that if our decision rules allow our opponent to take advantage of us, he will do so. Hence we make decisions in such a way that the gain of utility cannot be affected no matter what outcome is attained. The reasoning is taken from the Theory of Games where it may be appropriate; except in certain types of competitive situations, it seems unlikely, however, that we need to make such pessimistic assumptions. Either the outcomes are not chosen by a rational opponent or the opponent's aims may not be opposed to our own. In either case, if we know or can find the relative frequencies of the outcomes, we can use such information in making our decision.

Generalized Maximin. To overcome some of these objectives, Hurwicz (1951) suggested a more general criterion, which makes possible varying degrees of optimism. The Hurwicz criterion is

$$\max_{C_i} \{\alpha \max_{O_j} [U(O_j, C_i)] + (1 - \alpha) \min_{C_i} [U(O_j, C_i)]\} \qquad (2.7)$$

where $0 \leq \alpha \leq 1$. The term α may be thought of as an index of optimism. If $\alpha = 0$, the Hurwicz criterion reduces to *maximin*. On the other hand, if $\alpha = 1$, the criterion becomes *maximax:* it would direct selection of that course of action which maximizes the "maximum gain." Suppose that we set $\alpha = 0.6$ and apply it to the payoff matrix shown in Table 2.2. Then, if the decision maker selects C_1, the maximum gain is 5 and the minimum is 1. Therefore,

$$0.6(5) + 0.4(1) = 3.4.$$

Similarly, if he selects C_2, then

$$0.6(3) + 0.4(2) = 2.6.$$

Therefore, C_1 is best by this criterion.

Note that α acts like a probability term: if α is interpreted as a subjective estimate of probability, this criterion is equivalent to *maximizing expected utility*.

Minimax Regret. Savage (1954) has suggested a third criterion. To employ his criterion, the payoff matrix must be converted to a regret matrix. In each cell we enter the difference between what the decision maker would have done if he had known which outcome would occur, and the choice represented by that cell. For example, the payoff matrix shown in Table 2.5a converts into the regret matrix shown in Table 2.5b. If the decision maker knew that O_1 would occur, he would select C_2; therefore, if he selected C_1 and O_1 did occur, his regret would be $2 - 1 = 1$. Had he selected C_2 and O_1 occurred, he would have no regret. Similarly, if he knew O_2 would occur, he would select C_1 and gain 5. Therefore, if he selects C_2 and O_2 occurs, his regret is $5 - 3 = 2$. Once the regret matrix is formed, the minimax criterion can be applied to it to select the "best" course of action. In this particular case a mixed strategy would be required. However, it does not seem appropriate to use a strategy against nature; only against an opponent who (1) is rational, (2) cannot know our decision before making his own, and (3) can himself employ a mixed strategy against us, which is designed to minimize our gains or maximize our regret.

The following is an example of the application of a "regret analysis." A company that was entering a new business found it necessary to build a plant to produce the new product. The plant could be built with either one, two, or

TABLE 2.5

	O_1	O_2
C_1	1	5
C_2	2	3

(a) Payoff

	O_1	O_2
C_1	1	0
C_2	0	2

(b) Regret

three production units. Forecasts of annual sales were prepared for the next ten years. For each year three forecasts were made: pessimistic, conservative, and optimistic. The one-unit plant was best if the pessimistic forecast were true; the two-unit plant, if the conservative forecast were true; and the three-unit plant, if the optimistic forecast were true. The basis for the forecasts was not firm; hence it was impossible to assign objective probabilities to them. The managers could not agree on a set of subjective estimates, because some of them were pessimistic, some conservative, and some optimistic. The problem was resolved by using the regret principle. For each forecast, the present value of future profits for each initial plant size was determined. This yielded a 3 × 3 payoff matrix, which was converted to a regret matrix. In this case regret was minimized by building the three-unit plant. The managers agreed to proceed on this basis, because it seemed reasonable to them and it avoided a complex resolution of their differences of opinion concerning the future.

The existence of three criteria of choice in uncertainty problems creates the need for a metacriterion to determine which of the three is the best criterion in any specific situation. No such metacriterion has yet been developed. Hence the researcher must resort to his own or the manager's intuition.

MEASUREMENT OF EFFICIENCY

Only in a completely deterministic situation, such as a controlled game, would a course of action always consume exactly the same input and yield exactly the same output. The kinds of situations with which OR deals are seldom, if ever, deterministic, although they are sometimes assumed to be in order to simplify the problem. In many, if not most problems, however, it is necessary to estimate the outcome probabilities associated with the controlled variables.

Estimates of probabilities are of two types: *objective* and *subjective*. Objective probabilities are estimated from the observed ratio of the number of occurrences of the event of interest to the total number of observed outcomes. Procedures for deriving such estimates from observed "relative frequencies" are well established in mathematical statistics and need not occupy us here.

Science has traditionally tried to shy away from subjective probabilities. The work of Savage (1954) and Churchman (1961), however, has shown that subjective estimates of probability cannot be avoided in science. Churchman has shown that even estimates of objective probability presuppose estimates of subjective probability. Consequently, procedures for obtaining subjective estimates have been receiving increased attention. One such procedure is described here.

Suppose that we have two exclusive and exhaustive outcomes, O_1 and O_2, whose utilities are not equal, and two courses of action, C_1 and C_2. We wish to determine what the decision maker's estimates of $P(O_1 \mid C_1)$ and $P(O_1 \mid C_2)$ are. From these we can estimate $P(O_2 \mid C_1)$ and $P(O_2 \mid C_2)$, because we postulate that $P(O_2 \mid C_1) = 1 - P(O_1 \mid C_1)$ and $P(O_2 \mid C_2) = 1 - P(O_1 \mid C_2)$. We can, of course, simply ask the decision maker for his estimates, but we may want to check their reliability. We can do so as follows.

Using the decision maker's initial estimates of probabilities, we can calculate the expected utility of each choice. Let α represent the ratio of the smaller expected utility to the larger; hence $0 \leq \alpha \leq 1$. Suppose that $EU(C_1) > EU(C_2)$ and $EU(C_2)/EU(C_1) = \alpha = 0.8$. Now offer the decision maker the following choice:

> If you select C_1, we will select a number at random from 1 to 10. If we obtain any number from 1 to 8 inclusive, you can follow through with C_1; but if we obtain a 9 or a 10, you can do nothing. If, on the other hand, you select C_2, you can pursue it with certainty. Which do you prefer?

If the decision maker has no preference (i.e., he is indifferent to the alternatives) under these circumstances, his original estimates of outcome probabilities can be left as they are. Otherwise the estimates will have to be modified until they yield an α such that when the type of choice described is offered, there is no preference.

For example, suppose that the payoff matrix is that shown in Table 2.6 and the subject's estimates of outcome probabilities are $P_{11} = 0.4$, $P_{12} = 0.6$, $P_{21} = 0.7$, $P_{22} = 0.3$.[5] Then

$$EU(C_1) = 0.4(2) + 0.6(5) = 3.8$$
$$EU(C_2) = 0.7(3) + 0.3(1) = 2.4.$$

In this case $\alpha = 2.4/3.8 = 0.63$. Now, if we offer the choice $0.63C_1$ or C_2, there should be no preference. If, however, $0.63C_1$ is preferred to C_2, either P_{12} or P_{22} must be decreased. If C_2 is preferred to $0.63C_1$, either P_{12} or P_{22} must be increased. Adjustments should be made until the α that produces indifference is obtained. If more than two courses of action are involved,

TABLE 2.6 *A*
Payoff Matrix

	O_1	O_2
C_1	2	5
C_2	3	1

they would be considered as a pair until all necessary adjustments are made. If more than two outcomes are involved, the adjustment of probability estimates would require taking more such estimates into account.

When possible, it is desirable to get the decision maker's estimates of the highest and lowest value that he believes each probability can assume, as well as his "best" estimate. One can then determine whether changes of the value within these ranges make a difference in the evaluation of alternative courses of action. For example, suppose that in the last example the range on P_{11} were 0.2–0.6 (hence P_{12} would range from 0.8 to 0.4), and on P_{21}, 0.6–0.8 (hence P_{22} would range from 0.4 to 0.2). We can evaluate the most favorable case to C_1:

$$P_{12} = (1 - P_{11})$$

$$EU(C_1) = 0.2(2) + 0.8(5) = 4.4$$
$$EU(C_2) = 0.6(3) + 0.4(1) = 2.2;$$

and the most favorable case to C_2:

$$EU(C_1) = 0.6(2) + 0.4(5) = 3.2$$
$$EU(C_2) = 0.8(3) + 0.2(1) = 2.6.$$

Hence in this case variations within the "expected range" make no difference because C_1 is best in each case. Isaacs (1963) has shown how to calculate

[5] For the sake of simplicity, we let $P_{ij} = P(O_j \mid C_i)$.

the ranges of probabilities within which no change in choice is required for problems of this type. His procedure applies to more than two courses of action.

TRADEOFF FUNCTIONS

Tradeoff functions, like estimates of outcome probabilities, may be obtained either objectively or subjectively. First we examine objective procedures, which are based on the behavior of the system under study.

Objective Tradeoffs

Consider the following simplifications of a real case. A merchandising firm receives mail orders for goods selected by customers from a catalogue. The

Figure 2.5

orders are filled by clerks who draw the required goods from stocks, package, and mail them. In this case the company wanted to determine how large a staff of order clerks it should maintain. Two objectives were involved: the company desired to minimize the cost of its operations (conservation objective), and it also sought to minimize the time the customer must wait for receipt of the goods ordered (avoidance objective).

It seemed clear that it would be desirable to express the (negative) value of delay to the customer as a cost. Consequently, the research team studied the system to ascertain the cost of order-filling delay to the company. First, records were examined to determine what proportion of orders were returned to the company by the customer because of delay and how this proportion varied for various delays in receipt of goods by the customer. This analysis revealed a function of the form shown in Figure 2.5. That is, delays of up to a few days had practically no effect on the return rate; for longer delays the proportion of returns increased at a relatively constant rate. Beyond a certain delay time the return rate remained relatively constant, rising almost imperceptibly.

Next, analysis was performed to determine whether the value of the goods was in any way related to the delay in shipment. No relationship was found. This meant that the length of a delay in shipping did not depend on the size or value of an order.

It was then necessary to determine the cost of a returned order. This cost involved both direct outlays and customer dissatisfaction. Hence an analysis was made of the salvage value of returned orders. Salvage value was expressed as a percentage of the sale value and as such was found to be relatively constant.

By studying the distribution of the sizes of orders, the average dollar loss resulting from a returned order could be determined. To this expected cost

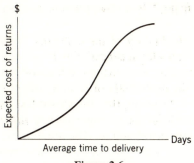

Figure 2.6

was added the cost of shipping itself. Finally, by multiplying this combined cost of return by the probability of return, a function of the form shown in Figure 2.6 was obtained. This, then, provided a transformation function, in which the expected cost associated with various delays could be obtained.

The question remained whether customers were lost by long delays and, consequently, whether loss of future sales also had to be taken into account. On examination of the records, however, it was found that delays of the frequency and magnitude that actually had been experienced by customers did not affect the amount or frequency of their orders. Therefore the transformation could be used without adjustment for loss of future business. It was very likely, of course, that repetitive delays of longer duration than customers had previously experienced would affect future business, but the range of delays within which the company was willing to operate (i.e., the constraints it imposed) made the probability of a sequence of long delays very unlikely.

The underlying principle in this procedure is very simple: it involves determining what is the loss of the resource that is to be conserved if the event to be avoided occurs. Determination of this loss, however, may be very complicated or even impractical. If, for example, in the case just considered, customers were lost because of repetition of delays, it would have been a much more difficult problem, although not necessarily an impossible one.

In another problem, in which the event to be avoided was the cancellation of a scheduled flight of a commercial airline, it was not possible (nor, as it turned out, necessary) to determine the effect on future business of such a cancellation. A variation of the transformation procedure just described was used.

The problem of the commercial airline involved determining how many stewardesses should be located at each base. The objectives were "to minimize the cost of stewardesses" (the size of the stewardess staff at each base) and "to minimize the number of instances on which stewardesses were not available for a scheduled flight." If a stewardess is not available for a flight, it cannot be flown.

An examination of the history of the company revealed—to the surprise of the research team—that a flight cancellation because of lack of stewardesses had never taken place. This was surprising because it could be shown that with the existing staff the probability of running out of stewardesses was not negligible. It turned out, however, that the stewardess administrators at each base had advance knowledge as to when such a runout would occur and therefore could take preventive action. The administrator would obtain the aid of a former stewardess who lived in the city and could be enlisted on an emergency basis at an additional cost to the company. In this case, then, the cost of a runout was the cost of the emergency measure (expediting) that was taken. This cost was not a linear function of the number of simultaneous runouts. That is, it was increasingly difficult for the administrator to obtain emergency stewardesses as the number required increased. An examination of the records indicated that these costs increased approximately as the square of the number of stewardesses required, that is, quadratically.

It should be observed that the cost of prevention might exceed the cost of the event to be avoided. But if it does not, the correct policy is to prevent rather than to incur the undesirable outcome, and the "cost" of such an event as "running out" is the cost of preventing that outcome if the event occurs.

A similar problem arose in connection with production control in a pharmaceutical company. Here the objectives were "to minimize production and inventory costs" and (again) "to minimize the lateness of delivery of customers orders." An examination of records indicated that delays beyond promised delivery dates practically never occurred. This was due to the fact that when there was a shortage of a product relative to an order in hand, a special production run was initiated and expedited under the direction of a manager so as to be certain that the promised delivery date was met.

Here the cost of expediting involved two components: the cost of the labor (managerial and other) required to perform the necessary expediting, and the cost added to scheduled production by the interruptions in the schedule. To determine the second component of cost was difficult but possible.

The general logic of the second objective procedure for making an objective transformation, then, is to determine the cost (in terms of the resources to be conserved) of avoiding or preventing the event to be avoided. This method assumes that avoidance is always possible. Justification of this assumption may be difficult, but is nevertheless necessary for the legitimate application of the procedure.

Subjective Tradeoffs

If an objective procedure cannot be used, the researcher may employ the procedure described earlier, in which one controlled variable is minimized or maximized for a number of selected values of the other. The plotted results are presented to the decision maker for selection of the pair of values of O_1 and O_2 that he prefers.

The researcher can also ask the decision maker to sketch his believed tradeoff function on graph paper. If there are several decision makers, each should be asked to do so independently of the others. They should then discuss the results together and resolve their differences. In practice, agreement does not seem difficult to obtain.

These two subjective but explicit procedures open the possibility of future objective evaluation of the tradeoff used. It is important to remember that a decision about two or more objectives that involve different units or measures requires tradeoff decisions. They cannot be avoided, but they can be hidden and kept from conscious evaluation.

MEASUREMENT OF UTILITY

Attempts to measure the utility of objects, events, states, and their properties date back at least to Jeremy Bentham (1789), but it was not until the recent work of von Neumann and Morgenstern (1953) that a procedure was developed in which scientists have placed any confidence. Since then a number of procedures have been worked out,[6] two of which are discussed here.

The first procedure is a simplification of that proposed by von Neumann and Morgenstern. It can be applied either to go–no-go outcomes or to different outcomes on the same or different scales.

The procedure is based on the assumption that if the utility of O is U and the probability of attaining O is p, the utility of this situation is pU. That is, we would be indifferent to an outcome with utility pU and to an outcome with

[6] For detailed discussion, see Fishburn (1964) and (1967).

utility U and probability p of occurring. This is a fundamental assumption about human behavior that may not be valid in some circumstances.

Given any two outcomes (objects, events, states, or properties of these), one can estimate their utility to the decision maker by the following methods:

1. Determining which outcome is preferred; say, O_1 is preferred to O_2: $O_1 > O_2$.

2. Finding a probability α such that the decision maker has no preference between (is indifferent to) αO_1 and O_2; that is, the preferred outcome with probability α and O_2 with certainty.

Once we have an α such that $\alpha O_1 = O_2$, we can set the utility of O_2 equal to 1 and express the utility of O_1 as $1/\alpha$.

In general, then, given a set of n outcomes, we can have the decision maker rank them in order of his preference and then proceed by considering pairs. For example, suppose that there are three outcomes (O_1, O_2, and O_3) with O_1 the most preferred and O_3 the least preferred. First we find α_1 such that

$$\alpha_1 O_1 = O_3.$$

We set O_3's utility equal to 1; the utility of O_1 is then $1/\alpha_1$. Next we find α_2 such that

$$\alpha_2 O_2 = O_3$$

and solve for the utility of O_2: $1/\alpha_2$.

It is desirable to check the reliability of the results by also finding α_3 such that

$$\alpha_3 O_1 = O_2,$$

using the previously obtained utility of O_2. For example, if

$$0.5(O_2) = O_3, \quad \text{then } U(O_2) = 1/0.5 = 2.0$$
$$0.25(O_1) = O_3, \quad \text{then } U(O_3) = 1/0.25 = 4.0.$$

Then if we find α_3 such that

$$\alpha_3(O_1) = U(O_2) = 2.0,$$

α_3 should be equal to $2.0/4.0 = 0.5$. Otherwise we would have an inconsistent result, which should be corrected. The number of possible checks on reliability increases with an increase in the number of outcomes, n. For $n = 3$, there is one reliability check. For $n = 4$, three checks possible: O_1 and O_3, O_1 and O_2, and O_2 and O_3. In general, there are $1 + 2 + \cdots + (n - 2)$ possible checks and the initial evaluation.

An alternative procedure that does not involve the use of probabilities but is applicable only to go–no-go outcomes with independent utilities was developed by Churchman and Ackoff (1954). It is based on the following assumptions:

1. To every outcome, O_j, there corresponds a real nonnegative number, U_j, to be interpreted as a measure of the true relative importance of O_j.
2. If O_j is more important than O_k, then $U_j > U_k$, and if O_j and O_k are equally important, $U_j = U_k$.
3. If O_j and O_k have utilities U_j and U_k, respectively, the utility of the combined outcome O_j-and-O_k is $U_j + U_k$.

This assumption will fail if O_j and O_k are mutually exclusive outcomes, hence cannot occur together. It will also fail if the occurrence of O_j implies the occurrence of O_k, but O_k does not imply the occurrence of O_j; for example, if $O_j =$ to earn at least \$10,000 per year, and $O_k =$ to earn at least \$5000 per year.

Assumption (3) is called the *additivity* assumption. It has the following important corollaries:

3a. If O_j is preferred to O_k, and O_k is preferred to O_l, combined outcome O_j-and-O_k is preferred to O_l.

This assumption might fail, for example, if $O_j =$ having a steak for dinner tonight, and $O_k =$ having lobster for dinner tonight. If "tonight" is removed from the definitions of these outcomes, they might satisfy the assumption.

3b. $U(O_j\text{-and-}O_k) = U(O_k\text{-and-}O_j)$; that is, the order of presentation of the outcomes does not alter the combined utility.

3c. If $U(O_j\text{-and-}O_k) = U(O_k)$, then $U_j = 0$.

Fishburn (1964) has considered how to treat outcomes that do not satisfy the additivity assumption and its corallaries. Although the three assumptions are restrictive in principle, they have turned out to be widely applicable in practice.

We now describe the procedure of generating utilities under the assumptions given above:

1. Have the decision maker rank the n outcomes in order of preference. Let O_1 represent the most preferred and O_n the least preferred.
2. Assign "1" to the utility of O_n and have the decision maker assign numbers to the remaining outcomes that reflect their relative value to him. (Conceal these numbers during the next step.)
3. Present him with the program of choices shown in Table 2.7 or Table 2.8. (The augmented program shown in Table 2.8 will yield more precise results than the program in Table 2.7, but it requires more time and patience.) Offer the choices indicated starting from the top of the left-hand column. If the

TABLE 2.7   *Program for Churchman-Ackoff Evaluation of Outcomes*

Start O_1 or $O_2 + O_3 + \cdots + O_n$	O_2 or $O_3 + O_4 + \cdots + O_n$	$\cdots$	O_{n-2} or $O_{n-1} + O_n$
O_1 or $O_2 + O_3 + \cdots + O_{n-1}$	O_2 or $O_3 + O_4 + \cdots + O_{n-1}$	$\cdots$	Stop
O_1 or $O_2 + O_3 + \cdots + O_{n-2}$	O_2 or $O_3 + O_4 + \cdots + O_{n-2}$	$\cdots$	
.	.	.	
.	.	.	
.	.		
O_1 or $O_2 + O_3$	O_2 or $O_3 + O_4$		
Next Column	Next column		

left-hand side of a choice is preferred or equal to the right-hand side, proceed to the top of the next column to the right; otherwise continue down the column.

4. Check the numbers assigned in step (2) to determine if they are consistent with the inequalities obtained in step (3). If not, modify the numbers as little as possible to make them consistent with the inequalities.

Suppose, for example, that an individual ranks five outcomes and assigns the following weights to them.

$$O_1: 7$$
$$O_2: 4$$
$$O_3: 2$$
$$O_4: 1.5$$
$$O_5: 1$$

Assume that by using the augmented program of choices (Table 2.8) we obtain the following judgments from him ($>$ means "is preferred to" and $<$ means "is less preferred than"):

$$(1)\ O_1 < O_2 + O_3 + O_4 + O_5$$
$$(2)\ O_1 < O_2 + O_3 + O_4$$
$$(3)\ O_1 < O_2 + O_3 + O_5$$
$$(4)\ O_1 > O_2 + O_3$$
$$(5)\ O_2 < O_3 + O_4 + O_5$$
$$(6)\ O_2 > O_3 + O_4$$
$$(7)\ O_3 > O_4 + O_5$$

We now check the inequalities and numbers, beginning with the last judgment:

(7) The numbers are inconsistent with this inequality; they are most easily corrected by changing the number assigned to O_3 from 2.0 to 3.0.

(6) is now inconsistent; change number assigned to O_2 to 5.0.

(5) is now consistent.

(4) is inconsistent; change number assigned to O_1 to 9.0.

TABLE 2.8 *John Plummer's Augmented Program of Churchman-Ackoff Utility Choices*

Start O_1 or $O_2 + O_3 + \cdots + O_n$	O_2 or $O_3 + O_4 + \cdots + O_n$		O_{n-2} or $O_{n-1} + O_n$
O_1 or $O_2 + O_3 + \cdots + O_{n-1}$	O_2 or $O_3 + O_4 + \cdots + O_{n-1}$		Stop
$^aO_1$ or $O_2 + O_3 + \cdots + O_{n-2} + O_n$	O_2 or $O_3 + O_4 + \cdots + O_{n-2} + O_n$		
O_1 or $O_2 + O_3 + \cdots + O_{n-2}$			
$^aO_1$ or $O_2 + O_3 + \cdots + O_{n-3} + O_{n-1} + O_n$			
$^aO_1$ or $O_2 + O_3 + \cdots + O_{n-3} + O_{n-1}$			
$^aO_1$ or $O_2 + O_3 + \cdots + O_{n-3} + O_n$			
O_1 or $O_2 + O_3 + \cdots + O_{n-3}$			
$^aO_1$ or $O_2 + O_3 + \cdots + O_{n-4} + O_{n-2} + O_{n-1} + O_n$			
$^aO_1$ or $O_2 + O_3 + \cdots + O_{n-4} + O_{n-2} + O_{n-1}$			
$^aO_1$ or $O_2 + O_3 + \cdots + O_{n-4} + O_{n-2} + O_n$			
$^aO_1$ or $O_2 + O_3 + \cdots + O_{n-4} + O_{n-1} + O_n$			
$^aO_1$ or $O_2 + O_3 + \cdots + O_{n-4} + O_{n-1}$			
O_1 or $O_2 + O_3 + \cdots + O_{n-4} + O_n$			
O_1 or $O_2 + O_3$ Next column	O_2 or $O_3 + O_4$ Next column		

^{a} Choices not in program of Table 2.7.

(3) is inconsistent; change number assigned to O_1 to 8.5 so that (4) remains consistent.

(2) is consistent.

(1) is consistent.

The resulting utilities, then, are

$$O_1: 8.5$$
$$O_2: 5$$
$$O_3: 3$$
$$O_4: 1.5$$
$$O_5: 1$$

It is clear that this procedure becomes unwieldy for large numbers of outcomes, but a slight modification of the procedure makes it possible to handle any number of outcomes. Up to 200 outcomes have been considered in practice. Suppose that we have seventeen outcomes, $O_1, \ldots, O_{17}$. Practice has shown that sets containing more than eight outcomes are difficult to handle and that sets of six are the most desirable. Therefore, we would like to divide the seventeen outcomes into three groups of approximately equal size. We proceed as follows.

1. Select one outcome at random, say O_4.

2. Divide the remaining sixteen outcomes randomly into three groups, two containing five outcomes and one containing six. We can now form three groups, each containing the outcome selected in step (1) in each. For example,

$$
\begin{array}{ccc}
O_4 & O_4 & O_4 \quad \Rightarrow \text{ STD oR BASIS}\\
O_1 & O_3 & O_5 \\
O_9 & O_2 & O_7 \\
O_{10} & O_6 & O_{11} \\
O_{15} & O_8 & O_{12} \\
O_{17} & O_{14} & O_{13} \\
& & O_{16}
\end{array}
$$

3. The procedure described above can now be applied to each group of outcomes separately. Before doing so, assign a number to O_4, say 10, and give this to the decision maker when he performs step (2) of the original procedure. He is not permitted to change this number. Also, when adjustments are made in the numbers in step (4) of the original procedure, this number is never changed, but each of the others may be.

In effect, what we have done is to insert a standard or a basis of comparison into each subset of outcomes. The reliability of the utility measures obtained can easily be determined by forming new subsets that use a different standard, and repeating the process. If inconsistency is revealed, an examination of the problem with the decision maker can usually resolve it.

In the use of this procedure, and any other procedure for measuring utility, a problem arises when there are two or more decision makers. There are essentially two kinds of procedures that can be used in such situations.

1. *Open decisions*. An open vote can be taken on each choice offered to the decision makers, and some criterion such as "majority rules" can be applied to the outcome. The criterion selected should be the same one used in their normal decision-making procedure.

2. *Closed decisions*. Each decision maker goes through the evaluation procedure privately. Then the utility assigned to each outcome is some function of the utilities of the individuals; for example, the average. In some cases the individual decision makers may themselves be weighted by a superior who desires to have the value that he places on their judgments reflected in the ultimate utilities. The superior can be put through the Churchman-Ackoff procedure to obtain weights on each manager, W_k. Then we obtain each manager's (k) utility of the jth outcome, U_{jk}. The final utility of an outcome can then be

$$\sum_k W_k U_{jk}.$$

For a discussion of the various ways of aggregating different utility measures into one measure, see Minas and Ackoff (1964).

In some problem situations the utility measure can perform the central role in obtaining a solution. The following certainty problem situation, which actually occurred, is a case in point.

A large research organization consisting of fifteen divisions is given an annual budget by its parent organization for the purchase of major pieces of equipment. Each division head was asked to submit a list of the equipment he wanted. Typically, when a consolidated list was prepared and the individual items were priced, the total cost was usually several times as large as the amount available in the budget. The problem was to find a way of selecting from the list of items (usually about two hundred) those that "should" be purchased. The procedure developed was the following:

1. Each division head and the head of the organizational unit were put through the Churchman-Ackoff procedure to determine the utility of divisions; that is, they were each asked to rank the divisions in order of importance to the organization's overall function, assign numbers to them, and then go through the program of choices. Contrary to expectations, the results were very consistent. Division heads did not place their own divisions first and suppress the needs of all the others. The utilities obtained in this way were averaged to obtain a division weight W_k ($1 \leq k \leq 15$).

2. Each division head was asked to indicate those items on the consolidated list for which he had any use. Some items were useful to more than one division, and every item, of course, was selected by at least one division.

3. Each division head was put through the Churchman-Ackoff procedure to obtain the utilities that he placed on each item. The utilities assigned were totaled for each division head, and each number that he had assigned was divided by the total so that the sum of his utilities equaled 1.00. Let U_{jk} represent the normalized utilities of the jth item to the kth division head.

4. For each item the sum of the weighted utilities, $\sum_k W_k U_{jk}$ was found. These were divided by the cost of the item to give the utility per dollar. The items were ranked in order of decreasing utility per dollar. Items were then selected from the top down until the budget was spent.

This procedure, then, maximized the estimated utility obtained by the organization for the budget available to it. Each division received at least some of the items that it wanted. Although all details of the procedure are not explained here, it can be seen that the procedure is essentially fair. In fact, two of its principal payoffs were the reduction of time required to prepare the purchase list and the reduction of hostility among the division heads that the previous procedure had stimulated each year.

SUMMARY

One person or a group of persons can be said to have a problem if (1) they have one or more desired outcomes, (2) are confronted with two or more courses of action that have some, but unequal, efficiency for the desired objective(s), and (3) are in doubt about which course of action is "best." Formulating their problem requires

(*a*) defining their possible courses of action, hence identifying the controllable variables;

(*b*) defining their environment, hence identifying the uncontrolled variables; and

(*c*) defining a criterion of choice, hence identifying their objectives and determining their relative importance.

Problems were classified into *certainty*, *uncertainty*, and *risk* types depending on what knowledge the decision maker has concerning the probabilities that outcomes follow courses of action. When he believes that one and only one outcome can follow each course of action (certainty), the criterion of choice is normally *maximum utility*. When he has no basis for believing that any one outcome is more likely or less likely than another outcome (uncertainty), he can employ three criteria that have been proposed and are used: *maximin* (and minimax), the *generalized maximin*, and *minimax regret*. We still have no scientific way of determining which of these criteria is "best" in any particular situation, but, as indicated, uncertainty problems cannot (or at least seldom do) arise in other than contrived situations, unless we prefer to ignore what knowledge we have or can obtain. If the decision maker has estimates of, or knows, the probability of each outcome occurring after each course of action (risk), the criterion that is usually employed is *maximum expected utility*.

In order to maximize expected utility, estimates of the probability of occurrence of each outcome following each course of action (measures of *efficiency*) are necessary. These may be obtained objectively (based on observations of relative frequency) or subjectively (based on the decision maker's judgment). If the outcomes are characterized as points or intervals along two or more different scales, it is also necessary to find *tradeoffs* between the different scales. These may also be found objectively and/or subjectively. Finally, in the case of quantitative outcomes the relative value (utility) of points or intervals on the "standard" scale must be found, or in the case of qualitative outcomes, their utilities must be found. Techniques applicable to both types of situation were considered.

DISCUSSION TOPICS AND PROBLEMS

1. Select some activity or operation in your college (e.g., the operations of its library or its admissions office) and perform a systems analysis of it. Prepare a diagram showing your results.
2. Discuss how you might find the tradeoffs between net profit and share of the market, and between net profit and return on investment.
3. Identify and define your objectives in buying a car. Determine the appropriate tradeoffs and utilities.
4. Take a decision recently made by the administration of your school and determine what objectives were involved and what criterion was used, implicitly or explicitly, in selecting a course of action.
5. What are the objectives of the department in charge of streets in your community? What is the collective utility that your class or group places on them?
6. Select six common objects of a value less than $5.00 and determine a friend's relative value of them. Repeat after a lapse of a day or more and compare the results. Do the same with several people.

Suggested Readings

Very little of a systematic character has been written on problem formulation. A treatment similar to that given here but more detailed can be found in Ackoff (1962, Chapters 2 and 3).

Normative decision theory, the newly developing body of knowledge relevant to selecting decision criteria, is discussed in many places; for example, Arrow (1958),

Chernoff (1954), and Radnor and Marschak (1954). A complete treatment of the measurement of utility and a discussion of problems associated with it can be found in Churchman (1961) and Fishburn (1964).

To get a conception of the literature on decision theory, Gore and Silander (1959), Wasserman and Silander (1958), and Thrall, Coombs, and Davis (1954) are particularly useful.

Bibliography

Ackoff, R. L., *Scientific Method: Optimizing Applied Research Decisions*, John Wiley and Sons, New York, 1962.

Arrow, K. J., "Utilities, Attitudes, Choices: A Review Note," *Econometrica*, **26** (1958), 1–23.

Chernoff, H., "Rational Selection of Decision Functions," *Econometrica*, **22** (1954), 422–443.

———, and L. E. Moses, *Elementary Decision Theory*, John Wiley and Sons, New York, 1959.

Churchman, C. W., "Problems of Value Measurement for a Theory of Induction and Decisions," *Proceedings of the Third Berkeley Symposium on Mathematical Statistics and Probability*, University of California Press, Berkeley, 1955, 53–59.

———, *Prediction and Optimal Decision*. Prentice-Hall, Englewood Cliffs, N.J., 1961.

———, "Decision and Value Theory," in *Progress in Operations Research*, Vol. I R. L. Ackoff (Ed.), John Wiley and Sons, New York, 1961, pp. 35–64.

———, and R. L. Ackoff, "An Approximate Measure of Value," *Operations Research*, **2** (1954), 172–180.

Edwards, W., "Theory of Decision-Making," *Psychological Bulletin*, **51** (1954), 380–417.

Feeney, G. F., "A Basis for Strategic Decisions on Inventory Control Operations," *Management Science*, **2** (1955), 69–82.

Fishburn, P. C., *Decision and Value Theory*, John Wiley and Sons, New York, 1964.

———, "Methods of Estimating Additive Utilities," *Management Science*, **13** (1967), 435–453.

Gore, W. S., and F. S. Silander, "A Bibliographical Essay on Decision-Making," *Administrative Science Quarterly*, **4** (1959), 97–121.

Hurwicz, L., "Optimality Criteria for Decision Making under Ignorance," *Cowles Commission Discussion Paper, Statistics*, No. 370, 1951. (Mimeographed.)

Isaacs, H. H., "Sensitivity of Decisions to Probability Estimation Error," *Operations Research*, **11** (1963), 536–552.

Luce, R. D., and H. Raiffa, *Games and Decisions*, John Wiley and Sons, New York, 1957.

Markowitz, H., "The Utility of Wealth," *Journal of Political Economy*, **60** (1952), 151–158.

Minas, J. Sayer, and R. L. Ackoff, "Individual and Collective Value Judgments," in *Human Judgment and Optimality*, M. Shelly and G. Bryan (eds.), John Wiley and Sons, New York, 1964.

Radner, R., and J. Marschak, "Note on Some Proposed Decision Criteria," in Thrall, Coombs, and Davis (1954).

Savage, L. J., "The Theory of Statistical Decisions," *Journal of the American Statistical Association*, **46** (1951), 55–67.

Simon, H. A., *Models of Man*, John Wiley and Sons, New York, 1957.

Thrall, R. M., C. H. Coombs, and R. L. Davis (eds.), *Decision Processes*, John Wiley and Sons, New York, 1954.

Von Neumann, J., and O. Morgenstern, *Theory of Games and Economic Behavior*, 3rd ed. Princeton University Press, Princeton, N.J., 1953.

Wasserman, P., and F. S. Silander, *Decision-Making: An Annotated Bibliography*. Graduate School of Business and Public Administration, Cornell University, Ithaca, N.Y., 1958.

CHAPTER 3

Model Construction

INTRODUCTION

Models are representations of reality. If they were as complex and difficult to control as reality, there would be no advantage in their use. Fortunately, we can usually construct models that are much simpler than reality and still be able to use them to predict and explain phenomena with a high degree of accuracy. The reason is that although a very large number of variables may be required to predict a phenomenon with perfect accuracy, a small number of variables usually account for most of it. The trick, of course, is to find the right variables and the correct relationship between them.

TYPES OF MODELS

Three types of models are commonly used in OR as well as in most of science: *iconic, analogue, and symbolic*.

In *iconic* models the relevant properties of the real thing are represented by the properties themselves, usually with a change of scale. Hence iconic models generally look like what they represent but differ in size; they are *images*. Some common examples are photographs, drawings, maps, and "model" airplanes, ships, and automobiles. Iconic models of the sun and its planets such as are usually housed in planetariums are scaled down, whereas models of the atom (e.g., Bohr's) is scaled up. Iconic models are generally specific, concrete, and difficult to manipulate for experimental purposes.

Analogues use one set of properties to represent another set of properties. Contour lines on a map, for example, are analogues of elevation. A hydraulic system can be used as an analogue of electrical, traffic, and economic systems. Graphs are analogues that use geometrical magnitudes and location to represent a wide variety of variables and the relationships between them. In general, analogues are less specific, less concrete, but easier to manipulate than are iconic models.

60

Symbolic models use letters, numbers, and other types of symbols to represent variables and the relationships between them. Hence they are the most general and most abstract type of model. They are usually the easiest to manipulate experimentally. Symbolic models take the form of mathematical relationships (usually equations or "inequations") that reflect the structure of that which they represent.

In many research projects all three types of models are used in sequence; iconic models and analogues are sometimes used as initial approximations, which are subsequently refined into a symbolic model. The flow diagram produced by a system analysis is such an initial representation; it is usually made up of a combination of iconic and analogue elements. The preliminary and tentative representations of the system that are frequently used in the development of the model that is ultimately used to obtain a solution, are often called *conceptual models*. These models often are diagrams that record our conception of what variables are relevant and how they are related. The relationships are usually described quantitatively; it may be stated, for example, that as one variable increases, it produces a decrease in another variable. Figures 3.8 and 3.9, which appear later in the chapter, are examples of such conceptual models whose use in constructing symbolic models is explained in the discussion of the cases with which they are associated.

In OR, symbolic models are sought wherever possible not only because they are easier to manipulate, but because they usually yield more accurate results under manipulation than do either iconic or analogue models.

Descriptive and Explanatory Models

It is important to distinguish between models (1) that contain controlled variables and (2) those that do not. In general, those that do are *explanatory* and those that do not are *descriptive*. Decision models of the form previously considered, $U = f(X, Y)$, are explanatory. It is frequently necessary, however, to construct descriptive models as a preliminary step toward developing an explanatory decision model. This is illustrated in the following case.

An oil company wanted to predict how much business it would do if it were to build service stations at certain prospective sites. It wanted to avoid erecting stations at sites that would turn out to be unprofitable. The problem was given to an internal group of market researchers, who interviewed a wide variety of personnel in the company and collected opinions as to which properties of a service station and its location contributed to sales. About 65 variables were identified. Data were collected on each variable for several hundred stations, and a multiple linear regression of sales on these variables was run. About one half of the variables turned out to be "statistically significant." The resulting regression model, however, did not yield predictions sufficiently accurate to avoid most of the unfavorable site selections.

An OR team was later asked to reexamine the problem. The team was opposed to dealing with large numbers of variables because it believed that, in general, the extent to which a phenomenon is understood is inversely proportional to the number of variables required to explain it. It decided, therefore, to see how far it could go with one variable. It believed that volume of traffic was probably the most important variable in the discarded regression model and decided, therefore, to concentrate its initial efforts on understanding *why* this variable was important even though it is not controllable.

First, a precise way of describing traffic was developed. There are sixteen possible routes[1] by which a car can go through an intersection of the normal type (including turnarounds through service stations). A study of traffic classified by these routes showed that only a few of the routes contributed significantly to service-station sales. A ranking of routes by the *percentage* of cars stopping suggested the possibility that as the time lost in stopping for service increased, the percentage of cars that stopped decreased. This hypothesis was then tested and confirmed. The way in which lost time affected percentage of cars stopping was also explained. Then the other variables that had been "significant" in the earlier regression analysis were examined to determine if any of these were related to lost time. Most were found to be so related; for example, number of entrances and exits, number of pumps, location of entrances and exits, number of attendants, and automatic shutoffs on pumps. Their effects on lost time were estimated on purely theoretical grounds. These estimates were then tested and confirmed empirically. This made it possible to construct a model in which numerous station characteristics appeared as decision variables, enabling the company not only to choose better sites for new stations, but also to design new (and redesign old) stations to obtain as large a share of the potential business as possible.

The initial regression model was descriptive and predictive, but did not make control possible because it did not explain station performance. Explanation and control can be obtained only when the *causal* connections between the variables, controllable and uncontrollable, and performance are understood.

In problems involving systems most of whose relevant variables are subject to control—for example, production and inventory systems—causal relationships are usually revealed by direct examination of the system. If the system is less subject to control—for example, marketing—the causal relationships are seldom apparent. In such problems a good deal of analysis and experimentation is generally required before enough is known to build an explanatory model. The more obscure a system's structure—that is, the causal relationships between its variables—the more difficult it is to model.

---

[1] Four possible entries combined in all ways with four possible exits. Some of these, of course, may be illegal.

Differences in degree of obscurity have therefore produced different patterns of model construction.

PATTERNS OF MODEL CONSTRUCTION

The quality of a model depends very much on the imagination and creativity of the research team. Intuition, insight, and other mental operations that are essentially unregulatable play a major role in the process. It is not possible, therefore, to prepare a manual of instructions for model building. If such a manual could be prepared, it would be more likely to constrain than promote creativity. Nevertheless, when past experience in model building is examined, certain patterns emerge. Awareness of these patterns may stimulate imagination and guide creativity. These patterns vary depending on both the obscurity of the structure of the system under study and the amount of access that the researcher has into the inner workings of the system.

We shall consider five patterns, starting with the simplest and proceeding to the most complex. It should be borne in mind that these patterns are neither exclusive nor exhaustive. Particular model-building experiences may not fit any one pattern or a combination of them, although most seem to do so.

Pattern 1

This pattern occurs when the structure of the system is sufficiently simple and transparent to be understood by inspection and/or discussion with those involved in and with the system.

Consider the situation of a newsboy who must decide how many newspapers to order to maximize his expected profit. He buys a certain number of newspapers each day and sells some or all of them. He makes a profit on each one he sells. He can return unsold newspapers, but at a loss. The number of people who want newspapers varies from day to day, but the probability that any specified number of newspapers will be sold on a particular day can be determined by analyzing past data.

The causal structure of this situation is transparent. We can begin to model it by identifying the relevant variables and selecting symbols to represent them. Let

n = the number of newspapers ordered per day;
a = the profit made on each newspaper sold;
b = the loss incurred on each newspaper returned;
d = the demand, that is, the number that could be sold per day if $n \geq d$;
$p(d)$ = the probability that the demand will equal d on a randomly selected day;
P = net profit per day (negative P represents a loss).

If the demand on a particular day exceeds the number ordered, that is, if $d > n$, his profit would be

$$P(d > n) = na. \tag{3.1}$$

On the other hand, if demand does not exceed the number ordered, his profit is

$$P(n \geq d) = da - (n - d)b. \tag{3.2}$$

Then the expected net profit per day ($\bar{P}$) can be expressed as

$$\bar{P} = \sum_{d=0}^{n} p(d)[da - (n - d)b] + \sum_{d=n+1}^{\infty} p(d)na. \tag{3.3}$$

This is a decision model of the risk type. $\bar{P}$ is the measure of performance, n is the controlled variable, d is an uncontrolled variable, and a and b are uncontrolled constants. To solve the problem represented by this model it is necessary to find the value of n that maximizes $\bar{P}$. This "newsboy" model is obviously applicable to the ordering of many perishable products.

Many if not most of the prototype models to be discussed in later chapters represent situations whose structure is as (or nearly as) transparent as that involving the newsboy. Hence in very simple situations one can sometimes (but not often) go directly from an examination of the system to the appropriate ready-made model. But even when an appropriate model is easy to construct or find, the uncontrolled variables and constants (i.e., the *parameters*) may be very difficult or impossible to evaluate. The data situation may require modification of the model, so that parameters that do appear in it can be evaluated. These modifications are frequently more difficult than the original analysis and may require following one of the patterns that are still to be described. We shall return to this point after discussing each of the patterns.

Pattern 2

In situations in which the structure is relatively apparent but the way to represent it symbolically is not equally apparent, we may sometimes recognize a similarity of the structure of the problem system to another whose structure is better known. We may then use either the other *analogous* system itself or a symbolic model of it (with or without modification) as a model of the problem system.

For example, suppose that our problem is to locate a new warehouse, which is to supply a specified set of variously situated customers. Each customer's requirement per time period in tons is relatively constant and is known. The cost of transporting each customer's requirement to him is, in first approximation, equal to the shipment's weight times the distance times a unit cost per unit weight per unit distance. The problem is to locate the warehouse so as to minimize the total transportation cost per period. Many who have been confronted with this common problem have recognized that it has a very good physical analogue, which can be constructed rather easily as follows:

1. Locate each customer on a map that is drawn on as large a scale as can reasonably be handled.

2. Glue the map to the surface of a large flat board, such as a sheet of plywood or composition board.

3. Rest the board flat on horses or some other suitable supports leaving the map side up and clear space under that part of the board which has the map on it.

4. Drill a small hole through the map and board at each customer's location and insert a smooth plastic bushing.

5. Drop the end of a piece of smooth cord or string through each hole and tie a weight to the end of the cord under the board, each weight being some specified fraction of the weight of the shipments to that customer. For example, an ounce may be used to represent a ton.

6. Tie the ends of the string above the board to a small smooth ring so that when the ring is on the map, all weights are suspended above the floor.

If this construction were free of friction, the ring would move to an equilibrium point. The location in the center of the ring would then be the one that minimizes the sum of the products of the weights and the distances of the customers' locations from the center of the ring. Hence this is the optimal location of the warehouse. In practice some friction is always present, which must be overcome by some "jiggling" of the board to enable the ring to find its equilibrium point. More sophisticated versions of this physical analogue can be constructed, and the analogue can be extended to take account of more complicated conditions.

Representation of existing transport paths furnishes one of the many examples of such sophistication: a number of smooth plastic pegs are inserted in holes drilled along such paths, and appropriate cords are placed between the pegs so that they would be restricted to the existing paths. Multiple warehouses and pipeline networks furnish other examples.

It is also possible for an analogue (physical or other) to provide or suggest a symbolic model. This is illustrated in the following case in which, it will be noted, the "solution" was derived experimentally.

A study that was recently completed in India found so much interference between trains moving over the same tracks, in either the same or opposite direction, that the passing delay was excessive and, correspondingly, the average speed of advance very low (5 mph for freight trains, primarily because of their low priority relative to passenger trains). Could anything be done to remedy this undesirable situation? One possibility was to make a computer simulation in which each train would be individually represented in all of its states (moving at various speeds in each of many subdivisions of the track, held on a passing track, and so on). Such a program was judged to be impractical under existing conditions; another approach was necessary if the project were not to be abandoned.

A very cursory observation showed that trains were almost invariably behind schedule by a randomly distributed amount. In fact, the whole situation was reminiscent of the movement of gas molecules as envisaged in the kinetic theory of gases, except that it was one-dimensional instead of three-dimensional. In pursuing the physical analogy, trains were grouped by type ("crack" passenger, passenger, "crack" freight, freight, and so on) and by running speed and direction. The passing of a train of one class by a train of another was likened to the collision between two gas molecules, with a statistically distributed delay of the train of lower priority. The theoretical results so obtained were very enlightening as to the factors affecting average speed of advance, and they suggested how the controllable variables (primarily the dispatching procedures) could be manipulated to increase the average speed. To carry out the suggestions in practice, however, it would have been necessary to measure a number of parameters and to determine the optimal operating procedures by a lengthy computer calculation.

However, the gas-kinetic model had already yielded great insight into the *directions* of the needed changes in operational procedures, and it was therefore decided to conduct an operational experiment consisting of gradually increased changes in the indicated directions. In three weeks of such cautious experimentation, the average speed of advance of freight trains increased by 50 per cent along the trial section of 200 miles, without in any way interfering with the 100 per cent priority of all passenger trains over all freight trains; the "stabling" of freight trains, on which the crew had worked for 12 hours or more, was completely eliminated.

The logical considerations that led to this excellent result were as follows. First, an analogy was drawn with a physical system of which much is known, namely a collection of randomly moving gas molecules. Second, a mathematical-statistical model of the system was developed by appropriate modification of the gas model. Third, this model was solved by the use of rough guesses about the values of unknown parameters, which thus gave a good idea of the *direction* of desirable changes in operational procedures, although not of the proper magnitude of these changes. Fourth, using the desired directions of change as a guide, cautious experiments were performed on the system itself (this system is its own identical model), which yielded a large, although probably not optimal, improvement. Even though this result might have been obtained without the gas-molecule analogue, the analogue was nevertheless found to be very useful.

Pattern 3

In this type of situation the structure of the system is not apparent but can be extracted by analysis of the data that describe the operation of the system. The data may be available or may need to be collected, but in either case analysis of them is sufficient to reveal the system's structure. Actually, analysis yields structural hypotheses that require confirmation by use of data other than those used in generating the hypotheses.

The development of an explanatory model for the service-station site-selection problem discussed above illustrates this pattern. Analysis of traffic movement and customers' routes provided a hypothesis involving subjective perception of time lost in stopping for service. Inferences were drawn deductively from this tentative theory and tested by analysis of data that were collected for this purpose.

Pattern 4

In situations in which it is not possible to isolate the effects of individual variables by analysis of operating data, it may be necessary to resort to experimentation to determine which variables are relevant and how they affect the system's performance. The use of experimentation is the essential characteristic of this pattern.

To illustrate this pattern, we consider the case of a company whose principal product is a packaged food. Its management asked an OR group that was already working for it in other areas to aid in preparing an appropriate annual advertising budget for its principal product. The managers did not want the research to interfere with the duties of the company's advertising agency, that is, with the preparation of commercials, selection of media, geographical allocation, and so on. They only wanted to know how much to spend; the method of expenditure was to remain unchanged.

The company's annual advertising budget had been increasing for many years by an amount approximately proportional to anticipated increases in sales; at the time it was about $20,000,000 per year.

In previous studies of marketing (which had involved unrelated products) the OR team had found that increased expenditures of money or effort do not always produce an increase in sales. Therefore the team made the initial assumption that whatever the shape of the curve representing the effect of advertising expenditures on sales, the curve had a plateau. This assumption is represented graphically in Figure 3.1.

The segment of a function with a plateau suggested to the team that advertising might be viewed as a *stimulus*, and sales as a *response*. It was then argued, from knowledge of characteristic forms of stimulus-response functions found by psychologists, that the response curve probably had the shape shown in Figure 3.2.

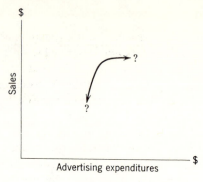

Figure 3.1

Further speculation was directed to the right-hand side of this response function, and the upper limit was considered in the following way. Suppose that all the advertising in the country dealt with only one product; what effect would this be likely to have on the sales of this product? Or, more realistically, if a salesman were to spend all his working hours with only one customer, what would happen? It seems clear that the customer would try to eject him and would certainly refuse to buy his wares. It seemed reasonable to assume, therefore, that there is an amount of advertising beyond which the effect on sales would be harmful. This line of thinking resulted in the completed hypothetical advertising-response function shown in Figure 3.3.

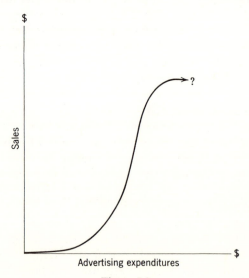

Figure 3.2

The exact shape and the parameters of this curve were, of course, completely unknown. They could not be obtained by an analysis of past expenditures, because the method of setting the budget had established a strong positive correlation between these expenditures and sales. Therefore, the OR team felt that some experimentation was necessary and suggested it to management. Management was reluctant to "play" with its markets and risk loss of sales, but it was persuaded to allow experimental use of eighteen of its two hundred and fifty market areas. The areas were selected by the research team, subject to minor constraints imposed by management.

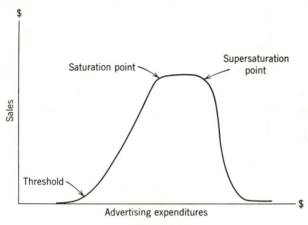

Figure 3.3

An experiment was designed and conducted in which three groups of nine markets were randomly selected from the permissible set of markets. One group was continued at its current level of advertising, one group had its budget increased by 50 per cent, and group's budget was reduced by 25 per cent.

Because advertising is only one of the factors that affect sales, and certainly not more important than all others taken together, it was necessary to reduce the effect of other variables, so that the effect that advertising does have could be observed and the effects of the other principal factors on the way in which advertising affects sales (interactions) could be determined. This was done by using a three-factor experiment, each at three levels, and by developing a forecasting procedure for market areas which, when tested retrospectively, was shown to account for much of the variation of sales between markets and from month to month within a market. The dependent variable, then, was the percentage of deviation of each month's sales from the predicted sales.

After the experiment had been running for six months, significant differences were observed between the three levels of advertising, differences whose significance became stronger in the next six months. But the results were completely unexpected because the configuration of the three points obtained was the only configuration that could be inconsistent with the hypothesized advertising response function. These points appeared as shown in Figure 3.4.

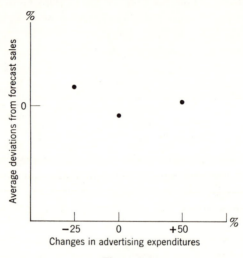

Figure 3.4

At this point the team was confronted with the apparent need to reject either the theory or the experimental results. Not inclined to do either, the team looked for a possible explanation of the experimental results that was consistent with the theory. It found one.

Suppose that the population of consumers were divided into two groups, each with a different response function, but both having the hypothesized shape. This supposition and its consequences are shown in Figure 3.5. Was there a reason for accepting the supposition? There was. It had appeared during the development of the forecasting procedure. The researchers had observed that the amount of the product consumed was related to income. The population was then divided into two income groups, one accounting for slightly more of the total sales than the other. Further analysis of the experimental results strongly confirmed this hypothesis.

Management was surprised to learn that a 25 per cent reduction in advertising had yielded a larger increase in sales than a 50 per cent increase. Nevertheless, it was unwilling to act on this result because it felt that an insufficient number of areas and of variations in advertising levels had been used. The OR team fully agreed.

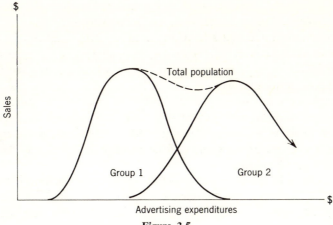

Figure 3.5

An extended experiment was conducted in which there were areas with *no* advertising, 50 per cent and 25 per cent reductions, and 50, 100, and 200 per cent increases. This experiment confirmed the earlier results and, of course, augmented them. The plot through the points was as shown in Figure 3.6.

Another inconsistency with the theory now appeared. The left-hand side of the function had not come down to zero. An explanation consistent with the theory was again sought and found. It involved bringing in another variable, *time*. It was argued that a product that had been on the market for many years during which it had been well advertised would "coast" on its past advertising for a while before sliding downhill. How long would it do so?

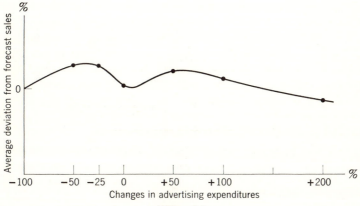

Figure 3.6

Another experiment was designed and conducted to find the answer; the product "coasted" much longer than had been expected.

This result suggested that advertising need not be continued at a constant level; by varying the level (i.e., by *pulsing*) the same effects on sales could be obtained at lower cost. Experiments were designed and conducted that confirmed this suggestion as well.

Although we need not go further with this case for our purposes, it is worth noting that the model eventually took into account the effectiveness of each advertising medium (television, radio, magazines, newspapers, and billboards), the measurable quality of the message delivered, and the amount of competitive advertising.

In the pattern of model building just illustrated it is apparent that analysis of available data played an important role, but the critical procedure was experimental. Although such a procedure usually is very time-consuming, often it is not necessary to wait until the "end" to extract conclusions that can be fruitfully implemented. This was true of the case just described. Because the structure was not initially known, knowledge of it, once obtained, tended to yield large improvements in the system's performance.

Pattern 5

In this last and most difficult situation sufficient descriptive data on the system's operations are not available or obtainable, and experimentation on

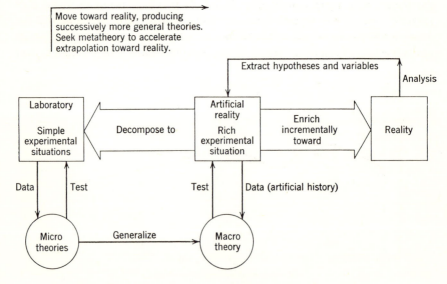

Figure 3.7   Schematic diagram of model-construction pattern 5.

the system is precluded. This may seem to be a hopeless situation, but it is not necessarily so.

Consider the case of research directed toward discovering how to control the escalation of large-scale social conflicts such as strikes or cold and hot wars. The type of data required for quantitative analysis of such situations are not available and cannot be generated. Nor would society allow experiments in this domain even if they could be carried out. The structure of such situations, of course, is almost a complete mystery. Then how might we go about constructing a model suitable to such conflict?

Models of conflict between two individuals or small groups exist, which have been extracted from experiments conducted in a laboratory. But unfortunately inferences cannot be drawn from these very simple artificial situations to the complexities of the real world. More complicated and more realistic experiments have also been conducted on conflict between larger groups, but the addition of complexity and realism to laboratory experiments has resulted in the loss of the ability to model such experimental situations. A procedure is required that incorporates the advantages of both approaches and avoids their shortcomings.

Such a method is shown schematically in Figure 3.7. First, a relatively complex experimental situation (in this case a "rich" game) is constructed, which is the simplest one that satisfies the following conditions:

1. It must be rich enough to test a large number of hypotheses that have been formulated about the system under study; in this case, the dynamics of large-scale social conflict. Clearly, such tests cannot confirm any hypotheses, but they can define limits on their generality and suggest how they can be generalized. The purpose of this requirement is to link the experimental situation to reality. The nature of the linkage is made explicit by the second condition.

2. There must be an explicit formulation of the variables and their scales along which simplification of reality has taken place. This makes it possible to successively enrich the experimental situation by the addition of complexities one at a time or in combination.

3. The relevant behavior in the experimental situation must be describable in quantitative terms.

4. The situation must be decomposable into a set of simpler experimental situations and, wherever possible, these simpler situations should be the ones that have already been experimented on, or they should closely resemble situations on which work has been done.

The experimental situation that satisfies these conditions is used as an "artificial reality." It is *not* used as a model of reality, but rather as *a reality to be modeled*. The artificial reality is used to generate a history, which is to be explained by a theory that is to be constructed. The history is generated by systematically testing hypotheses that have been formulated about the real world in this artificial one.

Experiments are also conducted with the decomposed parts of the artificial reality, that is, with simple conflict games. Either separate "micro" theories for each of the simple experiments are developed, or a general "micro" theory of such simple experimental situations is constructed in which situation characteristics enter as parameters. An effort is then made to aggregate or generalize these models into a model of the artificial reality.

A simultaneous effort is made to formulate a theory of the artificial reality by direct "macro" analysis of the history that it generates. These two modeling efforts interact until a satisfactory model (M_1) of the artificial reality is developed.

The artificial reality is then modified along a well-defined scale in the direction of reality, and efforts are made to generalize the earlier model, M_1. The output is a more general model, M_2, of which M_1 is a special case. This procedure is continued with the hope of producing a set of successively more general models, $M_1, M_2, \ldots, M_n$. As this set expands, it is analyzed to find principles that explain how the models must be generalized as the artificial reality approaches reality. The development of such a *metatheory* (a theory of model or theory construction) should make it possible to proceed by larger jumps toward reality and possibly to reach reality. In this way a theory of the dynamics of large-scale social conflict that will be useful in the real world may eventually be developed.

This pattern of model construction has begun to emerge only recently, simultaneously with the increased scope and complexity of the types of problem undertaken by OR. This is particularly true with respect to broad problems of social planning. Because this pattern requires many years for completion, there are as yet no completed projects that have used it, but a number are in process.

DATA AVAILABILITY AND MODEL CONSTRUCTION

As we have pointed out, it is sometimes necessary to modify an otherwise acceptable model because it is not possible or practical to evaluate one or more of its parameters. Even when the initial model construction is simple, the stages of modification may not be. It may be necessary to go through several cycles of model construction and search for data. Each model leads to a search for data. The search may not yield the required information, but when it does not, it usually suggests how the model might be modified to improve the matching of the data that are available. It is not uncommon to go through as many as six cycles.

Differences in availability and quality of data between organizations are also often responsible for the fact that a model that is suitable in one situation is not suitable in another situation that at first glance appears to be very similar.

The interaction of data generation and model construction is illustrated in experience with the problem of budgeting research and development activities in different companies.

Research and development (R&D) budgeting problems are relatively easy to solve in principle, but they are usually extremely difficult to solve in practice. The difficulty generally is caused by the fact that records maintained in R&D departments have not been designed to provide the data that are needed for developing rational budgeting procedures. This is particularly true in organizations in which R&D is taken to be a "good thing" and in which, consequently, expenditures on it do not usually require strong defense.

The R&D budgeting problem involves three questions, each of which normally occurs at a different level of management. They are as follows:

1. *Corporate budgeting:* what should be the total amount allocated to the R&D function for the next (and possibly subsequent) planning period(s)?

2. *Functional budgeting:* how should the total amount available to R&D be allocated to various types of R&D; for example, basic research, applied research, and development?

3. *Subfunctional budgeting:* which specific projects should be initiated, which continued, and what level of support should be given to each?

These questions are not independent. In fact, it is easy to show that if the last question could be answered in terms of corporate objectives, answers to the first and second questions would become unnecessary. Therefore, the ideal approach to R&D budgeting would be to first consider the lowest-level question, and which involves project selection and support.

If we knew

(*a*) the probability of "success" of each project as a function of the amount invested in it, and

(*b*) the probability density function of present value of net return for each project (or some other suitable measure),

we could easily find how to allocate a fixed total budget so as to optimize performance. We could then iterate for a range of possible budgets and find that which yields the best return.

This idealized procedure usually cannot be carried out; one of the main reasons is that the probability of project success and the probability density function of return either cannot be estimated at all or cannot be estimated with any measurable or acceptable accuracy and precision. We can, of course, guesstimate them, and this has been done. But unless we had some measure of the accuracy and precision of such guesstimates, we would be proceeding purely by faith. It can easily be shown that the payoff is greatly dependent on the accuracy of these estimates, hence the subjective approach is not very comforting.

In the first of the two cases to be described, which involved a large chemical company with a centralized R&D activity, an effort was initially made to obtain historical cost and return data on individual projects. The records did not permit the extraction of such data. Consequently, an approach was taken that involved classification of projects into basic and applied research. The definitions of these types of research were those used by the National Science Foundation in its national surveys of R&D. However, these concepts could not be used. The company did not classify its research in this way, and it was not possible to go back and assign past projects to either one or the other class. Many projects belonged to both classes, and it was not possible to allocate their cost to the two categories in any reasonable way. Efforts were made to do so but they produced very unreliable results. The fact was that research managers did not use these concepts in the performance of their functions.

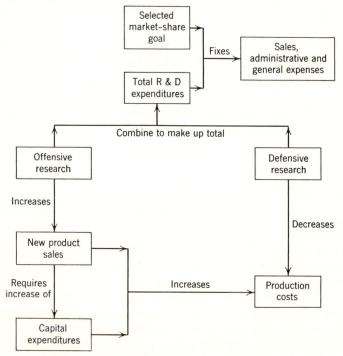

Figure 3.8 Conceptual model of budgeting process.

Several efforts were made to retain the concepts of basic and applied research by modifying their definitions. These efforts were equally fruitless. Eventually an attempt was made to determine whether *any* classification scheme was used either implicitly or explicitly by research management when it made its budget allocations. It was found that no classification scheme was used explicitly, but probing revealed two categories that "made sense" to R&D managers and which, they felt, were "in the back of their minds" when budgeting:

1. *Offensive research:* research directed toward producing "new" products; that is, products that would provide additional sources of income to the company.

2. *Defensive research:* research directed toward reducing production costs by process improvement or modification of existing products.

These definitions emerged from a number of efforts to have managers classify projects in a meaningful way. In each test a number of managers carried out classifications independently. The tests were continued until a classification scheme was obtained that yielded a consistent set of results.

The offensive-defensive classification of research projects suggested a conceptual model that, when modified by analysis of the system and performance records, appeared as shown in Figure 3.8.

This model in turn suggested a measure of performance that, when tempered by company practices and data availability, resulted in the following scheme:

Return on gross value of plant = (sales revenue − production costs
− sales, administrative, and general
expenses − R&D costs)/
(gross value of plant)

The reason for grouping sales, administrative, and general expenses in the measure of performance lies in another data-availability problem. It was not possible to allocate selling costs of previous years to old and new products, nor was it possible to find a suitable relationship between R&D expenditures and selling costs. After internal sources of data were explored thoroughly without useful results, attention was turned to external sources of (industry) data. A source was found in which total annual R&D expenses and aggregated annual sales, administrative, and general (SAG) expenses were available from sixteen chemical companies for the period 1947 to 1957. From this data the descriptive relationships shown in Table 3.1 were found. The variances of the average ratios in the right-hand column were significantly less within groups than between groups. Consequently, by using (*a*) a trial value of the R&D budget and (*b*) the company's market-share objective for next year, it was possible to obtain an estimate of SAG expenses for next year.

TABLE 3.1

Market Share	Average (R&D Dollars/Year ÷ SAG Dollars/Year)
0.2 − 0.5%	0.20
0.5 − 2.0	0.22
2.0 − 4.0	0.27
4.0 +	0.36

A mathematical model based on the conceptual model shown in Figure 3.8 was constructed and a solution to the budgeting problem was devised, which yielded a significant improvement in the company's performance.

After this study was completed, an effort was made to apply the results in several other chemical companies. Modifications were required in each case because of differences in the type of data that were available. More recently an attempt was made to apply this model to a company in another basic industry with equal lack of success, but it was possible to continue from this initial failure to the development of another model that appears to work.

First, a few words about the organization of the company. It has a divisional structure based on product lines. There is a centralized corporate R&D division and similar activities within each product-line division. In the product-line divisions efforts are predominantly (but not exclusively) developmental, and corporate efforts are predominantly (but not exclusively) directed toward research. It was not possible, however, to separate past expenditures into research and development by location, nor was it possible to separate research at the corporate level into basic and applied. Therefore, an effort was made to use the offensive-defensive categories.

These concepts were not applicable without modification because much of the research conducted at the corporate level appeared to be truly fundamental. Furthermore, other aspects of the previously developed model did not match this company:

1. "Share of the market" is a meaningful concept for some of the company's product lines, but not for others; hence it cannot be applied to the company as a whole. That is, the company as a whole does not service a well-defined market for which share data are available or even meaningful.

2. Better data on marketing development and selling costs were available in this company than in the first company discussed.

3. Return on investment in gross plant was not an acceptable measure to this company's management because unlike the first company it had more than an adequate supply of capital; hence it was considerably more profit-oriented than return-oriented.

A second attempt to develop a useful classification of types of R&D yielded the following categories:

1. Research on fundamental ideas.
2. Research on applied ideas.
3. Research on potential processes, materials, and products.
4. Development of processes, materials, and products.

The available data did not make the task of classification easy. Classification pretests that involved a number of senior scientists indicated that it would take a large part of their time for about one year to do the amount of classifying required. This was both too costly and too time-consuming.

After four successive revisions in the classification scheme, one to which the available data could be "fitted" was finally obtained. Then an appropriate measure of performance was developed:

Net profit before taxes = sales revenue — cost of production
— cost of capital invested in additional plant
— selling, administrative, and overhead expenses
— R&D expenditures

It will be observed that the components of this measure and that used in the first case that we described are essentially the same but are differently "arranged."

The classification scheme and the conceptual model that was based on it are shown in Figure 3.9. A usable mathematical model was constructed on this foundation: it was the best model that the data permitted, but it was considerably less than what the researchers had hoped for. Fortunately, it provided much that management had not had before, from which we can extract the adage: *an approximate model of a system that improves its performance is much better than an exact model that does not.*

MODELS AS APPROXIMATIONS

Model builders are confronted by conflicting objectives: to make the model as easy to solve as possible and to make it as accurate as possible. They must also keep in mind the mathematical complexity of the solution, because the decision maker must understand the solution and be capable of using it. Consequently, in constructing a model it is usually desirable to simplify reality but only to the point where there is no significant loss of accuracy.

It is not always easy to obtain the proper balance. Good judgment, the ease that comes with practice, and sensitivity to the organization's capabilities can, however, be developed with experience if the researcher recognizes the problem and keeps his eyes, ears, and mind open.

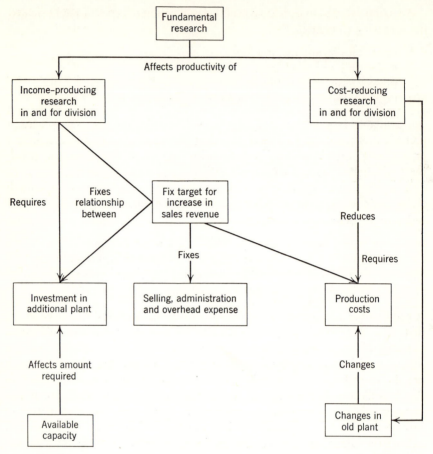

Figure 3.9   Conceptual model for budgeting R&D in product-line divisions.

Simplification of reality can be obtained by

(*a*) omitting relevant variables,
(*b*) changing the nature of variables,
(*c*) changing the relationship between variables, and
(*d*) modifying constraints.

We shall consider each of these in turn.

Omitting Relevant Variables

Clearly, we do not want to omit variables that have a large effect on the system's performance. It may require some study, however, to determine which variables have and which do not have significant effects. Certainly, the deliberate omission of a variable should always be justified in as rigorous a way as possible.

In subsequent discussions of production and inventory control models, for example, you will find that the effect of production-run sizes on in-process inventory costs is not usually taken into account. Examination of most production processes will show that (*a*) in-process inventory is affected by run size and (*b*) the effect is very small compared to the effects of other variables that are treated in the models. In most cases these costs account for only a fraction of one per cent of the total cost, but in some cases they are significant. The only way to avoid overlooking a potentially significant variable is to take it into account initially and to eliminate it only when there is an explicit justification for so doing.

Because many ready-made models are now available, there is a temptation to select one that appears to fit a problem and apply it without reexamining the simplifying assumptions inherent in it. These assumptions may not be explicitly stated in the source from which the model is drawn. Therefore, the assumptions underlying any model so selected should be considered with care.

Aggregating Variables. In many problems the number of controllable variables is very large. For example, some inventory problems involve determination of the purchase quantities of more than one million items. To solve such problems, the controlled variables are grouped into "families." A family of items is then treated as though all of its members were identical. A common principle of "family" formation in such problems involves the use of four classes of items:

1. High usage, high cost.
2. High usage, low cost.
3. Low usage, high cost.
4. Low usage, low cost.

If relatively few items appear in the first class, as is usually the case, they can be treated separately.

Estimates of the error of aggregation can be obtained by solving individually for a random sample of items in each family, and determining the difference from the solution obtained by treating them as identical with the "average" item used to characterize the family.

When variables are aggregated, the error in the estimate of the outcome that results is roughly proportional to the ratio of the within-aggregation-variance to the between-aggregation-variance. Hence it is desirable to aggregate things that are as nearly alike as possible and to separate those that are not.

Changing the Nature of Variables

The three most common ways of changing the nature of a variable are (1) to treat it as a constant, (2) to treat a discrete variable as continuous, and (3) to treat a continuous variable as discrete.

It is quite common to treat as a constant a variable whose value is set equal to the mean of the variable's distribution. For example, in a very simple "toy" model of the form

$$U = X + \frac{Y}{X}, \tag{3.4}$$

Y may be a variable (say, demand) that is treated as a constant equal to $\bar{Y}$, the expected value of Y. U should then be treated as an expected value. Such a model does not account for the variations in Y. If these variations are large relative to the magnitude of the mean (i.e., if $\sigma_y / \bar{Y}$ is large), use of the model could be very deceptive. For example, the value of X that minimizes U is found as follows:

$$\frac{dU}{dX} = 1 - \frac{Y}{X^2} = 0 \tag{3.5}$$

$$X^0 = \sqrt{Y}. \tag{3.6}$$

Therefore, when Y is correctly estimated, the minimum value of U is

$$U^0 = \sqrt{\bar{Y}} + \frac{Y}{\sqrt{\bar{Y}}} = 2\sqrt{\bar{Y}}. \tag{3.7}$$

Suppose now that we use the value Y when its true value is $Y + \Delta Y$. Then the actual outcome will be

$$u = \sqrt{\bar{Y}} + \frac{Y + \Delta Y}{\sqrt{\bar{Y}}} = 2\sqrt{\bar{Y}} + \frac{\Delta Y}{\sqrt{\bar{Y}}}. \tag{3.8}$$

The true minimum would be

$$U^0 = \sqrt{Y + \Delta Y} + \frac{Y + \Delta Y}{\sqrt{Y + \Delta Y}} = 2\sqrt{Y + \Delta Y}. \tag{3.9}$$

Therefore, the cost of error is

$$u - U^0 = 2\sqrt{\bar{Y}} + \frac{\Delta Y}{\sqrt{\bar{Y}}} - 2\sqrt{Y + \Delta Y}. \tag{3.10}$$

It can be shown that this cost increases as $\Delta Y / Y$ increases.

One must be particularly careful when treating a controllable variable as a constant. For example, in most production-quantity models setup cost (the cost of preparing the machines for producing an item) is treated as a constant.

In fact, setup time is almost always a variable. Some of this variation is due to the variation in the workers' time, but frequently the amount of setup required is affected by the item that preceded it on the production line. For example, product *A* may be very similar to product *B* and very dissimilar to product *C*. Therefore, the setup for *A* after *B* may be much less costly than if it were made after *C*, and this may be controllable. In one such case we obtained greater improvements by controlling the order of production (hence setup costs) than by optimizing production quantities.

From a mathematical point of view it is frequently helpful to treat discrete variables as continuous. For example, withdrawals of items from stock that are actually discrete are frequently handled as though they were continuous at a constant rate over a planning period. By treating withdrawals as though they were made instantaneously at the beginning or end of the period, and by comparing the difference between these treatments, one can estimate the maximum cost per period that the continuity assumption can produce.

On the other hand, in many processes in which the time between events is a relevant variable, the model is considerably simplified by assuming that all events that occur within a period occur instantaneously at the beginning or end of the period. Calculation of the cost of this simplification can be carried out in essentially the same way as was described in the preceding paragraph.

Changing the Relationship between Variables

Models can frequently be simplified by modifying the functional form of part or all of the model. Linear approximations to nonlinear functions are quite common in all of science (e.g., in linear programming); in some cases a curve is approximated by a series of straight lines corresponding to consecutive segments of the curve (e.g., in nonlinear programming). Quadratic functions are also frequently used as approximations because their derivatives are linear (e.g., in quadratic programming). Discrete functions (e.g., the binomial and Poisson) are sometimes approximated by the continuous normal function. Probability density functions with no negative values are frequently approximated by functions that have negative values, if the probabilities associated with these values are very small.

Determination of the cost of such approximations requires comparison of the model with "reality." We shall consider such comparisons in the discussion of testing the model in Chapter 15.

One should be on guard against excessive use of the linear assumption, a tendency that B. O. Koopman (1956) has referred to as *linearitis*. In the marketing area this is particularly dangerous because sales responses to most forms of sales effort level off to a plateau and may even decline once the market is "saturated." Excessive amounts spent in advertising, for example, can usually be traced back to an assumed linear function that relates sales to the amount of advertising.

Modifying Constraints

Constraints can be added, subtracted, or otherwise modified to simplify the model.

If solving a model with constraints is difficult, the constraints can be ignored until a "solution" is obtained. If the "solution" satisfies the constraints, it can be accepted. If it does not, the constraints can be added one at a time, in order of increasing complexity, until a solution satisfying the constraints is obtained.

Sometimes the constraints can be worked in "backwards" more easily than they can be "frontwards." For example, suppose that we must determine the optimal production quantities for two items produced on the same machine. The time required to produce the quantities selected cannot exceed the amount of time available on the machine. It is possible to ignore this constraint and, if the two quantities determined lead to excessive production time, to reduce these quantities in such a way as to minimize the cost of so doing.

In problems involving the selection of production or purchase quantities, where demand for the items is variable, possible shortages must be taken into account. To do so in the model requires an estimate of shortage costs. It may be very difficult to obtain these estimates objectively, and the decision makers may be unwilling to provide subjective estimates. However, they may be willing to stipulate that shortages should occur no more frequently under the new policy than they did under the old. That is, they are willing to *satisfice* relative to shortages. Then it is possible to determine what the frequency of shortages has been and to introduce the constraint that future shortages do not exceed this amount.

In general, when constraints are removed, the solution derived will be optimistic (it will yield better performance than the "true" solution); when constraints are added, the solution will be pessimistic. Hence manipulation of constraints can be used to *bound* the solution: to estimate the range within which the solution will fall. Such a procedure is often useful in making "quick and dirty" estimates of potential payoffs in feasibility and exploratory studies.

MULTIPLE MODELS

In some cases the model of a problem situation may be either too complicated or too large to solve. It is frequently possible to decompose the model into parts that are solvable individually, and to take the output of one model as an input to another. Consider, for example, the problem of determining the number of maintenance shops that a military organization should have for the repair of heavy equipment.

First, a model was constructed from which, for any specified number of shops, n, the optimally sized work force at each shop could be determined. This model was used for a variety of values of n. A second model was constructed, which used n and the shop-operating cost associated with n and also took into account transportation costs and the cost of time lost in transportation. Then that n was selected which yielded minimum costs in the second model.

A model for a more complicated version of this problem was discussed as follows in the final report of a study of maintenance logistics:[2]

The total expected incremental cost of the maintenance system (C) can be expressed as

$$C = P + E + S + T$$

where P = the total expected cost of *parts* (ordering, purchase cost, stocking, excessing, etc.).

E = the total expected cost of the *end items* (major equipment) in the system.

S = the total expected *shop* cost (including direct personnel, indirect personnel, tools, facilities, etc.).

T = the total expected cost of *transporting* equipment to and from the shops.

Ideally, one should expand this equation by expressing each of the above costs as functions of the controllable and uncontrollable variables. Then by mathematical methods, one would seek to minimize the total expected incremental cost by selecting the proper values of the controllable variables. However, this approach is not mathematically feasible. Consequently, an alternative approach was developed. It involves constructing three "submodels": one for *shops*, one for *parts*, and one for *method of repair* (sub-assembly versus part replacement).

In order to break this problem into three parts, certain interactions between these parts had to be accounted for. First the number and size of the parts inventories required depend on the number of shops and hence the number of inventory locations. It was found, however, that for the alternate number of shops which were feasible, the effect of this number on parts inventory requirements was sufficiently small so that the optimal solution is not significantly altered by considering these variables independently.

Secondly, the method of repair affects both the parts and shop costs. Decisions concerning parts inventory and the number and size of shops were made assuming parts replacement. Then the possible improvements to be obtained by sub-assembly replacement were considered.

---

[2] *Maintenance Logistics for Major Mechanical Equipment*, prepared by the Operations Research Group of Case Institute of Technology for the U.S. Army Corps of Engineers, 1960, pp. 8–9.

A separate submodel was not required for the cost of end-items. The additional end-item requirements (above availability requirements) can be broken down into

(1) equipment waiting for repairs,
(2) equipment being repaired,
(3) equipment in transit, and
(4) equipment waiting for parts.

The costs associated with these four types of additional end-items . . . appear in the shops and parts submodel.

SEQUENTIAL DECISION MODELS

In practical problems involving probabilistic variables a model is constructed that contains assumptions concerning the distributions of probabilistic variables relative to either their form (e.g., normal, Poisson, exponential) or the values of the distribution's parameters. At least one additional assumption is made: the characteristics of the distribution that pertained in the past will also pertain in the future. In general, such an assumption becomes less justified as the time of applying the model becomes more distant from the time at which the model was developed. There are advantages, therefore, in evaluating the variables in a model and making a decision based on it at the last possible moment.

One obvious advantage of making a decision as late as possible is the maximum amount of relevant information that is then available. A late decision also makes it possible to treat the *particular* state of affairs that pertains at the time of the decision. One need not deal with the "average" characteristics of such situations. This frequently allows research economies and better decisions. This fact, for example, is responsible for the power of sequential sampling. In normal sampling procedures the sample size is determined on the basis of previously available information. In sequential sampling the sample size is not fixed in advance, but observations are made one at a time or in small blocks.

After each observation or block a research decision is reached as to whether enough information is available to make the estimate required or whether the collection of data should be continued. Those who developed sequential sampling realized that the data that are obtained during sampling can be used to determine more efficiently the required size of the sample. As a consequence, sequential sampling, where applicable, saves about one third of the observations required by a fixed sampling plan relative to any specified degree of precision.[3]

[3] The maximum exploitation of available information and its continuous revision and reevaluation lie at the root of what is called the Bayesian approach to statistics. For further discussion of this type of statistics, see Chernoff and Moses (1959).

Sequential decision models, then, do not "average" over future decision situations on the basis of past experience; they deal with each situation separately. For example, in some inventory situations the average demand and the average time to replenish stock are used to determine reorder quantities and frequencies. These average quantities and frequencies are then used regardless of what happens in any particular period. In sequential inventory models a prior decision as to when to order (e.g., every week or every month) is not made, but the reorder point is specified by a certain stock level. This level is determined by using average replenishment times. But the time of ordering becomes a variable in this treatment, a variable that reflects the characteristics of the period at hand. Here, then, the sequential concept is introduced in a limited way. If the stock level at which reordering takes place is also permitted to vary as a function of production or purchasing experience during the current period, another sequential element is introduced.

To see more clearly the significance of sequential models, consider a replacement problem involving a large number of low-cost items that fail. A number of identical items such as light bulbs, vacuum tubes, and air filters are installed at a certain time, $t = 0$. These are subsequently subjected to usage at an identical rate. All have the same probability-density function of length of life, $f(t)$. When an item fails, it is immediately replaced by an identical item of age zero.

Given such a population of items, it is often desired to carry out the replacement process in some optimal manner. In industrial situations, a policy of replacement that minimizes the total cost of operation is generally sought. The usual nonsequential solution to this problem specifies individual replacement of items as they fail and group replacement of all items at a specified fixed interval. Such a policy assumes that the form and parameters of the probability-density function $f(t)$ are known. There are two good reasons for questioning this assumption:

1. If the data on which these assumptions are based come from the manufacturer, the chances are that he obtained them under conditions different from those in which the user will operate. For example, he may have tested light bulbs by burning them continuously to failure under relatively constant environmental conditions. But it is known that lamp life depends on the frequency of turning the lamps off and on, temperature changes, jarring, and so on; in brief, conditions in the laboratory may differ from those in the installation involved in the problem.

Furthermore, even if the data were obtained from the installation itself, operating conditions may vary significantly from period to period (e.g., winter and summer); hence the distribution of times to failure may vary significantly from period to period.

2. The distribution of life-spans, even if accurate, is obtained for a very large sample; hence the actual distribution of failures for a smaller number of bulbs may differ significantly from it.

The use of a sequential model involves observing the failures as they occur and using this information to decide, at the time of a failure, whether to group-replace or to continue replacing each item individually.

Rutenberg (1961) has developed a sequential model that takes advantage of random fluctuations of failures about the mean of a given distribution. It yields a policy in which group replacement is not carried out at a point in time corresponding to the minimum expected cost, but at a time at which the actual sequence of failure is estimated to yield a minimum cost *for that particular sequence.*

Some other problems to which sequential modeling techniques are applicable are the following:

1. A publisher puts out a new book and watches sales week after week. On the basis of the sales information he wishes to make the following decisions: should a new edition be printed and, if so, how large should it be?

2. A theater puts on a new show and counts the tickets sold each night. Should the show be continued or dropped?

3. An enemy missile is detected on the radar screen. As more radar observations are obtained, its trajectory can be determined with better accuracy; on the other hand, precious time is lost. When should the countermeasures be activated?

4. In certain servicing operations (e.g., operation of a fleet of delivery trucks) additions to facilities can be made on short notice (e.g., by renting trucks and hiring drivers by the day). Here, too, observations on accumulation of units waiting for service can be made until a change in requirements is indicated.

A number of characteristics are common to these examples:

(*a*) The information available at the outset is general in nature, but the relevant parameters are estimated, rather than known. As more information is collected, a more precise estimate of the parameters can be obtained.

(*b*) A cost is attached to errors of estimation.

(*c*) A cost is attached to deferring the decision in order to collect additional information.

Under these conditions use of sequential decision models is frequently advantageous. Decision rules derived from such models have two important advantages in addition to those already considered:

1. Control (maintenance) of the solution under changing conditions is inherent in the decision process itself instead of being dependent on a separately designed control procedure such as that discussed in Chapter 16.

2. Situations in which very little information is available initially can nevertheless be handled systematically by sequential decision rules, and the informational input to these may undergo continuous improvement as time passes. Therefore, such rules are *adaptive* and provide those who use them with an opportunity for learning how to do so more effectively.

MODELS AS HEURISTIC INSTRUMENTS

Models are normally thought of as instruments for selecting the best (or at least a good) course of action from that set of courses of action that is "covered" by the model. However, models have another very important use that is frequently overlooked: they can be used *heuristically*, that is, as an instrument of discovery. They provide an effective tool with which to explore the structure of a problem and to uncover possible courses of action that were previously overlooked. The discovery of such courses of action may often be the most important use to which the model can be put. Many of the most successful applications of operations research have involved use of the model to uncover possibilities not normally considered in the literature on the relevant type of theory. The value of such exploration cannot be overemphasized. We should like to stress it here by considering several cases in which the heuristic use of a model played the key role in solving the problem. In these, as in most such cases, the course of action uncovered is so obviously superior to the possibilities that were previously considered, that a model is hardly needed to justify their choice.

Case 1

A series of analytic studies of inventories in one factory and in the large number of warehouses that it supplied had failed to yield significant decreases in the relevant costs. Industrial consumers of the products that were involved purchased them directly from the warehouses, that is, over the counter. Because the products deteriorated under normal atmospheric conditions, they were normally purchased in very small quantities. The supplier had attempted, without success, to induce customers to buy larger quantities by offering a generous quantity discount. Expected losses in storage made the offer unattractive to customers. The OR team observed that inventories could be reduced if the customer gave advance notice of what he wanted and when he wanted it. This type of lead time is not normally considered in inventory theory. Appropriate models were developed, and the potential improvements that the increased lead time provided by the customer could yield were calculated. A discounting plan was developed in which the price of the product was made a step function of the lead time provided by the customer. This plan was put into operation. Customers took advantage of it because it did not affect their storage and inventory in any way and they usually knew what they would require some time in advance. This made it possible for the warehouses to launch a "stock-to-order" policy that resulted in a considerable reduction in inventories.

Case 2

A company with a very large product line found only a small percentage of these products profitable. It felt compelled to continue the unprofitable items because, management argued, these products were purchased by customers who also purchased profitable items in large quantities and who would not continue to do so if a complete line were not offered. The managers also argued that they could not increase the price of these products, because their competitors were both willing and able to sell these unprofitable products at the current prices. The large number of small production runs of these items disrupted production of the profitable large-volume items. Therefore, management said, it wanted to schedule production so as to minimize this disruptive effect.

The OR team found the argument for continuing the unprofitable items less than well substantiated by any objective evidence, but management was firm in its conviction. The researchers found that salesmen were paid a base salary plus a commission based on the dollar volume of their sales. An alternative commission scheme for salesmen was developed, in which commissions were based on profitability of sales, no commissions being offered for unprofitable sales. The commission rates were so established as not to affect the earnings of the salesmen, provided that they continued to obtain the same volume and variety of sales.

Management considered the scheme a fair one and installed it. Sales of unprofitable items immediately decreased and those of the profitable items were not affected. It was possible after a short time to drop a number of the unprofitable items from the line. Their elimination permitted considerable production economies relative to the profitable large-volume items.

Case 3

A company that produced large, industrially consumed equipment found that demand for its product would increase by more than a factor of two in some years and would decrease by one half or more in other years. This created a serious production-smoothing problem because of the short supply of the highly skilled workers that were required for production. Study showed that demand for the product followed general economic conditions quite closely, but that these conditions could not be forecasted with sufficient accuracy to allow optimal decision rules to yield much improvement. After a considerable amount of effort to improve the forecasts had had no significant success, another line of attack was taken. It was directed toward determining how the company's production schedule could be made less sensitive to general economic conditions. The question itself suggested an answer: to take on another product line that moved counter to the economy and required the same technology and production facilities as did the original class of products. A search was initiated and a suitable class of products was found. It was added to the line. Today the new class of products accounts for a large portion of the company's considerably enlarged and stabilized business.

Case 4

An international fleet of military transport vehicles required a large number of maintenance centers spread over the world. Each center carried a large stock of replacement parts and subassemblies. Inventories were large and costly. The problem was to bring them under control. Parts used in repair were classified by annual demand and their cost. Two important discoveries resulted. First, the large majority of items were of very low demand, and requirements for them could more than adequately be met by cannibalizing equipment that was no longer fit for use. Second, the purchase price of the five hundred most used parts bought one at a time was greater than that of the vehicle itself. This suggested that spare parts be carried in stock in the form of extra vehicles. Not only did this reduce the cost of stock, but it also reduced handling costs and downtime of vehicles. It also increased the mobility of the stock. By having extra vehicles in the system it was possible to take needed parts from that vehicle in a maintenance queue whose repair required the most work.

SUMMARY

Models play such a fundamental role in OR that some practitioners claim that it is their use that distinguishes OR from other fields that also conduct research on management problems. Models provide distilled and economic descriptions and explanations of the operations of the systems that they represent. By analyzing or experimenting on them, we can usually determine how changes in the relevant system will affect its performance. These procedures frequently substitute for experimentation on the system itself. Experimentation on the systems of interest in OR is usually either impossible or too costly. Even when experiments can be conducted on the system itself, models enable us to design such experiments more effectively than we otherwise could.

Three types of models were identified: iconic, analogue, and symbolic. Iconic and analogue models are usually employed in the development of symbolic models, which, although more abstract, are easier to manipulate and yield more accurate and precise predictions than the others do.

The procedures by which models are constructed fall into patterns according to the complexity of the system and the amount of access that the researchers have to the system's structure. Five such patterns have been considered, which are characterized by their use of (1) direct examination of system operations, (2) an analogue, (3) analysis of data, (4) experimentation, and (5) an "artificial reality."

We also considered how the availability of data interacts with model construction, often necessitating the development of a model that is less precise than was hoped for, but is nevertheless useful. Usable approximate models are much better than more exact models that cannot be used.

Models are never as complex as the phenomena that they represent; they are simplified as much as possible without significant loss of accuracy. In order to simplify the representation of the system under study, variables may be omitted, aggregated, or simplified in form; relationships may also be modified to make them easier to deal with, and constraints may be added or subtracted.

Complex systems may require representation by a set of models, each of a subsystem, that are linked together.

For problems requiring repeated solution under changing conditions, sequential decision models are being developed that exploit all relevant information available at the time of decision. These models can also be used to determine the time for action.

Finally, we considered the use of models as instruments to uncover courses of action not previously considered. Such use often yields solutions that are so clearly superior to those previously considered that this superiority hardly requires proof.

DISCUSSION TOPICS AND PROBLEMS

1. Take a familiar process, such as shoppers coming to a check-out counter in a supermarket or the operation of a two-man barbershop, and discuss how an iconic, analogue, and symbolic model of the operation can be constructed.
2. Examine some case studies in the OR literature and determine which pattern of model construction was used in each.
3. In any of the cases examined in (2), was the nature of the model used affected by the kinds of data available? If so, how?
4. In one of the cases found in the literature identify each of the ways in which the model simplifies reality.
5. Did any of the cases involve the use of two or more models in combination? If so, how were the models made to interact?

6. Find some cases in the history of science or technology in which a model or a theory led to the discovery of new facts or possibilities.

Suggested Reading

Very little has been written on models in general, but a great deal has been written on particular types of models. A few general discussions can be found in Ackoff (1962), Beach (1957), Camp (1957–1958), Rutenberg (1961), and Beer (1966).

Bibliography

Ackoff, R. L., *Scientific Method: Optimizing Applied Research Decisions*, John Wiley and Sons, New York, 1962.

Beach, E. F., *Economic Models*, John Wiley and Sons, New York, 1957.

Beer, Stafford, *Decision and Control*, John Wiley and Sons, New York, 1966.

Camp, G. D., "Approximation and Bounding in Operations Research," in *Operations Research*, Vol. II, Record of the 1957–1958 Seminar in Operations Research, University of Michigan, Ann Arbor, Mich.

Chernoff, H., and L. E. Moses, *Elementary Decision Theory*, John Wiley and Sons, New York, 1959.

Koopman, B. O., "Fallacies in Operations Research," *Operations Research*, **4** (1956), 422–426.

Rutenberg, Y. H., *Sequential Decision Models*, Ph.D. thesis, Case Institute of Technology, Cleveland, 1961.

CHAPTER 4

Deriving Solutions from Models

TYPES OF SOLUTION

We have seen that the general model of a decision process takes the form

$$U = f(X, Y), \tag{4.1}$$

where X represents the controlled variables, Y the uncontrolled variables, and U the expected value or utility.[1] In addition, there may be constraints:

$$\phi(X, Y) \geq 0. \tag{4.2}$$

The solution of such a model is obtained by determining the value of X (as a function of Y) that maximizes U, and all the tools of classical mathematics, such as differential calculus and finite differences, are available for this task. Such techniques work well provided that the constraints (4.2) consist mainly of strict equalities and there are only a few controlled variables. Methods of this type, which proceed directly to the solution in terms of a general value of Y, are called *deductive*.

It may be impossible, particularly in probabilistic situations, to express U as a simple function of X and Y. Instead we may have a set of rules that enable us to compute the utility gained for any particular realization of X and Y. By studying a suitable sample of values of Y, we can compute the expected utility U by *inductive* methods. In such cases classical methods are of little assistance in finding optimal decisions. When classical methods fail—for lack of a closed expression for U or because of the complexity of the constraints or of the number of variables—we are usually forced to use an *iterative* procedure. Such a procedure starts with a trial solution and a set of rules for improving it. The trial solution is then replaced by the improved solution, and the process is repeated until either no further improvement is possible or the cost of further calculation cannot be justified.

---

[1] X, Y, and ϕ may be thought of as vectors; U is a scalar.

In this book we assume that the reader is familiar with classical deductive techniques, but we shall discuss some of the newer methods that have been developed for solving problems in operations research. Particular models and their solutions will be found in subsequent chapters; at this point we wish to consider some of the more general techniques that are available.

Iterative Solutions

Most of the now well-known algorithms of linear, nonlinear, and dynamic programming are iterative techniques. The following is a very simple example of how iteration works. Suppose that a salesman has a total of ten hours to divide among three accounts (*A*, *B*, and *C*). The amount of sales that he obtains for each hour with each account is known and is shown in Table 4.1.

TABLE 4.1   *Example of an Iterative Procedure*

	Accounts		
Hours	*A*	*B*	*C*
1	20	18	21
2	17	16	16
3	12	14	15
4	10	13	14
5	8	9	11

The entries are incremental; that is, if he spends two hours with *A*, he sells $20 + 17 = 37$; if he spends three hours with *A*, he obtains $20 + 17 + 12 = 49$. Note that the increments are monotonically decreasing.

An iterative procedure for dividing the 10 hours so as to maximize sales is the following:

1. Make an arbitrary allocation of the 10 hours; say, 4 to *A*, 3 to *B*, and 3 to *C*.
2. Identify the largest increase that can be obtained by adding 1 hour. In this case we can gain 14 by adding 1 hour to *C*.
3. Identify the smallest decrease that would result by decreasing time by 1 hour. In this case it is 10 that is lost by removing 1 hour from *A*.
4. If the number obtained in step (3) is less than the number obtained in step (2), exchange hours between the relevant accounts. In this case we would allocate 3 to *A*, 3 to *B*, and 4 to *C*.

5. Repeat steps (2), (3), and (4) until the largest gain that can be obtained by adding 1 hour is less than the smallest loss that would be sustained if 1 hour is removed. In this case we can make one more exchange: add 1 hour to B (gain 13) and subtract 1 hour from A (lose 12). The solution is 2 to A, 4 to B, and 4 to C.

The Las Vegas Technique

Iterative procedures fall into three groups. In the first group, we know that each iteration will improve the solution and that after a finite number of repetitions no further improvement will be possible. In the second group, although successive iterations improve the solution, we are only guaranteed the solution as a limit of an infinite process. In the third group we include trial and error methods; we only know that successive trials tend to improve the result, without being sure of monotonic improvement.

In the first group, provided that we have a test to tell us that no further improvement is possible, we can be certain the computations will terminate. However, they may be unduly lengthy, and in all three groups we will wish to decide when we have reached the point at which further improvements will not justify the computational expense that they require. The Las Vegas technique enables us to make this decision. We shall first describe it in terms of a deterministic model and then show how it may be extended to cover probabilistic systems.

Suppose that, given the values of the controlled variables X and the uncontrolled variables Y, we can compute the utility, $U = f(X, Y)$. For a given value of Y we now compute U for a series of values of X, say $X_1, X_2, \ldots$, with corresponding utility $U_1, U_2, \ldots$. If possible, we would like to have a rule for deriving X_{n+1} from $X_1, X_2, \ldots, X_n$ and $U_1, U_2, \ldots, U_n$ in such a way that $U_{n+1} > U_n$. Lacking such a rule, we would like one which makes it highly probable that $U_{n+1} > U_n$. However, this is not necessary; the technique will work even if the successive X's are chosen at random.

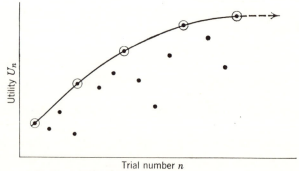

Figure 4.1 A Las Vegas plot.

The next step is to plot the utility achieved against the trial number (Figure 4.1). We then circle any point that represents the maximum utility achieved so far. By sketching a freehand curve through the circled points and by extrapolating, we can estimate the gain in utility for one further iteration. Comparison with the cost of the computation will show whether it is worth continuing.

Many of the iterative procedures used in OR have been developed very recently; therefore, we shall not assume that the reader is familiar with them and shall consider them in detail when discussing the models with which they are usually associated. Most of the deductive procedures used in OR, on the other hand—the calculus and differential and difference equations—are familiar to graduates in science and engineering. Whenever the mathematics required to solve a model goes beyond these, we shall explain the procedure.

In this chapter we consider derivations of solutions that are obtained by the following methods:

1. *Simulation:* experimentation on the model.
2. *Gaming:* a type of simulation that involves real decision makers.
3. *Experimental optimization:* experimentation on the system itself.

SIMULATION

Models *represent* reality, simulation *imitates* it. Simulation always involves the manipulation of a model; it is, in effect, a way of manipulating a model so that it yields a motion picture of reality. Simulation normally involves large amounts of computation; hence it would frequently be impractical were it not for the availability of high-speed electronic computers. Even so there are situations in which the amount of computation may be prohibitive relative to the "size" of the problem.

Simulation in OR has a number of important uses other than that in deriving solutions from models; these uses will be discussed after we have considered the process in more detail.

We shall be primarily concerned with simulations that are based on symbolic models, but it should be observed that simulation can employ iconic or analogue models.

Iconic simulation involves the manipulation of an iconic model under real or iconically represented conditions. Such simulation is widely used in testing the design of large complex systems with respect to selected properties of the system. For example, the aerodynamic properties of proposed aircraft are usually tested by use of a small-scale iconic model of the craft in a wind tunnel (an iconic model of the relevant environment). Ship models may be tested in tow tanks for their hydrodynamic properties. Similarly, pilot plants in the chemical industry are iconic models of proposed production systems.

A hydraulic model of the British economy, the MONIAC, has been constructed at the London School of Economics. This analogue can be used to simulate the effect of such changes in the economic system as devaluation of the pound and increases or decreases in tax or interest rates.

In symbolic simulation we wish to evaluate an expression in an equation, or the entire equation, where one or more of the components are *stochastic* variables. A stochastic variable is one whose value at any moment of time is a random selection from some probability distribution of possible values.

For example, suppose that we wish to evaluate an expression $\overline{z^2}$, the average value of z^2 where z can assume any value from 0 to 9, inclusive, with equal probability (i.e., 1/10). We can evaluate this expression numerically as follows:

$$0.1(0^2) + 0.1(1^2) + 0.1(2^2) + \cdots + 0.1(9^2) = 28.5;$$

but let us try to evaluate it in another way.

Using a table of random numbers, we can select values of z from 0 to 9 with equal probability, square each, and calculate the sample average. We can use this average as an estimate of $\overline{z^2}$. Such a procedure is shown in

TABLE 4.2 *Estimating $\overline{X^2}$*

X_i	X_i^2	Cumulative Average	X_i	X_i^2	Cumulative Average
0	0		4	16	
5	25		1	1	
4	16		3	9	
0	0		9	81	
8	64		8	64	
		21.0			26.0
0	0		9	81	
0	0		4	16	
2	4		2	4	
5	25		1	1	
7	49		0	0	
		18.3			24.9
5	25		6	36	
8	64		6	36	
4	16		6	36	
6	36		7	49	
5	25		9	81	
		23.3			28.7

Table 4.2, where the averages are calculated accumulatively after every five observations, for a sample of thirty.

The basis of simulation is random sampling of a variable's values from a distribution of that variable. This is sometimes called the *Monte Carlo* technique but, strictly speaking, Monte Carlo refers to the use of sampling methods to estimate the value of nonstochastic variables. For example, suppose that we wish to estimate the size of an arc marked on the perimeter of a roulette wheel. By spinning the wheel a number of times, we could determine the fraction of times that it stops within the arc. This fraction multiplied by 360° would give us an estimate of the number of degrees in the arc.

In random sampling from a probability distribution, we usually require three things:

1. A set of random numbers.
2. A way of converting these numbers into another set of numbers, random variates, which have the same distribution as the variable involved.
3. A sampling-estimating procedure.

We shall consider each of these aspects of simulation in turn.

Random Numbers

There is no problem in obtaining random numbers for simulations performed by hand. Numerous tables of such numbers are available, of which the most extensive are those published by the RAND Corporation (1955). When a computer is to be used in simulation, however, we can seldom afford to fill the computer's memory with a large number of random digits. Consequently, programs have been developed for generating what are called *pseudorandom numbers*. Two of the more commonly used generating procedures are the *midsquare* and *congruential* techniques.

The midsquare procedure consists of taking a four-digit number,[2] preferably (but not necessarily) selected at random, squaring it, taking the four digits starting at the third from the left, recording them, squaring them, and so on. For example, if we start with 3182, by squaring we obtain 10,125,124. We then take the four digits, 1251, record them, square them, and so on. Eventually this procedure will return to the number with which it started. The length of the cycle generally falls between 10^4 and 10^6.

The congruential procedure, although more complicated, may yield cycles as large as 10^{12}. This procedure consists of letting

$$X_{n+1} = KX_n(\text{mod } M).$$

---

[2] More elaborate techniques may use up to ten digits.

That is, X_{n+1} is equal to the number that remains after KX_n is divided by M. This method was first reported by Lehmer (1951), who used $K = 23$, $M = 10^8 + 1$. He obtained a sequence of eight-digit numbers with a cycle length of 5,882,352. Taussky and Todd (in Meyer, 1956) report that in using $K = 5^{17}$, $X_0 = 1$, and $M = 2^{42}$ they obtained a sequence of approximately 10^{12} numbers before cycling.

For a detailed discussion of testing and generating random numbers, see Taussky and Todd (1956) and Tocher (in "Symposium on Monte Carlo Methods," 1954).

Random Variates from a Specified Probability Distribution

The procedure for converting random numbers into numbers drawn from a specified probability distribution is a relatively simple one in principle,

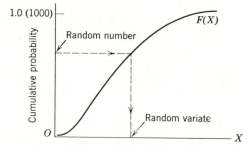

Figure 4.2 Conversion of a random number to a random variate from a specified distribution.

although it may be quite difficult in practice. Suppose that we plot the relevant distribution in a cumulative form as in Figure 4.2. We divide the vertical scale of probability into, say, one thousand parts. When a random number is selected, it is located on this scale and projected horizontally over to the function. Then one projects down to the abscissa and reads the corresponding random variate. It can be seen that variates under the steepest parts of the function—where the probability is most dense—are most likely to be selected.[3]

Tables of random variates from the normal distribution are available (RAND, 1955). Random variates from the exponential distribution can be generated by taking the logarithm of random numbers. Detailed discussion of this problem can be found in Lytle and Butler (in Meyer, 1956).

In some cases when a set of observations have been made on a stochastic variable, a probability density function cannot be fitted to it very well. In

---

[3] We wish to choose a value x such that $Pr\{x \leq X\} = F(X)$. Let y be the random variable chosen. Then $Pr\{x \leq X\} = Pr\{y \leq F(X)\}$, which is as required.

such cases, if the observations are independent of each other, one can order the observations and use random numbers to select from the set of actually observed values those values that are to be used in the simulation. There is a danger in doing this if the number of observations is not large: one may miss extreme values. On the other hand, one does avoid the distortion that fitting a function may introduce.

Sampling-Estimating Procedures

Because of the large amount of computation that is usually required in simulation, it is desirable to employ a sampling-estimating procedure that gives the most precise results possible for the fewest "observations" possible. This is particularly true when the computations are done by hand. Sampling-estimating procedures that either increase precision of estimates for a fixed sample size or decrease the sample size required to obtain a fixed degree of precision, are called *variance-reducing* techniques.

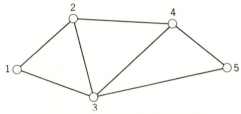

Figure 4.3   A simplified network.

The very simple telephone network shown in Figure 4.3 may help in describing these techniques. Each link in this network has some probability of being busy. We wish to determine the probability of communicating between 1 and 5 at a random instant. The problem can be solved analytically, but the solution is not easy and the difficulty increases with the number of links. However, if we know which links are not busy, it is easy to determine whether or not communication is possible. For example, we cannot communicate between 1 and 5 if links (35) and (45) are busy.

Let p_{ij} be the probability that link (ij) is busy, and let x_{ij} be a random variable that takes the value 0 if (ij) is busy and 1 if (ij) is free. We might also set $x_{ij} = 0$ if there is no link between i and j; in these cases $p_{ij} = 1$. Thus at any instant the state of the system is completely described by the matrix $[x_{ij}]$, and from it we can infer whether or not communication from 1 to 5 is possible.

Now suppose that we choose random numbers, r_{ij}, between 0 and 100, and for each $p_{ij} \neq 0$, if $r_{ij} \leq 100 p_{ij}$, we set $x_{ij} = 0$; otherwise $x_{ij} = 1$. We then repeat the process and count the fraction of occasions in which communication is possible. Hand calculations, which can be tedious in complex networks, are simple for this one.

We wish to estimate the probability of communication between 1 and 5. Table 4.3 gives the probabilities that each link is open.

The simplest procedure consists of taking sets of seven single-digit random numbers corresponding to the seven links: (12), (13), (23), (24), (34), (35), and (45). If the first random digit is 0, 1, 2, 3, 4, 5, or 6, we shall assume that link (12) is open; otherwise it is closed, and so on. Table 4.4 shows the

TABLE 4.3 $(1 - p_{ij})$

j \ i	1	2	3	4	5
1					
2	0.7				
3	0.2	0.3			
4		0.6	0.3		
5			0.2	0.7	

result of twenty trials in six of which communication is possible. We estimate the probability P of an open line between 1 and 5 as 0.3. The estimate of the variance is

$$\frac{p(1 - p)}{20} = \frac{0.3 \times 0.7}{20} = 0.0105.$$

There are several techniques for reducing the variance, if it is too large, by modifying the experimental design and estimation procedure.

Importance Sampling. Suppose that we change the probability of the link (12) being busy from p to p' and that we allow for this in estimating P. This can easily be done by weighting the trials in which communication is possible depending on whether or not link (12) is open. When we use p' instead of p, the link will be busy p'/p times too frequently, and it will be open $(1 - p')/(1 - p)$ too often. Thus each trial in which the link is open is counted $(1 - p)/(1 - p')$ times and each trial in which it is closed is counted p/p' times. If out of n trials there are n_1 cases in which communication is possible and (12) is open, and n_2 cases in which communication is possible and (12) is busy, we would estimate P by

$$P = \frac{\left(\dfrac{1 - p}{1 - p'}\right)^n 1 + \dfrac{p}{p'}\, n_2}{n}.$$

TABLE 4.4 *Random Numbers Used in Simulation of Telephone Network*

Link:	12	13	23	24	34	35	45	15 Open	15 Open if 12 Open	15 Open if 12 Closed
$1-P_{ij}$	0.7	0.2	0.3	0.6	0.3	0.2	0.7			
Trial 1	⓪ᵃ	3	4	7	4	3	8			
2	9	7	7	④	②	4	⑥		×	
3	①	6	7	6	6	2	②			
4	①	2	5	⑤	8	5	9			
5	⑤	5	5	9	5	6	③			
6	①	6	②	②	7	7	9		×	
7	8	4	4	②	①	7	⑤		×	
8	⑥	3	⓪	①	6	3	7			
9	③	3	②	①	①	2	③	×	×	
10	⑤	7	6	⓪	8	6	③	×	×	
11	①	8	①	8	⓪	7	9			
12	②	6	6	②	3	8	9			
13	②	3	4	②	4	⓪	8			
14	⑤	2	3	6	②	8	①			
15	③	7	8	⑤	9	4	③	×	×	
16	7	⓪	②	9	①	7	①	×	×	×
17	⑤	6	6	②	①	8	③	×	×	
18	9	9	4	9	5	7	②			
19	①	6	⓪	8	①	5	⓪	×	×	
20	③	①	①	6	9	3	③			

ᵃ The encircled numbers indicate open link.

It may be shown that the best value for p' is given by

$$\frac{1-p'}{p'} = \left(\frac{1-p}{p}\right)\sqrt{\frac{K_1}{K_2}}, \tag{4.3}$$

where K_1 is the probability that communication between 1 and 5 is possible given that link (12) is busy, and K_2 is the corresponding probability given that (12) is open. Of course, K_1 and K_2 are not known at the outset, but they can be estimated from the first few trials for subsequent use. With p' having been determined from (4.3), it can be shown that the variance (V) of estimates based on n trials is reduced by

$$\frac{1}{n} p (1 - p)(\sqrt{K_1} - \sqrt{K_2})^2, \tag{4.4}$$

a quantity that is never negative and may be quite large if p is near 0.5 and K_1 and K_2 are different.

If, in the example, we ignore the random numbers for the link (12) and assume that it is always closed, we find one case in which communication is possible and we estimate $K_1 = 0.05$. If we assume that (12) is open, we find eight cases and estimate $K_2 = 0.4$. Thus

$$\frac{1 - p'}{p'} = \frac{0.7}{0.3} \sqrt{\frac{0.05}{0.4}}$$

or $p' = 0.55$.

The estimated reduction of variance for an estimate based on 20 trials is 0.0018, or about 17 per cent.

Russian Roulette and Splitting.   In 20 trials we had to generate $20 \times 7 = 140$ random numbers. Now it is clear that if links (12) and (13) are busy, no communication is possible, so that there is no point in examining the remaining links. Such cases arise with probability $p_{12}p_{13} = 0.3 \times 0.8 = 0.24$. Therefore, if we terminated any trial in which this occurs, we would reduce the average amount of random numbers per trial from 7 to $7(1 - p_{12}p_{13}) + 2p_{12}p_{13} = 6.52$. Alternatively, by using the same amount of random numbers we could increase the number of trials in the ratio 7/6.52, or about 8 per cent. The variance of the estimate of P would be reduced by the same amount. In the example there are three such cases, and the five "wasted" random numbers in each would permit two more trials, which is about what we would expect.

This process of "killing" a trial in midstream is called *Russian Roulette*. In some cases, instead of terminating a trial with certainty when a given event occurs partway through, we may assign some probability to its termination. Alternatively, we may arrange to draw two or more random numbers for each subsequent stage if a certain event occurs. If we draw k random numbers, each receives a weight of $1/k$ in counting successes. This process is called *splitting*.

Both Russian Roulette and splitting are based on the idea that some intermediate outcomes are more "interesting" than others. We try to increase the relative frequency of interesting outcomes.

The Use of Expected Values.   In discussing importance sampling we pointed out that we could estimate the conditional probabilities K_1 and K_2 of communication depending on whether (12) is busy or not. If the estimates are k_1 and k_2, the probability of communication is estimated by $p_{12}k_1 + (1 - p_{12})k_2$, where p_{12} is known. The variance of such an estimate, assuming that K_1 and K_2 are estimated from two independent sets—each of n independent observations—is

$$\frac{1}{n} [p_{12}^2 K_1(1 - K_1) + (1 - p_{12})^2 K_2(1 - K_2)]. \tag{4.5}$$

Each observation requires 6 random numbers; thus with the 140 random numbers used in the simple sampling scheme above we could obtain two independent sets of 12 observations.

On the other hand, if we use the same data to estimate both K_1 and K_2, a single set of n observations would produce a variance of

$$\frac{1}{n}[p_{12}{}^2 K_1(1 - K_1) + (1 - p_{12})^2 K_2(1 - K_2)$$

$$+ 2p_{12}(1 - p_{21}) \text{ cov } (K_1 K_2)], \quad (4.6)$$

where the cov $(K_1 K_2)$ is the covariance of k_1 and k_2 when measured on the same sample. Usually this will be difficult to compute, but if we had, say, 100 observations we could proceed as follows:

1. Split the 100 observations into five sets of 20 each.
2. Estimate K_1 and K_2 from each subset.
3. Compute the covariance.
4. Compare the variance of the estimates of P resulting from using all 100 observations for both K_1 and K_2 with those resulting from using the first 50 for K_1 and the second 50 for K_2.

Systematic Sampling. Sometimes the generation of random numbers can be avoided by systematically associating numbers with events. In our example we might assign the number 0 to link (ij) in trials 1, 11, 21, 31, . . . ; the number 1 in trials 2, 12, 22, . . . ; 2 in trials 3, 13, 23, . . . ; and so on up to the number 9 in trials 10, 20, 30, ... For any trial in which the assigned number is less than 7 we assume that link (12) is open. This procedure will give assurance that (12) is open in the correct proportion of time.

Stratified Sampling. It may be possible to combine systematic sampling and importance sampling. Suppose that we assign a probability p' to link (12) being closed (instead of the true value p_{12}). This will have the effect of changing the number of cases in which we study the possibility of communication with (12) busy. If we use systematic sampling with p', we are certain that of a total of n trials, we shall have $p'n$ in which (12) is busy and $(1 - p')n$ in which it is open. Let k_1 and k_2 be the corresponding estimates of K_1 and K_2. The estimate of P is $p_{12} k_1 + (1 - p_{12})k_2$, and the variance is

$$\frac{p_{12}{}^2 K_1(1 - K_1)}{p'n} + \frac{(1 - p_{12})^2 K_2(1 - K_2)}{(1 - p')n}. \quad (4.7)$$

If we differentiate (4.7), it is apparent that the variance is minimized by setting

$$\frac{1 - p'}{p'} = \left(\frac{1 - p_{12}}{p_{12}}\right) \sqrt{\frac{K_1}{K_2}}. \quad (4.8)$$

Correlation and Regression. It may happen that we wish to estimate a quantity y when a given number of observations would result in a variance σ^2. Suppose that y is correlated with x and that our procedure would permit an estimate of x with a much lower variance. It is possible that y can be estimated with lower variance by observing x.

Suppose, for example, that we have estimated P in the communication problem and now wish to study the effect of an additional link, say from 2 to 5, which will be busy with probability p. There is no need to simulate the entire operation. We can go back to our study of the original network, select those cases in which communication was not possible, and find the fraction of these in which the link (25) would have made a difference. If this fraction is p', the addition of (25) to the network will increase P by $(1 - p)p'$.

Some of the variance-reducing techniques are better than others, but in most practical situations we do not have enough information to choose the most powerful of the techniques. For example, the idea of importance sampling could be extended by modifying several of the probabilities instead of only that of link (12). It is not difficult to see how to weight results if this is done, but computing the effect on variance may be as difficult as an analytical solution to the original problem. Consequently, the changes made are usually the result of intuition and insight rather than calculation. For any given design and estimating procedure, it is easy enough to estimate the sampling variance by dividing the data into blocks, estimating the parameter for each block, and calculating its variance, thus verifying the results of intuition.

Kahn (1956, p. 156) has the following methodological observation on the six techniques just described:

> Techniques described under the headings of Importance Sampling, Russian Roulette and Splitting, and Stratified Sampling have the property that in many calculations they will give a tremendous increase in efficiency if properly used; if, however the intuition of the calculator is faulty and he does not use a reasonable design, then they can be very unreliable and actually increase the variance. The other techniques are more stable in that it is almost impossible for the experimenter to worsen the sampling variance by misusing them, even if he has a bad intuition.

Variance-reducing techniques can in some instances yield startling reductions in the number of computations required to obtain a specified level of precision. In the problem reported by Arnold, Bucher, Trotter, and Tukey [in Meyer (1956, pp. 80 ff)], by the use of a procedure that combines splitting and what these authors call conditional calculations, a gain of a factor of about 5000 over standard simple random-sampling techniques was obtained.

The quotation from Marshall [in Meyer (1956, p. 8)] provides a succinct summary of the methodological aspects of variance reduction in Monte Carlo procedures:

The increase in the speed of [computing] machines has tended to make variance reducing techniques relatively less interesting, but has by no means eliminated their usefulness. The effect of increased computing speed in the newer machines is to make the cost of designing and coding a problem increase relative to the cost of machine running time. The use of variance reducing techniques shortens running time but at the expense of (1) increasing the time spent in designing the computations so as to adapt the classical techniques to the particular problem or in the invention of a new, more suitable technique, and (2) complicating the coding because of the more elaborate bookkeeping and calculations these techniques usually require. On the whole, however, if there is one thing that would generally increase the usefulness of Monte Carlo it is the discovery of new variance reducing techniques, or the application of known variance reducing techniques as a matter of course to the ordinary run of problems. Not only should these techniques be used whenever it is economical to do so but, in addition, since the variance reducing techniques are not yet well known there should be a bias toward using them even when they are not economical for the problem at hand. This is a way to learn about them for use in later and more suitable problems. The use of new techniques in marginal cases is almost always justified as a method of building intellectual capital. In the long run one would suppose that real thought on the design of Monte Carlo problems will be confined to problems of a basically new type whenever they first appear; standard variance reducing techniques will be available, and used, for other problems on the basis that sub-routines for computing common functions now are.

Marshall's statement about "building intellectual capital" shows explicit recognition of the obligation of scientists working on either pure or applied problems to take responsibility for the methodological and technical development of research procedures.

By now it is probably clear to the reader that the problem of reducing variance in estimates obtained by simulation is very similar to that faced in any application of sampling procedures: "For this reason, it is very valuable to have professional statistical help in designing these calculations" [Kahn (1956 p. 190)].

Variance and Computers in Simulation

In some instances in which a statistic of two or more distributions is taken jointly the variance of this statistic can be determined analytically. In most instances in which simulation is required it cannot be analytically determined. Therefore, the researcher usually cannot determine in advance how many simulation "runs" he will need. For this reason, the application of sampling in stages (at least double sampling) is particularly well suited for simulation. When the simulation is done by hand, the variance of the estimate sought can be recomputed after each trial. When a computer is used, however, it is costly and time-consuming to divide the simulation into stages. What is frequently overlooked, on the other hand, is that it may be more costly and time-consuming to select a sample size arbitrarily and to make too many or too few observations. Even when a computer is used, several hand-runs of the simulation are usually required in order to check out the computer program. These runs can also be employed to obtain at least a crude estimate of the variance, which can then be used to estimate the required sample size. Given an estimate of the variance, the procedures for determining optimal sample size can be applied, perhaps with modification to suit the characteristics of the situation.

The question whether or not a computer should be used in a simulation entails considerations of economy as well as of accuracy. In complex simulations the opportunities for nonsampling errors are considerable. These errors have the same characteristics, in general, as observer errors and can be analyzed in the same way. The cost of using a computer involves not only running time but also programming and the inevitable "debugging."

Other Uses of Simulation

In addition to deriving solutions from models, simulation in OR can also be used for other important purposes.

1. *To study transitional processes.* When a model can be solved analytically, the solution often specifies only the terminal or steady state that results from changing the values of the variables, and not the intermediate states—the states of transition. Simulation exposes the transition to as careful a study as the researcher may care to make. For example, the solution of a complex inventory problem involving the purchasing, storage, and use of a large number of items (e.g., spare parts for aircraft) may show that the current stock levels of some items are too high and of others too low. The solution obtained analytically may tell us what the average inventory investment will be after the changes have been made and after the system has settled down to a steady state. While the inventory is moving from its current state to its steady state, items that are understocked according to the solution can usually be brought up to the level indicated by the solution rather quickly by buying more of them. But items that are overstocked will be reduced to the appropriate level only with use, which may take time. Consequently, although the inventory investment may *eventually* decrease if the solution is followed, it will usually increase during the transition. It may be important to know by how much it will increase and how long the period will be before the steady state is reached. Simulation makes it possible for us to "map" this transition and determine its characteristics.

2. *To estimate values of model parameters or the model's functional form.* Sometimes we may be able to construct a model but be unable to evaluate all its parameters (uncontrolled variables) because of lack of data. We may, however, have good and plentiful data on past outcomes and values of the

controlled variables. Then we can use simulation to try out a number of possible values of the parameters together with known past values of the controlled variables, until we obtain one or more sets of values that yield outcomes that correspond well to the known past outcomes. The same kind of procedure can be used to explore functional forms of the model.

3. *To treat courses of action that cannot be formulated into the model*. In some problems the performance of an entity under a set of specified conditions may be one of the important variables, but we may not be able to enumerate or characterize all of its possible courses of action in advance. Even if we can enumerate them, we may not be able to characterize them by a set of quantitative variables. Such a problem is quite common when the entity is a decision maker and the conditions involve either cooperative or competitive decision makers. When such an entity's performance cannot be modeled, the entity itself may be placed in a modeled situation to determine the effects of its behavior, as well as of the behavior of other variables, on outcomes. When this entity is human, such simulation is called *operational gaming*.

OPERATIONAL GAMING

A simulation in which decision making is performed by one or more real decision makers is called *operational gaming*. This term is sometimes restricted to simulations in which two or more competing decision makers take part. However, the term will not be so restricted here.

Gaming has come into increasing use in the last decade, particularly in the study of complex military and industrial operations. It is now used in the study of governmental problems at the municipal, national, and international levels.[4] Gaming, particularly in the military context, has a long history, which is described in detail by Young (1957) and Thomas (1961), but its use as a research tool is recent. As Hoggatt (1959) has observed, its principal application has been as "a teaching device and in making the play of the game interesting for the participants" (p. 192). It is also being increasingly used to select and train personnel, to familiarize personnel with the operations of a complex system, and to demonstrate a new idea about a complex system. For a discussion of gaming as other than a research tool, see Thomas and Deemer (1957) and Cohen and Rhenman (1960). Bibliographies on gaming may be found in Malcolm (1960) and Shubik (1960).

The uses of gaming in problem-solving research fall into three general classes: (1) to help develop a decision model, (2) to help find the solution to such a model, and (3) to help evaluate proposed solutions to problems

[4] Gaming has been used in solving municipal problems by Professor Nathan Grundstein at the University of Pittsburgh and Professor Richard Meier at the University of Michigan. An example of its application in the study of international problems can be found in Guetzkow (1959).

modeled by the game. Gaming can aid in constructing a model by providing a basis for testing the relevance of variables or the functional form of the model (i.e., the relationship between the variables). It can also be used both to help uncover possible courses of action and decision strategies and to compare the alternatives. In cases in which a completely specified course of action or decision procedure cannot be derived analytically from a model, but a partially specified action or procedure can, the effect of the action or procedure may be determined by gaming.

Gaming is essentially experimentation in which the behavior of decision makers is observed under controlled conditions. It differs from most psychological and social experimentation only in that the conditions under which the "play" is observed represent some situation outside the laboratory about which knowledge is sought. The experimental situation, then, is deliberately constructed as an iconic or analogue model of the type of real situation in which the researcher is interested.

Often games have been developed without a clear idea about how they can or should be used. Rationalizations for the effort are occasionally offered, but in general these games have been developed either for the scientific exercise involved or for the purpose of exploring the uses to which they can be put. Claims have been made that games are useful in training and selecting personnel in demonstrating the operation of complex systems. As yet, however, there has been little or no controlled evaluation of their use for any of these purposes.[5]

Thomas and Deemer (1957) have discussed extensively the methodological problems associated with the use of gaming as an applied-research technique. The quotation is from their article (pp. 19–21):

Beyond [the] difficulty of knowing when one has solved the "right" problem, there is the difficulty . . . of knowing when one has solved any problem . . . . In gaming, generally, there is no way of knowing with certainty when a sample of plays is both strategically and statistically adequate for a required decision . . . .

Despite the absence of logical proof, operational gaming inspires its practitioners with a remarkable confidence in its results. Sometimes an implausible result is accepted with special relish because of its implausibility. The plausible results are often accepted as being now beyond dispute . . . .

In the formulation of a game one is beset by conflicting objectives that induce an ambivalent attitude toward elaboration. On the one hand, it is desirable to formulate a game the solution of which is highly relevant to the competitive situation being investigated. This consideration encourages one to add more and more details in an effort to acquire realism. On the other hand it is desirable to formulate a game the solution of which is possible, at least to the required accuracy. This constraint tends to inhibit the addition of details . . . .

[5] For a detailed discussion of this point, see Thomas and Deemer (1957) and Cohen and Rhenman (1960).

The common tendency toward excessive elaboration in operational gaming may be regarded as another instance of that misplaced emphasis on the "appearance of reality" . . . It is an easy mistake to make. The search for the "essence of reality" is arduous and difficult, the goal difficult to recognize. One often feels that by incorporating a few more details in a model of reality he is that much more certain of capturing the essence. When, as in operational gaming, the increased difficulty of solution easily escapes notice, the temptation to enlarge the model becomes all the greater.

But this temptation to elaborate should be the more strongly resisted in gaming. For to yield is to court delusion. Not only is there the doubly diminished effectiveness of solution mentioned before as a consequence of excessive elaboration, but there is also another difficulty that arises in interpreting the results of gaming. One tends to forget that the game is not reality itself. The "appearance of reality," so useful in teaching, becomes dangerous in application.

Gaming: Analogy or Analogue?

The fundamental weakness of current gaming is the inability to draw strong inferences from the play of the game to decisions in the situation that the game models. Thomas and Deemer argue that the inferences that are drawn are weakened by the complexity of the game. A model, whether an equation or a game, is always a simplification of reality, and only for this reason is it useful in science. It is important, however, to understand the nature and significance of the simplification because only then can we justify inferences from the model to reality.

In current applications of operational games there is a tendency to confuse the use of analogies and analogues. These are not the same thing. We can usually draw only very weak inferences (if any) by analogy, but such inferences are sometimes given a degree of credibility that they would deserve only if they had been derived from manipulation of an adequate analogue or other type of model.

It is important to understand the difference between an analogue and an analogy, as these terms are used here. In both an analogy and an analogue we use one situation as a model of another. The difference lies in what we know of the correspondence of the models to the "real" situation. In an analogy we know only that two situations have certain properties in common; we know nothing about the correspondence of the *structure* of the two situations. That is, in an analogy we do not know the function f, which relates the outcome to the variables; hence we do not know how well or how badly it corresponds to the structure of the real situation. In an analogue we self-consciously design into the model a structure that, based on analysis or experimentation, we believe to correspond in some acceptable degree to the real one.

The structure of a game corresponds to the structure of the modeled situation to the extent that the same types of decisions yield the same performance in both situations. Such correspondence of output for related input must be established before inferences can be drawn from the game to the real situation.

We simply cannot argue from a correspondence of properties to a correspondence of structure. We can construct a game and manipulate its structure until the relation between its inputs and outputs corresponds to that of the real situation. In this way the game can be used to explore structural relationships that yield a particular kind of input-output relation. But because a particular input-output relationship over a certain set of values of inputs may be produced by a large number of different structures, it is dangerous to use the game to infer input-output relationships involving inputs of values different from those that have been tested. Therefore, it is also important to establish the range of inputs over which the structure is asserted to yield outputs corresponding to the real situation. The last observation is similar to the statement that a linear approximation to an S-shaped curve over a certain region of values of the independent variable may be good, but that it generally fits badly outside that range.

The more aspects of reality are represented in a game, the more difficult it becomes to analyze its structure (i.e., to represent it by a mathematical model). On the other hand, unless enough of the relevant aspects of reality are included, it cannot be an adequate model of reality. Gradation between excessive simplicity and complexity can be attained only by experimenting with the game itself. Considerably more time is generally required to develop a game that will be useful in problem solving, than to use the game once it is developed.

If a game fails to correspond adequately to reality or if the degree of the correspondence is difficult to establish, the researcher is likely to become interested in the game for its own sake, and not as an analogue. At this point gaming either becomes "ordinary" experimentation or is used for other purposes than research, such as the training of personnel.

Games Used Inferentially

Some games have been constructed that can be used to infer approximate solutions to real problems. They are generally simple and involve a mathematical model of a major portion of the "real" situation. Such games are less dramatic and more modest than those that receive most attention in the literature, but they do show the way to the productive use of gaming for other than scientific exploration. The following is a simple example of such a game developed to help solve a noncompetitive problem.

In an industrial problem reported by Hare and Hugli (1955) it was necessary to find the order in which items requiring production should be processed over an assembly line. The setup costs[6] associated with each product depended

---

[6] Costs incurred in adjusting the machinery for a production run.

on which item preceded it over the assembly line. The problem, which was to minimize the sum of the setup costs subject to certain inventory requirements, could be represented by a matrix in which the cost of making each product after each other product was shown. The matrix was not symmetrical, because the cost of setting up product A after product B was not necessarily the same as that of setting up product B after product A. It was recognized that this was an "asymmetrical traveling-salesman problem."[7] A general solution to this type of problem was not available at that time. Study of the problem revealed several decision rules that appeared to yield lower costs than one would expect by using intuition and experience to sequence the production runs. The rules, however, did not completely specify the decision to be made in any situation. Some judgment by the decision maker was still required.

The researchers replanned the production of the last three years, using the proposed decision rules and their judgment where required, and compared the resulting costs with those actually incurred. A substantial reduction was obtained. The question remained, however, whether such improvements could be obtained by the people who actually planned production in the plant. A game was set up involving the rescheduling of production over a three-year period. The people who actually had scheduled production over that period were taught the new decision rules and asked to reschedule production over the period. They did so, and the results showed the same improvement that had been obtained by the researchers. On the strength of these results the rules were adopted and subsequently showed a continuing improvement over previous methods.

Few would argue with the inference that the improvement in performance obtained by use of the decision rules in this game was a legitimate basis for forecasting an improvement if the rules were applied in reality. The confidence one has in such an inference derives from the adequacy of the model of the problem situation: the correspondence of the game's structure to the situation which it modeled.

EXPERIMENTAL OPTIMIZATION

There are some situations in which we may not be able to construct a model of the problem because of its complexity or our relative state of ignorance of the situation. There are other situations in which, although we can construct a model, we cannot solve it even by use of simulation. In these cases it may be possible to find the optimal solution by use of the recently developed technique of *experimental optimization*. One can, in some cases, conduct experiments on the system under study in such a way as to locate an optimal solution to the problem at hand.

[7] This type of problem will be discussed in Chapter 12.

There are two types of designs for seeking optimal solutions experiment-ally—*simultaneous* and *sequential*. In simultaneous designs all the combina-tions of controlled values at which observations are to be made are selected in advance, whereas in sequential designs only a few are selected in advance, other choices being made as data become available. In general, sequential designs are more efficient from a statistical point of view, but they require greater flexibility in manipulating the system and more time to conduct than do simultaneous designs.

In simultaneous experimental designs the observations may be made either simultaneously or sequentially. In sequential designs most, if not all, of the observations are made in sequence. If observations are made sequentially, the same "subject" may be used over and over again or different "equivalent subjects" may be employed. For example, in experiments to determine the combination of speed and altitude of a bomber that yields minimum dis-persion of bombs dropped on a point target, different bombs and even different targets may be used.

If the observations are made simultaneously, different but "equivalent" subjects may have to be used. Either or both of these requirements may be impossible in practical situations. In marketing research, for example, it may not be possible to duplicate a specific market. Furthermore, a market may be changed by the experiment, so that it cannot be used again as the same market.

In both simultaneous and sequential designs the uncontrolled variables must either remain constant, vary in a statistically stable way, or be capable of being "canceled out" (e.g., by use of the analysis of covariance). That is, the variations in observed outcomes must be attributable either to the vari-ables that are controlled in the experiment or to random and measurable effects of the uncontrolled variables. Even if stability is attained during the experiment, it may not continue thereafter, thus invalidating the solution yielded by the experiment.

Because experimental optimization requires a degree of control and stability of the system that can seldom be obtained in the systems with which OR deals, it has not been used often in OR. But it may become increasingly useful as the techniques for conducting it are improved and the opportunities for control of systems by OR teams increase.

A description of the principal designs for experimental optimization can be found in Cochran and Cox (1957), together with references to more detailed expositions. Here we only identify and briefly describe these designs.

In order to describe the four principal designs that are employed in experimental optimization, we shall consider a situation in which performance of the system is a function of two controlled variables, X_1 and X_2. General-ization of the remarks that follow to larger numbers of controlled variables is straightforward.

The two principal simultaneous designs are the *random* and the *factorial* designs. In the former, ranges on the X_1- and X_2-scales are selected within which the optimal values of X_1 and X_2 are believed to lie. Randomly selected values of X_1 are then paired with randomly selected values of X_2. Observations on the system, or its parts, are made at these paired values. Either that pair which yields the best performance is selected as the solution or the region of the pair is explored in more detail, usually employing a factorial design.

In the factorial design, ranges on the X_1 and X_2 scale are similarly chosen. These are then broken into the smallest intervals between which differences in the controlled variables are thought to produce significant differences in performance. Therefore, the X_1-scale is broken into a set of points (x_{11}, $x_{12}, \ldots, x_{1m}$), and so is the X_2-scale ($x_{21}, x_{22}, \ldots, x_{2n}$). Pairs of values are formed by combining each value of X_1 with each value of X_2, yielding mn points. Observations are made at each of these and the best pair is selected, or its region is further explored in detail (Anderson, 1953).

The two principal sequential designs are the *single-step* and *steepest-ascent* designs. The single-step method (suggested by Friedman and Savage, 1947) begins by estimating which of the controlled variables has the greater effect on performance, say X_1. An estimate of the optimal pair of X_1- and X_2-values is made. A first observation is made at this point. One then moves out along the X_1-scale in the direction in which improvement is believed possible, holding X_2 constant. The interval of the move is the smallest one within which significant change of performance is believed possible. If the observation shows improved performance, movement continues in the same direction along the X_1-scale; otherwise it is started in the opposite direction from the origin. When a reduction of performance is obtained, one returns to that X_1-value at which the best performance has been observed and begins to probe along the X_2-scale in the same way. When further improvement along this scale is no longer possible, one again selects the best X_2-value and resumes changes on the X_1-scale. This process continues until no further improvements are obtained and the best point is selected.

The steepest-ascent procedure (Box and Wilson, 1951) tries to approach the optimum by the shortest possible route, rather than by horizontal and vertical steps. It begins with the selection of what is believed to be the best pair of values. Four points in the form of a rectangle, with the original point in the center, are selected; the intervals between the points are selected as in the previous procedures. Observations are made at these five points and a plane is fitted to the data by the method of least squares. One then proceeds along the line of steepest ascent lying in the plane in the direction of improved performance, using an interval proportional to those selected earlier. One continues so long as improvement is obtained and the fit remains good. If the fit deteriorates, a new rectangle is set down on the last point and a new

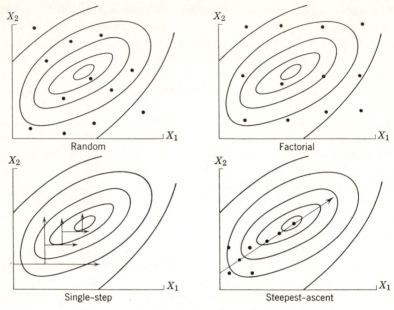

Figure 4.4 Designs for experimental optimization.

linear fit made. If the result is not satisfactory, one goes to higher-ordered curves. When the coefficients of the fit become small this indicates that a plateau has been reached. The peak of the plateau is estimated and used as the solution.

The differences between the four designs are illustrated in Figure 4.4.

A completely general comparison of the four procedures cannot be made. They have been compared in specific cases (see, for example, Brooks, 1955). It is generally felt, however, that the steepest-ascent procedure is the most efficient; the single-step method is placed next, then factorial, and finally random. But it should be noted that the first two give much less assurance than the last two that the optimum has been found when there are more than one minimum or maximum of the function. Therefore, when the presence of more than one minimum or maximum is suspected, one of the last two procedures may be used first to locate the region of the maximum in a gross way; further exploration may then use one of the first two procedures.

SUMMARY

Solving a model consists of finding the values of the controlled variables that optimize the measure of performance, or of estimating them approximately. The tools of classical mathematics may be used in some cases to obtain solutions *deductively*. When deductive solutions are not possible, solutions may frequently be obtained *inductively* by use of *numerical analysis*. Computational rules that incline successive trials toward a solution are called *iterative*. The Las Vegas technique is one that tells us when the expected improvement on the next trial is no greater than the cost of the trial; hence it provides a computational cutoff point when exact solutions are too costly to obtain.

Simulation is a way of manipulating a model so that it imitates reality. It has particular value when the model contains stochastic expressions that are difficult or impossible to evaluate analytically. The basis of simulation is random sampling of a variable's possible values. Therefore, to carry it out random numbers are required, and they must be converted into random variates from the relevant distribution. Routines are available for generating (pseudo) random numbers and for converting them into random variates. A number of techniques can be used for reducing the variance of estimates obtained from simulation: importance sampling, Russian Roulette and splitting, the use of expected values, systematic sampling, stratified sampling, and correlation and regression.

Simulation is useful for studying transitional processes, for estimating values of model parameters, and for treating courses of action that cannot be formulated into the model. To accomplish the last purpose, *operational gaming* is used.

Operational gaming is a form of simulation in which real decision makers are observed in simulated environments. Its usefulness for optimization is restricted, but it can be an effective heuristic device in developing models for situations involving interacting decision makers.

In situations in which models cannot be constructed but experiments can be conducted, *experimental optimization* may be possible if the system is statistically stable. Four optimum-searching techniques were discussed: random, factorial, single-step, and steepest-ascent. None give assurance of finding the optimum of a function that has more than one maximum or minimum. Additional information is required to be certain that *the* optimum has been located; for example, to be sure that the function has only one maximum or minimum or to know what the region of the optimum is.

DISCUSSION TOPICS AND PROBLEMS

1. By simulation determine the probability of beating the following hand in five-card stud poker: three aces (spade, heart, and club), a king of spades, and a queen of hearts.
2. Build a simulation model of a supermarket check-out counter. Collect the necessary data. Determine the effect on average waiting time of customers for two different numbers of operating counters.

3. Find a discussion of an operational game in the literature. Evaluate the game and the use to which it has been put.
4. Discuss how you would go about evaluating the pedagogic effectiveness of a management game. If you have played one game, use it as a basis of your discussion.
5. How would you design an experiment to determine the relative effectiveness of various experimental optimization procedures?
6. Discuss why experimental optimization can or cannot be used to determine the combination of price and amount of advertising that would maximize gross profit from the sale of such items as canned soup and laundry detergent.

Suggested Readings

A recent general treatment of the design and use of simulation can be found in Tocher (1963). A good survey of the state of the art is provided by Morgenthaler (1961). Discussion of many detailed problems associated with simulation can be found in Meyer (1956).

For a general discussion of gaming see Cohen and Rhenman (1960), Thomas (1961), and Thomas and Deemer (1957). All of these are critical of gaming and are likely to prevent abuses of the technique.

Bibliographies on simulation and gaming are provided by Malcolm (1960) and Shubik (1960).

Experimental optimization is covered in breadth but not in depth by Cochran and Cox (1957). Detailed discussions are available in the works of Box and Anderson (1953), and Friedman and Savage (1947).

Bibliography

Anderson, R. L., "Recent Advances in Finding Best Operating Conditions," *Journal of the American Statistical Association*, **48** (1953), 789–798.

Box, G. E. P., "Multifactor Designs of First Order," *Biometrika*, **39** (1952), 49–57.

——, "The Exploration and Exploitation of Response Surfaces; Some General Considerations and Examples," *Biometrics*, **10** (1954), 16–61.

——, and J. S. Hunter, "Multifactor Designs," Report prepared under Office of Ordnance Contract No. DA-36-034-ORD-1177 (RD) (1954).

——, and J. S. Hunter, "Experimental Designs for Exploring Response Surfaces," in *Experimental Designs in Industry*, Victor Chew (ed.), John Wiley and Sons, New York, 1958, pp. 138–190.

——, and K. B. Wilson, "On the Experimental Attainment of Optimum Conditions," *Journal of the Royal Statistical Society*, Series B, **13** (1951), 1–45.

——, and P. U. Youle, "The Exploration and Exploitation of Response Surfaces and Examples of the Link between the Fitted Surface and the Basic Mechanism of the System," *Biometrics*, **11** (1955), 287–323.

Brooks, S., *Comparison of Methods for Estimating the Optimal Factor Combination,* Sc. D. thesis, Johns Hopkins University, 1955.

Cochran, W. G., and G. M. Cox, *Experimental Designs,* 2nd ed., John Wiley and Sons, New York, 1957.

Cohen, K. S., and Eric Rhenman, "The Role of Management Games in Education and Research," *Working Paper* No. 22, Graduate School of Industrial Administration, Carnegie Institute of Technology, Pittsburgh, Pa., September 1960.

Davies, O. L. (ed.), *Design and Analysis of Industrial Experiments,* Hafner Publishing Co., New York, 1956.

Friedman, M., and L. J. Savage, "Planning Experiments Seeking Maxima," in *Techniques of Statistical Analysis,* Statistical Research Group, Columbia University, McGraw-Hill Book Co., New York, 1947.

Guetzkow, Harold, "A Use of Simulation in the Study of Inter-Nation Relations," *Behavioral Science,* **4** (1959), 183–191.

Hare, V. C., Jr., and W. C. Hugli, "Applications of Operations Research to Production Scheduling and Inventory Control, II," in *What is Operations Research Accomplishing in Industry?,* Case Institute of Technology, Cleveland, Ohio, 1955.

Hoggatt, A. C., "An Experimental Business Game," *Behavioral Science,* **4** (1959), 192–203.

Hotelling, H., "Experimental Determination of the Maximum of a Function," *Annals of Mathematical Satistics,* **12** (1941), 20–45.

Kahn, H., "Use of Different Monte Carlo Sampling Techniques," in Meyer (1956), pp. 146–190.

Lehmer, D. H., "Mathematical Methods on Large Scale Computing Units," *Annals of the Harvard University Computing Laboratory,* **26** (1951), 141–146.

Malcolm, D. G., "Bibliography on the Use of Simulation in Management Analysis," *Operations Research,* **8** (1960), 169–177.

Meyer, H. A. (ed.), *Symposium on Monte Carlo Methods,* John Wiley and Sons, New York, 1956.

Morgenthaler, G. W., "The Theory and Application of Simulation in Operations Research," in *Progress in Operations Research,* Vol. I, R. L. Ackoff (ed.), John Wiley and Sons, New York, 1961, pp. 363–419.

The RAND Corporation, *A Million Random Digits,* The Free Press, Glencoe, Ill., 1955.

Plackett, R. L., and J. P. Burman, "The Design of Optimum Multi-Factor Experiments," *Biometrika,* **33** (1946), 305–325.

Shubik, Martin, "Bibliography on Simulation, Gaming, Artificial Intelligence and Allied Topics," *Journal of the American Statistical Association,* **55** (1960), 736–751.

"Symposium on Monte Carlo Methods," *Journal of the Royal Statistical Society,* Series B, **16** (1954), 23–75.

Taussky, Olga, and John Todd, "Generation of Pseudo Random Numbers," in Meyer (1956), pp. 15–28.

Thomas, C. J., "Military Gaming," in *Progress in Operations Research*, Vol. I, R. L. Ackoff (ed.), John Wiley and Sons, New York, 1961, pp. 421–463.

——, and W. L. Deemer, Jr., "The Role of Operational Gaming in Operations Research," *Operations Research*, **5** (1957), 1–27.

Tocher, K. D., *The Art of Simulation*, D. Van Nostrand, Princeton, N.J., 1963.

Young, J. P., "History and Bibliography of War Gaming," *Staff Paper* ORO-SP-13, Operations Research Office, The Johns Hopkins University, Chevy Chase, Md., April 1957.

CHAPTER 5

Allocation Problems: The Assignment And Distribution of Resources

INTRODUCTION

Allocation problems involve the allocation of resources to jobs that need to be done. They occur when the available resources are not sufficient to allow each job to be carried out in the most efficient manner. Therefore, the objective is to allot the resources to the jobs in such a way as to either minimize the total cost or maximize the total return.

Most allocation problems can be represented by a matrix such as is shown in Table 5.1. The entries in the cells, c_{ij}, represent the cost or return that

TABLE 5.1 *Typical Allocation Problem*

Resources	Jobs to Be Done						Amount of Resources Available
	J_1	J_2	$\cdots$	J_j	$\cdots$	J_n	
R_1	c_{11}	c_{12}	$\cdots$	c_{ij}	$\cdots$	c_{1n}	b_1
R_2	c_{21}	c_{22}	$\cdots$	c_{2j}	$\cdots$	c_{2n}	b_2
.	.	.		.		.	.
.	.	.	$\cdots$	.	$\cdots$	.	.
.	.	.		.		.	.
R_i	c_{i1}	c_{i2}	$\cdots$	c_{ij}	$\cdots$	c_{in}	b_i
.	.	.		.		.	.
.	.	.	$\cdots$	.	$\cdots$	.	.
.	.	.		.		.	.
R_m	c_{m1}	c_{m2}	$\cdots$	c_{mj}	$\cdots$	c_{mn}	b_m
Amount of resources required	a_1	a_2	$\cdots$	a_j	$\cdots$	a_n	

results from allocating one unit of resource R_i to job J_j. The c_{ij}'s may be either *independent* or *interdependent*. For example, the cost of assigning one truck to a particular delivery route does not depend on the way in which other trucks are assigned to other routes. On the other hand, in company budgeting, the return from spending a certain amount of money by one function of a business (e.g., production) usually depends on what is spent by other functions (e.g., marketing). Almost all of allocation theory has been concerned with problems involving independent cost or payoffs. Independent allocation problems are not more important, but they are considerably easier to model and solve.

If the cost (or return) from allocating an amount x_{ij} of resource i to job j is equal to $x_{ij}c_{ij}$, we have a linear allocation problem. Allocation problems with independent linear cost (or return) functions have been studied the most intensively because of the availability of powerful iterative procedures for solving them: the techniques of *linear programming*. However, techniques for solving some nonlinear allocation problems also are available, including those that involve linear approximations.

The allocation of resources made in one period of time may or may not affect allocations that must be made in subsequent periods. If each of a sequence of allocations is independent of the others, the problem is said to be *static;* otherwise it is called *dynamic*. More attention has been given to static problems than to dynamic ones, but such techniques as dynamic linear programming and dynamic programming can be applied to some types of dynamic allocation problems. *Stochastic programming* is applicable to some dynamic problems in which current decisions are based on estimates of probable future values of parameters (e.g., unit costs, selling price, demands, etc.) that have unchanging probability distributions.

The principal techniques available for solving allocation problems—in particular, linear programming—involve the assumption that the amounts of resources available (b_i), the amounts required (a_j), and the costs (c_{ij}) are known without error. This is not always the case. Hence it is sometimes desirable to determine how sensitive a solution to an allocation problem is to possible errors in these coefficients. Such *sensitivity analyses* are provided by *parametric linear programming*, but at present this technique can be applied in only a very limited number of cases.

If the sum of the available resources, $\sum_{i=1}^{m} b_i$ is equal to the sum of the resources required, $\sum_{j=1}^{n} a_j$, we have a *balanced* allocation problem. However, if

$$\sum_{j=1}^{n} a_j \neq \sum_{i=1}^{m} b_i,$$

we have an *unbalanced* problem that requires not only allocation of resources to jobs, but also the determination of either what jobs should not be done (if $\sum_{i=1}^{m} b_i < \sum_{j=1}^{n} a_j$), or what resources should not be used (if $\sum_{i=1}^{m} b_i > \sum_{j=1}^{n} a_j$). For example, when demand for a product decreases, it may be necessary to determine which machines, production lines, or even plants should be shut down. With an excess of demand, it may be necessary to determine which orders not to fill, or what kind of a new plant to acquire and what its characteristics should be (e.g., size and location). We shall consider both balanced and unbalanced allocation problems.

The last distinction to be made between allocation problems involves their mathematical structure. If the amounts of resources available and required per job are all equal to one, that is, if $a_j = b_i = 1$ for all i and j (and in addition all allocations $x_{ij} = 1$ or 0), we have an *assignment problem*. In such a problem each job requires one and only one resource, and each resource can be used on one and only one job. Resources are not divisible among jobs, nor are jobs divisible into resources.

If resources can be divided among jobs, some jobs may be done with a combination of resources; if both jobs and resources are expressed in units on the same scale, we have what is generally called the *transportation problem*, but what might better be called the *distribution problem*. If the jobs and resources are not expressed in the same units, we have the *general allocation problem*.

An assignment problem may consist of assigning men to offices or jobs, trucks to delivery routes, drivers to trucks, classes to rooms, or problems to research teams. A typical transportation problem is one that involves the distribution of empty freight cars to locations requiring them, or the assignment of orders to be filled to stocks at warehouses or factories. The general allocation problem may consist of determining which machines should be employed to make products that require use of alternative sets of machines, or what set of feasible products should be manufactured in a plant during a particular period—the product-mix problem.

We shall consider each of these types of problem in turn.

THE TRANSPORTATION PROBLEM

Consider the problem faced by the transportation department of a company that has three plants and four regional warehouses. Each month a list of requirements for each warehouse is available and the production capacities of plants are known. In addition, the cost of shipping a unit from each plant to each warehouse is known. The problem is to determine which plants should supply which warehouses in such a way as to minimize the total transportation costs. It should be noticed that this criterion of optimality is appropriate only when the total capacity of the plants is precisely sufficient to meet the total requirements, that is, when the problem is balanced. If capacity is insufficient, it is necessary to consider, in addition to transportation costs, the costs of shortages at each warehouse. If we have excess capacity, it is necessary to consider production costs at each plant. Otherwise we may be using the full capacity of a high-cost plant when the production savings elsewhere may have more than offset higher transportation charges. Another practical consideration is the possibility of increasing capacity, in plants near markets, by the use of overtime. This may result in higher production costs, which are offset by lower transportation charges. We shall see later that these complications can be handled within the same basic model; therefore, we start with the simplest case.

TABLE 5.2   *A Transportation Problem*

Plants	Warehouses				Amount Available
	1	2	3	4	
1	19	30	50	10	7
2	70	30	40	60	9
3	40	8	70	20	18
Amount required	5	8	7	14	34

Let us assume that costs of transportation between any two cities are proportional to the quantities shipped. This is usually quite close to the truth, provided that shipments are not too small. For example, if we are shipping by rail, the shipments must be integral multiples of carload quantities. The charges per ton for less-than-carload (LCL) quantities will be quite different.

Suppose that plant capacities, warehouse requirements, and unit transportation costs are those shown in Table 5.2.

Finding an Initial Feasible Solution

The first step in solving such a problem is to find an allocation that is feasible; we than make successive improvements until no further cost reduction is possible. Clearly, if we start with a good allocation, there will be fewer improvements to make. Before we discuss a procedure for finding a good initial allocation, we shall describe a simple technique that always yields a feasible allocation (i.e., one that meets requirements using only available resources), although it may be an expensive one.

Let x_{ij} represent the quantity shipped from plant i to warehouse j, and c_{ij} the unit cost of such a shipment. The steps are shown in Table 5.3. We start

TABLE 5.3   *An Initial Feasible Solution to the Problem in Table 5.2*

Plants	Warehouses 1	2	3	4	Amount Available
1	5(19)	2(20)			7
2		6(30)	3(40)		9
3			4(70)	14(20)	18
Amount required	5	8	7	14	34

with cell (1, 1) and find that the largest possible entry (x_{11}) is 5 because that is all that warehouse 1 requires. We make this allocation and proceed to cell (1, 2), because no other allocations are required in column 1. The most that we can allocate in this cell is 2, because this is all that is left of plant 1's capacity after $x_{11} = 5$ has been made. Therefore, we make $x_{12} = 2$. Now we go to cell (2, 2) because warehouse 2 still requires 6 units. We can allocate this number in (2, 2); therefore, we make $x_{22} = 6$. Now warehouse 2 is taken care of, and we proceed to cell (2, 3). The most that we can allocate here is the 3 units that are left from plant 2; hence we make $x_{23} = 3$. Because warehouse 3 still requires 4 units, we go to cell (3, 3) and find that we can allocate the required 4 units; we make $x_{33} = 4$. We proceed to cell (3, 4) and make $x_{34} = 14$. The cost of the solution shown in Table 5.3 is

$$5(19) + 2(30) + 6(30) + 3(40) + 4(70) + 14(20) = 1015.$$

Obviously, we can obtain a better initial feasible solution by using common sense as follows (see Table 5.4). The lowest-cost entry (8) in Table 5.2 is in

TABLE 5.4   *An Improved Initial Feasible Solution*

Plants	Warehouses 1	2	3	4	Amount Available
1				7(10)	7
2	2(70)		7(40)		9
3	3(40)	8(8)		7(20)	18
Amount required	5	8	7	14	34

TABLE 5.5 *Penalties Associated with Second-Best Allocations*

| | Warehouses | | | | | |
Plants	1	2	3	4	Available	Penalties
1	19	30	50	10	7	9
2	70	30	40	60	19	10
3	40	8	70	20	18	12
Required	5	8	7	14		
Penalties	21	22	10	10		

cell (3, 2); therefore, we start here and allocate as much as we can, making $x_{32} = 8$. The next lowest cost (10) is in (1, 4) where we again allocate as much as we can, making $x_{14} = 7$. The next lowest entry (19) is in cell (1, 1). Here we can make no allocation because the capacity of plant 1 was used up in (1, 4). We proceed to cell (3, 4) where the most that we can allocate yields $x_{34} = 7$. Now there are two cells with entries of 30 (1, 2) and (2, 2), but warehouse 2 has been allocated all that it requires; therefore, we proceed to cell (2, 3) and make $x_{23} = 7$. Continuing this process, we obtain the results shown in Table 5.4. The total cost of the solution shown in Table 5.4 is

$$2(70) + 3(40) + 8(8) + 7(40) + 7(10) + 7(20) = 814.$$

This is a reduction in cost of 201 units as compared to the solution shown in Table 5.3. However, we can go one step further. In the last procedure we tried to use the smallest costs but could not always do so. Recall that we could not make an allocation to cell (1, 1), which has the second lowest cost

TABLE 5.6 *First Reduced Penalty Matrix*

| | Warehouses | | | | |
Plants	1	3	4	Available	Penalties
1	19	50	10	7	9
2	70	40	60	9	20
3	40	70	20	10	20
Required	5	7	14		
Penalties	21	10	10		

TABLE 5.7   *Second Reduced Penalty Matrix*

	Warehouses			
Plants	3	4	Available	Penalties
1	50	10	2	40
2	40	60	9	20
3	70	20	10	50
Required	7	14		
Penalties	10	10		

in the matrix. It is obvious that we must make an allocation in at least one cell of each row and in at least one cell of each column. Therefore, in the following procedure we examine the penalties associated with not using the lowest cost in each row and column. The penalties are the differences between the lowest cost in a row or column and the second lowest cost. These are shown in Table 5.5.

We start with the cell that has the largest penalty, cell $(3, 2)$ with a penalty of 22, and allocate as much as we can, making $x_{32} = 8$. Now we can eliminate column 2, which necessitates our recomputing the new penalties and correcting the amount available from plant 3. The results are shown in Table 5.6.

The largest penalty (21) is now associated with cell $(1, 1)$; therefore, we allocate here as much as we can, making $x_{11} = 5$. This eliminates column 1, requiring recalculation of row penalties and the amount available from plant 1 as is shown in Table 5.7.

The largest penalty (50) is now associated with $(3, 4)$; therefore, we make $x_{34} = 10$ and reduce and adjust the matrix as is shown in Table 5.8.

The largest penalty (50) is now associated with $(1, 4)$; therefore, we make $x_{14} = 2$. This leaves only plant 2 with 9 units available and warehouses 3

TABLE 5.8   *Third Reduced Penalty Matrix*

	Warehouses			
Plants	3	4	Available	Penalties
1	50	10	2	40
2	40	60	9	20
Required	7	4		
Penalties	10	50		

TABLE 5.9 *A Further Improved Initial Feasible Solution*

| Plants | Warehouses | | | | Available |
	1	2	3	4	
1	5(19)			2(10)	7
2			7(40)	2(60)	9
3		8(8)		10(20)	18
Required	5	8	7	14	

and 4 requiring 7 and 2 units, respectively. Therefore, we make $x_{23} = 7$ and $x_{24} = 2$. The resulting initial feasible allocation is shown in Table 5.9 and involves a cost of

$$5(19) + 8(8) + 7(40) + 2(10) + 2(60) + 10(20) = 779,$$

which is 35 cost units less than the previous initial feasible solution.

Finding an Optimal Solution

Even the solution shown in Table 5.9 is not the best that is possible, although the procedure by which it was obtained often yields an optimal solution. To determine whether a feasible solution minimizes costs, we must find how costs would be affected if we were to allocate one unit using a source-destination (i.e., plant-warehouse) pair that is not used in the feasible solution. To see how this can be done, let us begin with the feasible solution shown in Table 5.4. That solution and the relevant data appear in Table 5.10.

Suppose that we wish to ship our unit from plant 1 to warehouse 1. We shall have to subtract 1 unit from (1, 4) to keep the row total the same, that is, we make $x_{14} = 6$. The unit removed from (1, 4) will have to be moved to

TABLE 5.10 *An Initial Feasible Solution to the Problem in Table 5.2*

| Plants | Warehouses | | | | Available |
	1	2	3	4	
1	(19)	(30)	(50)	7(10)	7
2	2(70)	(30)	7(40)	(60)	9
3	3(40)	8(8)	(70)	7(20)	18
Required	5	8	7	14	

another cell in the solution: to (3, 4), making $x_{34} = 8$. Now we must remove one unit from row 3 and, if possible, put it into (1, 1). This can be done by moving a unit from (3, 1) to (1, 1), making $x_{31} = 2$. The net change in cost, which we represent by d_{11}, is equal to

$$d_{11} = c_{11} - c_{14} + c_{34} - c_{31} = 19 - 10 + 20 - 40 = -11.$$

We call $d_{11} = -11$ the evaluation of cell (1, 1). This evaluation shows that we can save 11 cost units for each unit that we can allocate to (1, 1). But before

TABLE 5.11   *Improved Solution*

Plant			Warehouses		
	1	2	3	4	Available
1	3(19)	(30)	(50)	4(10)	7
2	2(70)	(30)	7(40)	(60)	
3	(40)	8(8)	(70)	10(20)	
Required	5	8	7	14	

we make such an allocation, we should evaluate each empty cell. The evaluations are as follows:

$$d_{12} = c_{12} - c_{14} + c_{34} - c_{32} = 32$$
$$d_{13} = c_{13} - c_{14} + c_{34} - c_{31} + c_{21} - c_{23} = 50$$
$$d_{22} = c_{22} - c_{21} + c_{31} - c_{32} = -8$$
$$d_{24} = c_{24} - c_{21} + c_{31} - c_{34} = 10$$
$$d_{33} = c_{33} - c_{31} + c_{21} - c_{23} = 60.$$

From these results it is clear that we can improve by reallocating to (1, 1) or (2, 2), but that we can improve most be the use of (1, 1). The largest number of units that we can move into (1, 1) is 3 from (3, 1). To do so, we must move 3 units from (1, 4) to (3, 4). The results of so doing is shown in Table 5.11. The net saving obtained is 3(11) = 33.

Now we must reevaluate each of the empty cells. The results are as follows:

$$d_{12} = c_{12} - c_{14} + c_{34} - c_{32} = 32$$
$$d_{13} = c_{13} - c_{11} + c_{21} - c_{23} = 61$$
$$d_{22} = c_{22} - c_{21} + c_{11} - c_{14} + c_{34} - c_{32} = -19$$
$$d_{24} = c_{24} - c_{21} + c_{11} - c_{14} = -1$$
$$d_{31} = c_{31} - c_{34} + c_{14} - c_{11} = 11$$
$$d_{33} = c_{33} - c_{34} + c_{14} - c_{11} + c_{21} - c_{23} = 71.$$

Because savings are still possible, in (2, 2) and (2, 4) we take the larger one and reallocate. The most that we can move into (2, 2) is determined by the most that we can move out of row 2 into a solution cell, which is 2 out of (2, 1). The result of doing so is shown in Table 5.12. The net saving is 2(19) = 38.

TABLE 5.12   *Optimal Solution to Problem in Table* 5.2

Plant	Warehouses				Available
	1	2	3	4	
1	5(19)	(30)	(50)	2(10)	
2	(70)	2(30)	7(40)	(60)	9
3	(40)	6(8)	(70)	12(20)	18
Required	5	8	7	14	

Once again we must reevaluate the empty cells. The results are as follows:

$$d_{12} = c_{12} - c_{14} + c_{34} - c_{32} = 21$$
$$d_{13} = c_{13} - c_{14} + c_{34} - c_{32} + c_{22} - c_{23} = 50$$
$$d_{21} = c_{21} - c_{22} + c_{32} - c_{34} + c_{14} - c_{11} = 11$$
$$d_{24} = c_{24} - c_{22} + c_{32} - c_{34} = 18$$
$$d_{31} = c_{31} - c_{34} + c_{14} - c_{11} = 11$$
$$d_{33} = c_{33} - c_{32} + c_{22} - c_{23} = 52.$$

Since no further improvements are possible (because of the absence of any further possible net reductions in cost), the solution shown in Table 5.12 is optimal. Its cost is

$$5(19) + 2(30) + 6(8) + 7(40) + 2(10) + 12(20) = 743,$$

an improvement of 36 units over the best initial solution that we obtained previously (Table 5.9).

If at the optimal stage some of the evaluations of empty cells are equal to zero, alternative optimal solutions exist. Reallocations into such cells will yield them.

An Alternative Procedure for Evaluating Cells.   Computation of all values by the procedure described can be difficult as well as tedious in large problems, because the costs to be added and subtracted are not always apparent. There is an alternative procedure that is often easier and faster. Before trying to show more rigorously the mathematical basis for the procedure, we use an intuitive argument and an example.

TABLE 5.13

	1	2	Available
1	1(10)	1(20)	2
2	(50)	1(40)	1
Required	1	2	

Consider the "toy" transportation and its solution shown in Table 5.13. The evaluation of cell (2, 1) is

$$d_{21} = c_{21} - c_{22} + c_{12} - c_{11} = 50 - 40 + 20 - 10 = 20.$$

If we could reduce the coefficients c_{22}, c_{12}, and c_{11} that appear in the solution so that they would be equal to zero, even if we have to adjust c_{21} in the process, the evaluation would be considerably simplified. Suppose that we proceeded as follows. In order to reduce $c_{11} = 10$ to 0, let us subtract 10 from the coefficients in column 1:

	1	2
1	0	20
2	40	40

Subtracted   10

To reduce the 20 in (1, 2) to 0, let us subtract 20 from column 2:

	1	2
1	0	0
2	40	20

Subtracted   10   20

Finally, to reduce the 20 in (2, 2), let us subtract 20 from row 2:

		Subtracted
0	0	0
20	0	20

Subtracted   10   20

TABLE 5.14 *Reducing Solution Cell Coefficients to Zero*

Plant	Warehouses				Subtracted
	1	2	3	4	
1	(19)	(30)	(50)	7(10)	−10(7)
2	2(70)	(30)	7(40)	(60)	30(4)
3	3(40)	8(8)	(70)	7(20)	0(2)
Subtracted	40(3)	8(1)	10(5)	20(6)	

Note that the new value in (2, 1) is equal to d_{21}. Furthermore, to obtain the original coefficient in any cell, we only need to add the amount subtracted from its column and row to the entry in any cell.

Let us now use this procedure on a larger scale by considering again the initial feasible solution shown in Table 5.4, to the problem shown in Table 5.2. The amounts that can reduce, by subtraction from each row and column, the coefficients in the solution cells to zero, are shown in Table 5.14. The parenthesis beside the amounts subtracted indicate the order in which they were obtained. There are more than one set of subtracted quantities that will reduce the coefficients in the solution cells to zero. Another set is shown in Table 5.15.

The evaluations of the empty cells resulting from the use of Table 15.5 are shown in Table 5.16. These evaluations are the same as those obtained by the other procedure from Table 5.11. A reallocation is now made to cell (1, 1), and the amounts to be subtracted to reduce the solution-cell coefficients are recalculated. The process is continued until there are no further negative entries in any cells.

TABLE 5.15 *Alternative Way of Reducing Solution-Cell Coefficients to Zero*

Plants	Warehouses				Subtracted
	1	2	3	4	
1	(19)	(30)	(50)	7(10)	0(2)
2	2(70)	(30)	7(40)	(60)	40(6)
3	3(40)	8(8)	(70)	7(20)	10(3)
Subtracted	30(5)	−2(4)	0(7)	10(1)	

Now we turn to the mathematical ideas behind this procedure. We do so by considering the following algebraic problem. Let a, b, c, d, p, and q be given constants and suppose that

$$Z = aw + bx + cy + dz \tag{5.1}$$

where

$$w + x - p = 0, \tag{5.2}$$

$$y + z - q = 0, \tag{5.3}$$

and

$$w \geq 0, \qquad x \geq 0, \qquad y \geq 0, \qquad z \geq 0. \tag{5.4}$$

Suppose that we have chosen $x = y = 0$ and that we wish to find how an increase in x (or y) will affect Z. We cannot determine the nature of this

TABLE 5.16   *Evaluation of Cells Yielded by Table 5.15*

| | Warehouses | | | | |
Plants	1	2	3	4	Subtracted
1	−11	32	50	0	0
2	0	−8	0	10	40
3	0	0	60	0	10
Subtracted	30	−2	0	10	

effect from (5.1), because a change in x will cause a change in w [see (5.2)] and a change in y will cause a change in z [see (5.3)]. But note that we can multiply (5.2) and (5.3) by a constant without affecting its zero value; hence we can subtract the result from (5.1) without changing the value of Z. Then let us subtract a times (5.2) and d times (5.3) from (5.1). We obtain

$$Z = aw + bx + cy - dz - aw - au + ap - dy - dz + dq$$
$$= (b - a)x + (c - d)y + ap + dq. \tag{5.5}$$

From (5.5) we can determine the effects of a unit change in x or y, because the nonzero variables w and z do not appear in it.

The transportation problem is similar to the one just described. The total cost, Z, that is to be minimized can be written as

$$Z = c_{11}x_{11} + c_{12}x_{12} + \cdots + c_{in}x_{in} + c_{21}x_{21} + \cdots + c_{mn}x_{mn}, \tag{5.6}$$

where none of the x's are negative and where the row and column totals are fixed; that is (see Table 5.1),

$$\sum_i x_{ij} = a_j$$

and

$$\sum_j x_{ij} = b_i, \tag{5.7}$$

where a_j and b_i are constants. These constraints can be used to eliminate all nonzero x's from (5.6). The coefficients in the resulting expression will show how Z will change if we increase any zero variable and compensate for the increase by adjusting the nonzero variables. To see how this works, let us return to the problem shown in Table 5.2 and the initial feasible solution to it shown in Table 5.10. The first column total is

$$x_{11} + x_{21} + x_{31} = 5.$$

Therefore,

$$x_{11} + x_{21} + x_{31} - 5 = 0. \tag{5.8}$$

Because $c_{31} = 40$, we shall eliminate x_{31} from Z if we subtract 40 times (5.8), and the coefficient c_{31} will become

$$d_{31} = 40 - 40 = 0.$$

The coefficients c_{11} and c_{21} become

$$d_{11} = 19 - 40 = -21$$
$$d_{21} = 70 - 40 = 30$$

To eliminate x_{21} from Z we multiply

$$x_{21} + x_{22} + x_{23} + x_{24} - 9 = 0$$

by $c_{21} = 30$ and subtract it from Z. Continuing this process, we can eliminate all nonzero x's from the cost function. The remaining coefficients would then show the change in Z for each of the zero variables and would be the same as the cell evaluations. The computational procedure can be considerably simplified by way of the following reasoning.

We wish to have a set of weights $(u_1, \ldots, u_m)$, one for each row, and another set $(v_1, \ldots, v_n)$, one for each column, such that if

$$x_{ij} > 0, \quad \text{then} \quad c_{ij} - u_i - v_j = 0 \tag{5.9}$$

and if

$$x_{ij} = 0, \quad \text{then} \quad c_{ij}' = c_{ij} - u_i - v_j \tag{5.10}$$

It may be shown, in general, that there are $m + n - 1$ nonzero x's; therefore, (5.9) yields $m + n - 1$ equations in $m + n$ variables: $u_1, \ldots, u_m, v_1, \ldots, v_n$. This means that we can select one u or one v arbitrarily and then find the others. Furthermore, it will be found that if the u's and v's are computed in the correct order, each successive equation involves only one unknown.

Computer programs, or their equivalent, that can carry out the procedure described here, are readily available.

(Exercises $1a$ and $1b$ should be done at this point.)

DEGENERACY

We have seen how the transportation problem can be solved, provided that we are able to obtain a set of numbers $u_1, \ldots, u_m, v_1, \ldots, v_n$ such that for all nonzero x's in a proposed solution

$$c_{ij} = u_i + v_j. \qquad (5.11)$$

Because we are interested only in the sums $u_i + v_j$, we can derive an infinity of sets $\{u_i\}, \{v_j\}$ from any given set. We merely take $\{u_i + \alpha\}, \{v_j - \alpha\}$ to be another set; α may have any value we choose. This permits us to select one value at will (say $u_1 = 0$) and to determine the others from (5.11). This will work provided that there are $m + n - 1$ equations in (5.11), which will generally be the case. However, it can happen that a solution is found which consists of fewer than $m + n - 1$ nonzero x_{ij}'s. Such cases are called *degenerate*, and some modifications of the previously described procedure are required for their solution. For example, consider the problem shown in Table 5.17.

TABLE 5.17 *A Degenerate Transportation Problem*

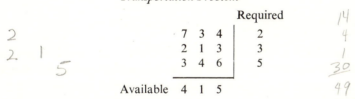

			Required
7	3	4	2
2	1	3	3
3	4	6	5

Available 4 1 5

It is easy to see in Table 5.17 that $x_{11} = 2$, $x_{21} = 2$, $x_{22} = 1$, and $x_{33} = 5$ is a possible solution, but we have only 4 nonzero x_{ij}'s instead of the 5 that we require. This occurs because when we set $x_{22} = 1$, we satisfy the requirements for row 2 ($x_{21} + x_{22} = 3$) and the availability for column 2 ($x_{22} = 1$) simultaneously. In general, each nonzero x_{ij} that is inserted completes *either* a row *or* a column, but not both. If the row had not been completed, we would have had $x_{23} > 0$, and if the column had not been completed, we would have had $x_{32} > 0$. Either addition would provide a set of equations for determining the $\{u_i\}, \{v_j\}$. We may as well use the one with the smaller c_{ij}, that is, treat x_{23} as if it were greater than zero, because $c_{23} < c_{32}$. It is

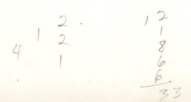

usual to set $x_{23} = \epsilon$ to remind us of what we have done. Here ϵ is to be treated as a very small quantity, subject to the following rules:

1. $\epsilon < x_{ij}$ for all $x_{ij} > 0$.
2. $\epsilon + 0 = \epsilon$.
3. $x_{ij} \pm \epsilon = x_{ij}$, $x_{ij} > 0$.
4. If there are two or more ϵ's in the solution, $\epsilon < \epsilon'$ whenever ϵ is above ϵ'. If ϵ and ϵ' are in the same row, $\epsilon < \epsilon'$ when ϵ is to the left of ϵ'.

The last rule is arbitrary; we merely need a procedure to ensure that we distinguish between various ϵ's. Otherwise one iteration might reverse the modification of the previous stage.

One way to think of what we have done is to imagine that the original problem is slightly distorted, so that it is not degenerate. Consider the problem shown in Table 5.18 and its solution.

TABLE 5.18   *A Distortion of the Problem Shown in Table* 5.17

			Required
7	3	4	2
2	1	3	$3 + \epsilon$
3	4	6	5

Available   4   1 $5 + \epsilon$

We start with the solution $x_{11} = 2$, $x_{21} = 2$, $x_{22} = 1$, $x_{23} = \epsilon$, $x_{33} = 5$; we set $u_1 = 0$, and we find $u_2 = -5$, $u_3 = 8$, $v_1 = 7$, $v_2 = 6$, $v_3 = -2$. The solution and cell evaluations $c_{ij} - u_i - v_j$ are:

Solution			Evaluation		
2	0	0	0	-3	-4
2	1	ϵ	0	0	0
0	0	5	-2	0	0

We decide to increase x_{13} and see that this requires decreases in x_{23} and x_{11} and an increase in x_{21}. By rule 1, $x_{23} = \epsilon < x_{11} = 2$; therefore, we obtain the solution and evaluation:

Solution			Evaluation			u_i
$2 - \epsilon$	0	ϵ	0	-3	0	0
$2 + \epsilon$	1	0	0	0	4	-5
0	0	5	-6	-4	0	2
			v_j 7	6	4	

We decide to increase x_{31}, which requires decreases in x_{33} and x_{11} and an increase in x_{13}. We obtain:

Solution			Evaluation			u_j
0	0	2	6	3	0	0
$2 + \epsilon$	1	0	0	0	-2	1
$2 - \epsilon$	0	$3 + \epsilon$	0	2	0	2

$$v_j \quad 1 \quad 0 \quad 4$$

We decide to increase x_{23}, which requires decreases in x_{33} and x_{21} and an increase in x_{31}. We obtain:

Solution			Evaluation			u_i
0	0	2	6	1	0	0
0	1	$2 + \epsilon$	1	0	0	-1
4	0	1	0	0	0	2

$$v_j \quad 1 \quad 2 \quad 4$$

We conclude that this solution is optimal, because all evaluations are non-negative. Because the evaluation of cell (3, 2) is zero and $x_{32} = 0$, we conclude that alternative solutions are possible with $x_{32} > 0$. The final result is written without reference to epsilon, which was introduced only to facilitate computation.

In practice, we need to write ϵ in the calculation only where it appears alone. It may be omitted whenever it is added to (or subtracted from) a nonzero quantity.

The use of epsilons on a digital computer would require a special program, which is not convenient. It is preferable to distort all problems slightly, so that we know that degeneracy will not arise, and to remove the distortion at the end. In Table 5.18 we had $a_1 = 2$, $a_2 = 3$, $a_3 = 5$, $b_1 = 4$, $b_2 = 1$, and $b_3 = 5$. Degeneracy arose because $a_1 + a_2 = b_1 + b_2$. Let us modify these quantities so that $a_1 = 2.00002$, $a_2 = 3.00004$, $a_3 = 5.00006$, $b_1 = 4$, $b_2 = 1$, and $b_3 = 5.000012$. If we solve the modified problem and round up the nearest integers, we shall have the solution to the original degenerate problem, and degeneracy will not arise during the calculations.

The reason for degeneracy is that some subset of the a's total the same amount as some subset of the b's. Suppose that the a's and b's are integers between zero and 100 and that there are more a's than b's. Then we can be certain of avoiding degeneracy by adding $2 \cdot 10^{-5}$, $4 \cdot 10^{-5}$, $6 \cdot 10^{-5}$, $\ldots$, $2n \cdot 10^{-5}$ to the n successive a's and $10^{-5}[2 + 4 + 6 + \cdots + 2n] = n(n + 1)10^{-5}$ to the last b. Because no subset of the additions to the a's totals the same as a subset of additions to the b's, we cannot now have degeneracy, even if the original problem were degenerate. When we have solved the distorted problem, we simply round up to the nearest integers to obtain the solution of the original problem.

(Exercises 2a and 2b should be done at this point.)

UNBALANCED TRANSPORTATION PROBLEMS

The transportation problem, in the sense in which we have dealt with it so far, has an amount of available resources equal to the amount of required resources. In the introduction to this chapter such an allocation problem was called "balanced." If the available and required resources do not balance, either some available resources will remain unused or some requirements will remain unfilled.

If more capacity than is required is available and if there are no costs associated with the failure to use capacity, we add a "dummy destination" (e.g., a warehouse in the problem that we have been considering) and make its requirements equal to the unused capacity. The costs of shipping to this dummy destination are set equal to zero. The problem can then be solved in the same way as one that is balanced. If there is a cost associated with unused capacity (e.g., maintenance) and this cost is linear, it too can easily be treated.

If there is insufficient capacity to meet requirements, it is necessary to add a dummy source to "fill" excess requirements. The cost of an unfilled requirement is seldom zero. It may involve a lost sale, a costly delay, or the use of a more costly substitute. If the costs of shortages are the same at all destinations, they can be distributed arbitrarily. If this is not so, considerable research effort may be required to estimate the costs of shortage.

In some cases additional capacity can be obtained by the use of overtime at one or more sources. Suppose, for example, that we have three plants and four warehouses, as is shown in Table 5.19. Overtime can be used to raise

TABLE 5.19   *An Unbalanced Transportation Problem*

| Plant | Warehouses | | | | Available |
	1	2	3	4	
1	25	17	25	14	300
2	15	10	18	24	500
3	16	20	8	13	600
Required	300	300	500	500	1400 / 1600

capacity by 50 per cent at each plant, but it adds 10, 15, and 20 to the unit costs of production at each plant, respectively. If we were to use all of the overtime capacity, we would have an excess; hence we should add a dummy warehouse. We can put the overtime into the problem by adding three "overtime plants," as is shown in Table 5.20. The solution to this problem will automatically guarantee us that no plant will do overtime until all of its

TABLE 5.20   *Balancing the Problem in Table 5.19 with Overtime*

| Plant | Warehouses | | | | | |
	1	2	3	4	Dummy	Available
1	25	17	25	14	0	300
2	15	10	18	24	0	500
3	16	20	8	13	0	600
1 Overtime	35	27	35	24	0	150
2 Overtime	30	25	33	39	0	250
3 Overtime	36	40	28	33	0	300
Required	300	300	500	500	500	2100

regular capacity is used. Why? The solving of this problem is left as an exercise.

(Exercise 3 should be done at this point.)

THE ASSIGNMENT PROBLEM

It will be recalled from our discussion of degeneracy that an allocation problem is degenerate if, in making a feasible allocation, an entry in any cell but the last satisfies column requirements and uses all available resources in the row. It will also be recalled from the introductory discussion in this chapter that in an assignment problem each resource can be assigned to only one job and each job requires only one resource. Hence the assignment problem is a completely degenerate form of the transportation problem.

Consider the following problem. Five men are available to do five different jobs. From past records, the time that each man takes to do each job is known. The data are shown in Table 5.21. In this case the c_{ij}'s are the times required for each man to do each job and the x_{ij}'s are 1 or 0: 1 if a man is assigned to a job, 0 otherwise. The problem, therefore, is to minimize

$$Z = \sum_{i=1}^{n} \sum_{j=1}^{n} x_{ij} c_{ij}$$

subject to the following conditions:

$$\sum_{i=1}^{n} x_{ij} = 1 \qquad j = 1, 2, \ldots, n$$

$$\sum_{j=1}^{n} x_{ij} = 1 \qquad i = 1, 2, \ldots, n$$

and

$$x_{ij} = 0 \quad \text{or} \quad 1.$$

The last condition may also be written as

$$x_{ij} = x_{ij}^2.$$

We see that if the last condition is dropped and replaced by $x_{ij} \geq 0$, we have a transportation problem with all requirements and available resources equal

TABLE 5.21   *An Assignment Problem*

			Jobs			
Men	1	2	3	4	5	Available
1	2	9	2	7	1	1
2	6	8	7	6	1	1
3	4	6	5	3	1	1
4	4	2	7	3	1	1
5	5	3	9	5	1	1
Required	1	1	1	1	1	5

to one. The optimal solution will have x_{ij} equal to an integer or zero, and clearly the only possible integer is one.[1] Thus the solution to the transportation problem will automatically yield $x_{ij} = x_{ij}^2$.

However, because of the degeneracy, the transportation technique is not very useful. Whenever we make an assignment, we automatically satisfy a row and column requirement and therefore obtain n nonzero x_{ij} instead of $2n - 1$. We have to fill in $n - 1$ epsilons, and it could happen that the nonzero x_{ij}'s are optimal but the test fails to show optimality because the epsilons are wrongly placed.

The method of solution relies on two fairly obvious theorems. The first asserts that the solution is unchanged if we add or subtract a constant to any

[1] It is not difficult to show that if the a_j's and b_j's in a transportation problem are all integers, the optimal solution is also a set of integers.

row or column of the c_{ij} matrix. It can be stated more precisely as follows:

Theorem 1 If $x_{ij} = X_{ij}$ minimizes $Z = \sum_{i=1}^{n} \sum_{j=1}^{n} x_{ij} c_{ij}$ over all x_{ij} such that $x_{ij} \geq 0$ and $\sum_{i=1}^{n} x_{ij} = \sum_{j=1}^{n} x_{ij} = 1$, then $x_{ij} = X_{ij}$ also minimizes $Z' = \sum_{i=1}^{n} \sum_{j=1}^{n} x_{ij} c_{ij}{}'$ where $c_{ij}{}' = c_{ij} - u_i - v_j$ for all i and $j = 1, \ldots, n$.

Theorem 2 If all $c_{ij} \geq 0$ and we can find a set $x_{ij} = X_{ij}$ such that

$$\sum_{i=1}^{n} \sum_{j=1}^{n} x_{ij} c_{ij} = 0,$$

then this solution is optimal.

The second theorem is obvious. To prove the first, note that

$$Z' = \sum_{i=1}^{n} \sum_{j=1}^{n} (c_{ij} - u_i - v_j) x_{ij}$$
$$= \sum_{i=1}^{n} \sum_{j=1}^{n} c_{ij} c_{ij} - \sum_{i=1}^{n} u_i \sum_{j=1}^{n} x_{ij} - \sum_{j=1}^{n} v_j \sum_{i=1}^{n} x_{ij}$$
$$= Z - \sum_{i=1}^{n} u_i - \sum_{j=1}^{n} v_j.$$

TABLE 5.22 *Reduced Matrices of Table* 5.21

	(a)						(b)					
	1	2	3	4	5	Subtracted	1	2	3	4	5	Subtracted
1	1	8	1	6	1	1	0	7	(0)	4	0	1
2	5	7	6	5	0	1	(4)	6	5	3	0	1
3	3	5	4	2	0	1	2	4	3	(0)	0	1
4	3	1	6	2	0	1	2	(0)	5	0	0	1
5	4	2	8	4	0	1	3	1	7	2	(0)	1
						Subtracted	1	1	1	2	1	

Because the terms that are subtracted from Z to yield Z' are independent of the x_{ij}'s, it follows that Z' is minimized whenever Z is minimized, and conversely.

The method of solution consists of adding and subtracting constants to rows and columns until sufficient c_{ij}'s have become zero to yield a solution with a value of zero.

We start by subtracting the smallest element from each row, and then do the same for each column. For the example in Table 5.21, the results are shown in Table 5.22. A total of 10 was subtracted from the rows and columns. Therefore, any solution that we obtain by using Table 5.22b must have 10 added to it for its proper evaluation.

We first look for a solution involving only those cells in Table 5.22*b* that have zero entries, for such a solution, if we can find it, would be the best one possible. There may be several solutions, however, that are equally good. In this case, no such solution can be found. A feasible solution is indicated in Table 5.22*b* by the cells whose entries are enclosed in parentheses. But to determine whether an improvement is possible, the following procedure can be used.

Note that any further subtraction from a row or column, although possibly adding zeros, will also add negative numbers, and a solution among zeros need no longer be optimum. However, the negatives could be removed by suitable additions to columns or rows. For example, if in Table 5.22*b* we subtract 2 from column 1, we shall have -2 in row 1. If we add 2 to row 1, we shall again have a nonnegative array. The problem is to insert additional zeros in this fashion in such a way that we eventually obtain an array with a solution among the zeros. The following procedure can be proved to solve this problem.

1. Draw the minimum number of horizontal and vertical lines necessary to cover all zeros at least once. (It can be shown that in all $n \times n$ matrices fewer than n lines will cover the zeros only where there is no solution among them. Conversely, if the minimum number of lines is n, there is a solution.) Carrying out this step on Table 5.22*b* gives the result shown in Table 5.23.

TABLE 5.23

	1	2	3	4	5
1	0	7	0	4	0
2	4	6	5	3	0
3	2	4	3	0	0
4	2	0	5	0	0
5	3	1	7	2	0

Note that only four lines are used; hence there is no optimal solution among the zero cells.

2. Select the smallest number that does not have a line through it. In this example, it is 1 in (5, 2).

3. Subtract this number from all elements that have no lines through them and add it to all elements that have *two* lines through them. In this example, this yields the result shown in Table 5.24. This procedure must add a zero where one did not previously exist; in this case in (5, 2).

4. Try for a solution among the new set of zeros. (In this case one cannot be found.) If one cannot be found, repeat step 1 and continue until a solution is found. Continuing the example, we obtain the result shown in Table 5.25.

TABLE 5.24

	1	2	3	4	5
1	0	7	0	4	1
2	5	7	6	4	0
3	2	4	3	0	1
4	2	0	5	0	1
5	2	0	7	3	0

The smallest uncovered number is now 2. Therefore, we next obtain Table 5.26. A solution, as indicated by the parenthesis, can be found here. Its value is 13, which is an improvement of 1 over the initial feasible solution.

The reader should show that step 3 in the procedure is equivalent to subtracting from certain rows and adding to certain columns, so that Theorem 1 applies.

TABLE 5.25

	1	2	3	4	5
1	0	7	0	4	1
2	5	7	6	4	0
3	2	4	3	0	1
4	2	0	5	0	1
5	2	0	7	3	0

Now let us consider a more complex assignment problem that arises in the operation of a commercial airline. Consider an airline that has flights in both directions between two cities, say New York and Chicago. If a crew is based in New York and arrives in Chicago on a given flight, it must return to New York on a later flight (perhaps the following day). The company wishes to

TABLE 5.26

	1	2	3	4	5
1	0	9	(0)	6	3
2	3	7	4	4	(0)
3	0	4	1	(0)	1
4	0	(0)	3	0	1
5	(0)	0	5	3	0

choose the return flight so as to minimize the time spent on the ground away from home. Given the timetable, two types of decisions are required:

1. Which flights are to be paired? If two flights are paired, the same crew flies east on one of them and west on the other.

2. Given the pairs of flights, where should the crews be based?

Both decisions are to be made so as to minimize the time on the ground away from home, subject to a minimum interval of one hour between arrival and departure.

We might have a timetable similar to that shown in Table 5.27, which has been simplified to make the arithmetic less tedious. Note first that all times

TABLE 5.27   *Airline Flight Schedule*

Flight	Departs New York	Arrives Chicago	Flight	Departs Chicago	Arrives New York
1	0730	0900	2	0700	1000
3	0815	0945	4	0745	1045
5	1400	1530	6	1100	1400
7	1745	1915	8	1800	2100
9	1900	2030	10	1930	2230

are local; therefore, Chicago is one hour behind New York. It will also be observed that flights westward are longer than those eastward because of prevailing winds.

We start by drawing up two tables (Table 5.28) that show layover times; we assume that each possible pair of flights is based in New York or Chicago. (Times are shown in multiples of quarter-hour intervals.) Note the pairing of 7 and 10 based in New York; because the layover time is less than one hour, twenty four hours must be added. The next step is to combine both tables, using the base that results in the smaller layover time for each pairing. The composite table is shown in Table 5.29. Entries marked by a single

TABLE 5.28   *Layover Times*

	(a) Based in New York					(b) Based in Chicago				
	2	4	6	8	10	2	4	6	8	10
1	88	91	8	36	42	86	83	70	42	36
3	85	88	5	33	39	89	86	73	45	39
5	62	65	78	10	16	16	13	96	68	62
7	47	50	63	91	97	31	28	15	83	77
9	42	45	58	86	92	36	33	20	88	82

TABLE 5.29 *Minimum Layover Times*

	2	4	6	8	10
1	86	83	8*	36*	36
3	85*	86	5*	33*	39**
5	16	13	78*	10*	16
7	31	28	15	83	77
9	36	33	20	36*	82

asterisk refer to flights based in New York; those not so marked are based in Chicago. A double asterisk indicates equal layover times at each base. The solution of this assignment problem is left as an exercise.

(Exercises 4 and 5 should be done at this point.)

SUMMARY

An allocation problem is one that involves determining how resources should be used so as to perform a set of jobs in the best way. In the kind of allocation problem that we considered in this chapter, and shall consider in the next, the measure of performance over the set of jobs is equal to the sum of the measures that are applied to each combination of resources and jobs.

In this chapter we considered two relatively simple types of allocation problem—assignment and transportation.

The transportation (or distribution) problem involves allocating resources from one or more sources to jobs requiring them (destinations), when the jobs may be performed by combining resources from several sources. Most problems involving the redistribution of empty freight cars, trucks, and planes are of this type, as are problems of supplying demand at many locations from several supply points. Here, as in the assignment problem, we can determine how to add or subtract resources or jobs.

In the assignment problem we seek a unique one-to-one pairing of resources and jobs so as to minimize the sum of the measures of performance of each pairing that is made. Such problems arise, for example, in assigning planes or crews to commercial airline flights, trucks or drivers to delivery routes, men to offices, and space to departments. If there are more jobs to do than can be done, we can decide either which job to leave undone or what resources to add.

Both the assignment and the transportation problems are special cases of the more general allocation problem that is discussed in the next chapter. Suggested Readings that are relevant to this chapter and a bibliography appear at the end of the next chapter.

EXERCISES

1. Solve the following nondegenerate transportation problems:

(a)

				a_i
21	16	25	13	11
17	18	14	23	13
32	27	18	41	19
b_j 6	10	12	15	43

(b)

			a_i
16	19	12	14
22	13	19	16
14	28	8	12
b_j 10	15	17	42

2. Solve the following degenerate transportation problems:

(a)

					a_i
95	33	95	22	18	13
90	84	60	79	24	19
46	40	62	98	54	16
20	31	89	43	38	10
b_j 7	14	21	8	8	58

(b)

				a_i
14	56	48	27	71
82	35	21	81	47
99	31	71	63	93
b_j 71	35	45	60	211

3. A company has four plants, each of which manufactures the same product. Production costs differ from one plant to another, as do the costs of raw mater-

TABLE 5.30

Plant: Production (Other Than Raw Materials): Raw Materials:		1 15 10	2 18 9	3 14 12	4 13 8	Sales Price	Maximum Sales
	Warehouse						
Transportation	1	3	9	5	4	34	80
Costs	2	1	7	4	5	32	110
	3	5	8	3	6	31	150
	4	7	3	8	2	31	100
	5	4	5	6	7	31	150
Capacity		150	200	175	100		

ials. There are five regional warehouses, and customers pay different prices at each. Given the data in Table 5.30, what is the best production and distribution schedule?

This problem has a number of features that make it different from a standard transportation problem.

(a) The objective is to *maximize* profit instead of *minimizing* costs. This can be overcome by treating profits as negative losses and minimizing. For example, the profit per unit on shipping from plant 1 to warehouse 1 is $34 - (15 + 10 + 3) = 6$ and the loss is -6.

(b) There is surplus production capacity; we must, therefore, add a dummy warehouse, shipments from which result in zero profit.

(c) Certain shipments will result in a loss (for example, the *profit* from plant 2 to warehouse 1 is $34 - (18 + 9 + 9) = -2$). The standard transportation solution will force all warehouse requirements to be met, even if some shipments are at a loss. Unless management insists on supplying all customers, it is better to add a dummy plant with an unknown capacity x, and zero profits for all shipments. If x is sufficiently large, then all feasible solutions to the augmented problem are bound to show a non-zero shipment from the dummy plant to the dummy warehouse. It may be shown that any optimal solution to the augmented problem which has a shipment between the dummies, will also be the optimal solution to the profit maximization problem. Provided x is large enough, the actual value of x will not affect shipments between real plants and warehouses. A sufficiently large value of x is the greater of the total capacity of all plants, or the total maximum sales of all warehouses.

4. Solve the following assignment problems:

(a)
8	4	2	6	1
0	9	5	5	4
3	8	9	2	6
4	3	1	0	3
9	5	8	9	5

(b)
5	0	6	8	7	4
5	2	3	0	6	7
3	4	4	3	5	2
3	9	7	2	7	6
9	8	7	8	4	5
1	8	7	4	2	3

5. An airline that operates 7 days a week has the timetable shown in Table 5.31. Crews must have a minimum layover of 5 hours between flights. Obtain the pairing of flights that minimizes layover time away from home. Note that crews flying from A to B can be based either at A or B. For any given pairing they will be based at the city that results in the smaller layover.

TABLE 5.31

Cleveland–New York			New York–Cleveland		
Flight Number	Depart	Arrive	Flight Number	Depart	Arrive
1	7:00 A.M.	8:00 A.M.	101	8:00 A.M.	9:15 A.M.
2	8:00 A.M.	9:00 A.M.	102	8:30 A.M.	9:45 A.M.
3	1:30 P.M.	2:30 P.M.	103	12 noon	1:15 P.M.
4	6:30 P.M.	7:30 P.M.	104	5:30 P.M.	6:45 P.M.
5	8:00 P.M.	9:00 P.M.	105	7:00 P.M.	8:15 P.M.
6	11:30 P.M.	0:30 A.M.	106	10:00 P.M.	11:15 P.M.

CHAPTER 6

The General Linear Allocation Problem

INTRODUCTION

It will be recalled that the general allocation problem involves resources and tasks that are expressed in different kinds of units. For example, a factory manufactures n different products in amounts $x_1, x_2, \ldots, x_n$ using various combinations of m different machines. Each unit of product j requires a_{ij} units of time on machine i ($j = 1, 2, \ldots, n; i = 1, 2, \ldots, m$). The same task may require more time on one machine (e.g., an older one) than on another

TABLE 6.1 *Number of Units of Time Required to Produce one Unit of Each Product*

		Product				Number of Hours Available/Planning Period
		1	2	$\cdots$	n	
Machines $i =$	1	a_{11}	a_{12}	$\cdots$	a_{1n}	b_1
	2	a_{21}	a_{22}	$\cdots$	a_{2n}	b_2
	.	.	.	.	.	.
	.	.	.	$\cdots$	.	.
	.	.	.	.	.	.
	m	a_{m1}	a_{m2}	$\cdots$	a_{mn}	b_m
Profit/unit		c_1	c_2	$\cdots$	c_n	

(newer) one. The total amount of time available on the ith machine is b_i per planning period. Finally, the profit on each unit of product j that is sold is c_j. This situation is shown in Table 6.1.

This problem, and many other problems of allocation, can be expressed as the maximization of a linear function subject to linear inequality constraints.

148

A NUMERICAL EXAMPLE

Let us consider a very simple numerical example. A small plant makes two types of automobile parts. It buys castings that are machined, bored, and polished. The data shown in Table 6.2 are given.

Castings for Part *A* cost $2 each; for Part *B* they cost $3 each. They sell for $5 and $6, respectively. The three machines have running costs of $20,

TABLE 6.2 *Capacities*

	Part *A*	Part *B*
Machining capacity	25 per hour	40 per hour
Boring capacity	28 per hour	35 per hour
Polishing capacity	35 per hour	25 per hour

$14, and $17.50 per hour. Assuming that any combination of Parts *A* and *B* can be sold, what product mix maximizes profit?

The first step is to calculate the profit per part. This is done in Table 6.3. From the results shown there it is apparent that if on the average we make x of Part *A* and y of Part *B* per hour, our net profit is

$$Z = 1.20x + 1.40y. \tag{6.1}$$

Because there is no meaning for negative x and y, we must have

$$x \geq 0, \quad y \geq 0. \tag{6.2}$$

TABLE 6.3 *Costs and Profit per Part*

	Part *A*	Part *B*
Machining	$20/25 = 0.80$	$20/40 = 0.50$
Boring	$14/28 = 0.50$	$14/35 = 0.40$
Polishing	$17.50/35 = 0.50$	$17.50/25 = 0.70$
Purchase	2.00	3.00
Total cost	3.80	4.60
Sales price	5.00	6.00
Profit	1.20	1.40

We are not able to choose x and y freely, because we must take into account the capacity limits. These yield the following results:

Machining $\qquad \dfrac{x}{25} + \dfrac{y}{40} \leq 1$

Boring $\qquad \dfrac{x}{28} + \dfrac{y}{40} \leq 1$

Polishing $\qquad \dfrac{x}{35} + \dfrac{y}{25} \leq 1$

By multiplying through to clear fractions, we obtain:

$$
\begin{array}{lll}
\text{Machining} & 40x + 25y \leq 1000 & \\
\text{Boring} & 35x + 28y \leq 980 & (6.3) \\
\text{Polishing} & 25x + 35y \leq 875 &
\end{array}
$$

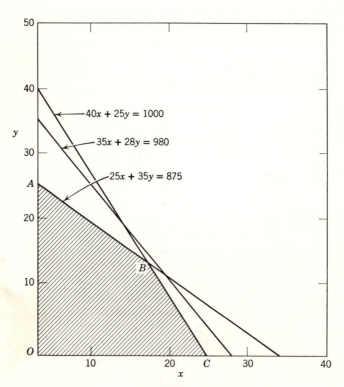

Figure 6.1

When we plot the equation $40x + 25y = 1000$, we obtain a line that divides the plane into two regions (Figure 6.1). In the region that includes the origin $40x + 25y < 1000$; in the other region $40x + 25y > 1000$. The other two inequalities in (6.3) divide the plane in a similar fashion. Thus if we regard our decision about the values of x and y as selecting a point in a plane, we see that the point must lie within or on the boundaries of the region $OABC$. Because the line $35x + 28y = 980$ lies outside this region, the boring constraint is redundant. In other words, any combination of x and y that satisfy the machining and polishing constraints will automatically be within the boring capacity.

The key result that permits us to solve the problem states that the point (x, y) for which profits attain their maximum must lie at one of the corners of $OABC$. It is easy enough to verify that the possible maximizing values are $0(0, 0)$, $A(0, 25)$, $B(16.93, 12.90)$, and $C(25, 0)$. The corresponding profits are $Z_0 = 0$, $Z_A = 35$, $Z_B = 38.39$, and $Z_C = 30$, so that the best production plan is 16.93 of A per hour and 12.90 of B per hour. These must be interpreted as average rates. We could probably run for several hours (or even days) on Part A and then run for several hours on Part B. All that is required to maximize profit is to keep the amounts produced in the ratio 16.93 to 12.90.

The slight surplus capacity in boring raises a practical point about the costs. We were told that the boring machine costs \$14 per hour; to complete the solution we really ought to know if this cost remains the same whether or not the machine runs continually. Implicit in our calculation is the assumption that the cost is at the *rate* of \$14 per hour only when the machine is in use and there are no other costs. It may well be that there are fixed costs of \$10 per hour plus variable cost of \$14 per hour. If this is so, the magnitude of the fixed cost is not relevant in maximizing profit, but it will determine whether or not the net profit is positive or negative (i.e., a loss).

It is not hard to see why the maximizing point (x, y) must lie at a corner. Consider the geometric interpretation of equation (6.1), which is restated here for convenience:

$$Z = 1.20x + 1.40y. \tag{6.1}$$

If we keep Z fixed (say $Z = 20$), then as x and y vary, (6.1) must be represented by a line of equal profit. If we choose another value of Z (say $Z = 25$), we shall obtain a parallel line further away from the origin O. This is shown in Figure 6.2. As we increase Z, we obtain family a of parallel lines. Clearly, Z is maximized by finding the line of the family furthest from the origin which has at least one point within or on the boundary of $OABC$. Such a line passes through B. The reader should convince himself that no matter what boundary figure we draw, the maximizing line must pass through a corner. This immediately provides us with a graphical method for solving

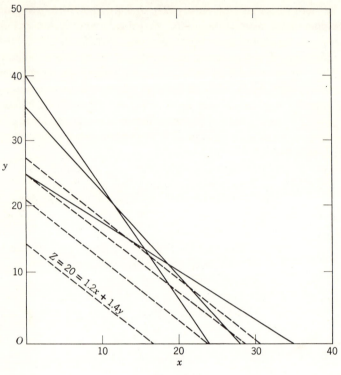

Figure 6.2

problems with two variables, and by analogy we can devise a computational procedure for more complex problems.

(Exercise 1 should be done at this point.)

COMPUTATIONAL PROCEDURE: THE SIMPLEX METHOD

It is much easier to handle equalities than inequalities. Therefore, we convert (6.3) to equations by introducing *slack variables: u, v,* and *w*. These are the differences between the two sides of the inequalities; thus

$$40x + 25y + u = 1000$$
$$35x + 28y + v = 980 \qquad (6.4)$$
$$25x + 35y + w = 875.$$

Clearly, in order for (6.3) to hold, we must specify that u, v, and w be nonnegative.

It can be shown that at any corner of the boundary $OABC$ (Figure 6.1), two of the five variables (x, y, u, v, and w) are zero and the other three are greater than zero. In a more general problem with n variables and m inequality constraints, we require m slack variables, and the solution that maximizes has, out of a total of $m + n$ variables including slacks, exactly m that are not zero. A set of values satisfying the constraints with m nonzero and n zero, is called a *feasible solution*. The calculation starts with a feasible solution, tests to see if it is optimal; if not, it finds an improved feasible solution, repeating the procedure until further improvement is not possible. This procedure can be divided into four steps.

1. An obvious feasible solution to (6.4) is to set $x = y = 0$ and to read off $u = 1000$, $v = 980$, and $w = 875$. This solution can be altered by increasing either x or y. From (6.1), $Z = 1.2x + 1.4y$, we see that the *rate* of increase in Z is 1.2 if we increase x, and 1.4 if we increase y. Therefore we decide to increase y.

2. An increase in y will result in decreases in u, v, and w, and we can increase y until one of u, v, and w becomes zero. From the first equation of (6.4) we see that $u = 0$ when $y = 40$; from the second equation, $v = 0$ when $y = 35$; and from the third, $w = 0$ when $y = 25$.

3. Thus y can be increased to 25, which makes $u = 375$, $v = 280$, and $w = 0$. This calculation can be made easily because:

(a) Z does not contain the nonzero variables u, v, and w;

(b) each of the equations (6.4) contains exactly one of the nonzero variables u, v, and w, and the coefficients of each of these is one.

4. We now rearrange Z and equations (6.4) so that (a) and (b) hold for the new nonzero variables y, u, and v. The third equation of (6.4) is the only one containing the variable w that has become zero. We divide this equation by 35, which is the coefficient of the new nonzero variable y, obtain

$$\tfrac{5}{7}x + y + \frac{w}{35} = 25, \tag{6.5}$$

and subtract suitable multiples (25 and 28) of (6.5) from the other equations to eliminate y from them. We obtain

$$\tfrac{155}{7}x + u - \tfrac{5}{7}w = 375 \tag{6.6}$$

$$15x + v - \tfrac{4}{5}w = 280. \tag{6.7}$$

Now from (6.5), $\tfrac{5}{7}x + y + (w/35) - 25 = 0$; therefore, if we subtract multiples of this from Z, we shall not change Z. If we subtract 1.4 times this expression from Z, we shall eliminate y. Thus $Z = 0.2x - 0.04w + 35$. We see that of the two zero variables x and w, only x will increase Z as it is increased from zero. To find how much x can be increased, we divide the coefficients of x in (6.5), (6.6), and (6.7) into the constants on the right. We obtain 35, $16\frac{29}{31}$ and $18\frac{2}{3}$ and conclude that increasing x to $16\frac{29}{31}$ will decrease u to zero and will leave $y = 12\frac{28}{31}$ and $v = 25\frac{30}{31}$. When we divide (6.6) by the coefficient of x and transpose the constant, we obtain

$$x + \tfrac{7}{155}u - \frac{w}{31} - 16\tfrac{29}{31} = 0; \qquad (6.8)$$

if we take 0.2 times (6.8) from

$$Z = 0.2x - 0.04w + 35,$$

we obtain

$$Z = -\frac{1.4}{155}u - \tfrac{26}{775}w + 38\tfrac{12}{31}.$$

We conclude that an increase in either w or u will diminish Z; hence the maximum value of Z has been found. Note that the corresponding value of Z is $38\frac{12}{31}$, which agrees with the value found previously.

In practice the calculations may be written in tabular form without writing the variables in each equation. We set up a table (see Table 6.4) with rows labeled P_3, P_4, and P_5 to correspond to the first set of nonzero variables:

TABLE 6.4

	P_1	P_2	P_3	P_4	P_5	P_0
P_3	40	25	1			1000
P_4	35	28		1		980
P_5	25	35			1	875
Δ	1.2	1.4				

u, v, and w. The columns are labeled P_1, P_2, P_3, P_4, and P_5 to correspond to x, y, u, v, and w. A final column, P_0, is added to correspond to the constants in the equations, and a final row, Δ, is added to show the coefficients in Z. Equations (6.1) and (6.3) are completely represented in Table 6.4. Blanks are left in the table for zero entries.

Using Table 6.4, we can again proceed in four steps, which correspond to the four through which we have just worked.

1. Select the column that has the largest positive entry in row Δ. In this case it is P_2 with entry 1.4.

2. Divide the *positive* entries in the column selected in step 1 into the corresponding entries in P_0 and select the smallest. In this case we selected P_2. For P_3 the result is $1000/25 = 40$; for P_4, $980/28 = 35$, and for P_5, $875/35 = 25$. Therefore, we select row P_5.

3. Divide the row selected in step 2 by the entry in the column selected in step 1 and relabel the result with the heading of the column selected. In this case, we divide the entries in row P_5 by 35 and relabel the row P_2. This yields

	P_1	P_2	P_3	P_4	P_5	P_0
P_2	5/7	1			1/35	25

4. Eliminate the entries in all rows other than that changed in step 3 (including the Δ row) by subtracting suitable multiples of the relabeled row obtained in step 3. If all Δ entries are negative or zero, the optimal solution

TABLE 6.5

	P_1	P_2	P_3	P_4	P_5	P_0
P_2	5/7	1			1/35	25
P_3	155/7		1		−5/7	375
P_4	15			1	−4/5	280
Δ	1/5				−1/25	

has been found. If not, return to step 1. In this case we multiply row P_2 by 25 and subtract it from row P_3. We proceed similarly for row P_4 (multiplying P_2 by 28) and for row Δ (multiplying by 1.4). This yields Table 6.5. The constant obtained when eliminating from the Δ row is not required at subsequent steps; hence it is usually omitted.

Because there still is a positive entry in row Δ, we return to step 1 and repeat the four steps. This yields Table 6.6. Because both entries in row Δ of Table 6.6 are negative, we conclude that $P_1 = x = 16\frac{29}{31}$, and $P_2 = y = 12\frac{28}{31}$ maximize Z.

Note that step 2 in the procedure just described fails if none of the entries (other than Δ) in the column selected at step 1 are positive. In this case the variable selected at step 1 can be increased indefinitely without violating a

TABLE 6.6

	P_1	P_2	P_3	P_4	P_5	P_0
P_1	1		7/155		−1/31	$16\frac{29}{31}$
P_2		1	−1/31		8/155	$12\frac{28}{31}$
P_4			−21/31	1	−49/155	$25\frac{30}{31}$
Δ			−1.4/155		−26/775	

constraint. If the data are supposed to represent a real problem, this usually means that the *real* problem is nonlinear or that a constraint has been omitted.

(Exercises 2 to 7 should be done at this point.)

DUALITY

The method of calculation described permits us to solve any linear programming problem, but it may happen that we can guess the solution and that we merely wish to verify our guess without going through the entire calculation. Suppose that in the parts problem, the sales price of one of the parts changes slightly. It is likely that the optimal amounts that are to be produced remain the same, although the maximum profit will change. We shall now show how a proposed solution can be checked.

We know that in the Δ row of the last block in the calculation, the entries are zero in the columns corresponding to variables that are greater than zero and negative, or zero, in the columns corresponding to zero variables.

We now wish to use our knowledge of the values of the control variables to compute the final Δ row without going through the entire calculation. At any stage, the new Δ row is obtained from the previous Δ row by subtracting some multiple of a P row from the previous stage, and the P rows are obtained from the previous P rows, either by dividing through by a constant or by subtracting some multiple of another P row. In other words, the final Δ row consists of the original row less a weighted sum of the original P rows. The original Δ row consisted of the coefficients in Z, together with a set of zeros corresponding to the slack variables. A little reflection will show that P rows which correspond to nonzero slack variables are not included in the weighted sum. The weights are only greater than zero for constraints with zero slack variables, that is for constraints that have been satisfied as strict equalities. Now, corresponding to any variable that is not zero, we must have a zero entry in the Δ row, and these conditions are enough to allow us to compute the weights and from them the complete Δ row. We proceed as follows.

1. Form equations for the weights $w_1, w_2, \ldots, w_m$ by reading down the columns of the nonzero variables and equating the result to the corresponding cost coefficient.

For example, let us test the solution obtained to the parts problem that we have just considered where $Z = 1.2x + 1.4y$; the constraints were:

$$40x + 25y \leq 1000$$

$$35x + 28y \leq 980$$

$$25x + 35y \leq 875.$$

In the solution, x and y were both greater than zero, so that the weighted sum of their columns (P_1 and P_2) must equal their coefficients in Z; that is,

$$40w_1 + 35w_2 + 25w_3 = 1.2$$
$$25w_1 + 28w_2 + 35w_3 = 1.4.$$

2. Set to zero those weights corresponding to constraints that are satisfied as strict inequalities and solve the equation for the remaining weights.

Returning to the example, when we check the numerical solution values of x (16.93) and y (12.90) in the constraints, we find that the first and third values are exactly satisfied and that the second is a strict inequality. Therefore, $w_2 = 0$, and we can now solve for w_1 and w_3 as follows:

$$40w_1 + 25w_3 = 1.2 \quad \text{or} \quad w_1 + 0.625w_3 = 0.03$$
$$25w_1 + 35w_3 = 1.4 \quad \text{or} \quad w_1 + 1.4w_3 = 0.056.$$

By subtraction we obtain:

$$0.775w_3 = 0.026 \quad \text{or} \quad w_3 = 0.0335.$$

Therefore, $w_1 = 0.0091$.

3. Except for the Δ row, multiply the entries other than P_0 in each column by the appropriate weights, add them, and subtract the result from the entries in the original Δ row (i.e., the original coefficients in Z) or from zero in the case of slack variables.

In the example, for column P_1 clearly $40(0.0091) + 35(0) + 25(0.0335) = 1.2$; for P_2, $25(0.0091) + 28(0) + 35(0.0335) = 1.4$; for P_3, $1(0.0091) = 0.0091$; for P_4, $1(0) = 0$; and for P_5, $1(0.0335) = 0.0335$. Then, subtracting from the entries in the Δ row, we have for P_1, $1.2 - 1.2 = 0$; for P_2, $1.4 - 1.4 = 0$; for P_3, $0 - 0.0091 = -0.0091$; for P_4, $0 - 0 = 0$; and for P_5, $0 - 0.0335 = -0.0335$.

4. We now have the complete Δ row. If none of the entries are greater than zero, the proposed solution has been verified.

Clearly, in the example, none of the revised entries in the Δ row are greater than zero; therefore, the solution is verified.

Notice that because, in the original column corresponding to a slack variable, the only entry is a *one* in its own row, it follows from steps 3 and 4 that the weights are minus the entries in the *final* Δ row corresponding to slack variables. It follows that if any weight is negative, the proposed solution cannot be optimal and step 3 can be omitted.

The weights have another interpretation. From the way they were obtained, when we multiply them by the entries in the original P_0 column and add, we obtain the optimal value of Z. The reason is that Z equals its original expression minus the weighted sum of the original rows with the P_0 column transposed. (The amounts subtracted are all zero.) In the example,

$$Z = 1.2x + 1.4y - 0.0091(40x + 25y + u - 1000)$$
$$- 0.0335(25x + 35y + w - 875)$$
$$= -0.0091u - 0.0335w + [0.0091 \times 1000 + 0.0335 \times 875].$$

In this form either the coefficients are zero (as in the cases of x, y, and v) or the variables have zero values (as in the case of u and w). The only remaining terms are the weighted sum of the entries in the P_0 column; thus the weighted sum equals the value of Z.

Let us consider the set of all nonnegative weights with the property that the weighted sum of all original columns (other than P_0) is not less than the corresponding entry in the Δ row. One member of this set was found in the procedure for verifying a proposed solution; the weighted sums were made to equal the Δ entries for nonzero variables, and the solution was verified if and only if the sums were not less than the Δ entries for zero variables. We shall show that all such weights also have the following properties:

1. None of the feasible values of Z exceed the weighted sum of the P_0 column.

2. If any such weighted sum of the P_0 column *equals* a feasible value of Z, we have the maximum value of Z and the minimum value of the weighted sums.

Thus the w's found in the example minimize

$$Y = 1000w_1 + 980w_2 + 875w_3$$

over all w_1, w_2, w_3 such that

$$w_1 \geq 0, w_2 \geq 0, w_3 \geq 0$$

and

$$40w_1 + 35w_2 + 25w_3 \geq 1.2$$
$$25w_1 + 28w_2 + 35w_3 \geq 1.4.$$

Let us write the original problem in the following way. Maximize

$$Z = c_1x_1 + c_2x_2 + \cdots + c_nx_n$$

over all $x_1, \ldots, x_n$ such that

$$x_1 \geq 0, x_2 \geq 0, \ldots, x_n \geq 0 \qquad (6.9)$$

and

$$a_{11}x_1 + a_{12}x_2 + \cdots + a_{1n}x_n \leq b_1$$
$$a_{21}x_1 + \cdots\cdots\cdots + a_{2n}x_n \leq b_2 \qquad (6.10)$$
$$\cdot$$
$$\cdot$$
$$\cdot$$
$$a_{m1}x_1 + \cdots\cdots\cdots + a_{mn}x_n \leq b_m.$$

We define Y by the equation

$$Y = b_1w_1 + b_2w_2 + \cdots + b_mw_m$$

where

$$w_1 \geq 0, \; w_2 \geq 0, \ldots, \; w_m \geq 0 \qquad (6.11)$$

and

$$a_{11}w_1 + a_{21}w_2 + \cdots + a_{m1}w_m \geq c_1$$
$$a_{12}w_1 + a_{22}w_2 + \cdots + a_{m2}w_m \geq c_2$$
$$\cdot \qquad\qquad\qquad\qquad\qquad\qquad (6.12)$$
$$\cdot$$
$$\cdot$$
$$a_{1n}w_1 + a_{2n}w_2 + \cdots + a_{mn}w_m \geq c_n.$$

Because all the x's are greater than or equal to zero, we can multiply the successive inequalities of (6.12) by $x_1, x_2, \ldots, x_n$ and add. We obtain, after rearrangement,

$$w_1(a_{11}x_1 + a_{12}x_2 + \cdots + a_{1n}x_n)$$
$$+ \; w_2(a_{21}x_1 + a_{22}x_2 + \cdots + a_{2n}x_n)$$
$$+$$
$$\cdot$$
$$\cdot$$
$$\cdot$$
$$+ \; w_m(a_{m1}x_1 + a_{m2}x_2 + \cdots + a_{mn}x_n) \geq c_1x_1 + c_2x_2 + \cdots + c_nx_n = Z.$$

But from (6.10), each of the quantities in brackets is less than or equal to the corresponding $b_1, b_2, \ldots, b_m$. It follows that

$$w_1b_1 + w_2b_2 + \cdots + w_mb_m \geq c_1x_1 + c_2x_2 + \cdots + c_nx_n;$$

that is, $Y \geq Z$ for *all* $(x_1, \ldots, x_n)$ and $(w_1, \ldots, w_m)$ satisfying the conditions (6.9) to (6.12).

It follows that if we find a set of x's and a set of w's for which $Y = Z$, we have the maximum Z and the minimum Y. If Y were not a minimum, the minimum Y would be less than some Z, which is impossible, and conversely.

The problem of minimizing Y is called the *dual* problem, and the problem of maximizing Z is called the *primal* problem.

We have seen how to obtain the dual solution from the primal; we can easily solve the primal problem from the dual for the following reasons:

(a) when $a_{j1}w_1 + a_{j2}w_2 + \cdots + a_{jm}w_m \geq c_j$, we must have $x_j = 0$, and

(b) when $w_i > 0$, we must have $a_{i1}x_1 + a_{i2}x_2 + \cdots + a_{in}x_n = b_i$.

Sometimes we can guess the solution to the dual problem. If we obtain the solution to the primal from (a) and (b) *and* if it satisfies *all* conditions for the primal, we simultaneously verify both solutions.

Example: A Warehouse Problem

A man is engaged in buying and selling identical items. He operates from a warehouse that can hold 500 items. Each month he can sell any quantity that he chooses up to the stock at the beginning of the month. Each month he can buy as much as he wishes for delivery at the end of the month, so long as his total stock does not exceed 500 items. For the next six months, he has the following error-free forecast of costs and sales prices:

Month	i	1	2	3	4	5	6
Cost	c_i	27	24	26	28	22	21
Sales price	p_i	28	25	25	27	23	23

If he currently has a stock of 200 units, what should his policy be?

In this example we have ignored the costs of storage. After studying the solution, the reader should formulate and solve the problem for the case in which storage costs each month are 0.25 times the average of the stock on the first of the month and the stock immediately before delivery at the end of the month.

Let x_i be the quantity purchased in month i and let y_i be the quantity sold. The net profit is

$$Z = 28y_1 + 25y_2 + 25y_3 + 27y_4 + 23y_5 + 23y_6$$
$$- 27x_1 - 24x_2 - 26x_3 - 28x_4 - 22x_5 - 21x_6.$$

Now, he cannot sell anything that he does not own; therefore, for each month $n = 1, 2, \ldots, 6$

$$200 + \sum_{i=1}^{n-1} (x_i - y_i) \geq y_n \quad \text{(for } n = 1 \text{ ignore the summation)},$$

which yields

$$\sum_{i=1}^{n} y_i - \sum_{i=1}^{n-1} x_i \leq 200. \tag{6.13}$$

Also, he cannot overstock the warehouse; therefore, for each month

$$200 + \sum_{i=1}^{n} (x_i - y_i) \le 500$$

or   (6.14)

$$\sum_{i=1}^{n} x_i - \sum_{i=1}^{n} y_i \le 300.$$

Thus the problem is to maximize Z over $x_1 \ge 0, x_2 \ge 0, \ldots, x_6 \ge 0, y_1 \ge 0,$ $y_2 \ge 0, \ldots, y_6 \ge 0$, which satisfy (6.13) and (6.14).

Instead of solving this directly, we shall first solve the dual problem. Let $u_1, u_2, u_3, u_4, u_5, u_6$ be the dual variables corresponding to (6.13) and let $v_1, v_2,$ v_3, v_4, v_5, v_6 correspond to (6.14). The primal problem may be written, with detached coefficients, as shown in Table 6.7. Thus the dual problem is to minimize

$$Y = 200(u_1 + u_2 + \cdots + u_6) + 300(v_1 + v_2 + \cdots + v_6) \quad (6.15)$$

TABLE 6.7

	x_1	x_2	x_3	x_4	x_5	x_6	y_1	y_2	y_3	y_4	y_5	y_6	
u_1							1						200
u_2	-1						1	1					200
u_3	-1	-1					1	1	1				200
u_4	-1	-1	-1				1	1	1	1			200
u_5	-1	-1	-1	-1			1	1	1	1	1		200
u_6	-1	-1	-1	-1	-1		1	1	1	1	1	1	200
v_1	1						-1						300
v_2	1	1					-1	-1					300
v_3	1	1	1				-1	-1	-1				300
v_4	1	1	1	1			-1	-1	-1	-1			300
v_5	1	1	1	1	1		-1	-1	-1	-1	-1		300
v_6	1	1	1	1	1	1	-1	-1	-1	-1	-1	-1	300
Δ	-27	-24	-26	-28	-22	-21	28	25	25	27	23	23	

subject to constraints that are found by reading down the columns. For example, from the column for x_1 we have

$$-(u_2 + u_3 + u_4 + u_5 + u_6) + (v_1 + v_2 + v_3 + v_4 + v_5 + v_6) \ge -27.$$

From the form of Y in (6.15) it seems likely that all u's and v's should be as small as possible. Also, they are nonnegative. From the column for x_6 we see that $v_6 \ge -21$; therefore, because v_6 is nonnegative, we must have $v_6 = 0$. Hence from the y_6 column, if $v_6 = 0$, then $u_6 = 23$.

If we tackle the dual constraints in the correct order, we find that each successive constraint contains one further unknown u or v, and so their values may be found. We now know that $v_6 = 0$ and $u_6 = 23$. From the x_5 column

$$-u_6 + v_5 + v_6 \ge -22;$$

on substituting the values for u_6 and v_6, we have

$$v_5 \geq 1;$$

hence $v_5 = 1$. From the y_5 column

$$u_5 + u_6 - v_5 - v_6 \geq 23;$$

on substituting known values, we obtain

$$u_5 \geq 1;$$

hence $u_5 = 1$.

We now use the columns in the order

$$x_4, y_4, x_3, y_3, x_2, y_2, x_1, y_1$$

and obtain the values

u_1	u_2	u_3	u_4	u_5	u_6	v_1	v_2	v_3	v_4	v_5	v_6
3	1	0	4	1	23	0	2	1	0	1	0.

If we assume that these values yield the solution to the dual problem, we can find the corresponding primal solution. The first step is to find which of the dual constraints have become strict equalities. This is done by substitution. For example, the first dual constraint is

$$-(u_2 + u_3 + u_4 + u_5 + u_6) + (v_1 + v_2 + v_3 + v_4 + v_5 + v_6) \geq -27$$

or

$$-(1 + 0 + 4 + 1 + 23) + (0 + 2 + 1 + 0 + 1 + 0) = -25 > -27.$$

We have seen that the x's and y's can only be nonzero when the corresponding dual constraint is a strict equality. We conclude that $x_1 = 0$, and in a similar fashion we find that x_4, x_6, and y_3 are all zero. We also know that corresponding to nonzero dual variables we must have strict equalities in the primal constraints.

Thus in the primal problem (Table 6.7), rows for u_1, u_2, u_4, u_5, u_6, v_2, v_3, and v_5 must be strict equalities, and (omitting the zero variables) we have:

$$y_1 = 200 \qquad (6.16)$$

$$y_1 + y_2 = 200 \qquad (6.17)$$

$$-(x_2 + x_3) + (y_1 + y_2 + y_4) = 200 \qquad (6.18)$$

$$-(x_2 + x_3) + (y_1 + y_2 + y_4 + y_5) = 200 \qquad (6.19)$$

$$-(x_2 + x_3 + x_5) + (y_1 + y_2 + y_4 + y_5 + y_6) = 200 \qquad (6.20)$$

$$x_2 - (y_1 + y_2) = 300 \qquad (6.21)$$

$$x_2 + x_3 - (y_1 + y_2) = 300 \qquad (6.22)$$

$$x_2 + x_3 + x_5 - (y_1 + y_2 + y_4 + y_5) = 300 \qquad (6.23)$$

From (6.16) we have $y_1 = 200$; from (6.17), $y_2 = 0$; from (6.21), $x_2 = 500$; and from (6.22), we have $x_3 = 0$. The remaining equations are solved in the order (6.18), (6.19), (6.23), and (6.20). The complete results are:

x_1	x_2	x_3	x_4	x_5	x_6	y_1	y_2	y_3	y_4	y_5	y_6
0	500	0	0	500	0	200	0	0	500	0	500

The final step required to verify that these values of x's and y's indeed maximize Z is to check that they satisfy all the constraints of the primal problem. Clearly, they are nonnegative, and from the way they were obtained they satisfy the constraints corresponding to $u_1, u_2, u_4, u_5, u_6, v_2, v_3, v_5$. Corresponding to u_3 we have $-(x_1 + x_2) + (y_1 + y_2 + y_3) \leq 200$, and corresponding to v_1, v_4, and v_6 we have

$$x_1 - y_1 \leq 200$$
$$(x_1 + x_2 + x_3 + x_4) - (y_1 + y_2 + y_3 + y_4) \leq 300$$
$$(x_1 + x_2 + x_3 + x_4 + x_5 + x_6) - (y_1 + y_2 + y_3 + y_4 + y_5 + y_6) \leq 300.$$

It is easy to see that the values satisfy all four conditions as strict inequalities, and we conclude that the best policy is to buy 500 in months 2 and 5 and to sell 200 in month 1 and 500 in months 4 and 6. The net profit is 7600.

It should be noted that the policy has the following form. Sell the entire stock in months 1, 4, and 6. Buy enough to fill the warehouse in months 2 and 5. The reader should now satisfy himself that this remains the best policy, no matter what the initial stock and warehouse capacity may be.

(Exercise 8 should be done at this point.)

PARAMETRIC PROGRAMMING

Even when we are certain that our problem is linear, there may be doubts about the values of some of the parameters. When we are certain of the constraints, but suspect the objective function, the methods described in the section on duality can be used to see what changes in the objective function would cause a change in the optimal solution. In the automobile parts problem at the beginning of this chapter, the objective function was

$$Z = 1.2x + 1.4y.$$

Suppose that we wish to find by how much the coefficient of y would have to change before the solution changes. Let us write

$$Z = 1.2x + cy$$

and find limits on c at which the solution changes. When $c = 1.4$, we know that the solution is

$$x = 16\tfrac{29}{31}, \ y = 12\tfrac{28}{31}.$$

Corresponding to this solution, the equations for the dual variables are

$$40w_1 + 25w_3 = 1.2 \tag{6.24}$$
$$25w_1 + 35w_3 = 1.4. \tag{6.25}$$

When we replace 1.4 by c, the second equation becomes

$$25w_1 + 35w_3 = c. \tag{6.26}$$

The solution of (6.24) and (6.26) is

$$w_1 = \frac{42 - 25c}{775,} \quad w_3 = \frac{40c - 30}{775}$$

For the solution to be optimal, we must have $w_1 \geq 0$, $w_3 \geq 0$. Thus, from w_1, we have

$$42 - 25c \geq 0 \quad \text{or} \quad c \leq \frac{42}{25} = 1.68$$

and, from w_3, we have

$$40c - 30 \geq 0 \quad \text{or} \quad c \geq \frac{30}{40} = 0.75.$$

We conclude that the optimal solution remains $x = 16\frac{29}{31}$, $y = 12\frac{28}{31}$ so long as

$$0.75 \leq c \leq 1.68.$$

Outside these limits we would have to recompute the last Δ row in the simplex calculation and continue to iterate until a new solution was found.

A similar technique can be used to explore the consequences of changes in the constants (the P_0 column) in the constraints. The basic notion that permits this investigation is that for a given set of nonzero variables the Δ row does not depend on the numerical values of the variables. Thus the optimal set of nonzero variables (but not their values) will only change where changes in the P_0 column reduce one of the nonzero variables to zero. In the automobile parts problem the constraints, with slack variables, were

$$40x + 25y + u = 1000$$
$$35x + 28y + v = 980 \tag{6.4}$$
$$25x + 35y + w = 875$$

We might have some doubt about the available hours, and the doubt might vary from one machine to another. This could be expressed by writing (6.4) as

$$40x + 25y + u = 1000 + 2\lambda$$
$$35x + 28y + v = 980 + \lambda \tag{6.27}$$
$$25x + 35y + w = 875 + 3\lambda$$

We know that if λ is close enough to zero, the optimal solution has $x > 0$, $y > 0$, $v > 0$ and $u = w = 0$. We wish to find how the solution varies with λ. We start by setting $u = w = 0$ in (6.27) and solving for x, y, and v. The results are:

$$x = 16\tfrac{29}{31} - \frac{\lambda}{155}; \qquad y = 12\tfrac{28}{31} + \frac{14\lambda}{155}; \qquad v = 25\tfrac{30}{31} - \frac{202\lambda}{155}.$$

Thus x remains positive as long as $\lambda \le 16\tfrac{29}{31} \times 155 = 2625$; y remains positive as long as $\lambda \ge -12\tfrac{28}{31} \times 155/14 = -2000/14 = -142\tfrac{6}{7}$; and v remains positive as long as $\lambda \le 25\tfrac{30}{31} \times 155/202 = 4025/202 = 19\tfrac{187}{202}$. We

TABLE 6.8

	P_1	P_2	P_3	P_4	P_5	P_0	λ
P_3	40	25	1			1000	2
P_4	35	28		1		980	1
P_5	25	35			1	875	3
Δ	1.2	1.4					
P_2	5/7	1			1/35	25	3/35
P_3	155/7		1		−5/7	375	−5/35
P_4	15			1	−4/5	280	−49/35
Δ	0.2				−0.04		
P_1	1		7/155		−1/31	$16\tfrac{29}{31}$	−1/155
P_2		1	−1/31		8/155	$12\tfrac{28}{31}$	14/155
P_4			−21/31	1	−49/155	$25\tfrac{30}{31}$	−202/155
Δ			−1.4/155		−26/775		

conclude that it is optimal to keep $u = w = 0$ and $x > 0$, $y > 0$, $v > 0$ as long as

$$-142\tfrac{6}{7} \le \lambda \le 19\tfrac{187}{202}.$$

As λ decreases below $-142\tfrac{6}{7}$, y becomes and remains zero; in this case either u or w must increase to preserve the equalities in (6.27). To decide between u and w, it is probably best to go back to the simplex tableux (Tables 6.4, 6.5, and 6.6). If we had started with the idea of exploring how the solution depended on λ, we would have added another column to keep track of λ. This is done in Table 6.8.

From the last P_2 row we see that

$$y - \frac{u}{31} + 8\frac{w}{155} = 12\tfrac{28}{31} + \frac{14\lambda}{155},$$

and if λ is such that the right-hand side is negative, when we set $y.= 0$ the only variable that can be increased to preserve the equality is u, because u has a negative coefficient. It should be clear that in general

(*a*) only variables with negative coefficients can be increased and if there is a choice, we could select the variable with the least negative entry in the Δ row;

(*b*) if all variables have positive coefficients, further decreases in λ will not yield a feasible solution at all.

Because we have decided that P_3 will enter the solution (that is $u > 0$) and P_2 will leave (that is $y = 0$), we compute the next simplex tableau accordingly. We divide the last P_2 row (Table 6.8) by the entry in the P_3 column (that is multiply by -31) and then eliminate P_3 from the remaining rows. The result is shown in Table 6.9.

TABLE 6.9

	P_1	P_2	P_3	P_4	P_5	P_0	λ
P_1	1	7/5			1/25	35	3/25
P_3		−31	1		−8/5	−400	−14/5
P_4		−21		1	−219/155	245	16/5
Δ		1.4/155			−37.2/775		

Note that the Δ entries are zero or negative; therefore, this solution is optimal, provided that λ is such that none of the variables are negative. On examining Table 6.9 we see that x becomes zero when $\lambda = -35 \times 25/3 = 875/3$. However, there are no negative entries in row P_1, and we conclude that if $\lambda < -875/3$, there is no feasible solution at all. The reader should now explore the situation as λ is increased above $19\frac{187}{202}$.

(Exercise 7 should be done at this point.)

SOME FURTHER DEVELOPMENTS

In this and the preceding chapter, we have discussed some procedures for solving linear allocation problems. It will be realized that for large problems that have many variables and constraints the computational difficulties are enormous, even when we are assisted by large digital computers. Much ingenuity has been expended on devising special methods to take advantage of particular features of the constraints in order to tackle large problems when computer facilities are limited. Sometimes the variables and constraints can be grouped so that the first set of constraints involve only the first set of variables and the second set of constraints involve the second set of variables, whereas the third set of constraints involve both sets of variables. If the constraints in the third set are relatively few, it is possible to *decompose* the problem into subproblems involving the first two sets of constraints and then to link up the parts by way of the third set of constraints. Suppose, for example, that a company has two plants and that it has a product mix problem. The first set of variables might be the mix at the first plant; the second set might be the mix at the second plant. The constraints would be the production capacities at each plant. There would be two separate problems, except for the additional constraints imposed by the total size of the market. Market limitations would apply to the combined output of both plants. However, there may be very few market constraints compared with the production constraints, and the total problem might well be decomposed and the separate pieces of the solutions recombined later.

It sometimes happens that in addition to other constraints certain variables can only take integral values. In the case of the assignment problem this presented no difficulty because the optimal solution necessarily consists of integers. In the general linear programming problem, the solution can take any values, and if integers are required, special methods must be used. Except when the variables take on large values (in the hundreds perhaps), rounding a solution to the nearest integer will not yield the best integer solution and may, in fact, be far from optimal. As an example of a case in which integers are required, consider the problem of the number of insertions of advertisements in a set of magazines. Attempts have been made to formulate this problem with a linear objective function and linear constraints (a monthly magazine cannot have more than twelve insertions per year). This is not the place to discuss the linearity assumptions (are two advertisements twice as good as one?), but it is obvious that the number of insertions must be an integer.

If either the constraints or the objective function is not linear, the problem is called a *nonlinear programming* problem. The advertising world, where quantity discounts are available for multiple insertions, provides a good example. Other cases arise in transportation, where less-than-carload quantities are carried at much increased prices per ton. In production, we often have nonlinear constraints on production capacities, the most obvious example being due to set-up and take-down times, which are often independent of the quantities produced. Some problems of this type are discussed in Chapter 7; in general, however, computations are lengthy and complex. It is possible by introducing new variables to change either the objective function or the constraints into linear forms, and we usually prefer linear constraints and a nonlinear objective. If the objective function is convex, which roughly speaking means that the marginal rates of profit decrease as the variables increase, it is possible to approximate the profit by a series of linear segments and to use linear programming methods. The technique is similar to that used in the overtime problem of Table 5.19. In more general cases, we often have to fall back on "hill-climbing" methods.

For a problem in two variables, we might imagine the objective function as the surface on a map. The maximum value is attained at the top of the highest hill. We start at any convenient point on the ground and proceed along the direction of steepest ascent until we reach either a peak or a boundary. When we reach a peak in the direction of movement, we turn to the steepest direction at that point and move along to the next peak. At a boundary we must avoid moving outside the constraints. Eventually we reach a position where movement in any direction means a descent, and at this stage we at least have a local maximum. There are two difficulties in practice. The first is the relatively slow rate of convergence, which to some extent has been overcome by methods for discovering better than steepest-ascent directions. The second difficulty is that the method only discovers local maxima, and there appears to be no general way of demonstrating that we have reached the absolute maximum. To safeguard against local maxima, it is usual to start the climb from several different positions and, if computations converge on different hills, we select the highest.

One group of nonlinear problems, in which the variables can be handled sequentially, has been studied extensively in recent years; a discussion will be found in Chapter 9. The method is very powerful but works only for problems that have the appropriate structure. Essentially, if we have k sequential decisions to make, we can arrange the calculations so that instead of one problem in k variables, we have k problems in one variable each. Because the amount of calculation with k variables tends to increase as the kth power of some number, this technique, called *dynamic programming* is a powerful aid in those problems for which it is suitable.

Before concluding this discussion of further developments, we wish to mention *chance-constrained* or *stochastic programming*. In the automobile parts problem, suppose that sales are related to the sales effort, but that instead of an exact mathematical relationship, we have a probabilistic one. Thus, if we spend t on selling the first part, sales might be distributed normally about $5t$ with a variance of 2, and if we spend z on the second part, sales might be distributed normally about $6z$ with a variance of 3. We now wish to determine how much of each part to make and how much to spend on sales effort in order to maximize profit, but subject to the condition that the probability of profits falling below $25 is less than 5 per cent. Techniques for solving such problems are now available, but they are beyond the scope of this book.

We might summarize this chapter by observing that for moderate-size problems, straightforward arithmetical procedures are available for maximizing linear functions, subject to linear inequality constraints. For special problems (such as the assignment and transportation problems), special algorithms are available to reduce the computational labor. For large problems (hundreds of variables and/or constraints), computations may exceed the capacities of large digital computers, but such problems can sometimes be decomposed into smaller ones that are computationally feasible. Methods also exist for solving more complex problems where integer solutions are required or where nonlinear functions or chance constraints are involved. However, the computations are much more involved, and (unlike in the simplex method) there is often no guarantee of convergence.

EXERCISES

1. Use the graphical method to maximize $Z = 8x + 9y$, where $x \geq 0$, $y \geq 0$, and $5x + 4y \leq 40$; $x + 2y \leq 12$; $5x + 19y \leq 95$.

2. Solve Exercise 1 by the simplex method.
   (*a*) Rewrite the three constraints as equalities by introducing slack variables u, v, w and state the obvious feasible solution. Set up the first table, including the Δ row.
   (*b*) Because y has the larger coefficient in Z, increase y first. Which slack variable will become zero?
   (*c*) Relabel the row whose slack variable becomes zero and eliminate y from the other rows.
   (*d*) Decide which variable is to be increased next and continue the calculation until the maximum value of Z has been found.

3. Solve the following problems:
   (*a*) Max $Z = 3x + 4y + 2z$, where $x \geq 0$, $y \geq 0$, $z \geq 0$, and

$$x + y + z \leq 12$$
$$x + 2y - z \leq 5$$
$$x - y + z \leq 2.$$

   (*b*) Max $Z = 4x_1 + 5x_2 + 7x_3 - x_4$, where $x_1 \geq 0, x_2 \geq 0, x_3 \geq 0, x_4 \geq 0$, and

$$2x_1 - x_2 + 3x_3 + 4x_4 \leq 10$$
$$x_1 + x_2 + x_3 - x_4 \leq 5$$
$$x_1 + 2x_2 - 2x_3 + 4x_4 \leq 12.$$

4. Find the maximum value of $Z = 4x_1 + 5x_2 + 2x_3 - x_4$, where $x_1 \geq 0, x_2 \geq 0$, $x_4 \geq 0$, x_3 may be either positive or negative, and

$$x_1 + x_2 + 2x_3 - x_4 \geq 1$$
$$2x_1 + 2x_2 - 3x_3 + x_4 \leq 3$$
$$x_1 + 4x_2 + 3x_3 + 2x_4 \leq 5.$$

(*Hints:* (a) Because one of the constraints has a "greater than" or "equal" sign, when we insert slack variables, a feasible solution is not obvious. However, if we rewrite the constraints as equalities, we have

$$x_1 + x_2 + 2x_3 - x_4 - x_5 = 1$$
$$2x_1 + 2x_2 - 3x_3 + x_4 + x_6 = 3$$
$$x_1 + 4x_2 + 3x_3 + 2x_4 + x_7 = 5,$$

and we see that $x_1 = 1$, $x_6 = 1$, $x_7 = 4$, and the remaining variables equal to zero are feasible. The first step is to eliminate x_1 from the second and third equations and from Z. For an alternative approach, see Exercise 5.

(b) If the entry is the Δ row in column P_3 is not zero, the solution cannot be optimal (why?). Thus we may as well make x_3 the first entering variable. In subsequent decisions about changes in other variables, it is not necessary to consider the row P_3. However, it is necessary to know the value of x_3, which means that once row P_3 is in the tableau, the only entry in it that we require is that in column P_0.)

5. Max $Z = 4x_1 + 5x_2 - 3x_3$, where $x_1 \geq 0$, $x_2 \geq 0$, $x_3 \geq 0$, and

$$x_1 + x_2 + x_3 = 10$$
$$x_1 - x_2 \geq 1$$
$$2x_1 + 3x_2 + x_3 \leq 20.$$

(*Hint:* For this problem $x_1 = x_2 = x_3 = 0$ is not a feasible solution because the first two constraints fail. Modify the problem to read: max $Z = 4x_1 + 5x_2 - 3x_3 - M_1 u - M_2 v - M_3 w$, where $x_1 \geq 0, x_2 \geq 0, x_3 \geq 0, u \geq 0, v \geq 0, w \geq 0$, $t \geq 0, z \geq 0$, and

$$x_1 + x_2 + x_3 + u - v = 10$$
$$x_1 - x_2 + w - t = 1$$
$$2x_1 + 3x_2 + x_3 + z = 20.$$

If M_1, M_2, and M_3 are very large numbers (say 10^6), the solution to the modified problem is bound to have $u = v = w = 0$. It follows that the values found for x_1, x_2, and x_3 will satisfy the constraints of the original problem and will be optimal for the original problem. For the modified problem, the obvious initial feasible solution is $x_1 = x_2 = x_3 = v = t = 0$ and $u = 10$, $w = 1$, $z = 20$.)

6. Write down the dual of the following problem: max $Z = 2x_1 + 3x_2 + 5x_3$ over all $x_1 \geq 0$, $x_2 \geq 0$, $x_3 \geq 0$, which satisfy

$$x_1 + x_2 + x_3 \leq 7$$
$$x_1 + 2x_2 + 2x_3 \leq 13$$
$$3x_1 - x_2 + x_3 \leq 5.$$

Verify that the solution is

$$x_1 = 0, \; x_2 = 0.75, \; x_3 = 5.75.$$

7. Explore how the solution to the following problems varies with λ.
   (a) Max $Z = 2x + (3 + \lambda)y$ over all nonnegative x and y, which satisfy

$$3x + 4y \leq 10$$
$$x + y \leq 5$$
$$2x + y \leq 7.$$

   (b) Max $Z = 4x + 3y$ over all nonnegative x and y, which satisfy

$$3x + 5y \leq 15 + \lambda$$
$$2x + 3y \leq 12 + 2\lambda$$
$$5x + 7y \leq 20 - \lambda.$$

   (*Hint:* Carry through the simplex calculations retaining the terms in λ in the P_0 column, but treating λ as zero when making decisions about variables that are to become nonzero. This will yield the optimal solution for $\lambda = 0$; then explore the effects of increasing and decreasing λ.)

8. An oil company produces two grades of gasoline, which it sells at 18 and 21 cents per gallon. The refinery can buy four different crudes with the following analyses and costs:

Crude	A	B	C	Price/Gallon
1	0.80	0.10	0.10	14¢
2	0.30	0.30	0.40	10¢
3	0.70	0.10	0.20	15¢
4	0.40	0.50	0.10	12¢

   The 21¢ grade must have at least 60 per cent of A and not more than 35 per cent of C. The 18¢ grade must not have more than 30 per cent of C. In the blending process 2 per cent of A and 1 per cent of B and C are lost because of evaporation. Show how to determine the relative amounts of the crudes to be used.

9. Solve the warehouse problem if, in addition to the costs mentioned, there is a holding cost of 0.5 for each item in stock immediately before deliveries at the end of each month.

10. An advertising agency has determined the relative sales value of a single advertisement in each of k different media. It has data on the costs of each medium and the audience (or readership) profile by time of day and/or season. Assuming that the effects of advertisement are additive, formulate the problem of media selection as a linear programming problem. Consider especially the types of constraints that may be involved.

11. Figure 6.3 shows the routing of three products through a plant. Given the data in Table 6.10, formulate the problem of deciding how much to produce of each product.

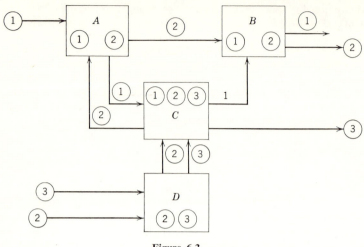

Figure 6.3

TABLE 6.10

		Machines			
Product		A	B	C	D
1	Rate per hour:	500	1000	1850	—
2		1200	1500	2300	1400
3		—	—	1600	800
	Running cost per hour:	500	450	800	600
	Percentage of downtime:	10	5	5	10

	Raw Materials		
	P	Q	R
Units per unit product 1:	1	1.25	2.0
Units per unit product 2:	—	2.0	2.5
Units per unit product 3:	1.5	—	1.75
Cost per unit raw material:	0.25	0.35	0.30

The selling prices for the three products are, 5.0, 4.5, and 3.5 respectively.

Suggested Readings

A comprehensive review of linear programming can be found in Arnoff and Sengupta (1961). This review article also includes an extensive bibliography. An earlier bibliography can be found in Riley and Gass (1958). A number of text-books are available; some of the more recent and better known are listed in the Bibliography. In Ford and Fulkerson (1962) an alternative way of solving the transportation problem is given.

Bibliography

Arnoff, E. L., and S. S. Sengupta, "Mathematical Programming," in *Progress in Operations Research*, Vol. I, R. L. Ackoff (ed.), John Wiley and Sons, New York, 1961, pp. 106–210.

Charnes, A., and W. W. Cooper, *An Introduction to Linear Programming*. John Wiley and Sons, New York, 1953.

————, *Management Models and Industrial Applications of Linear Programming*, Vols. 1 and 2, John Wiley and Sons, New York, 1961.

Chung, An-min, *Linear Programming*, Charles E. Merrill Books, Columbus, Ohio, 1963.

Dantzig, G., *Linear Programming and Extensions*, Princeton University Press, Princeton, N.J., 1963.

Dorfman, R., P. A. Samuelson, and R. M. Solow, *Linear Programming and Economic Analysis*, McGraw-Hill Book Co., New York, 1958.

Ferguson, R. O., and L. F. Sargent, *Linear Programming: Fundamentals and Applications*, McGraw-Hill Book Co., New York, 1958.

Ford, L. R., and D. R. Fulkerson, *Flows in Networks*, Princeton University Press, Princeton, N.J., 1962.

Garvin, W. W., *Introduction to Linear Programming*, McGraw-Hill Book Co., New York, 1960.

Gass, S. I. *Linear Programming: Methods and Applications*, McGraw-Hill Book Co., New York, 1958.

Hadley, G., *Linear Programming*, Addison-Wesley Publishing Co., Reading, Mass., 1962.

Karlin, S., *Mathematical Methods and Theory of Games, Programming and Economics*, Vols. 1 and 2, Addison-Wesley Publishing Co., Reading Mass., 1959.

Riley, V., and S. I. Gass, *Linear Programming and Associated Techniques: A Comprehensive Bibliography on Linear, Nonlinear and Dynamic Programming*, The Johns Hopkins Press, Baltimore, Md., 1958.

Valda, S., *Mathematical Programming*, Addison-Wesley Publishing Co., Reading, Mass., 1961.

CHAPTER 7

Inventory Problems

THE NATURE OF INVENTORY PROBLEMS

An inventory consists of usable but idle resources. The resources may be of any type; for example, men, materials, machines, or money. When the resource involved is material or goods in any stage of completion, inventory is usually referred to as "stock."

An inventory problem exists if the amount of the resources is subject to control and if there is at least one cost that decreases as inventory increases.

Normally, the objective is to minimize total (actual or expected) cost. If, however, inventory affects demand (the amount asked for by users), the objective may be to maximize (actual or expected) profit.

The variables that may be controlled, separately or in combination, are the following:

1. *The quantity acquired* (by purchase, production, or some other means); that is, *how much*. This may be set for each type of resource separately or for all items collectively; for example, the purchase or production level, or both. Decisions about the number of storage points also affect the quantity in stock.

2. *The frequency or timing of acquisition;* that is, *how often* or *when*.

The decision maker may have control over both or only one of these types of controlled variables. The housewife, for example, does not control the frequency of the milkman's visits (or does she?), but she does control how much of each product he leaves. In many chemical processes, on the other hand, production is always in *batch* quantities; hence control is exercised only over the frequency of batch production. In a typical job shop, managers usually can control both the quantity and the frequency of production.

3. *The stage of completion of stocked items.* The more finished the goods that are held in inventory, the less is the delay in supplying customers but the greater the cost of holding the item. The less finished the item (raw material in the extreme), the longer it takes to fill orders, but the less costly it is to carry the stock. Furthermore, forecasting errors for items in stock tend to increase the more finished the items are, hence the larger a buffer against uncertainty that is required. Finally, the number of different items that must be stocked normally increases rapidly with increases in the degree of completion of the items stocked.

Most of inventory theory has been concerned with only the first two types of controlled variables, hence these will be emphasized. But some consideration will be given to the type of inventory as well.

The uncontrolled variables in inventory problems are divisible into cost variables and others. The principal variables of each type are the following:

1. *Holding costs:* costs that increase in direct proportion to increases in inventory and the time for which stocks are held. The most obvious component, which is strictly proportional to stock level and time, is *the cost of invested capital.* This is an interest charge, and the exact figure often requires careful investigation. On the one hand, a company may be able to borrow capital at 6 per cent; on the other, its return on investment over the previous year may have averaged 20 per cent. Clearly, some investments returned more than others, so that it may not be appropriate to demand 20 per cent from investments in inventory. Yet 6 per cent may well be too low, partly because few companies will choose to exercise the limit of their credit except in extreme emergency, and partly because there may be alternative investments available that are expected to offer higher yields. Consequently, the appropriate rate depends primarily on what other use can be found for the money that is "tied up" in inventory. Selection of this rate is usually a matter that will be decided by the financial management.

In addition to capital costs we must consider *record-keeping* and *administrative charges.* Stocks are of little use unless we know whether or not the item required is in stock. Other relevant components of holding cost are:

(*a*) *Handling costs:* these include the costs of labor to move stock, of overhead cranes, gantries, forklift trucks, and other equipment used for this purpose.

(*b*) *Storage costs:* rent for space or interest and depreciation on owned space.

(*c*) *Insurance and taxes.*

(*d*) *Depreciation, deterioration, and obsolescence costs:* these are particularly relevant for fashion items or items that change chemically during storage, such as foods.

All such costs require investigation, but with the possible exceptions of fashion items and of drugs or foods with limited shelf life, the total holding costs typically vary from 1 to 2 per cent of the invested capital per month. The cost of storage, however, may depend on the amount of space set aside rather than the amount being used; hence it may be constant.

2. *Shortage or penalty costs:* costs that arise when an item that is requested is not available in stock. A physical shortage may not occur when emergency measures can be taken to see that deliveries are made on or before the date that customers require (i.e., expediting). However, there are costs involved in taking such measures: increased transportation charges (airfreight instead of truck); increased setup or overtime costs; administrative costs or the cost of disrupting a planned production schedule. There may also be the cost of standby production facilities which are used only in an emergency. Such facilities may be obsolescent or worn out and have higher production costs than the regular equipment.

When delivery dates are missed and physical shortages occur, the costs are often less tangible. For raw materials, semifinished goods, or spare parts the shortage costs may be those due to idle facilities or disrupted schedules. Alternatively, shortages may result in canceled orders and lost sales, which, in turn, may result in loss of goodwill. The latter involves a cost that is difficult to calculate, but by using the tradeoff techniques discussed in Chapter 2, it is frequently possible to obtain reasonable estimates of its magnitude.

Shortage costs are usually represented in one of two ways. The first assumes that the costs are proportional to both the quantity that is short and the duration of the shortage. This is appropriate only when shortages can be filled by back orders and thus do not result in lost demand. It represents the loss of goodwill or the cost of idle equipment. The second representation involves a fixed cost each time a shortage occurs. This cost covers at least the lost profit per order and may include a component to cover loss of goodwill.

3. *Costs due to changes in production rate.* They include setup costs that result from changing the production rate from zero to some positive amount. In the case of a purchase, they involve the fixed administrative costs of placing an order.

Other costs that depend on changes in production rates are those of hiring and training additional labor, and the corresponding costs of firing. The latter can be large, especially where union contracts enforce a seniority basis for moving personnel. A handful of dismissals can then result in new assignments for a large portion of the labor force. This causes a "learning process" to start while each man settles down to his new task. During such upheavals production rates may be relatively low, inspection rejects may be high, all with attendant high costs.

4. *Purchase price or direct production costs.* The unit cost of purchased items may depend on the quantity purchased because of "price breaks" or "quantity discounts." The unit cost of produced items may also be lower because of greater efficiency of men and machines in long continuous production runs.

5. *Demand:* the number of items required per period. Note that this is not necessarily the amount sold, because some demand may go unfilled because of shortages or delays. It is, in effect, the amount that would be sold if all that is required were available.

Demand may be (or may be assumed to be) known exactly. If this is so, each decision about replenishment has no impact on costs following subsequent decisions. On the other hand, we may have situations in which demand is known only probabilistically, that is, subject to a probability distribution. In such cases each decision may have an impact on those that follow.

As an example of the interdependence of sequential decisions consider a situation in which stocks are to be reviewed every month, and a decision is to be made about whether a production run shall be started. It may happen that stocks are such that the risk of shortage one month does not justify a setup cost. However, by next month we are almost certain to require a setup; therefore, after considering the costs for both months, we might find it profitable to start producing in the first month. Furthermore, when we do produce, we cannot decide on the run-size without considering its effect on the months to come. Problems of this nature are called *dynamic* and seldom have explicit mathematical solutions. However, some powerful techniques are available for computation of numerical approximations.

6. *Lead time:* the time between placing an order and its arrival in stock. If the lead time is known and is not equal to zero, and if demand is known, all that one needs to do is to order in advance by an amount of time equal to the lead time. If, however, it is a variable that is known only probabilistically, the question of when to order is a more difficult one. If either the demand or the lead time is known only probabilistically, the amount and timing of replenishment is found by considering expected costs of holding and shortage over the lead time period.

7. *Amount delivered.* If a quantity q is ordered for purchases or production, the amount delivered may vary around q with a known probability density function. As will be seen, the effect of such uncertainty is the same as the effect of uncertainty relative to demand or lead time.

THE CONTEXTS OF INVENTORY PROBLEMS

On reflection it will be apparent that inventory problems are pervasive and arise in many contexts. For example, the managements of commercial airlines must decide how often to conduct a class to train stewardesses and how large such classes should be. If too many stewardesses are "made," the company must pay salaries to the extra ones. If too few are "made," either flights will have to be cancelled or emergency measures will have to be taken, both of which involve shortage costs. Most "manpower" problems are of the inventory type.

Electric utility companies must determine when to add turboelectric generators to their systems and how large these generators should be. Although only one (multimillion-dollar) piece of equipment is involved, its capacity (quantity) is subject to choice. Therefore, this problem concerns both "how much" and "when." If too large a generator is purchased, or if one is obtained too soon, idle capacity results, which involves a cost (of depreciation and maintenance). If too little capacity is purchased, or if the purchase is made late, sales will be lost and customers and the utility commission will react unfavorably. These reactions involve shortage costs.

The question, How much operating capital should a company keep available? also presents an inventory problem. If too much capital is kept available, earnings from possible investments of the excess are lost—an inventory-carrying cost; if too little is kept available, additional capital will have to be borrowed at premium rates—a shortage cost. There are also setup and take-down costs associated with obtaining loans.

Although inventory problems may arise in a wide variety of contexts, the most common are in the purchasing and production of goods. Hence most of the discussion that follows will use illustrations drawn from this area, but the reader should keep in mind the wide range of contexts to which the discussion is applicable.

THE PERSISTENCE OF INVENTORY PROBLEMS

In any business, inventories provide a continuing source of management problems. This is probably because of all the variables over which managers have control, stock levels are among the easiest to manipulate. Moreover, the capital investment in inventories is readily apparent, so that when working capital is in short supply, it is easy to achieve a reduction in the amount required by curtailing stocks. Unfortunately, such a policy is often a short-run optimization and may ultimately result in increased production or selling costs.

A very simple example occurs when a setup cost is involved. Suppose that each time a batch of a particular item is made, a fixed amount of time is required to prepare the necessary machine tools. During this preparation or setup time no production takes place, but labor and other costs are incurred. If one item is required each day and no stocks are carried, a setup will occur every day; on the other hand, we could set up every other day, make two items for each setup, and carry one of them in inventory. The setup cost *per item* has been halved at the expense of some carrying costs. It is not uncommon for a company that is overly concerned with its investment in stocks to find itself short of production capacity solely because of the amount of nonproductive downtime required for setups. It is part of the task of inventory theory to strike a balance in these situations.

There are other reasons for carrying stocks. Suppose that competitors are prepared to deliver finished goods on three weeks' notice from customers and that the production process normally takes four weeks. If a company makes goods to order, either its customers will turn to other suppliers or the manufacturer will be faced with the problems and costs of expediting to meet delivery dates forced on it by competition. It may well be cheaper to stock finished or partly finished items, so that production does not have to start from scratch each time an order is received. If an item cannot be supplied when a customer requires delivery, we say that a shortage has occurred. Thus a shortage need not arise because an item is out of stock when a customer places an order; it will arise when special steps are required to meet delivery dates. Often the situation changes from time to time. Thus, for many years, steel pipe producers located in the northeastern and north central states were accustomed to ship supplies to Texas oil fields on only several weeks' notice. In effect, customers carried inventories that saw them through production lead times. However, with the advent of some local production and a falling-off in demand, some companies started to deliver from locally held stocks. This forced all suppliers to maintain local stocks for immediate delivery. The balance between lost sales because of shortages in local stocks and the cost of carrying the stocks became a pressing problem.

Still another reason for carrying inventories lies in the anticipation of rising prices. Except for pure speculators who have no other interest than buying and selling, most large companies which use raw materials that are bought and sold on the commodity markets endeavor to increase stocks when prices are deemed favorable. How to forecast prices and how to choose optimal purchasing policies provide many fascinating problems, but for the most part they are outside the scope of an introductory textbook.

THE STRUCTURE OF INVENTORY SYSTEMS

Figure 7.1 shows the structure of a typical inventory system. Such systems have a balance equation that relates stocks at time t to those at a later time t'. Let I_t be the stock at time t, S the quantity added to the inventory in the interval t to t', and D the demand. The physical stock at time t' is given by

$$I_{t'} = I_t + S - D, \tag{7.1}$$

provided that the quantity is positive.[1] However, if the demand exceeds supply, the physical stock will be zero. For bookkeeping purposes, two possible situations arise. If excess demand is back-ordered and is filled as soon as regular supplies become available, it is possible to think of the back orders as negative inventory and (7.1) holds for all values of I_t, S, and D. On the other hand, if excess demand is lost or is met in a special way (e.g., emergency procurement or expedited production), excess demand has no effect on inventory and $I_t = 0$ whenever $I_t + S - D$ is negative. It should be noted that from a mathematical point of view both loss of excess demand and meeting it from special sources have the same effect on inventory, but not on sales.

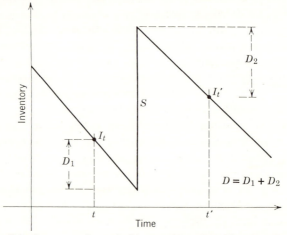

Figure 7.1 Structure of a typical inventory system: $I_t' = I_t + S - D$.

In most inventory problems the controlled variable is the quantity added to inventory, S. We seek the best quantities and the best timing of supply. Occasionally we may be able to control demand, D, or some of its properties. For example, when either the price of a product or the amount spent on advertising or selling it can be manipulated, demand can usually be at least partially controlled. In some cases we may be able to control the uncertainty associated with demand without affecting demand itself. Recall, for example, the case of the abrasive company discussed in Chapter 3. Typically customers ordered supplies almost daily for immediate delivery. This led to a wildly fluctuating demand that could be met only with substantial inventories. The usual technique in such situations is to endeavor to generate purchases in larger quantities by offering quantity discounts. In this case, however, probing revealed the customers' reasons for ordering in small quantities and very

---

[1] Strictly speaking, we should require the condition that the quantity S come into stock in such a way that the demand never reduces the stock to zero during the interval.

frequently. The abrasives, consisting of paper sheets on which the abrasive material was fixed, would curl unless stored under controlled-humidity conditions. The supplier had suitable storage facilities, but the customers did not. Analysis showed that small frequent purchases required a large inventory only if the aggregate demand per item could not be forecast accurately. If demand were known in advance, inventories could be drastically reduced no matter what the average quantity or frequency or purchase. When discounts, depending on customer lead time, were offered, most customers were glad to make use of them; they prepared their production schedules a month in advance and were in a position to supply the manufacturer with the information that he needed to reduce his inventories. This example is not typical of inventory problems, but it shows that the variables that can be controlled may not be as obvious as appears at first glance.

In some cases it may be easier to control demand than supply. In a hydroelectric water-storage facility, for example, the supply of water from rainfall and melting snow is not subject to control, but the demand for electricity on a particular facility in a network of such facilities is at least partially controllable.

When several items are involved, decisions about them need not be independent. Thus there may be limitations on the total inventory or total production costs. In some cases setup costs depend not only on the item to be made but also on the item preceding it. Thus in rolling steel strip it is relatively easy to increase or decrease the thickness (change in distance between rollers), but changing the width is much more expensive because this requires a different set of rollers.

The stock in question may be kept in a single storage facility or there may be one or more plant warehouses that supply regional warehouses, which in turn supply retail outlets. There is usually a time lag between retail orders and demands on the plant, so that simultaneous optimization of stocks at all levels becomes very complicated.

We next consider how to model simple inventory problems.

THE GENERAL DETERMINISTIC PROBLEM FOR ONE ITEM, ONE LEVEL

The deterministic assumptions (i.e., perfect knowledge of parameter values) that are used in this formulation are a gross oversimplification of most real situations. Nevertheless, such a formulation is widely used with considerable success. Actually, all models of inventory situations are approximate representations of reality, and although more elaborate formulas can be found that are not immediately open to criticism, the increased complexity may mask errors and cause an illusion of accuracy that is not always present.

In developing a general deterministic model, we shall spare the reader most of the details of mathematical manipulation, because even though they are straightforward to the mathematician, they are somewhat tedious. The analysis proceeds in three stages:

1. Find an expression for the average cost per unit time.
2. Simplify the expression by the use of relationships between certain variables to reduce the number of variables.
3. Find the values of the remaining variables that minimize the average cost.

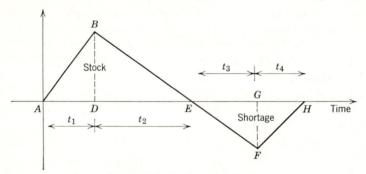

Figure 7.2   An inventory cycle.

The situation that we are going to consider is illustrated in Figure 7.2. Suppose that we wish to supply R units per time period T at a uniform rate $r = R/T$. Production takes place at a uniform rate $k(> r)$, and unfilled orders may be back-ordered. Let

$c_1 =$ holding cost per unit per unit time
$c_2 =$ shortage cost per unit per unit time
$c_3 =$ setup cost per production run
$r =$ demand rate
$k =$ production rate
$q =$ quantity produced per production run
$K =$ average cost per unit time
t_1, t_2, t_3, and t_4 are the times shown in Figure 7.2.

Figure 7.2 shows that there is an inventory cycle. Stocks start at zero and increase for a period t_1. They then decline for a period t_2 until they again reach zero, at which point a backlog piles up for a time t_3. At the end of t_3, production starts, and the backlog is diminished for a time t_4, when the backlog reaches zero. The cycle then repeats itself, after total time of $t_1 + t_2 + t_3 + t_4$.

From Figure 7.2 we see that the holding cost is given by c_1 times the area of triangle ABE. The height of this triangle BD is the maximum stock, which we will denote by S, and the base AE is $t_1 + t_2$. Therefore, the holding cost is

$$\frac{c_1 S(t_1 + t_2)}{2}.$$

The shortage cost is c_2 times the area of triangle EFH. The height of EFH is the maximum shortage, which we denote by s, and the base is $(t_3 + t_4)$. The shortage cost thus is

$$\frac{c_2 s(t_3 + t_4)}{2}.$$

When we add the shortage plus holding costs to the setup cost and divide by the cycle time, $t_1 + t_2 + t_3 + t_4$, we obtain the average cost per unit time K:

$$K + \frac{\frac{1}{2}[c_1 S(t_1 + t_2) + c_2 s(t_3 + t_4)] + c_3}{t_1 + t_2 + t_3 + t_4}. \tag{7.2}$$

At first sight, K is a function of six variables (S, s, t_1, t_2, t_3, and t_4) but there are four relationships, which can be derived from the geometry of Figure 7.2 and which permit us to eliminate all but two variables. An inventory policy is given when we know how much to produce, q, and when to start production, and the latter is given when we know s. However, the algebra is simplified if we express K in terms of t_2 and t_3, and then find the optimal values of t_2 and t_3. We can then use the geometric relationships to find the optimal q and s.

The initial inventory is zero at time A, when the cycle starts, and production continues for a time t_1, until D. During this period an amount kt_1 is produced, but because orders are being filled at a rate r, the net increase in inventory during t_1 is $kt_1 - rt_1 = t_1(k - r)$, and the net increase in inventory is the maximum stock S. Thus

$$S = t_1(k - r). \tag{7.3}$$

The stock S is used up during t_2 and, because the rate of use is r, we have

$$S = t_2 r. \tag{7.4}$$

From (7.4) and (7.3) we see that

$$t_1 = \frac{S}{k - r} = \frac{t_2 r}{k - r}. \tag{7.5}$$

During t_3 shortages accumulate at a rate r; therefore,

$$s = t_3 r. \tag{7.6}$$

During t_4 production is at a rate k and demand at a rate r, so that the net rate of reduction of shortage is $k - r$, and we have

$$s = t_4(k - r). \tag{7.7}$$

From (7.6) and (7.7) it follows that

$$t_4 = \frac{s}{k - r} = \frac{t_3 r}{k - r}. \tag{7.8}$$

Finally, because the total cycle $t_1 + t_2 + t_3 + t_4$ and production is just sufficient to meet demand, we have

$$q = r(t_1 + t_2 + t_3 + t_4), \tag{7.9}$$

and the use of (7.5) and (7.8) in (7.9) yields

$$q = \frac{(t_2 + t_3)k}{k - r}. \tag{7.10}$$

When we substitute from (7.5), (7.6), (7.7), and (7.8) into the equation (7.2), for K we obtain, after some manipulation,

$$K = \frac{\frac{1}{2}kr(c_1 t_2{}^2 + c_2 t_3{}^2) + c_3(k - r)}{k(t_2 + t_3)}. \tag{7.11}$$

To find the best values $t_2{}^0$ and $t_3{}^0$ of t_2 and t_3, we differentiate K with respect to t_2 and t_3 and set the results equal to zero. The resulting equations are then solved. We will omit the details and state the results:

$$t_2{}^0 = \sqrt{\frac{2c_2 c_3(1 - r/k)}{r(c_1 + c_2)c_1}} \tag{7.12}$$

$$t_3{}^0 = \sqrt{\frac{2c_1 c_3(1 - r/k)}{r(c_1 + c_2)c_2}}, \tag{7.13}$$

and with the aid of (7.3) to (7.10) we find (again omitting the details)

$$q^0 = \sqrt{\left(\frac{2rc_3}{c_1}\right)\left(\frac{1}{1 - r/k}\right)\left(\frac{c_1 + c_2}{c_2}\right)} \tag{7.14}$$

$$s^0 = \sqrt{\frac{2rc_1 c_3(1 - r/k)}{(c_1 + c_2)c_2}}, \tag{7.15}$$

Finally, with the optimal values of the decision variables, the minimum value of K is

$$K^0 = \left[\frac{2rc_1 c_2 c_3(1 - r/k)}{c_1 + c_2}\right]^{\frac{1}{2}}. \tag{7.16}$$

Some Special Deterministic Cases

We have deliberately given an outline of a general deterministic model, although in practice further simplifying assumptions are often made. We shall now describe them briefly and show how they affect the results (7.12) to (7.16). The reader may wish to draw diagrams corresponding to Figure 7.2 and to obtain these results by direct analysis.

It often happens that the production rate, k, is so much greater than the demand rate, r, that the total production time, $(t_1 + t_4)$, can be neglected. This is equivalent to allowing k to tend to infinity, and in this case $1/k = 0$ and $(k - r)/k = 1$. When we divide the numerator and the denominator of (7.11) by k and use the results, we find that for *instantaneous production*

$$K = \frac{\frac{1}{2}r(c_1 t_2^2 + c_2 t_3^2) + c_3}{t_2 + t_3}. \tag{7.11a}$$

Equations (7.14), (7.15), and (7.16) become

$$q^0 = \sqrt{\left(\frac{2rc_3}{c_1}\right)\left(\frac{c_1 + c_2}{c_2}\right)} \tag{7.14a}$$

$$s^0 = \sqrt{\frac{2rc_1 c_3}{c_2(c_1 + c_2)}} \tag{7.15a}$$

$$K^0 = \sqrt{\frac{2rc_1 c_2 c_3}{c_1 + c_2}}. \tag{7.16a}$$

A further simplification can be obtained when shortages are not permitted. This is equivalent to allowing the cost of shortage, c_2, to tend to infinity, in which case the shortage part of the cycle, t_3, must become zero. It is worth observing that occasional shortages are inevitable, unless both the lead time and demand rate can be predicted without error. In deterministic models we make precisely this assumption. When c_2 tends to infinity, the ratio $c_2/(c_1 + c_2)$ becomes one. Hence corresponding to (7.11a), (7.14a), (7.15a), and (7.16a) we have[2]

$$K = \frac{1}{2}rc_1 t_2 + \frac{c_3}{t_2} \tag{7.11b}$$

$$q^0 = \sqrt{2r\frac{c_3}{c_1}} \qquad E.O.Q. \tag{7.14b}$$

$$s^0 = 0 \tag{7.15b}$$

$$K^0 = \sqrt{2rc_1 c_3}. \tag{7.16b}$$

---

[2] We shall have occasion to use (7.11b) with t_2 replaced by $t_2 = q/r$; this yields an alternative form for K:

$$K = \frac{1}{2}c_1 q + c_3 r/q .$$

The result (7.14b) is the classical economic lot-size formula. It may be worth-while to reiterate the assumptions on which it is based, although in practice it is often used even when these assumptions do not hold very precisely.

(a) demand is at a fixed, known rate;
(b) lead time is zero (or is known exactly);
(c) production is instantaneous;
(d) no shortages are permitted.

Variable Purchase or Production Costs

The reader may have noticed that, except from setup costs, the costs of production have been ignored so far. This is justified in some cases if the marginal production costs are constant per unit and if all demand is eventually met. Total production costs, excluding setup, do not then depend on inventory policy. In the more general case, we might assume that the cost of producing q units is a nondecreasing function, $f(q)$, with $f(0) = 0$.

In the case of a setup cost, c_3, there is an immediate jump of c_3 in the value of $f(q)$ as soon as q is greater than zero, and we say that $f(q)$ is *discontinuous* when $q = 0$. Often there are other discontinuities in $f(q)$, which must be treated specially when determining lot sizes.

Sometimes quantity discounts are available; that is, the cost per unit depends on the number of units purchased. For example, for purchases up to 1000 units, the unit cost may be one dollar. For purchases of a thousand units or more, the unit cost may be 95 cents. In such a case it would be cheaper to buy 1000 units than any amount between 950 and 1000, even if the surplus had to be discarded. In situations of this type it may be less expensive to exceed the economic lot-size quantity in order to take advantage of the discount.

Let r be the demand rate, C_1 the unit holding cost per unit time, C_3 the fixed cost of placing an order, p the variable cost per unit if we order less than Q, and p' (where $p' < p$) the variable cost if we order more than Q. Then

$$f(q) = \begin{cases} 0 & q = 0 \\ C_3 + qp & 0 < q < Q \\ C_3 + qp' & Q \le q \end{cases} \qquad (7.17)$$

The total cost per unit time when we order in batches of q (compare with equation (7.14b), when t_2 is replaced by $t_2 = q/r$), is

$$K(q) = \begin{cases} \dfrac{C_3 r}{q} + pr + \tfrac{1}{2}C_1 q & 0 < q < Q \\[3mm] \dfrac{C_3 r}{q} + p'r + \tfrac{1}{2}C_1 q & Q \le q \end{cases} \qquad (7.18)$$

Thus $K(q)$ has a discontinuity at $q = Q$, and it may be shown that the minimum value of K occurs either where $dK/dq = 0$ or at the point of discontinuity.

$$\frac{dK}{dq} = \frac{C_3 r}{q^2} + \tfrac{1}{2}C_1, \tag{7.19}$$

except at $q = Q$, where it is not defined. This leads to

$$q^0 = \sqrt{\frac{2C_3 r}{C_1}}. \tag{7.20}$$

We must now consider the case in which $q^0 > Q$, and the case in which $q^0 < Q$.

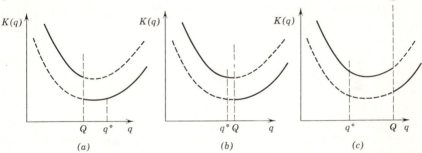

Figure 7.3 Three possible price-break situations. (*a*) $q^0 > Q$; (*b*) $q^0 < Q$; $K(Q) < K(q^0)$; (*c*) $q^0 > Q$; $K(Q) > K(q^0)$. The solid curves are the *actual* cost curves; the dotted curves are the costs that would be obtained without the price breaks.

If $Q \leq q^0$, the minimum value of K occurs when $q = q^0$, and by analogy with equation (7.16*b*) we have

$$K^0 = p'r + \sqrt{2C_1 C_3 r}. \tag{7.21}$$

If $Q > q^0$ and q^0 are purchased, the costs will be

$$pr + \sqrt{2C_1 C_3 r}. \tag{7.22}$$

On the other hand, if we order Q units and obtain the lower price, by analogy with (7.11*b*) the costs are

$$p'r + \frac{C_3 r}{Q} + \tfrac{1}{2}C_1 Q. \tag{7.23}$$

Therefore, it will pay to order Q only when

$$p - p' \geq \frac{1}{r}\left\{\frac{C_3 r}{Q} + \tfrac{1}{2}C_1 Q - \sqrt{2C_1 C_3 r}\right\}. \tag{7.24}$$

The possible situations are shown in Figure 7.3.

The reasoning that has been used in the case involving one price break may be extended to cases involving two or more such price changes.

In cases in which large-order quantities require overtime, the unit cost of production may increase. Suppose that when $q \leq Q$, each unit produced costs p and any units produced in excess of Q cost $p' > p$ each. Thus the production costs $f(q)$ are given by

$$f(q) = \begin{cases} 0 & q = 0 \\ C_3 + pq & 0 < q < Q \\ C_3 + pQ + p'(q - Q) & q \geq Q \end{cases} \qquad (7.25)$$

When $q \geq Q$, we may write $f(q)$ in the alternative form $f(q) = C_3 - (p' - p)Q + p'q$. As in other cases, the total costs per unit time are

$$K(q) = \begin{cases} \dfrac{C_3 r}{q} + pr + \frac{1}{2}C_1 q & 0 < q < Q \\ \dfrac{[C_3 - (p' - p)Q]r}{q} + p'r + \frac{1}{2}C_1 q & q \geq Q \end{cases} \qquad (7.26)$$

It should be clear that for $q > 0$ the function $K(q)$ is continuous; it is also differentiable when $q > 0$, except at $q = Q$. For a function of this type the minimum occurs either at a point where $K'(q) = 0$ or at the point where the derivative is undefined. There are three possible cases, which are shown in Figure 7.4. For clarity of exposition it is convenient to write

$$K_1(q) = \frac{C_3 r}{q} + pr + \frac{1}{2}C_1 q \qquad (7.27)$$

$$K_2(q) = \frac{[C_3 - (p' - P)Q]r}{q} + p'r + \frac{1}{2}C_1 q, \qquad (7.28)$$

so that

$$K(q) = \begin{cases} K_1(q) & q < Q \\ K_2(q) & q > Q \end{cases} \qquad (7.29)$$

Note that $K_1(Q) = K_2(Q)$.

MULTI-ITEM DETERMINISTIC PROBLEM, ONE LEVEL

When stocks consist of several items, limitations on storage capacity or production facilities may frequently prevent the consideration of each item separately. The simplest cases can be handled by means of the Lagrange multiplier technique. As an example consider n items; for the ith item, the setup cost is C_{3i}, the storage cost C_{1i}, and the demand rate r_i. For simplicity we will assume that production is instantaneous and that no shortages are permitted.

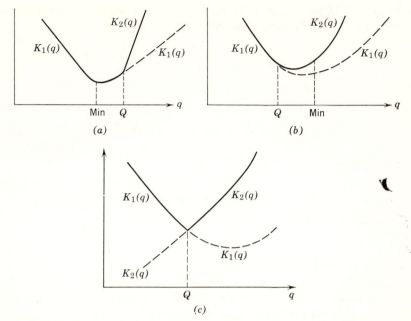

Figure 7.4 Three cases of price breaks. (*a*) $K_1'(q) = 0$ for some $q < Q$; $K_2'(q) > 0$ for all $q > Q$. (*b*) $K'(q) < 0$ for all $q < Q$; $K_2'(q) = 0$ for some $q > Q$. (*c*) $K_1'(q) < 0$ for all $q < Q$; $K_2'(q) > 0$ for all $q > Q$. Minimum is when $q = Q$.

The total cost per unit time is [by analogy with (7.11*b*) when t_2 is replaced by $t_2 = q/r$]

$$K = \sum_{i=1}^{n} \left\{ \tfrac{1}{2} C_{1i} q_i + \frac{C_{3i} r_i}{q_i} \right\}, \tag{7.30}$$

where q_i is the order quantity for item i.

We have

$$\frac{\partial K}{\partial q_i} = \tfrac{1}{2} C_{1i} - \frac{C_{3i} r_i}{q_i^2} \qquad i = 1, 2, \dots, n,$$

and the optimal value of q_i is

$$q_i^{\,0} = \sqrt{\frac{2 r_i C_{3i}}{C_{1i}}}. \tag{7.31}$$

If there is a limitation on inventories that requires that the average number of all stocked items not exceed I, we must minimize K subject to the condition that

$$\tfrac{1}{2} \sum_{i=1}^{n} q_i \leq I. \tag{7.32}$$

If $\sum_{i=1}^{n} q_i^0 < 2I$, there is no problem; if it is not, the equality condition must be imposed by reducing one or more of the q_i^0's. We set

$$L = \sum_{i=1}^{n} \left\{ \tfrac{1}{2} C_{1i} q_i + \frac{C_{3i} r_i}{q_i} \right\} + \lambda \{ \sum_{i=1}^{n} q_i - 2I \}. \tag{7.33}$$

(So long as the constraint is met, $L = K$.)

Now

$$\frac{\partial L}{\partial q_i} = \tfrac{1}{2} C_{1i} - \frac{C_{3i} r_i}{q_i^{2}} + \lambda = 0 \qquad i = 1, 2, \ldots, n, \tag{7.34}$$

which leads to

$$q_i^0 = \sqrt{\frac{2 C_{3i} r_i}{C_{1i} + 2\lambda}}. \tag{7.35}$$

We now have to find λ such that

$$\sum_{i=1}^{n} q_i^0 = 2I.$$

This is best done by trial and error.

Notice that the q_i^0 are chosen in such a way that $\partial K / \partial q_i = -\lambda$ for all i. In other words, the q_i^0 are selected so that the marginal cost of decreasing these quantities for each item is the same per unit.

Example.   Company management has decided that because of limitations on available capital, the average stock level must not exceed 750 items of all types. The company makes three products, and the following are given. What are the optimal production quantities?

Product	1	2	3
C_1	0.05	0.02	0.04
C_3	50	40	60
r	100	120	75

When we use the economic lot-size formula (7.31), we obtain

Product 1: $q_1^0 = \sqrt{\dfrac{2 \times 100 \times 50}{0.05}} = 100\sqrt{20} = 447$

Product 2: $q_2^0 = \sqrt{\dfrac{2 \times 120 \times 40}{0.02}} = 100\sqrt{48} = 693$

Product 3: $q_3^0 = \sqrt{\dfrac{2 \times 75 \times 60}{0.04}} = 100\sqrt{21.5} = 464$

The average inventory will be one-half the sum of these quantities, which is $1604 \div 2 = 802$ and exceeds the 750 allowed. We therefore use (7.35).

We first try $\lambda = 0.005$ and obtain

Product 1: $\qquad q_1^0 = \sqrt{\dfrac{2 \times 100 \times 50}{0.06}} = 100\sqrt{16.67} = 409$

Product 2: $\qquad q_2^0 = \sqrt{\dfrac{2 \times 120 \times 40}{0.03}} = 100\sqrt{32} = 566$

Product 3: $\qquad q_3^0 = \sqrt{\dfrac{2 \times 75 \times 60}{0.05}} = 100\sqrt{18} = 424$

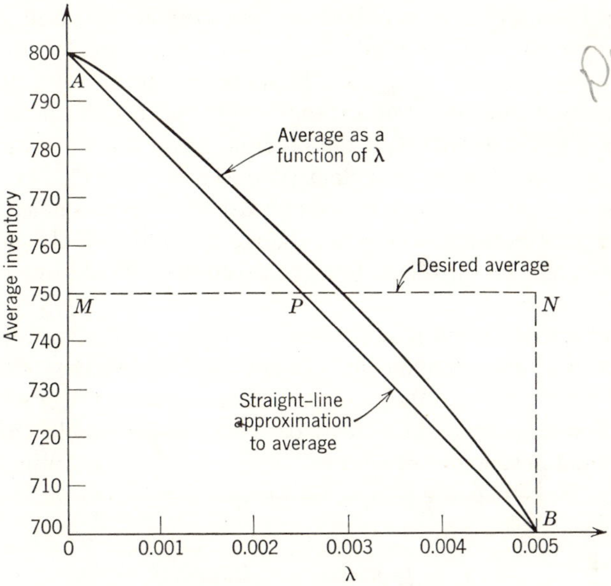

Figure 7.5 Interpolation for λ.

The average inventory will now be $\frac{1}{2}(409 + 566 + 424) \backsimeq 700$. Because this is too low, we require a smaller value of λ, and the best way of finding it is by interpolation. Suppose that we had computed average inventory as a function of λ and obtained Figure 7.5. We know the two points A and B corresponding to $\lambda = 0$ and $\lambda = 0.005$, and we argue that between A and B the unknown curve can be approximated by a straight line. In this case the point P where average inventories are 750 can be found from the similar triangles AMP and BNP. We have

$$\frac{MP}{AM} = \frac{NP}{NB} \quad \text{or} \quad MP = \left(\frac{MN - MP}{NB}\right) AM$$

$$= \left(\frac{0.005 - MP}{50}\right) 52 \quad \text{or} \quad MP = \lambda \backsimeq 0.0025.$$

We can either use this value of λ to recompute the production quantities or interpolate on the quantities found. Because the new value of λ is midway between the earlier values, we argue that the lot sizes will be approximately midway between those found previously. That is,

$$q_1{}^0 = \tfrac{1}{2}(447 + 409) = 428$$

$$q_2{}^0 = \tfrac{1}{2}(693 + 566) = 628$$

$$q_3{}^0 = \tfrac{1}{2}(464 + 424) = 444.$$

The average inventory is now 750, so that the problem is solved.

Another type of multi-item situation arises when items fall into families with a partially common setup cost. Suppose that there are n items in the family; if we have already set up for the family, the cost for starting production of item i is C_{3i}. However, if the previous setup was for an item not in the family, the cost for the first item produced is $C_3 + C_{3i}$. For example, consider the costs of a rolling mill. To increase the thickness of a bar requires altering the gaps between rollers. A change in width, on the other hand, requires a different set of rollers. In this case all bars of the same width form a family.

If demand is known and is at a rate r_i for item i, if holding costs are C_{1i}, and if acquisition is instantaneous, the situation is similar to the ordinary economic lot-size problem. We shall assume that every member of the family is made whenever any member is made. (The reader should consider this assumption and determine the circumstances in which it is optimal.)

Let t be the time between setups. From equation (7.11b) we have

$$K = \tfrac{1}{2}t \sum C_{1i}r_i + \frac{C_3 + \sum C_{3i}}{t}. \tag{7.36}$$

It is a straightforward matter to show that the optimal value of t is given by

$$t^0 = \sqrt{\frac{2(C_3 + \sum C_{3i})}{\sum r_i C_{1i}}} \tag{7.37}$$

and that the optimal production quantities are

$$q_i{}^0 = r_i t^0. \tag{7.38}$$

The reader should consider the case of several families with a constraint on total inventories.

The general problem of families of items in which some members are not made at every setup is one that requires integer programming. Let t be in the interval between family setups and suppose that item i is made at every

j_ith setup. Then the average cost per unit time is

$$K = \frac{C_3}{t} + \sum_i \frac{C_{3i}}{j_i t} + \tfrac{1}{2} \sum_i C_{1i} r_i j_i t. \tag{7.39}$$

We wish to choose $\{j_i\}$ and t so as to minimize K, subject to the constraints that the $\{j_i\}$ are integers and at least one $j_i = 1$. If we forget the constraints and equate $\partial K/\partial t$ and $\partial K/\partial j_i$ to zero, we obtain

$$t = \sqrt{\frac{2(C_3 + \sum C_{3i}/j_i)}{\sum r_i C_{1i} j_i}} \tag{7.40}$$

and

$$j_i = \frac{1}{t} \sqrt{\frac{2C_{3i}}{r_i C_{1i}}}. \tag{7.41}$$

When we substitute for j_i in t, we find $t = 0$, which corresponds to a maximum value of K. Instead, we start by assuming that $j_i = 1$ for all i, and compute the corresponding $t = t_1$ (which minimizes K for $j_i = 1$). We now compute

$$\frac{1}{t_1} \sqrt{\frac{2C_{3i}}{r_i C_{1i}}},$$

and the j_i that minimizes K is one of the integers on either side. Direct calculation easily verifies which one. If any j_i takes a value other than one, the calculations are repeated until we find a "matching set" of $\{j_i\}$ and t. For example, suppose that $C_3 = 22$, and

i	1	2	3
r_i	1	20	25
C_{1i}	1	2	1
C_{3i}	10	6	7

When $j_1 = j_2 = j_3 = 1$, we have $t_1 = \sqrt{90/66} = 1.17$. From t_1 we find $j_1 = 4$, $j_2 = 1, j_3 = 1$. Inserting these values in the formula for t yields $t = 1.09$ and again $j_1 = 4, j_2 = 1, j_3 = 1$. We conclude that these results are optimal.

(Exercises 1 to 6 should be done at this point.)

PROBABILISTIC PROBLEMS

In many situations it is not possible to predict demand exactly over the lead time and runs cannot always start when stocks are at a designated reorder level. As a result, the concept of a buffer stock arose. Suppose that there is a fixed known lead time L between the decision to produce (or buy) and the first deliveries to inventory. On the average we expect a demand for $L\bar{r}$ items (where $\bar{r}$ is the average rate of demand) during this time. Therefore, we would place orders at least by the time that stocks reach $L\bar{r}$. Such a policy would result in shortages about half the time. To avoid this we add a buffer stock of b units and place the order when stocks reach $L\bar{r} + b = s$, where b is so chosen that the probability of running short is small, say 0.05 or 0.01. Strictly speaking, the choice of b involves the relative costs of holding and shortage, and a more careful analysis shows that b and q cannot be optimized independently of each other.

Policies of this type, where stocks are kept under continuous review and fixed quantity orders are placed whenever stocks reach a predetermined level, are sometimes called "two-bin policies." Suppose that we wish to order a quantity q whenever stocks reach a level s. A simple control device, suitable for small items, is to have two containers (bins), one of which holds q and the other s. As soon as the q-bin is empty, an order is placed, and until it arrives we use the contents of the s-bin. When the order arrives, we fill the s-bin and put the remainder in the q-bin. This automatically takes care of reorders, without the need for written records.

It should be noted that if lead time is only known subject to a probability distribution and the demand rate is constant and known, the effect is much the same as a known constant lead time and varying demand. In either case, the reorder point is set so that the probability of shortage during the lead time is suitably low, say equal to α. This means that in the case of a fixed known lead time, we would have to predict the distribution of demand over the lead time and then select the amount of demand that would only be exceeded by a function α of the time. With known demand rate, say r, we would need to reorder when stocks reached s, where the probability of the lead time exceeding s/r is α. In some cases we shall have to consider the joint distribution of both demand rate and lead time.

It is clear that the more accurate the prediction of demand, the less safety stock will be required, and in recent years much attention has been given to methods of predicting future demand from past history. The interested reader should consult the book by R. G. Brown.

Periodic Review Policies

In some circumstances it may not be possible to maintain a continuous review of stocks, but they can be reviewed at fixed intervals. If the policy used in such situations requires a production run at each review, there are two decisions that must be made:

1. How frequently should the review be made?
2. How much should be made following each review?

Sometimes the policy calls only for a review at fixed intervals, and we then need to decide whether or not to produce before deciding how much to make.

Exact formulas for these circumstances are not simple, because they require some ability to manipulate the types of integrals that appear when we compute expected costs. The general pattern of analysis is to find an expression for the costs that would arise if demand were known exactly. There are usually two cases to consider depending on whether stocks are sufficient to meet demand or not. Because we do not know demand in advance, but only the probability of various amounts, we average the costs over the possible demands. This is done by multiplying by the probabilities and either adding or integrating. It is then possible to find optimizing values of the decision variables. Some examples of this type of analysis are treated by Sasieni et al. (1959), and an extensive treatment can be found in Naddor (1965).

Apart from the mathematical manipulation required to produce appropriate formulas, considerable numerical work is needed to obtain values in particular cases. The reason is that the values of the decision variables usually involve integrals that cannot be carried out in terms of tabulated functions. Thus, if there are more than one or two items to be stocked, an electronic computer is the only feasible method of computation. There are many cases in which the costs of such calculations cannot be justified, either because the theoretical savings over simpler approximations are small or because inaccuracies in the data on costs or demands are too large for the benefits of refined calculation.

For these reasons, the economic lot-size formula with forecasts of demand over the lead time is widely used in practical stock-control problems; we conclude this chapter with an illustration.

SOME PRACTICAL INVENTORY PROBLEMS—
AN ILLUSTRATION

As long as we may consider each item in stock to be controlled independently of all others, the analysis of the previous sections can be extended to cover cases of variable lead times and lost demand due to shortages. Numerous papers have been written on such problems, many of which are summarized and synthesized in the works of Hanssmann (1962), Hadley and Whitin (1963), and Wagner (1962). Our experience indicates that the results obtained from the more elaborate mathematical models seldom justify the additional computational effort that they require. Moreover, in cases in which a large number of items (perhaps 50,000, as in the large retail store) have to be controlled, and where such items interact, exact models become too cumbersome even for theoretical analysis.

Consider the following situation, which involves three items made from a common raw material. We shall assume that the raw material has an ordering cost (setup) of $1000 and that storage costs 1¢ per unit per day.

Deliveries of raw material take 7 days. For the finished items we have the data shown in Table 7.1. Shortages of finished items are back-ordered at the costs shown. Shortages of raw materials do not in themselves result in costs, but may cause production delays which, in turn, may cause shortages of finished items.

The first items to notice in Table 7.1 are the setup times and production rates. For example, it is impossible to set up all three items every day, because it takes either a half day or a full day to make the setup. It should also be noted that only the mean daily demand and standard deviations are given,

TABLE 7.1   *Data on Finished Items*

	Items		
	A	B	C
Mean daily demand, r	43	78	25
Standard deviation, σ	20	14	5
Holding cost per day, C_1	1	0.5	1.2
Shortage cost per day, C_2	20	10	30
Setup cost, C_3	800	1000	3000
Setup time, days	0.5	1.0	1.0
Production rate per day, k	192	385	90
Amount of raw material per unit	3	2	5

not the distribution functions. However, if we assume that the distribution functions are independent, then with any reasonably symmetric demand function, the law of large numbers assures us that the total demand over several days (perhaps 10 or more) will be approximately normally distributed.

Let us start by computing the mean daily demand for raw material and its standard deviation. Because the three items require 3, 2, and 5 units of raw material respectively, the total daily demand for raw material averages[3]

$$3 \times 43 + 2 \times 78 + 5 \times 25 = 410$$

and the variance is

$$9 \times 20^2 + 4 \times 14^2 + 25 \times 5^2 = 5009.$$

The standard deviation is about 71.

---

[3] We are using the following results: if $Z = ax + by + cw$, then $\bar{z} = a\bar{x} + b\bar{y} + c\bar{w}$, and if in addition x, y, w are independent, then $V(z) = a^2 V(x) + b^2 V(y) + c^2 V(\bar{w})$, where bars denote averages and $V(\ )$ denotes variance. See any elementary text on probability or statistics.

Now, the economic lot-size equation (7.14*b*) gives the optimal order quantity as

$$q^0 = \sqrt{\frac{2C_3 r}{C_1}} = \sqrt{\frac{2 \times 1000 \times 410}{0.01}} \simeq 9000,$$

which is 22 days' supply. In practice, if the plant works seven days a week, we would probably order every three weeks. If the plant works a five-day week (and Table 7.1 refers to working days), we would order every month. To continue the example, we shall assume a seven-day week.

Because the amount ordered plus the amount on hand must last until the next delivery, which will occur after an order interval plus a lead time, that is, $22 + 7 = 29$ days, we shall need a total quantity of 29 days' demand plus a buffer stock to take care of the variance. Let us assume that 3 standard deviations will be a sufficient buffer. The daily standard deviation is 71. Therefore, for 29 days we shall require a buffer of $3 \times \sqrt{29} \times 71 = 1130$. Consequently, to cover all contingencies over 29 days, we need a quantity of $1130 + (29 \times 410) = 13,020$. Our ordering rule would be:

Every 22 days order enough to make the stock on hand together with that on order total 13,020.

Therefore, if the stock on hand is 3000, we would order $13,020 - 3000 = 10,020$.

An alternative policy would be to order an economic lot-size quantity (9000) every time the stock is just sufficient to last over the lead time (7 days). Thus orders would be placed whenever stocks drop to $7 \times 410 + 3\sqrt{7} \times 71 = 3431$. Such a policy would result in slightly lower stocks, but might involve the increased costs of a "continuous" review as contrasted with a regular review every 22 days.

Either of the policies considered will virtually assure the availability of raw material when it is required.

We now turn to the finished items, assuming that no shortages of raw material occur. Several types of policy are possible, and we shall discuss a few of them.

A Two-Bin or S-s Policy

Such policies require us to order S minus any stock on hand whenever the stock drops below s. The difficulty here is to determine s, because s should be approximately sufficient to cover demand until deliveries take place, and the lead time depends on what production must come before the work starts on the order in question. Thus, if there are no orders in process, deliveries of item *A* will start half a day from the order date and continue at a rate of 192 per day until the order is filled. On the other hand, if items *B* and *C* have to be produced first, production will not start for several days. This implies that the trigger level *s* either must vary from day to day depending on shop loadings or must be sufficient to cover the case in which the other two items must be produced first. The first policy would be very difficult to apply in practice, whereas the second could result in excessive stocks.

Order at Fixed Intervals for Each Product

We can compute the intervals for each product separately by using the economic lot-size formula. In order to produce a workable schedule, it would be necessary to adjust the intervals so that they were integral multiples of the smallest. This might work well if there were sufficient finished items to balance the production load in successive intervals, but with only three items this is not possible. It will be found that the optimal intervals are about 7, 5, and 15 days for items *A*, *B*, and *C*, respectively. We might approximate this by making *A* and *B* every week and *C* every other week. The production times including setups are as follows:

$$\text{Item } A: \quad 0.5 + \frac{7 \times 43}{192} = 2.0 \text{ days}$$

$$\text{Item } B: \quad 1.0 + \frac{7 \times 78}{385} = 2.5 \text{ days}$$

$$\text{Item } C: \quad 1.0 + \frac{14 \times 25}{90} = 4.9 \text{ days}$$

In week 1, in which *A* and *B* are made, production capacity is sufficient, but in week 2, when all three items are made, there would be work for $2.0 + 2.5 + 4.9 = 9.4$ days, which, of course would run into the following week. Overall capacity is sufficient because every 14 days we have $9.4 + (2.0 + 2.5) = 13.5$ days' work. However, the calculation of buffer stocks would be difficult, and a schedule of this type would be hard to operate.

These difficulties, due to unbalanced loadings, suggest that we try to use the same interval between production runs for all items.[4]

---

[4] This is probably the best policy in this example. In problems with large numbers of items, balancing of loads would be easier. We are not suggesting, however, that fixed intervals for all items is always the best policy.

Common Order Intervals for All Items

In order to derive a formula for the best common order interval, we shall use the following notation (see Figure 7.2):

C_{1i} = holding cost per item per day for item i
C_{2i} = shortage cost per item per day
C_{3i} = setup cost for item i
k_i = production rate
r_i = mean daily demand
t_{1i} = production part of cycle when stocks are positive
t_{2i} = nonproduction part of cycle when stocks are positive
t_{3i} = nonproduction part of cycle when stocks are negative
(i.e., when there is a backlog)
t_{4i} = production part of cycle when there is a backlog
$t = t_{1i} + t_{2i} + t_{3i} + t_{4i}$ = common cycle time
K = total cost per unit time.

The analysis is very similar to the reasoning used to obtain (7.11). For each separate item we have a cost K_i analogous to K on (7.11), and the total cost is simply the sum of the K_i. Thus

$$K_i = \frac{\frac{1}{2}k_i r_i (C_{1i} t_{2i}^2 + C_{2i} t_{3i}^2) + C_{3i}(k_i - r_i)}{k_i(t_{2i} + t_{3i})} . \tag{7.42}$$

The total cost per cycle **R** is

$$K = \sum K_i. \tag{7.43}$$

We now have to minimize K with respect to t_{1i}, t_{2i} subject to the condition of a common cycle time t, that is,

$$t_{1i} + t_{2i} + t_{3i} + t_{4i} = t. \tag{7.44}$$

We use results similar to (7.5) and (7.8) to express (7.44) in terms of t_{2i} and t_{3i} only. We obtain

$$t = \frac{(t_{2i} + t_{3i})k_i}{r_i(k_i - r_i)}, \tag{7.45}$$

and our problem is to minimize k subject to (7.45). This is done in two stages with the aid of a Lagrange multiplier. We start by assuming that t is known and find t_{2i}, t_{3i} in terms of t. We then obtain K as a function of t only, and complete the solution by finding the optimal t. The results are:

$$t^0 = \left[2 \sum c_{3i} / \sum \frac{r_i c_{1i} c_{2i}(1 - r_i/k_i)}{(c_{1i} + c_{2i})} \right]^{\frac{1}{2}} \tag{7.46}$$

and

$$q_i^0 = t^0 r_i. \tag{7.47}$$

When we insert the data of Table 7.1 into equation (7.46), we have

$$(t^0)^2 = \cfrac{2(800 + 1000 + 3000)}{\cfrac{1 \times 20 \times 43(1 - 43/192)}{20 + 1} + \cfrac{0.5 \times 10 \times 78(1 - 78/385)}{10 + 0.5}} \simeq 116$$

$$+ \cfrac{1.2 \times 30 \times 25(1 - 25/90)}{30 + 1.2}$$

Hence t^0 is about 10.

If all three items are made on a ten-day cycle, we may be able to make a decision on production quantities as each run starts, in which case the stock on hand and on order must be sufficient to meet ten days' demand. It is much more likely, however, that we will wish to draw up a schedule of production at the start of each ten-day cycle. If the items are made in the order A, B, C, then A has virtually no lead time and the stock (including the production quantity) must be sufficient for ten days. For item B there is a lead time of the production and setup times for A plus the setup time for B. For item C there is a lead time of the production and setup times for A and B plus the setup time for C. The production times will vary slightly depending on demand in the previous cycle, but we may take them to be the times to produce the average demand over ten days without serious error. The stocks actually required may be computed roughly as the average demand plus, say, two standard deviations.

The reader should compute the stock levels for each item.

We have simulated this problem on a computer, and it is of interest that the common cycle time, using rough calculations at the last stage, can yield costs that are about one half of those of a separate "two-bin" policy for each finished item.

SUMMARY

This chapter is a long one because inventory problems are much more varied than appears at first sight and because there have been many successful applications of operations research in this area. The practitioner must be aware of the pitfalls that occur in unreflective use of elegant inventory mathematics with which the literature abounds. What is usually wanted in a practical problem is a good approximation that has the merit of simplicity of computation and implementation and which is easy to explain to those who must accept and use it. One must remember that the tacit assumption of fixed and known parameters is often far from realistic and the assumption of a known distribution for demand (let alone deterministic demand) is seldom justified. Consequently, the installation of an inventory control system must usually be a compromise involving the costs of data collection and the degree of control that may be exercised. Clearly, the more accurate the forecast of demand, the greater is the degree of control that can be obtained. In many situations the critical problem is to forecast demand over the lead time.

EXERCISES

1. A certain item costs $235 per ton. The monthly requirements are 5 tons, and each time that the stock is replenished there is a setup cost of $1000. The cost of carrying inventory has been estimated at 10 per cent of the value of the stock per year. What is the optimal ordering quantity?

   If in estimating the carrying costs interest charges of 6 per cent per year were omitted, what would be the cost of the error (i.e., the difference between the true optimal policy cost and the actual cost using carrying costs of only 10 per cent)?

2. Develop an economic lot-size formula in the following circumstances:

   (*a*) Orders for replenishment can only be placed on the first day of a calendar month.
   (*b*) If an order is placed, delivery is immediate.
   (*c*) Demand is *r* per month and arises only on the 15th of each month.
   (*d*) Carrying costs are C_1 per unit per month.
   (*e*) No shortages are permitted.
   (*f*) Setup costs are C_3.

3. A factory produces *n* different items. For item $i = 1, 2, \ldots, n$ we have:

$$C_{1i} = \text{holding cost per unit per month}$$
$$C_{3i} = \text{setup cost}$$
$$r_i = \text{demand per month}$$
$$k_i = \text{production rate.}$$

No shortages are permitted and it is assumed that production capacity is sufficient to meet all demand; that is,

$$\sum_{i=1}^{n} > \frac{r_i}{k_i} \leq 1.$$

Because of limitations of skilled labor, the average number of setups per month for all items must not exceed *m*.

(a) Let q_i be the order quantity for item i; obtain an expression for the average number of setups per month.

(b) Find the optimal number of setups if we ingore m.

(c) Assuming that m is smaller than the number found in (b), show how to determine the optimal policy.

4. A factory supplies two depots. The holding cost at the factory is C_1 and the setup cost is C_3. Demand arises only at the depots and is r_1 and r_2 per month. There is a shipping setup cost of C_{31} and C_{32} at each depot and holding costs of C_{11} and C_{12}. Production takes place at rate k and shortages are not permitted. Find the optimal policy.

(*Hint:* Let q be the production quantity, and q_1 and q_2 the quantities sent to the depots in each shipment. Find the average inventory computed as if the demand were r_1 and r_2 at the factory, less the average inventories at the depot. Show that there will be no shortages, provided that we can find integers n_1 and n_2 such that

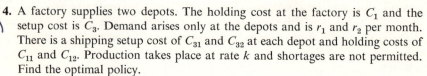

$$\frac{q}{r_1 + r_2} = \frac{n_1 q_1}{r_1} = \frac{n_2 q_2}{r_2}$$

Hence show how to find q, q_1, and q_2.)

5. The manufacture of a certain item is a two-stage process. The setup cost for the first stage is C_{31}. There are several machines available for the second stage, and for each setup there is a cost C_{32}. The capacity of the first stage is unlimited, but for the second stage each machine that is set up can produce any quantity up to Q. Thus if the first stage batch is $q \le Q$, exactly one second stage machine is needed; if $Q < q \le 2Q$, two stage machines are needed, and so on. The holding cost for finished items is C_1 per unit per unit time and the demand rate is r. If total production time is negligible, show how to find the optimal policy. Compute the policy when $r = 100$, $C_1 = 1$, $C_{31} = 500$, $C_{32} = 200$, and $Q = 120$.

6. A company makes three products, details of which are given in Table 7.2. It will be found that because of the time taken to make setups, there is insufficient capacity to make each product in the amount given by the economic lot-size formula $q = [2C_3 r / C_1 (1 - r/k)]^{\frac{1}{2}}$. What should the production quantities be? Note that the setup time on one product cannot start until production of the previous period has ended.

TABLE 7.2

Product, i	1	2	3
Daily demand r_i	100	200	150
Production rate k_i	500	800	300
Holding cost/day C_{1i}	0.01	0.016	0.012
Setup cost C_3	360	480	45
Setup time (days)	0.25	0.25	0.5

Suggested Readings

Books on inventory may be divided into two main groups—those that deal with theory and those that deal with practice. The former may also be classified by the level of mathematical sophistication required. An extensive bibliography is given by Hanssmann (1961), who also provides a review of progress in the field. Three books that require little mathematical knowledge and which are designed for practitioners are Bowman and Fetter (1961), Magee (1958), and Brown (1959). Brown provides an extended treatment of forecasting, particularly as it relates to inventory control. At a moderate level of mathematics are books by Buchan and Koenigsberg (1963), Fetter and Dalleck (1961), Hadley and Whitin (1963), Wagner (1962), Whitin (1953), and Hanssmann (1962). Hanssmann gives the most extended treatment of multilevel and multi-item problems. Finally, for an advanced treatment of the mathematical theory of inventory see Arrow, Karlin, and Scarf (1958).

Bibliography

Arrow, K. J., S. Karlin, and H. Scarf, *Studies in the Mathematical Theory of Inventory and Production*, Stanford University Press, Stanford, Calif., 1958.

Bowman, E. H., and R. B. Fetter, *Analysis for Production Management*, Richard Irwin, Homewood, Ill., 1961.

Brown, R., *Statistical Forecasting for Inventory Control*, McGraw-Hill Book Co., New York, 1959.

Buchan, J., and E. Koenigsberg, *Scientific Inventory Management*, Prentice-Hall, Englewood Cliffs, N.J., 1963.

Fetter, R. B., and W. C. Dalleck, *Decision Models for Inventory Management*, Richard Irwin, Homewood, Ill., 1961.

Hadley, G., and T. M. Whitin, *Analysis for Inventory Systems*, Prentice-Hall, Englewood Cliffs, N.J., 1963.

Hanssmann, F., "A Survey of Inventory Theory from the Operations Research Viewpoint", in *Progress in Operations Research*, Vol. I, R. L. Ackoff (ed.), John Wiley and Sons, New York, 1961, pp. 65–104.

———, *Operations Research in Production and Inventory Control*, John Wiley and Sons, New York, 1962.

Magee, J. F., *Production Planning and Inventory Control*, McGraw-Hill Book Co., New York, 1958.

Naddor, E., *Inventory Systems*, John Wiley and Sons, New York, 1965.

Sasieni, M. W., A. Yaspan, and L. Friedman, *Operations Research: Methods and Problems*, John Wiley and Sons, New York, 1959.

Wagner, H., *Statistical Management of Inventory Systems*, John Wiley and Sons, New York, 1962.

Whitin, T. M., *Theory of Inventory Management*, Princeton University Press, Princeton, N.J., 1953.

CHAPTER 8

Replacement, Maintenance, and Reliability Problems

INTRODUCTION

Almost all industrial and military equipment deteriorates with age or usage, unless action is taken to maintain it. In some cases instead of maintenance it may be more economical to replace the equipment altogether. It often happens that items are replaced not because they no longer perform to their designed standards, but because more modern equipment performs to higher standards. In this chapter we consider how decisions about replacement and maintenance should be made. In practice the two problems overlap; for example, replacing a generator on a truck is replacement as far as the generator is concerned and maintenance as far as the truck is concerned. Actually, most maintenance and repair consists of replacing subassemblies; the removed subassemblies may be scrapped or sent back to a specialized shop that repairs them. However, for purposes of analysis we shall distinguish three types of problems:

1. Major capital equipment, which often can be used indefinitely, but at a cost that steadily increases with age.
2. Equipment that is replaced in anticipation of complete failure, the probability of which increases with age.
3. The selection of a preventive maintenance scheme, which is designed to reduce the probability of failure.

CAPITAL EQUIPMENT

Suppose that we run a truck, which costs $3000 when new. We wish to determine how frequently it should be replaced, and we have the estimates shown in Table 8.1. The salvage value is the amount for which the truck

TABLE 8.1

Year	1	2	3	4	5	6	7
Salvage value	2000	1333	1000	750	500	300	300
Running cost	600	700	800	900	1000	1200	1500

could be sold at the end of the year, and the running costs are those of gasoline, taxes, insurance, maintenance, and repair during the year. We can now prepare Table 8.2. It is clear that the lowest average cost per year is achieved by replacing at the end of 5 years. Actually, the difference in costs for replacement at any age between 3 and 7 is so small that for practical purposes we might choose any age in this interval. In interpreting such computations it must be realized that the costs are only estimates and that the final decision might well depend on the price at which a new truck can be purchased.

The same type of reasoning may be used to decide which of several alternative pieces of equipment should be purchased. We compute the average cost per year for each, assuming replacement at the optimal age (it need not be the same for all items under consideration). We then choose the item with the lowest average cost.

Notice that this reasoning assumes implicitly that we will have a need for the equipment over an indefinite period in the future. This need not be so. Suppose that we have the data in Table 8.1 and that we will need a truck only for the next 7 years. If we presently have a one-year-old truck, what should our policy be? We prepare Table 8.3, in which all costs are from age one on. Depreciation is the difference between salvage value at age one ($2000) and salvage value at the age considered.

In addition to the costs during the remaining life of our present truck, we shall have the cost of a new truck for the balance of the next 7 years. For example, if we replace the present truck at age 5, we shall have to buy a new truck for the last 3 years at a cost (see Table 8.2) of $4100. Thus over the

TABLE 8.2

Age at Replacement	1	2	3	4	5	6	7
Total running cost	600	1300	2100	3000	4000	5200	6700
Depreciation[a]	1000	1667	2000	2250	2500	2700	2700
Total cost	1600	2967	4100	5250	6500	7900	9400
Cost per year	1600	1483	1367	1312	1300	1317	1343

[a] The difference between purchase price and salvage value.

TABLE 8.3

Age at Replacement	2	3	4	5	6	7
Total running cost	700	1500	2400	3400	4600	6100
Depreciation	667	1000	1250	1500	1700	1700
Total cost	1367	2500	3650	4900	6300	7800

TABLE 8.4

Age of Replacing Present Truck	2	3	4	5	6	7
Cost for present truck	1367	2500	3650	4900	6300	7800
Cost for new truck	7900	6500	5250	4100	2967	1600
Total cost	9276	9000	8900	9000	9267	9400

7 years the total cost would be $4100 + 4900 = 9000$. If we examine the other possible ages for replacing the present truck, we obtain Table 8.4. Thus we replace our present truck at age 4 and buy a new one for the last 4 years.

DISCOUNTING COSTS

The analysis above assumes that we are indifferent to the time at which money is spent. If we have to borrow or if we have alternative investments available, this may not be the case. Let us assume that money carries a rate of interest, i, per year. A dollar invested now will be worth $(1 + i)$ a year hence, $(1 + i)^2$ two years hence, and $(1 + i)^n$ in n years' time. It follows that if we have to make a payment of one dollar in n years' time, it is equivalent to a payment today of $(1 + i)^{-n}$. We say that the *present value* of one dollar due in n years is $(1 + i)^{-n}$ or if $v = (1 + i)^{-1}$, the present value is v^n.

Now suppose that a new truck costs C and that the salvage value at the end of year n is S_n. Let the running cost in year n be R_n, assumed to be payable at the start of the year.[1]

---

[1] If costs occur during the year, they may be discounted to the start of the year. We could assume that costs occur continuously over the year, in which case discounting requires the use of integral calculus. For most problems of the type considered, sufficient accuracy is obtained by assuming that expenditure takes place halfway through the year. Let j be the rate of interest per half year and i the rate per year. Then one dollar invested for six months becomes $(1 + j)$ dollars, and if this is invested for a second six months, the total at the end of the year is $(1 + j)^2$ dollars. Thus

$$1 + i = (1 + j)^2 \quad \text{or} \quad 1 + j = \sqrt{(1 + i)}.$$

It follows that one dollar due in six months' time has a present value of $1/\sqrt{(1 + i)} = \sqrt{v}$.

If we replace the truck at the end of year k, the present value of all the costs is

$$C - v^k S_k + \sum_{n=0}^{k-1} v^n R_n. \tag{8.1}$$

A present value of P is equivalent to payments of x at the start of each year for k years, where

$$P = x + vx^2 + \cdots + vx^{k-1}$$

$$= \frac{x(1 - v^k)}{1 - v}.$$

Thus

$$x = \frac{P(1 - v)}{(1 - v^k)}, \tag{8.2}$$

and the present value of all payments over the life of the truck is equivalent to fixed annual payments of

$$X = \frac{[C - v^k S_k + \sum_{n=0}^{k-1} v^n R_n](1 - v)}{1 - v^k}. \tag{8.3}$$

We wish to choose k to minimize the equivalent fixed cost, which is the same as minimizing $X/(1 - v)$ which we shall denote by $f(k)$:

$$f(k) = \frac{C - v^k S_k + \sum_{n=0}^{k-1} v^n R_n}{1 - v^k}. \tag{8.4}$$

The best way to compute the optimal k is to tabulate $f(k)$.

Again it should be noted that this reasoning needs modification if a truck is not required indefinitely.

As a numerical example we shall rework the truck problem, using the data of Table 8.1 and an interest rate of 10 per cent per year. We shall assume that running costs may be treated as if they occurred at midyear and shall discount them to the start of the year; to do so, we multiply them by $(1 + i)^{-\frac{1}{2}} = v^{\frac{1}{2}}$. When interest is at 10 per cent, we may compute $v^{\frac{1}{2}} = 1/\sqrt{1.1} = 0.95346$. The remaining calculations are shown in Table 8.5.

Table 8.5 is self-explanatory except for lines 9 and 10. Line 9 is the purchase price ($\$3000$) plus the discounted running costs (line 7) minus the discounted salvage value (line 8). Line 10 is line 9 divided by $1 - v^n$.

It can be seen that discounting has not affected the optimal replacement period, which is still five years. It will often happen that interest makes little or no difference to the optimal replacement age, especially for items that last only a few years. However, interest can affect profitability. For our example, at 10 per cent interest the equivalent constant annual cost (with five-year life) is

$$(1 - v)f(k) = 0.0909 \times 1528.3 = 1389.4$$

[see equations (8.3) and (8.4)].

This figure may be compared with an average annual cost of $1300 (Table 8.2) when no interest is charged. In other words, the truck would have to earn an annual revenue of $1300 to break even if we were not charging

TABLE 8.5

1. Year, n	1	2	3	4	5	6
2. Running cost (midyear) R_n'	600	700	800	900	1000	1200
3. Running cost (start of year) $R_n = v^{\frac{1}{2}}R_n'$	572.1	667.4	762.8	858.1	953.5	1144.2
4. v^n	0.9091	0.8264	0.7513	0.6830	0.6209	0.5736
5. Salvage value (year-end) S_n	2000	1333	1000	750	500	300
6. Discounted running cost $v^{n-1}R_n$	572.1	606.7	630.4	644.6	651.2	710.4
7. Total discounted running cost $\Sigma v^{n-1}R_n$	572.1	1177.9	1808.3	2453.3	3104.2	3814.6
8. Discounted salvage value $v^n S_n$	1818.2	1101.6	751.3	512.3	310.4	169.1
9. Total discounted costs (including purchase)	1753.9	3076.3	4057.0	4940.7	5793.8	6645.5
10. $f(n)$	1929.5	1772.1	1631.3	1558.6	1528.3	1558.5

interest, and a revenue of $1389.4 if the funds used to purchase and run the truck could be made to earn 10 per cent when invested elsewhere.

(Exercises 1, 2, and 3 should be done at this point.)

REPLACEMENT IN ANTICIPATION OF FAILURE

In the previous section we considered equipment that wears out or deteriorates with use, so that the costs of operation tend to increase with time. We then balanced the increased running costs against decreased depreciation, so that we could find an optimal life. In this section we turn to items that fail suddenly, thus precipitating costs of failure. The costs of failure may be quite high as compared to the value of the item itself. For example, a tube or condenser in aircraft navigational equipment is inexpensive, but failure may cause errors that could result in loss of an aircraft. In industrial equipment failures can cause loss of production and may result in damaged or faulty products. In some cases failures may involve safety risks to personnel.

To avoid the costs of sudden failures, we try to predict when they are likely to occur and try to replace the item before it actually fails. Sometimes inspection reveals minute defects, which permit the item to operate but indicate the likelihood of early failure. The question then arises of how frequently inspections should be made. Even when inspection does not reveal useful information, we can often predict the time of a failure by knowing the probability distribution of the age at which failure occurs.

TABLE 8.6 *Failure Probabilities*

Shifts since replacement	10	11	12	13	14	15	16	17	18	19	20	21	22	23	24	25
Probability of failure, if not failed previously (%)	0	4	9	14	19	26	33	40	47	54	61	68	76	84	92	100

We now examine how knowledge of the probability of failure can be used to determine a replacement policy. Consider a longwall coal mine, in which coal is cut and loaded onto a conveyor belt that runs along the coal face and may be 100 yards in length. If the belt breaks, loading stops and on the average one eighth of a shift's coal will be lost while the belt is being repaired. The output of such a face might be 500 tons per shift at a pithead price of $12. Thus the lost output per belt failure averages $750; in addition there is the cost of replacement, which might average $500 after allowing for salvage value. The probability of failure is given in Table 8.6. When should the belt be replaced? (Replacement can be made during a night shift when coal is not cut.) We now determine the best age of replacement (number of shifts) so as to minimize the average cost per shift. Let t be the age at replacement and let θ_t be the average number of shifts per belt. Let p_x be the probability that the belt fails at age x. Consider a large number, N, of new belts. Because a fraction p_x will last a time $x(x < t)$ and a fraction $p_t + p_{t+1} + p_{t+2} + \cdots$ will be removed at time t, the total number of "belt shifts" obtained is

$$Np_1 + 2Np_2 + 3Np_3 + \cdots + (t-1)Np_{t-1} + tN(p_t + p_{t+1} + \cdots);$$

on dividing by the number of belts, N, we obtain the average life θ_t. The terms in θ_t may be regrouped to yield a neater expression:

$$
\begin{aligned}
\theta_t = \; & (p_1 + p_2 + p_3 + \cdots + p_t + p_{t+1} + \cdots) \\
+ \; & \quad (p_2 + p_3 + \cdots + p_t + p_{t+1} + \cdots) \\
+ \; & \qquad\quad (p_3 + \cdots + p_t + p_{t+1} + \cdots) \\
+ \; & \\
\cdot \; & \\
\cdot \; & \\
\cdot \; & \\
+ \; & \qquad\qquad\qquad\qquad (p_{t-1} + p_t + p_{t+1} + \cdots) \\
+ \; & \qquad\qquad\qquad\qquad\qquad (p_t + p_{t+1} + \cdots).
\end{aligned}
$$

If we define P_x as the probability of failing after age x, the terms in parentheses are $P_0, P_1, \ldots, P_{t-1}$ and

$$\theta_t = P_0 + P_1 + \cdots + P_{t-1}; \tag{8.5}$$

the next step is to find the cost over a large number of shifts, T. In time T we shall use T/θ_t belts, and a fraction p_x will fail at age x. The total fraction that fail is $p_0 + p_1 + p_2 + \cdots + p_{t-1}$, and the remainder will be replaced at age t before failure. Thus $T(p_0 + p_1 + \cdots + p_{t-1})/\theta_t = T(1 - P_{t-1})/\theta_t$ will fail, and TP_{t-1}/θ_t will be replaced at age t without failure. The cost over time T is $[1250T(1 - P_{t-1}) + 500TP_{t-1}]/\theta_t$, and on dividing by T we obtain the average cost per shift:

$$K_t = \frac{1250(1 - P_{t-1}) + 500P_{t-1}}{\theta_t} = \frac{1250 - 750P_{t-1}}{\theta_t}. \tag{8.6}$$

To determine the best value of t, we tabulate K_t, but first we must compute P_{t-1}. The probability of failure at age x, if a previous failure has not occurred, is given in Table 8.6. If we denote this probability by q_x, then

$$q_x = \frac{p_x}{P_{x-1}}$$

or

$$p_x = P_{x-1}q_x. \tag{8.7}$$

from Table 8.6 we see that nothing fails before age 11; therefore,

$$P_{10} = \text{probability of failing after age } 10 = 1. \tag{8.8}$$

Again using Table 8.6, we see that $q_{11} = 0.04$, and when we consider (8.7) and (8.8), we obtain

$$p_{11} = 0.04.$$

Now $P_{11} = 1 - (p_0 + p_1 + \cdots + p_{11}) = 1 - 0.04 = 0.96$. Therefore, from (8.7) and Table 8.6 we see that

$$p_{12} = 0.96 \times 0.09 = 0.0864.$$

Therefore, $P_{12} = 1 - (0.04 + 0.0864) = 0.8736$ and $p_{13} = 0.8736 \times 0.14 = 0.1223$. Continuing in this fashion, we can compute Table 8.7.

The first four lines of Table 8.7 give x, p_x, P_x and θ_x. The next line gives $1250 - 750P_{x-1}$, which is the average cost per belt, and the last line gives K_x, which is the average cost per shift. It is clear that the belt should be replaced after 12 shifts if it has not failed previously.

It should be observed that preventive replacement cannot always be justified. In particular, when the conditional probability of failure is independent of age, there is as much chance of a new item failing as of an old item and preventive replacement is of no use. This situation arises when the principal cause of failure is an accident. Of course, if the additional costs of failure are very small, there may be no point in trying to anticipate them.

TABLE 8.7

x	10	11	12	13	14	15
p_x	0	0.04	0.0864	0.1223	0.1429	0.1583
P_x	1.0	0.96	0.8736	0.7519	0.6090	0.4507
$\theta_x = \sum_{i=0}^{x-1} P_i$	10	11	11.96	12.83	13.59	14.19
$1250 - 750P_{x-1}$	500	500	530	592.8	686.1	793.3
$K_x =$	50	45.6	44.3	46.2	50.5	56.2

The reader should now verify that if C_F is the cost of a failure (including replacement) and C_R is the cost of replacement alone, the general expression for K_t is

$$K_t = \frac{C_F - (C_F - C_R)P_{t-1}}{\theta_t}. \tag{8.9}$$

(Exercise 5 should be done at this point.)

GROUP REPLACEMENT

It often happens that a system contains a large number of identical low-cost items that are increasingly liable to failure with age and that there is a setup cost for replacement that is independent of the number replaced. In such cases it may be advantageous to replace all items at fixed intervals. Such a policy is called *group replacement* and is particularly attractive when the value of any individual item is so small that the cost of keeping records of individual ages cannot be justified. The classic example of such a policy is that used in replacing street light bulbs; the major cost of replacement is the cost of bringing a truck and crew to the defective bulb. Once the crew is on the street, the additional labor cost of replacing every bulb is extremely small.

The simplest model of a group replacement policy is one which assumes that items fail in the interval of time kt to $(k + 1)t$ are replaced individually at time $(k + 1)t$ and that all items in the system are replaced at intervals nt. For example, failed items are replaced at the end of the week of failure and all items are replaced every 26 weeks. Notice that when group replacement occurs, *all* items are replaced, including some which, being replacements, may be almost new.

Let p_k be the probability that a new item will fail in the interval kt to $(k + 1)t$, and let C_I be the cost of replacing an individual item that has failed. Let C_G be the cost per item of replacing the items as a group. We start by assuming that the system has a large number N of items, all new at time zero, and compute the replacements at time $t, 2t, 3t, \ldots, (n - 1)t$. At time nt all items are replaced. Let f_k be the replacement at time kt. Of the replacements at time $(k - 1)t$, there will be a fraction p_0 that fail by kt; of replacements at $(k - 2)t$, a fraction p_1 will fail between $(k - 1)t$ and kt; of replacements at $(k - 3)t$ a fraction p_2 will fail between $(k - 1)t$ and kt and so on. Hence we obtain the equations:

$$f_0 = N$$
$$f_1 = f_0 p_0$$
$$f_2 = f_0 p_1 + f_1 p_0$$
$$f_3 = f_0 p_2 + f_1 p_1 + f_2 p_0 \qquad (8.10)$$
$$\cdot$$
$$\cdot$$
$$\cdot$$
$$f_k = f_0 p_{k-1} + f_1 p_{k-2} + \cdots + f_{k-1} p_0.$$

Equations (8.10) provide a simple set of relationships from which $f_1, f_2, \ldots$ may be successively computed.

Once this has been done, we may find the total number of individual replacements by addition; that is, we compute

$$\sum_{k=1}^{n-1} f_i.$$

The total cost over n periods is

$$C_I \sum_{k=1}^{n-1} f_i + f_0 C_G.$$

The cost per interval t is

$$K = \frac{1}{n} \{ C_I \sum_{k=1}^{n-1} f_i + f_0 C_G \}. \qquad (8.11)$$

We wish to choose n so as to minimize K. There are two possibilities, as shown in Figure 8.1. In both parts of the figure the dotted line is the cost per period of replacing only on failure. In Figure 8.1*a* the first local minimum is less than this cost; in such cases the first local minimum is less than any other minimum. In Figure 8.1*b* the first minimum exceeds the cost of replacement only on failure. Successive minima form a decreasing sequence, but none of them are lower than the cost of replacement only on failure.

Thus to see if group replacement is justified, we compare the first minimum with the cost of never group-replacing, and group-replace only if the first minimum is smaller.

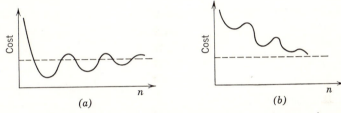

Figure 8.1   (*a*) Group replacement is worthwhile. (*b*) Group replacement is not justified.

To compute the cost of individual replacement, we need the limit as n tends to infinity of f_n. Let us assume that the limit exists and equals f. After we have been inserting f replacements for a long time, we shall have f survivors from those just replaced; $(1 - p_0)f$ survivors from insertions at time t previously; $(1 - p_0 - p_1)f$ survivors from time $2t$ ago; $(1 - p_0 - p_1 - p_2)f$ from $3t$ ago, and so on. Because the survivors must total N, the number in the system, we see that

$$
\begin{aligned}
N = f[1 &+ (1 - p_0) + (1 - p_0 - p_1) + (1 - p_0 - p_1 - p_2) + \cdots] \\
= f[p_0 &+ p_1 + p_2 + p_3 + \cdots \\
&+ p_1 + p_2 + p_3 + \cdots \\
&\quad\;\; + p_2 + p_3 + \cdots \\
&\qquad\quad + p_3 + \cdots \\
&\qquad\qquad\; + \cdots \\
&\qquad\qquad\quad \cdot \\
&\qquad\qquad\quad \cdot \\
&\qquad\qquad\quad \cdot] \\
= f[p_0 &+ 2p_1 + 3p_2 + 4p_3 + \cdots].
\end{aligned}
$$

The expression in brackets is the average life, assuming that the failures in the interval kt to $(k + 1)t$ occur at time $(k + 1)t$. This is essentially what we assumed when we said replacements would be at the end of the interval of failure.

Thus the average cost per period for individual replacement is

$$\frac{NC_I}{\text{average life}}.$$

This must be compared with the minimum value of K. This may be computed by tabulating K for $n = 1, 2, 3, \ldots$ until the first minimum is found.

Because all the costs that are involved are proportional to N, the value of N is irrelevent in making comparisons and we may compute with $N = 1$. (Exercise 4 should be done at this point.)

AN INSPECTION PROBLEM

Many preventive maintenance problems are similar in structure to replacement in anticipation of failure, but there is one class of problems, which we might call *preventive inspection*, that is different. Suppose that we have equipment that is used only in an emergency. Examples range from a firehose to guided missile systems. If such equipment deteriorates with age it may be unusable when we need it. The only way to make certain that it is in working order is to inspect it, but while it is being inspected, it is unavailable for use if the need arises. The problem is to find how often to inspect so as to maximize the proportion of time during which it is in working order. We make the following assumptions:

1. An item that is stored from age zero to age x, without inspection or repair, has a probability $F(x)$ of working at age x.
2. Inspections take a time t_1, and if defects are present, they will be found. If no defects are found, none are present.
3. If defects are found, the item is repaired, which takes a further time t_2. Repaired items are "as good as new."
4. An inspection is made at a time t following the last inspection or completion of repair.
5. Immediately following completion of inspection or repair, the item behaves as if it were new.

We wish to choose t so as to maximize the proportion of time during which the item is available for use in working order.

Suppose that at time zero we have a new item (or an inspected or repaired item) and that we consider the length of time until the item is next known to be working. It will be known to be working at the end of the next inspection or repair.

The probability that it is working at time t is $F(t)$, and in this case it will be as "good as new" at time $t + t_1$. If it is not working at time t, it is as "good as new" at $t + t_1 + t_2$. Thus the average time until it is known to be working is

$$(t + t_1)F(t) + (t + t_1 + t_2)[1 - F(t)] = t + t_1 + t_2[1 - F(t)].$$

The expected amount of time during which it is working is θ_t, and by analogy with equation (8.5) we have

$$\theta_t = \sum_{x=0}^{t-1} F(x).$$

Hence the proportion of useful time is $P(t)$, where

$$P(t) = \frac{\sum_0^{t-1} F(x)}{t + t_1 + t_2[1 - F(t)]}. \tag{8.11}$$

To maximize, it is necessary to tabulate $P(t)$.

It is worth comparing the implications of (8.9) and (8.11). The former gives the average costs for an item that is in continuous use and the latter gives the proportion of serviceable time for an item that is stored until required. We have already observed that in the first case preventive replacement is not justified when the primary cause of failure is accidental, but we shall now show that inspection is worthwhile because otherwise failures of stored items will not be detected until the item is needed, which may be too late.

When failures are accidental, let a be the probability that an item working at time x is still working at time $x + 1$. Then the probability that an item that works at time zero is still working at time t is a^t. Thus $F(x)$ in (8.11) is equal to a^x, and from (8.11) we have

$$P(t) = \frac{1 + a + a^2 + \cdots + a^{t-1}}{t + t_1 + t_2(1 - a^t)}$$

$$= \frac{1 - a^t}{(1 - a)[t + t_1 + t_2(1 - a^t)]}$$

and

$$\frac{1}{P(t)} = (1 - a)\left\{t_2 + \frac{t + t_1}{1 - a^t}\right\}. \tag{8.12}$$

Now, maximizing $P(t)$ is the same as minimizing $1/P(t)$, and from (8.12) we see that

$$P(0) = \infty \quad \text{and} \quad P(\infty) = \infty$$

Because for nonzero finite t, $P(t)$ is not infinite, it must have a minimum, and so we can justify inspection. On the other hand, consider (8.9) for the replacement problem:

$$K_t = \frac{C_F - (C_R - C_F)P_t}{\theta_t} \tag{8.9}$$

If failures are accidental, then $P_t = a^t$, and from (8.5) we have

$$\theta_t = 1 + a + a^2 + \cdots + a^{t-1} = \frac{1 - a^t}{1 - a}. \tag{8.13}$$

Thus

$$K_t = \frac{[C_F - (C_F - C_R)a^t](1 - a)}{1 - a^t}. \tag{8.14}$$

The only term involving t is $C_R a^t/(1 - a^t)$, which is equal to

$$C_R \left\{ \frac{1}{1 - a^t} - 1 \right\}.$$

Because a is a probability and thus less than one, it is clear that this expression always diminishes as t increases. It follows that the optimal value of t is infinite; in other words, preventive replacement is never justified.

THE GENERAL RENEWAL PROCESS

Many replacement and maintenance problems have the following general structure:

> At time 0 a new item is placed in the system and the probability that the system again has a new item for the first time at time t is $f(t)$. At time t there may literally be a new item or, by a process of inspection and maintenance, the item may be "as good as new." During the interval 0 to t, certain costs may be incurred, the probabilities of which are known. The interval 0 to t is called a cycle.

We shall now show that in the long run the average cost per unit time is:

$$\frac{\text{expected cost over one cycle}}{\text{expected duration of one cycle}}.$$

Let C be the expected cost over a cycle, that is, over the time between a new item being placed in the system and its first replacement or renovation. If g is the long-run average cost per unit time, for a long interval 0 to T the costs incurred will be equal to gT. Now suppose that with probability $f(u)$ the first item is replaced at time u. The costs from time u on will be $g(T - u)$. It follows that

$$gT = \sum_{u=0}^{T} (T - u)g f(u) + C. \tag{8.16}$$

Now, if T is large enough and if replacement must occur before T, it follows that

$$\sum_{0}^{T} f(u) = 1.$$

Hence

$$\sum_{0}^{T} Tg f(u) = Tg$$

and
$$\sum_0^T u f(u)\, du = \bar{u} = \text{average cycle length.}$$

Therefore, from (8.16)
$$gT = gT - g\bar{u} + C$$

or
$$g = \frac{C}{\bar{u}}. \tag{8.17}$$

The inspection and preventive replacement schemes already discussed are examples of the use of this formula. In the former case C consisted of the available service time per cycle, whereas in the latter it was a dollar cost. We now consider another example.

TABLE 8.8   *Tire Failures*

Age (thousands of miles)	10	11	12	13	14	15	16	17	18	19	20	21	22
Probability that tire becomes smooth							0.1	0.1	0.1	0.2	0.2	0.2	0.1
Probability that smooth tire can be recapped							0.8	0.8	0.7	0.7	0.5	0.5	0.3
Probability of failure of a recap	0.1	0.1	0.1	0.2	0.2	0.1							

A new tire costs \$25 and a recap costs \$15. A tire must be recapped or replaced when it wears smooth, but recapping is possible only when the tire walls have not deteriorated. Given the data in Table 8.8, find the average cost per thousand miles if

(*a*) we always replace with a new tire;
(*b*) we recap old tires whenever possible (assume that at most we can recap once).

The average age at which a new tire becomes smooth is found by multiplying each age by the probability of smoothness, and then adding. We shall assume that smoothness occurs at the midpoints of the milage intervals. The average age, in thousands of miles, is

$$16.5 \times 0.1 + 17.5 \times 0.1 + 18.5 \times 0.1 + 19.5 \times 0.2 + \cdots$$
$$+ 22.5 \times 0.1 = 19.8.$$

The cycle time is 20.8 and the cost per cycle is \$25. By (8.17), the average cost per thousand miles is $25/19.8 = 1.263$.

Similarly, the average age at which a recap must be replaced is

$$10.5 \times 0.1 + 11.5 \times 0.1 + \cdots + 16.5 \times 0.1 = 13.8.$$

The cost per thousand miles is $15/13.8 = 1.087$.

To find the cost per thousand miles of a new tire and a recap when possible, we must find the total average life of both. This is the average life of a new tire plus the probability that we can use a recap multiplied by the average life of a recap. The probability that we can use a recap is found by multiplying the probability of smoothness at each age by the probability that the tire can be recapped, and then adding. The probability that we can recap is

$$0.1 \times 0.8 + 0.1 \times 0.8 + 0.1 \times 0.7 + \cdots + 0.1 \times 0.3 = 0.6.$$

The total average life or cycle time until we again have a new tire is $19.8 + 0.6 \times 13.8 = 28.08$. The expected cost over the cycle is the cost of a new tire plus the cost of a recap times the probability of a recap, which is

$$25 + 0.6 \times 15 = 34.$$

The average cost per thousand miles, if we use recaps wherever possible, is

$$\frac{34}{28.08} = 1.210$$

(Exercises 6 and 7 can now be done.)

RELIABILITY

So far we have considered replacement and inspection as methods of ensuring that a system continues to work over time. There are some other possibilities that can be used at the *design* stage. We can either build the system of higher quality parts, that is, parts that last longer, or duplicate critical parts in such a way that the system will continue to work even if some components have failed. It is well known that multiengined aircraft will continue to fly after the loss of one engine, but they will not achieve their usual performance. A very simple example of a system that will achieve its designed performance, even after complete failure of one component, is the electric circuit shown in Figure 8.2. The bulb will light so long as[2]

(a) one of the lines AB and $A'B'$ is intact, *and*
(b) one of the lines XY and $X'Y'$ is intact.

Of course, if we can be certain that no failure will occur, we can save the cost of lines $A'B'$ and $X'Y'$, and the bulb will light. We say that $A'B'$ and $X'Y'$ are *redundant* with respect to AB and XY, respectively.

[2] We are assuming that there are no failures of the connectors, which this may not be warranted in practice.

In order to compare various designs, it is usually necessary to specify the desired lower limit of the life of the system. So long as failures of components are possible at all ages, the probability that any system will work at age T is bound to be a decreasing function of T. Usually we can agree on a desired working life, either on the basis of the cost of an inspection or overhaul or on the mission of the system. Thus we might compare aircraft engines on the probability that they

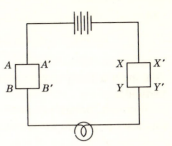

Figure 8.2   Redundant circuit.

will work for one thousand flying hours without major overhaul, because more frequent overhauls would be too expensive. For a missile guidance system a life of 30 minutes might be sufficient, because the flight time will never exceed this amount.

Let us suppose that we have determined the time T for which the system is to function and, for the moment, that there is a single critical part. That is, all other parts are so likely to be functioning at time T that we do not need to take their failure rates into consideration. We may suppose, at least in theory, that the probability that the critical part will function for a time t is a function of how much we spend on making it. Let $p(c)$ be the probability that it will function if we spend c on it. It is likely that there is an upper limit to $p(c)$, no matter what we spend; thus we shall assume that the cheapest part costs c_m and that $p(c)$ is an increasing function until $c = c_M$.

In the simplest case reliability can be increased by using n functionally identical parts in parallel (as AB and $A'B'$ in Figure 8.2), so that the system works if any one of these parts works. Then, provided that failures are *independent*, the probability that at least one part is working is

$$f(n) = 1 - [1 - p(c_1)][1 - p(c_2)] \cdots [1 - p(c_n)], \qquad (8.18)$$

where c_i is the cost of the ith part.

Usually, there is a limit on what we can spend; therefore, we wish to maximize $f(n)$ with respect to $c_1, c_2, \ldots$, and n subject to

$$c_m \leq c_i \leq c_M \qquad i = 1, 2, \ldots \qquad (8.19)$$

and

$$c_1 + c_2 + \cdots + c_n \leq C. \qquad (8.20)$$

It is clear intuitively that we shall spend C and that we shall spend the same amount on all components. Thus n will be chosen such that

$$c_m \leq \frac{C}{n} \leq c_M \qquad \text{or} \qquad \frac{C}{cM} \leq n \leq \frac{C}{cm}$$

and

$$f(n) = 1 - \left[1 - p\frac{C}{n}\right]^n. \tag{8.21}$$

It is now a fairly simple matter to find the best value of n by numerical methods.

Of course, design problems are not usually this simple. We have assumed that a series of components share some function and that if one of them fails,

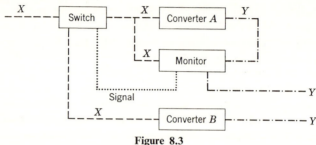

Figure 8.3

the others automatically take over its role. Two complications arise:

1. Recognition of a failure may not be automatic and some monitoring device is required.

2. When the monitoring device indicates a failure, a switching device is required to activate a working component and to eliminate the faulty component.

A good example of (1) is the light in the aircraft cockpit which goes on to indicate that the landing gear is locked into position. If the light fails to go on, the fault may be in one of two places—either the wheels are not locked or the monitoring device has failed (a burned-out bulb, perhaps). When the light fails to go on, the flight engineer acts as a switching device. He activates a hand pump and endeavors to force the wheels into position.

Because either the monitor or the switch may fail, redundancy may actually reduce the reliability of a system. Consider the system illustrated in Figure 8.3. Here A is intended to convert an input X into an output Y. The probability that A works successfully is p; to take care of failures we add a monitor that compares the input and output of A and decides if the correct conversion has been made. If not, the monitor suppresses the output from A and sends a signal to the switch, which then diverts the input from A to a second converter B that has the same probability p of functioning correctly. We shall assume that the monitor has a probability p_M of functioning correctly, that is, that

p_M = probability that the output is suppressed and a signal is sent to the switch, given that converter A has failed

and[3]

p_M = probability that the output is sent on and no signal is sent, given that converter A has worked correctly.

We shall also assume that if no signal is sent, the switch always routes via A, and that if a signal is sent, it routes via B with probability p_S.

The probability that the entire system will produce the desired output Y from an input X may be found by considering the various ways in which Y can be obtained. These are shown in Table 8.9. Here W means *works*, F means *fails* and a dash means either.

TABLE 8.9 *Conditions Required for the System of Figure* 8.3 *to Work*

Converter A	Monitor	Switch	Converter B	Probability
W	W	—	—	pp_M
F	W	W	W	$(1-p)p_Mp_Sp$
W	F	W	W	$p(1-p_M)p_Sp$
W	F	F	—	$p(1-p_M)(1-p_S)$

The total probability of the correct output is found by adding the probabilities in Table 8.9; it is called the *reliability* of the system. If we use R_{AB} to denote the reliability, then

$$R_{AB} = pp_M + (1-p)p_Mp_Sp + p(1-p_M)p_Sp + p(1-p_M)(1-p_S)$$
$$= p[1 - p_S(1-p)(2p_M - 1)]. \tag{8.22}$$

If the system consists of a single converter A, its reliability R_A is

$$R_A = p. \tag{8.23}$$

On comparing (8.22) and (8.23) we see that $R_{AB} < RA$ if $p_M < 0.5$. It is unlikely that $p_M < 0.5$, but it should now be clear that increasing reliability requires something more than duplication of components. Even if $R_{AB} > R_A$, the cost of the increased reliability may not be warranted. Sometimes cost in this context means *money*, but often the real limitations are on space or weight, and the cost in terms of these may be unwarranted.

---

[3] The two probabilities need not be the same; we assume them to be equal for the sake of simplicity.

If we have sufficient resources (money, space, weight, etc.) and if $p_M > 0.5$, we may feel that even though $R_{AB} > R_A$, it is still too small; the obvious way to increase reliability is to add another monitor to check on the output of B—another switch and another converter. If necessary we could add several such sets. Unfortunately, no matter how many sets we have, we cannot ensure 100 per cent reliability.

Let

P = probability that we obtain an output from the first converter and that it is correct

Q = probability that an input that has been switched to a given converter is subsequently switched to the next converter.

It is shown in Exercise 8 at the end of this chapter that as we increase the number of converters, the reliability cannot exceed[4]

$$L = \frac{P}{1 - Q} \tag{8.24}$$

It is also shown in Exercise 8 that

$$P = p(1 - p_S + p_S p_M), \tag{8.25}$$

$$Q = pp_S - 2pp_S + p_M p_S. \tag{8.26}$$

As a numerical example, suppose that $p = p_M = p_S = 0.9$; then $P = 0.819$ and $Q = 0.162$, so that from (8.23) the reliability cannot exceed $0.819/0.838 = 0.977$. If $p = p_M = p_S = 0.99$, then $P = 0.980199$ and $Q = 0.019602$. Thus $L = 0.980199/0.980398 = 0.99980$.

Because L is an upper limit, it cannot be attained in practice. It does serve as a guide, because it may tell us that this type of design will not satisfy our reliability needs. If this happens, we may be able to increase the reliability of the three basic components (by using higher-grade materials, purer alloys, etc.) or we may contemplate duplicating components. For example, suppose that the switch is actuated by a signal from the monitor and that, once actuated, it is unaffected by a second signal. If we replace every single monitor by $k > 1$ monitors, when the converter fails, the signal will reach the switch so long as any one monitor works, the probability of which is $p_M(k)$, where

$$p_M(k) = 1 - (1 - p_M)^k. \tag{8.27}$$

Thus we see that so long as $k > 1$, we have $p_M(k) > p_M$. On the other hand, if the converter works, the signal will reach the switch if any one monitor fails, so that a single failure means failure of the entire monitoring

---

[4] We are excluding the case in which $p_M < 0.5$, because it is unlikely to arise in practice. If $p_M < 0.5$, reliability *decreases* to the limit L as n increases.

subsystem. The probability that the subsystem works when the converter works, is $p_{M'}(k)$, where

$$p_{M'}(k) = p_M{}^k$$

Such a design has different reliabilities for the monitor according as the converter works or not. One is larger than p_M and the other smaller. Exercise 9 works out the details.

It will be realized that in principle it is possible to compute the probability that any given design will work once we are given the probabilities for the various components.[5] We must merely find the combinations of working components that will permit the system to work. Frequently, the possibilities are so numerous that some form of simulation is required. If a random number process is used on each trial to discover which components are working, it is usually simple enough to see whether the system will work.

Much work in reliability has been done on electronic systems, particularly guidance systems for aircraft and missiles. Components of such systems with extremely high reliability at least over the time spans required are now available. It is not easy to discover the reliability of, say, a transistor, where we have reason to believe that fewer than one in 10,000 will fail in less than 1000 hours. To test reliability, we would need thousands of similar transistors and several months of observations. By the time the experiment is completed, the transistor may have become obsolete. Instead, we try to find failure rates under conditions of extreme stress and to infer the rates under normal working conditions. The inferences are not easily made, because at the present time little is known about the physical causes of failure. Much work remains to be done in this area.

A further complication arises in analyzing systems that are not of a go–no-go nature. In our examples we have assumed that the system either works or fails. Frequently this is not the case. If the system is designed to convert an input X to an output $Y = f(X)$, where $f(X)$ is a given function, it may serve its purpose if the output Y lies in some range, say $f(X) \pm \alpha$. Furthermore, α may vary with time. In a device designed to land an aircraft, an error of 10 feet in the observation of altitude is probably of no importance at a 1000 feet but might be disastrous at 8 feet. Many faults are of an intermittent nature, so that it may happen that a component is not working well during a period when this is of little consequence, but may somehow revert to a working state by the time it is needed. Thus it is meaningless to talk of system reliability except against a background of the mission for which the system is designed; such a discussion is often complicated by our lack of detailed knowledge of the physical requirements of the mission and the failure rates of the components.

[5] In practice, minor changes in components can invalidate previous experience with failure rates. Thus an additional lug on an electrical connector may make its behavior change.

SUMMARY

We have discussed four types of problems:

1. *Replacement of capital equipment.* We seek the optimal life of equipment when increased age reduces efficiency. The aim is to balance increased running costs against annual depreciation costs.

2. *Replacement in anticipation of failures.* We seek a replacement policy that balances the wasted life of items replaced before failure against the costs incurred when items fail in service. In a system that has a large number of identical parts, no one of which is expensive, we can sometimes reduce the common setup cost per item replacement by a group-replacement policy.

3. *Inspection of emergency equipment.* If equipment deteriorates in storage, it is necessary to inspect it from time to time. Because equipment cannot be used while it is being inspected, we must balance the unavailable time during inspections against the increased probability of finding equipment unusable if it is not inspected.

4. *Reliability.* We briefly discussed the meaning of "reliability" and how duplication of components could lead to greater reliability at the design stage. Sometimes the problem is to balance increased cost (or weight or volume) against gains in reliability, but when we have to add devices to detect failures, the failures of the monitors may cause an upper limit to the reliability that is attainable.

Except for the deterministic models associated with capital equipment, all of the problems in this chapter require a knowledge of stochastic processes for their solution. In the problems of replacement and inspection we have assumed implicitly that the equipment will be required indefinitely. When this is not the case, it is often necessary to use the method of dynamic programming that is discussed in the next chapter.

EXERCISES

1. Given the data in Table 8.10, find the optimal replacement policy. Purchase price is $5000.

TABLE 8.10

Year	1	2	3	4	5	6	7	8
Running cost	1500	1600	1800	2100	2500	2900	3400	4000
Salvage value	3500	2500	1700	1200	800	500	500	500

2. Suppose that we have a piece of equipment of the type described in Exercise 1 and that it is 2 years old. If we need such equipment for 4 more years, what should we do?

3. Suppose, in Exercise 1, that the interest rate is 10 per cent per year and that the costs given can be considered as arising at the end of each year. Will this affect the replacement policy?

4. The probability p_n of failure just before age n are shown below. If individual replacement costs \$1.25 and group replacement costs \$0.50 per item, find the optimal group-replacement policy.

$n =$	1	2	3	4	5	6	7	8	9	10	11
$p_n =$	0.01	0.03	0.05	0.07	0.10	0.15	0.20	0.15	0.11	0.08	0.05

5. If an item fails in service, the total cost is \$100. Replacement before failure costs \$50. We are considering a policy of preventive maintenance that prolongs the life of the equipment but costs \$5 per week. Given the data in Table 8.11, what should the policy be?

TABLE 8.11

Week	1	2	3	4	5	6	7	8	9	10	11	12
Probability of failure at end of week	0.02	0.04	0.08	0.15	0.20	0.25	0.15	0.08	0.03			
Probability of failure at end of week with maintenance	0	0	0.05	0.08	0.10	0.15	0.20	0.15	0.10	0.07	05	0.05

6. The probability that a firehose will still be usable after it has been stored for t days is a^t, where $0 < a < 1$. It can be tested by removing it from its normal station and passing water through it under pressure. This takes t_1 days, but unfortunately there is a probability p that the test will damage a usable hose. If the hose is unusable at the end of the test, it takes t_2 days to replace it. Find the fraction of time for which we have a usable hose at its station.

   (*Hint:* There are two policies to consider. If we replace at age t without inspection, we can order the replacement at time $t - t_2$ for delivery at time t. The second policy is to test at time t, in which case a replacement, if needed, will arrive on station at time $t + t_1 + t_2$.)

7. Suppose, in Exercise 6, that a replacement hose costs c_1 and a pressure test costs c_2. Show that the average cost of a "no-test" policy is c_1/t and that the average cost of a testing policy is

$$\frac{c_1 + c_2[1 - (1 - p)a^t]}{t + t_1 + t_2[1 - (1 - p)a^t]}.$$

Given the following data, find a policy such that there is a chance of at least 92 per cent of a hose working at any time and such that the costs per day are a minimum of

$$c_1 = 10, \quad c_2 = 1, \quad p = 0.2, \quad a = 0.9, \quad t_1 = 1, \quad t_2 = 2.$$

(*Hint:* First find the value of t, which with inspection maximizes the probability that a single hose is working. Then find the number of hoses to give the required probability of at least one working. Compare the cost per day of this policy with a policy of no testing and suitably frequent replacement.)

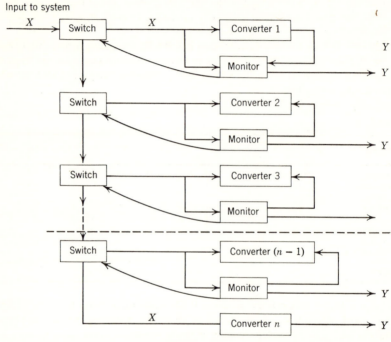

Figure 8.4

8. Figure 8.4 shows n converters arranged in parallel. Each has a monitor that can decide if the output is correct. If not, the output is canceled and a switch is changed so that the original input is sent to the next converter. The probability that any given converter will work is p; the probability that the monitor will work is p_M (i.e., p_M = probability of sending a signal to the switch when the converter has failed = probability of not sending a signal when the converter works). A switch will never move without a signal from the monitor, but the probability that it moves when a signal arrives is p_S.

Show that the probability of a correct output from converter 1 is

$$P = p(1 - p_S + p_S p_M)$$

and the probability that the input is diverted to converter $r + 1$, given that it has been diverted to converter $r \geqslant 1$, is

$$Q = pp_S - 2pp_Sp_M + p_Mp_S.$$

Hence show that the probability of a correct output from the system as a whole is

$$L_n = \frac{P[1 - Q^{n-1}]}{1 - Q} + pQ^{n-1}$$

and

$$L_{n+1} - L_n = Q^{n-1}pp_S(1 - p)(2p_M - 1).$$

Infer that as n is increased indefinitely, L_n approaches $L = P/(1 - Q)$, and that L_n increases or decreases according as p_M is more or less than one half.

9. Suppose that in an effort to increase the reliability of the system described in Exercise 8 we replace every monitor by a set of k monitors and that one or more signals from the set of monitors is sufficient to activate the switch. (See Figure 8.5.)

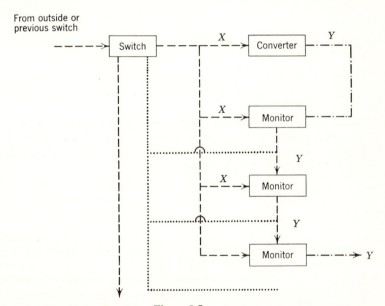

Figure 8.5

The probabilities p, p_M, and p_S have the same meanings as in Exercise 8. Show that the probabilities that the set of monitors work are:

(1) $p_M(k)$ = probability that the set of monitors send a signal to the switch when output is wrong and the wrong output is suppressed
$$= 1 - (1 - p_M)^k.$$

(2) $p_M'(k)$ = probability that no monitor sends signal and the output is sent on when it is correct

$$= p_M{}^k.$$

Show also that with the notation used previously

$$P = p[1 + p_M'p_S - p_S] \quad \text{and} \quad Q = pp_S - pp_S(p_M' + p_M) + p_Mp_S.$$

Compute L when $k = 2$, $p = p_S = p_M = 0.9$. Suppose that monitors are in short supply, but that we have several switches and converters. Which design is better?

1. Two converters, one switch, and two monitors in a set for the first converter.
2. Three converters, two switches and one monitor for each of the first two converters.

(Assume that $p = p_S = p_M = 0.9$.)

Suggested Readings

Relatively little has been written on replacement problems. The early books of J. Dean (1951) and Terborgh (1949) have not been brought up to date. A review of what work has been done can be found in B. V. Dean (1961).

Reliability, on the other hand, has had considerable treatment in the literature. Extensive bibliographies can be found in Barlow et al. (1965) and McCall (1965). Cox (1962) provides a brief but good introduction to the subject. A more detailed treatment can be found in Roberts (1964).

Bibliography

Alchian, A. A., *Economic Replacement Policy*, Rand Corp. Report R-224 (April 1952); reprinted as RM-2153 (April 9, 1958).

Barlow, R. E., and F. Prochan, *Mathematical Theory of Reliability*, John Wiley & Sons, New York, 1965.

Bazovsky, J., *Reliability: Theory and Practice*, Prentice-Hall, Englewood Cliffs, N.J., 1961.

Chorafas, D. N., *Statistical Processes in Reliability Engineering*, D. Van Nostrand, Princeton, N.J., 1960.

Cox D. R., *Renewal Theory*, Methuen & Co., London, 1962.

Dean, B. V., "Replacement Theory," in *Progress in Operations Research* Vol. I, R. L. Ackoff (ed.), John Wiley and Sons, New York, 1961, pp. 327–362.

Dean, J., *Capital Budgeting* (Chapter VI), Columbia University Press, New York, 1951.

Feller, W., *An Introduction to Probability Theory and Its Applications*, 2nd ed. (Chapter XIII), John Wiley and Sons, New York, 1957.

Lloyd, D. K., and M. Lepow, *Reliability, Management Methods and Mathematics*, Prentice-Hall, Englewood Cliffs, N.J., 1962.

McCall, J. J., "Maintenance Policies for Stochastically Failing Equipment: A Survey," *Management Science*, **11** (1965), 493–524.

Mendenhall, W., "A Bibliography on Life Testing and Related Topics," *Biometrica*, **45** (1958), 521–543.

Roberts, N. H., *Mathematical Methods in Reliability Engineering*, McGraw-Hill Book Co., New York, 1964.

Terborgh, B., *Dynamic Equipment Policy*, McGraw-Hill Book Co., New York, 1949.

CHAPTER 9

Dynamic Programming

INTRODUCTION

Chapters 5 to 8 of this book are organized around problems, rather than the mathematical techniques that are employed to solve them. The problems and techniques do not have a one-to-one correspondence; simulation, for example, has application in many types of problems, and so does linear programming. Most techniques, however, are primarily associated with a particular problem type (e.g., simulation with queueing and linear programming with allocation).

Classical mathematics has proved inadequate in handling many optimization problems that involve large numbers of decision variables and/or large numbers of inequality constraints. Until recently such problems could be handled only by trying to find optimal values for all decisions simultaneously, which rapidly leads to computations that are uneconomic or even infeasible within the limits of available computing equipment. There is an obvious attraction to splitting a large problem into subproblems, each of which involves only a few variables, and this is what *dynamic programming* does.

Dynamic programming is a mathematical technique whose development is largely due to Richard Bellman (1957). It is applicable to a wide variety of problems, including allocation, inventory, and replacement. We shall illustrate its application to each of these three types of problems, but we shall start by considering the structure of a problem involving the introduction of a new product line.

THE USE OF DECISION TREES

The research laboratories of a food processing company have discovered a new process for preserving foods and are considering launching a line of packaged meals to be sold through supermarkets. They have already produced some samples and have conducted taste tests on a small panel of housewives. The results indicate that the new line is considered equal to competing lines in all aspects and superior in some. Past experience and the considered judgment of the marketing department suggest that in these circumstances the chance of a successful national launch is 0.3, and it is agreed that a successful launch would result in an annual profit whose present value is three million dollars. Failure would mean a loss of $250,000. In practice the company has a whole series of possible decisions to make. They range from further testing of public acceptance to the design and timing of the marketing campaign, and include such production problems as the location of the plant, the building of new plants, and modifications of the existing plant. For purposes of illustration, we assume that the company can either drop the idea, or launch the product immediately, or try it in a test market (at a cost of $50,000). If a test market is used, there are three possible results:

1. Fewer than 10 per cent of the public try the new product.
2. More than 10 per cent try the product, but less than 50 per cent of those who try buy it on a second or subsequent occasion.
3. More than 10 per cent try the product and the repeat purchase rate is 50 per cent or more.

If the market test indicates that a national launch is not yet justified, the company has several possibilities open to it in practice. The product could be improved or the advertising altered; the price could be changed, or research could be conducted to find out why the product did not receive acceptance. In our example, however, we shall assume that, following the market test, the only possibilities are either to launch nationally or to drop the idea altogether. In these circumstances, how should decisions be made?

The first step is to draw a treelike diagram that shows the structure of the problem. In the *tree* shown in Figure 9.1, the branches represent various events that might occur and the nodes represent points at which alternatives arise. Where the nodes are circles, the selection among alternatives is made by the company, but square nodes represent "choices" outside the company's control. They are made by "nature" and the company can only estimate the probabilities of nature's choice. Thus node 1 is the decision either to drop the idea (D), to launch nationally (L), or to try a test market (T). If the company launches the new product, the next choice (2) is up to "nature." There is a probability of 0.3 of success (S) and of 0.7 of failure (F). The profit is shown at the end of each branch. Thus it is zero if D is chosen. It is $3,000,000 if L is chosen *and* it is successful; it is $-$250,000 if L is chosen *and* it fails. The expected monetary value, if the product is launched, is

$$\$3,000,000 \times 0.3 - \$250,000 \times 0.7 = \$725,000.$$

Thus if the decision to launch is made, the decision maker would be prepared to exchange his prospects for any cash payment exceeding $725,000. We

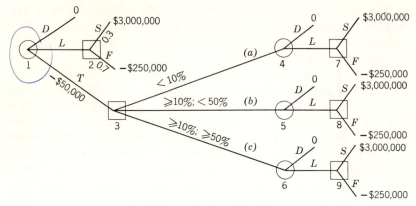

Figure 9.1 A decision tree.

would say that reaching node 2 is worth $725,000. We next examine the consequences of the decision to use a test market. First, we must pay $50,000 to reach node 3. However, the value of node 3 is not apparent, because there are several alternatives from node 3 onward. At node 3 nature chooses one of three paths:

(a) less than 10 per cent try;
(b) at least 10 per cent try, less than 50 per cent repeat;
(c) at least 10 per cent try, at least 50 per cent repeat.

Instead of estimating the value of node 3 directly, it is easier to go to the right-hand side of the tree and work backward. We start by assuming that we have reached nodes 7, 8, and 9, at each of which nature chooses the next path, either success (S) at a profit of $3,000,000 or failure (F) at a profit of − $250,000. To find the expected monetary value of these three nodes, we need the probabilities of S and F at each. These might be estimated by reference to similar product introductions in the past, but they are more likely to be obtained from subjective judgments of experts. Suppose that the experts provide the joint probabilities shown in Table 9.1.

TABLE 9.1   *Joint Probabilities*

	<10 Per Cent Try (a)	≥10 Per Cent Try, <50 Per Cent Repeat (b)	≥10 Per Cent Try, ≥50 Per Cent Repeat (c)	Probability
S (success)	0.03	0.07	0.20	0.30
F (failure)	0.47	0.18	0.05	0.70
Probability	0.50	0.25	0.25	1.00

The body of the entries in Table 9.1 show the joint probabilities (for example, the probabilities of the test market giving less than 10 per cent *and* failure are 0.47) and the marginal totals show the absolute probabilities of S, F, (a), (b), and (c).

We first compute the *conditional probabilities* of success or failure, given that (a) or (b) or (c) has occurred. We know that in 50 out of 100 test markets (a) will occur, and that 3 of the 50 will be successful if a launch follows. The probability of success (S) following (a) is 3 out of 50, or 0.06. The probability of failure (F) is 47 out of 50, or 0.94. Following (b) the probability of S is $7/25 = 0.28$ and the probability of F is $18/25 = 0.72$. Following (C) the probabilities of S and F are $20/25 = 0.8$ and $5/25 = 0.2$.

Node 7 is reached via (a); therefore, its expected monetary value is

$$\$3,000,000 \times 0.06 - \$250,000 \times 0.94 = -\$55,000.$$

Node 8 is reached via (b), and its expected monetary value is

$$\$3,000,000 \times 0.28 - \$250,000 \times 0.72 = \$660,000.$$

Node 9 is reached via (c), and its expected monetary value is

$$\$3,000,000 \times 0.8 - \$250,000 \times 0.2 = \$2,350,000.$$

Next suppose that we have reached node 4 and that we must make the decision to launch or drop. To launch means reaching node 7 and a profit of $-\$55,000$. To drop means a profit of zero. We decide to drop and give node 4 the value zero. At node 5 we can drop at zero profit or proceed to node 8 at an expected profit of $660,000. We would decide to launch and give node 5 the value $660,000. Similarly, node 6 has a value $2,350,000.

We now move backward in time and evaluate node 3. From node 3 we can, at nature's choice, reach either node 4, 5, or 6. To find the value of node 3 we again multiply the probabilities of each possibility by its value and add. From Table 9.1 the probabilities of (a), (b), and (c) are 0.50, 0.25, and 0.25. The monetary value of node 3, if we could reach it at no cost, would be:

$$0.50 \times 0 + 0.25 \times \$660,000 + 0.25 \times \$2,350,000 = \$752,500.$$

However, to reach node 3 we must pay $50,000 for the test market. Therefore, the net monetary value of node 3 is $\$(752,500 - 50,000) = \$702,500$.

Finally, we consider the decision at node 1. We have seen that dropping the idea results in no profit. An immediate launch results in $725,000, and use of a test market results in $702,500. In this example the cost of the test market is not justified; this is so despite the fact that the decision in the absence of a test would be to launch nationally and the decision on launching following a test (nodes 4, 5, 6) would depend on the test result. If the cost of a market test were less than $\$(752,500 - 725,000) = \$27,500$, we would find the test justified.

The principles behind this analysis may be summarized as follows:

1. At any node that "nature" chooses, the value depends only on future events and not on previous decision.

2. At any node that the decision maker chooses, the choice is made to move to the most profitable node one link away, and the value is the same as that of the node he reaches, less any cost of the movement.

3. Because of (1) and (2), the system may be evaluated and the optimal decisions found by imagining ourselves at the last nodes in real time and performing the calculations backward in real time.

The concept of decision trees provides a systematic approach to many problems that face management. The problem that we have just considered is typical of many, in which decision is a choice among a finite number of possibilities and in which the process terminates after some finite number of decisions. In the next section we shall see what happens when we relax these conditions.

(Exercise 1 should be done at this point.)

EXTENSION OF DECISION TREES TO AN INDEFINITE NUMBER OF DECISIONS

There are many situations in which the same decision is to be made at regular intervals and in which the process is expected to continue indefinitely. In such circumstances it is often convenient to plan decisions so as to maximize the *performance per decision*, rather than the total performance over an indefinite time period.

A MAINTENANCE PROBLEM

Suppose that we have a piece of equipment that is either running or broken down. If it runs throughout one week, it makes a gross profit of $100. If it fails during the week, gross profit is zero. If it is running at the start of the week and we perform preventive maintenance, the probability that it will fail during the week is 0.4. If we do not perform such maintenance, the probability of failure is 0.7. However, maintenance will cost $20. When the equipment has failed, it can be replaced at a cost of $120, or a repair can be attempted. Repairs cost $40 and have a 0.50 chance of success. Replacement always results in a machine that works. We wish to choose an optimal repair and maintenance policy.

In this problem the initial decision may be made in one of two circumstances. Either the equipment is working (*W*), in which case we must decide

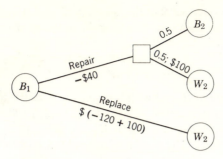

Figure 9.2a Starting in condition *B*.

whether to perform preventive maintenance or not, or it has broken down (*B*), in which case we must decide whether to repair or replace. Whatever the condition of the equipment at the time of the first decision, and whatever decisions we make, the next decision is also made with a similar machine, either in condition *W* or in condition *B*. Figures 9.2*a* and 9.2*b* show the relevant decision trees.

We again use round nodes for our decisions and square nodes for those of "nature." On each branch we show the decision or the probability and the profit. Following each node that has a 2 in it we have the same pattern as follows the corresponding node with a 1, and the process repeats indefinitely. Now suppose that all future returns beyond the B_2 nodes are worth x and those beyond the W_2 nodes are worth y. If we knew x and y, we could work backward and find the values of nodes B_1 and W_1. Because we do not know x and y, we cannot even see what decisions to take at B_1 and W_1. However,

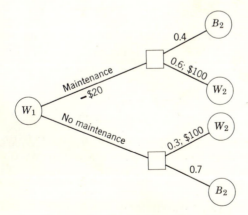

Figure 9.2b Starting in condition *W*.

it is reasonable to suppose[1] that the values of B_1 and W_1 will differ from those of B_2 and W_2 by the gain or profit, g, to be obtained over the week that lies between them. Thus

$$\text{value of } B_1 = x + g$$
$$\text{value of } W_1 = y + g.$$

Suppose that we are at B_1 and wish to make the decision to *repair* or *replace*. If we replace, there is a cost of $120 and a gain of $(100 + y)$ for a net gain of $(y - 20)$. If we repair and reach W_2, we gain $(100 + y)$; if we rapair and reach B_2, we gain x. The chance of either is 0.5. In addition, there is a cost of $40. The expected monetary value of a repair is thus $0.5(100 + y) + 0.5x - 40 = 0.5x + 0.5y + 10$. The decision will be to repair or replace depending on which of $y - 20$ and $0.5x + 0.5y + 10$ is the greater. The value of this decision is $x + g$. Thus

$$x + g = \max \, [y - 20; \, 0.5x + 0.5y + 10]. \tag{9.1}$$

Similarly, by working backward in Figure 9.2*b* we see that

$$y + g = \max \, [0.4x + 0.6y + 40; \, 0.7x + 0.3y + 30]. \tag{9.2}$$

We now have two equations to solve for the three unknowns x, y, and g. Inspection of these equations shows that if x and y are each increased by the same amount, each of the terms to be maximized is also increased by the same amount, and the decision about which one is the greater is unaltered. It follows that the equations are sufficient only to find the relative values of x and y, and that one of them can be given an arbitrary value. Suppose that we set $y = 0$ and obtain

$$x + g = \max \, [-20; \, 0.5x + 10] \tag{9.3}$$
$$g = \max \, [0.4x + 40; \, 0.7x + 30]. \tag{9.4}$$

These simultaneous equations can be solved by an iterative routine. We start by guessing which of the terms is the larger and then solve the resulting equations for x and g. If $-20 > 0.5x + 10$ and $0.4x + 40 > 0.5x + 10$, we would have:

$$x + g = -20 \tag{9.5}$$
$$g = 0.4x + 40. \tag{9.6}$$

The solution to (9.5) and (9.6) is $x = -42.9$, $g = 22.9$. We now check to see if these values yield the maxima that we assumed. We should have

$$-20 > 0.5x + 10 \quad \text{or} \quad -20 > -0.5 \times 42.9 + 10 = -11.45$$

---

[1] The assumption that we are making is that the difference in value between B_1 and B_2 is the same as the difference between W_1 and W_2. This can be justified provided that a large number of subsequent decisions follow B_2 and W_2.

and

$$0.4x + 40 > 0.7x + 30 \quad \text{or} \quad -0.4 \times 42.9 + 40 > -0.7 \times 42.9 + 30$$

or

$$22.84 > -0.03.$$

Thus the first assumption is wrong and the second is correct. We now repeat the calculation, assuming that the term that is the largest when the value of x just found is used, will still be the largest with the correct value of x. This assumption yields

$$x + g = 0.5x + 10 \tag{9.7}$$

$$g = 0.4x + 40. \tag{9.8}$$

From (9.7) and (9.8) we obtain $x = -33.3$, $g = 26.7$, and with this value of x

$$0.5x + 10 > -20$$

$$0.4x + 40 > 0.7x + 30.$$

These are exactly what we assumed in calculating x and g. It may be shown that these values of x and g are the only solutions of equations (9.3) and (9.4), and from the way in which they were obtained we see that the best policy is to perform preventive maintenance and to repair a broken machine.

The reasoning is very general and can easily be extended to cases in which there are more than two types of nodes at which decisions are made and in which there are more than two alternatives at each node. Figure 9.3 shows a typical decision node in these circumstances. We have labeled the states or conditions in which each decision is made as $S_1, S_2, \ldots, S_n$.

Let $x_1, x_2, \ldots, x_n$ be the values of all future decisions following states $S_1(2), S_2(2), \ldots, S_n(2)$; let the payoff associated with decision k be $q_i{}^k$. Let $r_{ij}{}^k$ be the payoff associated with decision k and nature's choice of S_j. Finally, $p_{ij}{}^k$ is the probability that nature chooses S_j when we choose k.

Then the expected value of node $S_i(1)$, if we choose k, is

$$q_i{}^k + \sum_{j=1}^{n} p_{ij}{}^k (r_{ij}{}^k + x_j).$$

We must choose k to maximize this expression. Hence for $i = 1, 2, \ldots, n$,

$$x_i + g = \max_k \left[\left(q_i{}^k + \sum_{j=1}^{n} p_{ij}{}^k r_{ij}{}^k \right) + \sum_{j=1}^{n} p_{ij}{}^k x_j \right]. \tag{9.9}$$

As in the simpler example, one of $x_1, x_2, \ldots, x_n$ may be chosen arbitrarily, say $x_1 = 0$, and the equations (9.9) may be solved iteratively for $g, x_2, \ldots, x_n$. Because $q_i{}^k + \sum_{j=1}^{n} p_{ij}{}^k r_{ij}{}^k$ does not depend on the values of $x_1, \ldots, x_n$, its value can be computed once and for all at the start of the calculations. If we denote its value by $R_i{}^k$, equations (9.9) become

$$x_i + g = \max_k \left[R_i{}^k + \sum_{j=1}^{n} p_{ij}{}^k x_j \right]. \tag{9.10}$$

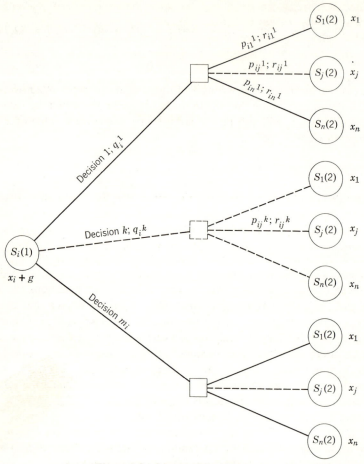

Figure 9.3 A general decision tree.

These equations may be solved in three steps:

1. Assume that for each i we know the value of k. We then obtain the linear equations

$$x_i + g = R_i^k + \sum_{j=1}^n p_{ij}^k x_j. \qquad (9.11)$$

Let $x_1 = 0$ and solve equations (9.11) for $x_2, \ldots, x_n$ and g.

2. Check the solution by computing for each possible decision k the value of

$$V_i^k = R_i^k + \sum_{j=1}^n p_{ij}^k x_j,$$

using the values of the x's found in step 1.

3. For each i find the value of k that maximizes V_i^k. If the maximizing values of k are those assumed at step 1, the assumed solution has been verified. If not, return to step 1, using the values of k found at step 3.

The three steps can be proved to solve the problem. At the end of the calculations the values of k that maximize V_i^k yield the optimum decisions and the value of g gives the long-run maximum average return per decision. The reader who wishes to have a rigorous demonstration of these results is referred to Howard (1960).

It should be emphasized that the method fails if the decision process is not to be continued indefinitely. However, in this case we have a finite decision tree that may be analyzed by using the same technique as was employed in the product-introduction problem of the previous section.

DETERMINISTIC PROBLEMS

It is obvious that the concept of a decision tree and the analysis that starts with the last decision and reasons backward in time to the initial decision, can also be used in deterministic problems in which decisions can be made sequentially. In many ways such problems are simpler, because there are no nodes corresponding to nature's decisions and no expected values to be handled. In such cases it is seldom necessary to draw the tree, although the underlying reasoning remains the same.

As an example consider the problem facing a production manager who has to schedule k different products. If the cost of holding a unit of product i in inventory is C_{1i} per month, the demand for i averages r_i per month and the setup cost each time a production run is started is C_{3i}, then (as we saw in Chapter 7) the average cost per month for all items is

$$K = \sum_{i=1}^{k} \left[\frac{C_{1i} r_i t_i}{2} + \frac{C_{3i}}{t_i} \right], \qquad (9.12)$$

where t_i is the interval between production runs for product i. It is easy enough to find the best value of t_i if there are no other conditions. Suppose, however, that in any one month resources limit the number of setups for all products to an average of n. Product i is made $1/t_i$ times per month, so that the total number of setups will be

$$\sum_{i=1}^{k} \frac{1}{t_i} \leq n. \qquad (9.13)$$

Thus the problem is to minimize (9.12) subject to $t_i \geq 0$ and (9.13). It will be a little easier to write

$$\frac{1}{t_i} = u_i,$$

so that

$$K = \sum_{i=1}^{k} \left[\frac{C_{1i} r_i}{2 u_i} + C_{3i} u_i \right] \qquad (9.14)$$

and

$$\sum_{i=1}^{k} u_i \leq n \tag{9.15}$$

It is clear that the cost of the best schedule depends on both n and k. It is an unknown function, which we denote by $f_k(n)$. As previously we start with the last decision. Suppose that we have managed to schedule all items except one, and that out of the original n setups that were available m remain for the last item. The best schedule for the last item is the one that has u setups and minimizes

$$K_1(u) = \frac{C_{11}r_1}{2u_1} + C_{31}u \tag{9.16}$$

subject to the condition that

$$0 \leq u \leq m. \tag{9.17}$$

When we have found the minimizing u, inserting its value into (9.16) will

TABLE 9.2   *Production Data*

Product i =	1	2	3
C_{1i}	1	2	1
C_{3i}	10	8	5
r_i	320	200	490

yield the minimum cost, which is $f_1(m)$. We usually write this as

$$f_1(m) = \min_{0 \leq u \leq m} \left\{ \frac{C_{11}r_1}{2u} + C_{31}u \right\}. \tag{9.18}$$

It may be shown (see Chapter 7) that if there are no restrictions on the number of setups, the best value of u is

$$u^0 = \sqrt{\frac{C_{11}r_1}{2C_{31}}}. \tag{9.19}$$

If we restrict u to being an integer, the best value is u^0, provided that u^0 is an integer. If u^0 is not an integer, the best value of u is one of the integers on either side of u^0. Of course, if any of these values exceed m, the best value of u is m. Once we have found the best value of u, we insert it into (9.16) and obtain the least possible cost, subject to (9.17), which is $f_1(m)$.

Suppose that we have the data shown in Table 9.2 and that we are limited to 12 setups per month. We will be interested in $f_1(m)$ for $m = 1, 2, 3, \ldots, 12$. From (9.19) and Table 9.2 we see that the optimal value of u, u^0, is given by

$$u^0 = \sqrt{\frac{1 \times 320}{20}} = 4.$$

Thus if $m \geq 4$, the best value of u is 4. If $m < 4$, the best value of u is m. We can now tabulate the function $f_1(m)$, which is done in Table 9.3.

Let us now consider the decision about product number 2. We imagine that after scheduling product number 3 we have m setups left for products 1 and 2. Suppose that we schedule u setups for product 2, leaving $(m - u)$ setups for product 1. It is clear that no matter what the value of $(m - u)$, we will refer to Table 9.2 for the decision about product 1. That is, we will schedule product 1 so as to minimize its costs, subject to $(m - u)$ or fewer setups. The cost for product 1 will be $f_1(m - u)$. The costs for product 2 will be analogous to (9.16). They will be

$$k_2(u) = \frac{C_{12}r_2}{2u} + C_{31}u. \qquad (9.20)$$

The total cost will be the sum of (9.19) and $f_1(m - u)$, and when u is chosen

TABLE 9.3 *Values of $f_1(m)$* Optimum Total Cost u 12 12

m	1	2	3	4	5	6	7	8	9	10	11	12
u	1	2	3	4	4	4	4	4	4	4	4	4
$f_1(m)$	170	100	83.3	80	80	80	80	80	80	80	80	80

to minimize this sum, we will have the function $f_2(m)$. Thus

$$f_2(m) = \min_{0 \leq u \leq m}\left\{\frac{C_{12}r_2}{2u} + C_{31}u + f_1(m - u)\right\}. \qquad (9.21)$$

The minimization is carried out by tabulating the expression in braces for various values of u. This is done in Table 9.4. The entries in the body of the table are found by adding $k_2(u)$ as shown in the second column to $f_1(m - u)$ as shown in the second row (e.g., $f_2(2)$ for $u = 1$ is $208 + 170 = 378$, and $f_2(3)$ for $u = 1$ is $208 + 100 = 308$). Once we have computed $f_2(m)$, the argument can be repeated to obtain $f_3(m)$. We would have

$$f_3(m) = \min_{0 \leq u \leq m}\left\{\frac{C_{13}r_3}{2u} + C_{31}u + f_2(m - u)\right\}. \qquad (9.22)$$

The reader should prepare a table similar to Table 9.4 and use it to show that $f_3(12) = 239.3$; the optimal policy is to make product 1 three times a month, product 2 four times a month, and product 3 five times a month. It may be of interest to note that if there were no constraints, the best policy would be to make three products 4, 5, and 7 times a month at a total monthly cost of 230. Thus the constraint costs 9.3 per item per month.

TABLE 9.4 · Computations for $f_2(m) = k_2(u) + f_1(m-1)$

u	$k_2(u) = 200/u + 8u$	$m = 1$ $f_1(m) = 170$	2	3	4	5	6	7	8	9	10	11	12
			100	83.3	80	80	80	80	80	80	80	80	80
1	208	—	378ᵃ	308	291.1	288	288	288	288	288	288	288	288
2	116	—	—	286ᵃ	216ᵃ	199.3	196	196	196	196	196	196	196
3	90.7	—	—	—	260.7	190.7ᵃ	174ᵃ	170.7	170.7	170.7	170.7	170.7	170.7
4	82	—	—	—	—	252	182	165.3ᵃ	162ᵃ	162	162	162	162
5	80	—	—	—	—	—	250	180	163.3	160ᵃ	160ᵃ	160ᵃ	160ᵃ
6	81.3	—	—	—	—	—	—	251.3	181.3	164.6	161.3	161.3	161.3
7	94.6	—	—	—	—	—	—	—	254.6	184.6	167.9	164.6	164.6
8	89	—	—	—	—	—	—	—	—	259	189	172.3	169
9	94.2	—	—	—	—	—	—	—	—	—	264.2	194.2	177.5
10	100	—	—	—	—	—	—	—	—	—	—	370	200
11	106.2	—	—	—	—	—	—	—	—	—	—	—	276.2
	$f_2(m) =$		378	286	216	190.7	174	165.3	162	160	160	160	160

ᵃ Minimum cost for each value of m.

242

It should be clear that this method of calculation can be extended to as many products as we wish. It has two advantages over the classical approach:[2]

1. Instead of solving one problem in k variables, we solve k problems each in a single variable.

2. We simultaneously solve the problem for a range of values of m.

When we are using any kind of search technique to locate optima, the amount of computation for k variables is roughly proportional to some constant to the kth power, whereas for k problems each in one variable it is proportional to k times the constant. For large k, the savings are considerable.

SUMMARY: THE GENERAL STRUCTURE OF DYNAMIC PROGRAMMING

We have considered some examples in which the optimal policy for a series of sequential decisions was found by considering the last decision first and working backward to the first decision. To do so we had to envisage all the circumstances in which the last decision might be made. We usually refer to the circumstances in which decisions are made as the *state* of the system. Roughly speaking, the state is a description of the system, which, together with future decisions, is sufficient for us to predict future behavior. It is not necessary to consider how the states arise or what the previous decisions were, which enables us to consider decisions one at a time. Whether the optimal decisions are found by tabulation followed by a search procedure or by analytical methods, it is usually quicker and more economical to take them one at a time. Unfortunately, not all decision processes lend themselves to this method. In order to use dynamic programming it is necessary that the payoffs from each decision are additive, and that no matter how a state arose, the consequences for the future are the same.

When the number of decisions is very large, it is possible to develop relative values for each state at successive decisions, and the values for each state at two successive decisions differ by a constant, which is the average return per decision. Although we have not discussed such a problem, it is also possible to discount the returns from future decisions. This may be necessary when decisions are infrequent, say once a year. No really new principles are involved, except that in the case of a large number of decisions we can usually show that the payoff functions converge to a limiting form, and we can find a functional equation that this form must satisfy. It is then no longer necessary to consider 1, 2, 3, . . . decisions until we reach a large value. Instead, we can work directly with the functional equation, usually at considerable economy in computation.

---

[2] The problem may also be solved with the use of a Lagrange multiplier; see page 188 for an example.

EXERCISES

1. The manufacturers of Thirstgon, which is a nationally distributed soft drink, currently sell 1,000,000 barrels per year at a profit of $5 per barrel. A large chain of supermarkets has proposed that Thirstgon, Inc. produce a private-label brand and offer a price that would yield a profit of $0.25 per barrel. Thirstgon believes that one fourth of the sales of the private brand would come out of their existing market. If they refuse to produce the private brand, one of their competitors may agree to do so, in which case Thirstgon can either do nothing, or increase the company's advertising appropriation by $350,000, or cut the price so that profit becomes $4.50 per unit. If they cut the price, their competitors may also do so. They have made subjective estimates of the probabilities as set out below. Should they agree to produce the private brand?

   (a) If Thirstgon agrees, the chance of losing 10 per cent of sales is 0.8, the chance of losing 20 per cent is 0.1, and the chance of losing 30 per cent is 0.1.
   (b) If it disagrees, the chance that a competitor agrees is 0.5.
   (c) If a competitor agrees and Thirstgon does nothing, sales losses could be 10 per cent, 20 per cent, and 30 per cent with probabilities 0.8, 0.1, and 0.1.
   (d) If a competitor agrees and Thirstgon spends an additional $350,000 on advertising, sales losses could be nothing, 5 per cent, and 10 per cent with probabilities 0.3, 0.4, and 0.3.
   (e) If instead of advertising more, Thirstgon cuts the price, the chance that competition also cuts price is 0.3. If both cut, possible sales losses are 5 per cent 10 per cent, and 15 per cent with probabilities 0.5, 0.2, and 0.3. If only Thirstgon cuts, the losses might be nothing, 5 per cent, and 10 per cent with probabilities 0.3, 0.5, and 0.2.

2. An automobile agency has classified its potential customers according to their past purchasing pattern and whether or not they received direct advertising (Table 9.5).

TABLE 9.5

Customer Group	Years Since Previous Purchase	Received Advertising Last Year
A	1	—
B	2	Yes
C	2	No
D	3 or more; never	Yes
E	3 or more; never	No

The average gross profit on a sale is $300, and it cost $5 per customer to advertise to group A, $10 to groups B and C, and $20 to groups D and E. The increased costs are due to errors in mailing lists and the need for telephone solicitation.

Past experience has shown that the probability of sales is as shown in Table 9.6. The sales manager points out that in categories D and E the increased sales to be

TABLE 9.6

Customer Group	No Advertisement	Advertisement
A	0.28	0.30
B	0.25	0.30
C	0.20	0.25
D	0.05	0.10
E	0.04	0.05

expected do not justify the cost of advertising and suggests that advertising to these groups should be dropped. Is he correct?

3. We wish to divide a quantity b into n parts so as to maximize their product. Let $f_n(b)$ be the maximum value. Show that $f_1(b) = b$ and

$$f_n(b) = \max_{0 \le z \le b} \{z f_{n-1}(b - z)\}.$$

Hence find $f_n(b)$ and the division that maximizes.

4. Consider the warehouse problem described on page 160. Let $f_n(b)$ be the maximum return when there are n months to go and the stock on hand is b ($n = 1$ is the last decision; $n = 6$ is the first). If p_n is the current sales price and c_n is the cost price, show that

$$f_1(b) = \max_{x,y} \{p_1 x - c_1 y\},$$

where x is the amount to be sold, y is the amount to be purchased, x, y satisfy the constraints

$$b \ge x \ge 0, \qquad b - x + y \le H, \qquad y \ge 0,$$

and H is the warehouse capacity.

Show also that

$$f_n(b) = \max_{x,y} \{p_n x - c_n y + f_{n-1}(b - x + y)\}$$

when x, y satisfy the constraints above. Use this method to solve the problem numerically.

5. The members of an interairline association have routes that permit passengers to travel between any pair of the n cities served, in some cases directly, and in others with intermediate stops and change of carrier. For any two cities i and j for which there is a direct link there is a published fare f_{ij}, but for two cities not directly linked there is an agreement that the fare shall be determined as the sum of the fares over the cheapest possible route. The problem is to devise the complete fare schedule between *any* two cities.

Let $f_{ij}^{(k)}$ be the least fare from i to j that uses k or fewer links, where $f_{ij}^{(1)} = f_{ij}$ if there is a direct link, $f_{ij}^{(1)} = \infty$ if there is no direct link. (If we were using a computer, we would set $f_{ij}^{(1)} = 10^{20}$ rather than ∞.) Find a relationship between $f_{ij}^{(k+1)}$ and $f_{ij}^{(k)}$, show that we have the complete schedule when for all ij we obtain $f_{ij}^{(k)} = f_{ij}^{(k-1)}$, and that this situation must arise for $k \leq n - 1$. Obtain the complete schedule for the data f_{ij} on Table 9.7.

TABLE 9.7

$i =$	1	2	3	4	5	6
$= 1$	0					
2	27	0				
3	63	∞	0			
4	26	∞	35	0		
5	∞	∞	∞	13	0	
6	∞	49	∞	∞	17	0

6. Suppose that we have n tasks to perform, one after the other, and that task i will take a time t_i. If task i is completed at time T_i, there is a cost $c_i T_i$. We wish to find the sequence of tasks that minimizes the total cost. Suppose that we perform task i first and task j second. Let $f_{n-2}(i, j)$ be the minimum cost of delays that occur after tasks i and j are completed, and let $f_n(i, j)$ be the total cost for all tasks. Show that

$$f_n(i, j) = (t_i + t_j) \sum_{k=1}^{n} c_k - t_j c_i + f_{n-2}(i, j).$$

Show also that

$$f_n(j, i) = (t_i + t_j) \sum_{k=1}^{n} c_k - t_i c_j + f_{n-2}(j, i)$$

and that

$$f_{n-2}(i, j) = f_{n-2}(j, i).$$

Infer that it is better to perform i before j if and only if

$$t_j c_i \geq t_i c_j.$$

Deduce that the optimal sequence may be found by ranking c_k/t_k in descending order.

7. A man wishes to sell a piece of real estate and has a firm offer of $100,000 that will expire in 10 days. He considers that in each of the next 10 days he will get a single offer and that the offers will come from a normal population, mean 100,000 and standard deviation of 10,000. If the property has not been sold before day 9, it is clear that he will accept any offer that exceeds $100,000. What is his expectation at the start of day 9 if the property has not been sold previously?

He decides that if the property has not been sold by the start of day $(10 - i)$, he will accept any bid that exceeds B_i. Let E_i be his expectation at the start of day $10 - i$. Obtain the relationship between E_{i+1}, B_{i+1}, and E_i. Hence compute the optimal values of $B_1, B_2, \ldots, B_9, B_{10}$ and his expectation at the start of the first day.

8. A machine that makes automobile tires has a part that may fail. The probability that it fails on making the $(i + 1)$th tire after it has already made i tires is p_i. When a failure occurs, the tire produced is scrap and the total cost of wasted materials and part replacement is C_F. To replace the part before failure costs $C_R < C_F$. Let $f_n(m)$ be the minimum expected cost of making n tires, when we start with a part that has already made m tires. Before each tire is made, we may choose to replace the part or to make the tire with the old part. Show that

$$f_n(m) = \min \begin{cases} \text{replace}: C_R + f_n(0) \\ \text{do not replace}: (1 - p_m)f_{n-1}(m + 1) + p_m[C_F + f_n(0)]. \end{cases}$$

Suppose that $C_R = 1$, $C_F = 1.5$, and for $i = 0, 1, 2, 3, 4, 5, 6, 7$, the values of P_i are $0, 0.1, 0.2, 0.3, 0.5, 0.7, 0.9$, and 1.0. Find $f_n(m)$ for $m = 0, 1, 2, 3, \ldots, 7$ and for $n = 1, 2, \ldots, 5$. For large values of n we may assume that the optimal policy is to replace the part at some fixed age. Use the methods of this chapter to find the replacement age that minimizes the average cost per tire produced.

Suggested Readings

It is not possible to discuss all details in one brief chapter. In any case, the mathematics tends to be difficult. The interested reader may refer to the Bibliography that follows, particularly Bellman (1957), Howard (1960), and Bellman and Dreyfus (1962).

Bibliography

Aris, R., *Discrete Dynamic Programming*, Blaisdell Publishing Co. New York, 1964.

Bellman, R., *Dynamic Programming*, Princeton University Press, Princeton, N.J., 1957.

———, *Adaptive Control Processes*, Princeton University Press, Princeton, N.J., 1961.

———, and S. Dreyfus, *Applied Dynamic Programming*, Princeton University Press, Princeton, N.J., 1962.

Hadley, G., *Non-Linear and Dynamic Programming*, Addison-Wesley Publishing Co., Reading, Mass., 1964.

Howard, R., *Dynamic Programming and Markov Processes*, John Wiley and Sons, New York, 1960.

READ

CHAPTER **10**

Queuing Problems

INTRODUCTION

Consider a facility at which work is done or a service is performed. Things requiring work or service come, or are brought, to the "service facility." These things are called "customers." They may be letters requiring signatures, cars to be parked, ships to be unloaded, parts to be assembled, people waiting for service, or anything else that requires work done on and for it. If the customers arrive "too frequently," they will have to wait for service or do without it. If they arrive too infrequently, the service facilities will have to wait (i.e., remain idle) until additional customers arrive. Waiting customers or idle facilities form a *waiting line* or *queue*. The order in which waiting customers are selected for service is called the *queue discipline*; it may be the order of "first come, first served," the order of age, urgency, or some priority system, and so on. Customers may even be selected randomly, as they appear to be by salesclerks at crowded counters.

A facility that can serve only one customer at a time is called a *service point*. If the service is performed in stages by a sequence of service points, the sequence is called a *line*. If there are several points or lines that can service customers simultaneously, they are called *channels*. All or some of the channels may provide the same service, or each or some may be specialized. On turnpikes, for example, there are usually several tollbooths for automobiles only and one or more for trucks. Cafeterias frequently have more than one channel—in some cases the same and in others different ones—each consisting of a number of service points. Several service points may feed into one subsequent service point; for example, several ticket booths at a theater may send all ticket holders to a single ticket collector at the entrance. On the other hand, a single service point may disperse customers among several channels that come after it; for example, an information clerk in a department store.

248

Whenever we have customers coming to a service point in such a way that either the customers or facilities may have to wait, we have a *queuing process*. A *queuing problem* arises in such a process

(*a*) if either the arrival rate of customers or the amount of service facilities available, or both are subject to control; and

(*b*) if there are costs associated with both the waiting time of customers and idle time of facilities.

A queuing problem consists of either *scheduling arrivals* or *providing facilities*, or both, so as to minimize the sum of the costs of waiting customers and idle facilities.

Since most of us spend a good deal of time in lines waiting to serve or be served, queuing processes and queuing problems are commonplace. A few examples are the following:

How many check-out counters to provide at a supermarket?
How many runways to provide at an airport?
How many berths for ships at a port?
How many parking spaces in a lot?
How many salesgirls in a department store?
How many maintenance crews in a factory?
How many doctors in a clinic?
How many beds in a hospital?
How to schedule airline flights into a city?
How to schedule trains or a trucking fleet?

A large class of maintenance problems can be treated as queuing problems. The equipment or items requiring repair are customers. The maintenance facilities may go to the customers, as service men do in repairing home appliances. The cost of customer waiting time may involve the loss of use of the item that is "down."

Some inventory problems may also be formulated as queuing processes. An arriving order that is to be filled from stock can be viewed as a customer. The storage facility can be looked at as a service facility that provides items from stock to customers. The service operation is the process of refilling the empty storage space by ordering another unit or units to fill the empty space. The queue is the number of these orders for replenishing stock which are unfilled. When demand is discontinuous and restricted to one or a few items at a time, inventory can be effectively treated as a queuing process. To solve such an inventory problem, a model of the queuing process is imbedded in an inventory model. For such treatment of inventories, see Morse (1958) and Prabhu (1965).

Some queues are said to be *circular*, because serviced items (i.e., those that have been discharged) may reenter the pool of potential customers and come back for service at a later date. For example, the trucks in a fleet may constitute a circular queue with respect to a company maintenance shop. If the pool of potential customers is very large, the circular queue behaves much as a linear queue in which discharged items do not return for service. The pools may be finite or virtually infinite in size. Very large pools are usually treated as though they were infinite, because of the mathematical simplification that is obtained by doing so.

The cost of waiting customers generally includes either the indirect cost of lost business (because people go somewhere else, buy less than they had intended to, or do not return in the future) or the direct cost of idle facilities and people; for example, the cost of truck drivers and equipment waiting to be unloaded or the cost of operating an airplane or ship that is waiting to land or dock. Lost business may not be easily observed. For example, automobile drivers wanting gasoline will avoid stations with long waiting lines at the pumps. To determine how much business is lost in such situations, some form of experimentation may be required or a detailed analysis of how demand has varied in the past with different levels of service that have been provided.

In some cases the cost of waiting customers can be obtained by appropriate analysis of "available" observations. For example, it will be recalled that in an illustration used in Chapter 2 a transformation was obtained of customer waiting time for receipt of mail orders into a cost resulting from returns of goods. In restaurants we can sometimes observe how the arrival rate of customers varies with the length of the waiting line; we can even observe how many go away as a function of the length of the waiting line, but it is more difficult to determine what longer-range effects this has on their returning. In circular queues, such as occur in truck-fleet maintenance systems, the cost of waiting customers (trucks waiting for repair) usually is the cost of the additional trucks required in the system to "cover" those that are "down," that is, the cost of "spares."

The cost of idle service facilities may affect other costs. For example, if an airline had only one maintenance location, much more time would be required to transport planes to and from this location than would be required if there were several dispersed locations.

In general, a model of a queuing problem expresses total cost as the sum of two costs—those of waiting customers and idle facilities. These costs are functions of the distributions of the two types of waiting time, which in turn are functions of the controlled variables: the number of facilities and/or the schedule of arrivals and the parameters of the queuing process. The difficulty in most queuing problems lies in determining waiting-time distributions, not in solving the "cost" model once the essential properties of the queues are known. For this reason queuing theory is preoccupied with the properties of queues, and not with cost models of queuing processes.

THE STATE OF THE SYSTEM

A basic concept in the analysis of a queuing process is that of a *state* of the system. Roughly speaking, a state is a description of the system that provides a sufficient basis for predicting probabilistically its future behavior. The essential point about such predictions is that they do *not* require information about *how* the state came about, only what it is. The concept can be illustrated as follows.

Suppose that a salesman calls on customers each month and that past experience shows that if a customer placed an order last month, the chance of an order this month is p_1, and if there was no order last month, p_0. It will be convenient to refer to this first month as month 0, the second month as month 1, and so on. Then in any month after the first one, each customer must be in one of two states:

state 0: placed no order last month
state 1: placed an order last month

Then, if we know a customer's present state and p_0 and p_1, we can predict his future behavior.

Let u_n be the probability of an order in month n for a customer who had placed no order in the first month, and let v_n be the corresponding probability for a customer who had placed an order in the first month. We can now construct the following equation for a customer who was in state 0 in month 1:

$$u_{n+1} = p_1 u_n + p_0(1 - u_n) \qquad n > 0; \tag{10.1}$$

for a customer who was in state 1 in month 1, the equation is

$$v_{n+1} = p_1 v_n + p_0(1 - v_n) \qquad n > 0. \tag{10.2}$$

But note that

$$u_1 = p_0 \tag{10.3}$$

and

$$v_1 = p_1. \tag{10.4}$$

It is not difficult to tabulate solutions to (10.1) through (10.4) if we can obtain numerical values for p_0 and p_1. For example, suppose that $p_0 = 0.3$ and $p_1 = 0.6$; then from (10.3) and (10.4) we see that $u_1 = 0.3$ and $v_1 = 0.6$. If we put $n = 1$ in (10.1), we obtain

$$u_2 = 0.6 \times 0.3 + 0.3 \times 0.7 = 0.39,$$

TABLE 10.1   *State Probabilities*

n	1	2	3	4	5	6	7	8
u_n	0.3	0.39	0.417	0.4251	0.4275	0.4283	0.4285	0.4286
v_n	0.6	0.48	0.444	0.433	0.430	0.429	0.4287	0.4286

and from (10.2) we see that

$$v_1 = 0.6 \times 0.6 + 0.3 \times 0.4 = 0.48.$$

Table 10.1 shows the results for $n = 1, 2, 3, \ldots, 8$.

Examination of Table 10.1 suggests that both u_n and v_n settle down to the same value as n becomes large, and in fact a rigorous proof that they do has been provided. If there is a value, v, such that for large n, $v = u_n = u_{n+1} = v_n = v_{n+1}$, then from (10.1) and (10.2) we see that v must satisfy

$$v = p_1 v + p_0(1 - v)$$
$$= 0.6v + 0.3 - 0.3v$$
$$= 0.3v + 0.3;$$

therefore, solving for v, we obtain

$$v = \frac{0.3}{0.7} = 0.4286,$$

which can be seen in Table 10.1 to be the value of u_n and v_n where $n = 8$.

We call v the *steady-state probability* of a sale. One interpretation of a steady-state probability is that in the *long-run*, independent of the state in the first month, there will be a sale for a fraction v of the time. Alternatively, if we imagine a large number of customers, then in any week, a long time hence, there will be sales to a fraction v.

Steady-state probabilities are of considerable interest, because they are useful in predicting *long-run* profits and costs. In most practical queuing problems, steady-state solutions exist independently of the initial state of the queue. Unless we know that the queuing process will terminate before it reaches a steady state or shortly thereafter, knowledge of the steady-state probabilities is usually sufficient to solve the queuing problem. Instead of states changing at fixed intervals, as in the salesman example, where they could only change once a week, in most queues arrivals and departures can take place at any point of time. This leads to partial differential equations rather than to difference equations such as (10.1) to (10.4).

RANDOM OR POISSON ARRIVALS AND
EXPONENTIAL SERVICE TIMES

In order to discuss a queuing system, we must specify the arrival and service patterns. Unless arrivals have been scheduled, it is convenient to assume for mathematical reasons that they are random,[1] that is, that they are equally likely to occur at any point of time. Put another way, the assumption states that the chance of the next arrival's occurrence is independent of the time that has passed since the last arrival. More precisely, if h is a sufficiently small amount of time and λ is the mean rate of arrivals (i.e., 1/the mean time between arrivals), the probability of an arrival in the interval t to $t + h$ is λh independent of the time t. The distribution of arrivals generated by this assumption is called *Poisson*, because it may be shown that the probability of n arrivals in any finite interval of time, t, is $e^{-\lambda t}(\lambda t)^n/n!$. This is the Poisson distribution with parameter λt. (The reader may wish to show that both the mean and variance of this Poisson distribution are λt.)

The probability of an interval exceeding t between two consecutive arrivals is the same as the probability of no arrivals in the interval t immediately following the first arrival. By setting $n = 0$ we see that this probability is $e^{-\lambda t}$. Thus under these assumptions the time between arrivals has an *exponential* distribution.

The assumption of Poisson arrivals, or the equivalent assumption that an arrival is equally likely to occur at any point of time, is more frequently justified than might appear at first sight. For example, iron-ore ships are scheduled to arrive at their destinations on given dates, but it has been observed that fluctuations in weather and tides cause schedules to be missed in such a way that actual arrivals follow a Poisson distribution. The same distribution has been observed for arriving flights at an airfield. At a busy airfield arrivals may be scheduled for every few minutes, but because planes are often early or late by amounts at least as great as the scheduled intervals between arrivals, the actual pattern is sufficiently similar to the Poisson distribution.

In the early years of this century a Danish telephone engineer, A. K. Erlang, observed that calls arrive at the exchange in such a way that the assumption of Poisson arrivals leads to useful conclusions about the necessary level of service.

---

[1] If in a real queuing situation this assumption is not justified, the results that follow from it are not relevant. The theory is complicated if other assumptions are made. It may become so complex that we must resort to simulation to learn what we want to know of the process.

There are two types of situation in which the Poisson assumption is likely to produce poor results:

1. When arrivals have been scheduled and the errors about the scheduled times are small compared to the planned interarrival interval.

2. When arrivals result from a time-dependent process, such as the need for maintenance on items that wear out. Here service is seldom required until some minimum time has elapsed since the previous occasion, and the assumption of equally likely arrivals at all times is unjustified.

In many other situations Poisson arrivals are a reasonable assumption, and even though data may fit other assumptions equally well, they are frequently not at great enough variance with this assumption for it to be rejected.

Although arrivals appear to be random in many situations, there is no obvious or consistent pattern for service times. Unless we assume exponentially distributed service times, however, or some extensions thereof that are discussed below, the mathematics rapidly become relatively complex. Because of the mathematical simplicity that exponential service times yield, they have been studied extensively. We discuss such service time here to illustrate how models of queuing processes are developed, not to develop a generally applicable queuing model.

It may be shown that a queuing system with any distribution of service times, which has m identical service channels, can reach a steady state provided that the mean rate of arrivals per channel (λ/m) is less than the mean service rate per channel (μ); that is, when

$$\frac{\frac{\lambda}{m}}{\mu} = \frac{\lambda}{m\mu} < 1.$$

If the arrival rate per channel is equal to the service rate per channel, unless the arrivals are spaced regularly at the mean service time, the queue will grow indefinitely. (Confirm this diagrammatically, assuming that $\lambda/m = \mu = 1$.) This result is a consequence of the fact that unused service time cannot be saved or made up.

Now, to see how the parameters of a queuing system are derived, consider a large number (N) of such systems in each of which, when n persons are present (waiting or being served), arrivals are Poisson at a rate λ_n and the service times are exponential with an average capacity of μ_n services per unit time. Let p_n be the steady-state probability that there are n persons present. Then at any instant the number of systems in the set with n persons present is $p_n N$. Because we are considering steady states, this number will not change with time. However, the systems with n present at one moment of time need not be the same ones that have n present at another moment of time. Arrivals occur at a rate λ_n, and an arrival will change a system with n persons present to one with $(n + 1)$ present. Similarly, completed services or departures occur at a rate of μ_n, and a departure will change an n-system to a $(n - 1)$-system. Hence, the rate at which n-systems become $(n + 1)$-systems is $\lambda_n p_n N$, and the rate at which they become $(n - 1)$-systems is $\mu_n p_n N$. Combining them, we obtain the rate at which n-systems change to either $(n + 1)$ or $(n - 1)$-systems:

$$\lambda_n p_n N + \mu_n p_n N = (\lambda_n + \mu_n) p_n N.$$

Because the number of n-systems remains constant, this rate must be balanced by the rate at which other (non-n) systems become n-systems. Therefore,

$$\lambda_{n-1} p_{n-1} N + \mu_{n+1} p_{n+1} N = (\lambda_n + \mu_n) p_n N$$

or, dividing by N,

$$\lambda_{n-1} p_{n-1} + \mu_{n+1} p_{n+1} + (\lambda_n + \mu_n) p_n. \tag{10.5}$$

Equation (10.5) will not hold when $n = 0$, because then p_{n-1} has no meaning. Furthermore, there can be no departures when $n = 0$ (i.e., $\mu_0 = 0$). Then, adjusting (10.5) appropriately for $n = 0$, we obtain

$$\mu_1 p_1 = \lambda_0 p_0. \tag{10.6}$$

To find the values of the p's we can proceed as follows. By rearranging (10.6) we obtain

$$p_1 = \frac{\lambda_0}{\mu_1} p_0 \tag{10.7}$$

and

$$\lambda_0 p_0 - \mu_1 p_1 = 0. \tag{10.8}$$

By rearranging (10.5), we obtain

$$\lambda_n p_n - \mu_{n+1} p_{n+1} = \lambda_{n-1} p_{n-1} - \mu_n p_n. \tag{10.9}$$

If we let $n = 1$ and use (10.8), (10.9) becomes

$$\lambda_1 p_1 - \mu_2 p_2 = \lambda_0 p_0 - \mu_1 p_1 = 0.$$

Again rearranging, we obtain

$$p_2 = \frac{\lambda_1}{\mu_2} p_1.$$

Now, when we use the value of p_1 from (10.7), the last equation becomes

$$p_2 = \frac{\lambda_0 \lambda_1}{\mu_1 \mu_1} p_0 \tag{10.10}$$

Continuing this procedure, we can obtain the values of p_n for all $n \geq 0$:

$$p_{n+1} = \frac{\lambda_n}{\mu_{n+1}} p_n \qquad (10.11)$$

and

$$p_n = \frac{\lambda_0 \lambda_1 \lambda_2 \cdots \lambda_{n-1}}{\mu_1 \mu_2 \cdots \mu_n} p_0. \qquad (10.12)$$

Finally, because some number $(0, 1, 2, \ldots)$ must be present, it follows that

$$p_0 + p_1 + p_2 + p_3 + \cdots = 1. \qquad (10.13)$$

Equation (10.12) permits us to express p_n in terms of p_0 and, provided that the series converges, equation (10.13) then yields p_0.

Single Channel with Constant Arrival and Service Rates

The simplest queuing system is one in which there is a single channel with a fixed arrival rate $(\lambda = \lambda_0 = \lambda_1 = \lambda_2 = \cdots)$ and a fixed service rate $(\mu = \mu_1 = \mu_2 = \mu_3 = \cdots)$. In this case (10.12) becomes

$$p_n = \frac{\lambda^n}{\mu^n} p_0 = \rho^n p_0 \qquad (10.14)$$

where

$$\rho = \frac{\lambda}{\mu}. \qquad (10.15)$$

The letter ρ is often referred to as the *traffic intensity*. Now, if we substitute (10.14) into (10.13), we obtain

$$p_0 + p_0 \rho + p_0 \rho^2 + p_0 \rho^3 + \cdots = 1$$

or

$$p_0(1 + \rho + \rho^2 + \rho^3 + \cdots) = 1.$$

But because $p = \lambda/\mu < 1$, we have

$$(1 + \rho + \rho^2 + \rho^3 + \cdots) = \frac{1}{1 - \rho},$$

and it follows that

$$\frac{p_0}{1 - \rho} = 1$$

or

$$p_0 = 1 - \rho. \qquad (10.16)$$

Then, from (10.14) and (10.16), we obtain

$$p_n = (1 - \rho)\rho^n.$$

The average number of customers in the system is

$$\bar{n} = p_1 + 2p_2 + 3p_3 + \cdots .$$

Substituting into this the value of p_n just obtained, we have

$$\bar{n} = (1 - \rho)\rho + 2(1 - \rho)\rho^2 + 3(1 - \rho)\rho^3 + \cdots$$
$$= (1 - \rho)[\rho + 2\rho^2 + 3\rho^3 + \cdots]$$
$$= (1 - \rho)\rho[1 + 2\rho + 3\rho^2 + \cdots].$$

Because it can be shown that the series $(1 + 2\rho + 3\rho^2 + \cdots)$ is equal to $1/(1 - \rho)^2$, it follows that

$$\bar{n} = (1 - \rho)\frac{\rho}{(1 - \rho)^2} = \frac{\rho}{1 - \rho} . \tag{10.17}$$

The average number in the queue (not counting the one, if any, that is in service) is

$$\bar{n}_q = p_2 + 2p_3 + 3p_4 + \cdots$$
$$= (1 - \rho)\,\rho^2(1 + 2\rho + 3\rho^2 + \cdots)$$
$$= (1 - \rho)\frac{\rho^2}{(1 - \rho)^2} = \frac{\rho^2}{1 - \rho} . \tag{10.18}$$

It is clear that $\bar{n}_q$ and $\bar{n}$ differ by the average number in service $(\bar{n}_s)$, which therefore is

$$\bar{n}_s = \frac{\rho}{1 - \rho} - \frac{\rho^2}{1 - \rho} = \rho. \tag{10.19}$$

We can also obtain $\bar{n}_s$ by observing that if one or more are present, there is one in service and that otherwise there is none. Hence

$$\bar{n}_s = 0 \times p_0 + 1 \times (1 - p_0) = 1 - (1 - \rho) = \rho.$$

The Multichannel Case

Consider a queuing process that has m channels, each with service rate μ. Then, when the number of customers present (n) is less than or equal to the number of channels (m)—that is, when $n \leq m$—there will be n busy channels and service will be at the rate $n\mu$. When $n > m$, all m channels are busy and service is at a rate $m\mu$. Hence,

$$\lambda_n = \lambda \qquad n = 0, 1, 2, \ldots$$

$$\mu_n = \begin{cases} n\mu & n = 1, 2, \ldots, m \\ m\mu & n = m + 1, m + 2, \ldots . \end{cases}$$

If $\rho = (\lambda/\mu) < m$, we may substitute these values of λ_n and μ_n in (10.12) to determine the values of p_n:

$$p_n = \left(\frac{\lambda^n}{\mu \times 2\mu \times 3\mu \times \cdots \times n\mu}\right) p_0 = \frac{\lambda^n}{n!\,\mu^n}\, p_0$$

$$= \frac{\rho^n}{n!}\, p_0 \qquad n = 0, 1, 2, \ldots, m \tag{10.20}$$

$$p_n = \left(\frac{\lambda^n}{\mu \times 2\mu \times \cdots \times m\mu \times \mu^{n-m}}\right) p_0 = \frac{\lambda^n}{\mu^n m!\, m^{n-m}}\, p_0$$

$$= \frac{\rho^n}{m!\, m^{n-m}}\, p_0 \qquad n = m + 1, m + 2, \ldots. \tag{10.21}$$

Substituting the values of p_n given in (10.20) and (10.21) into (10.13) yields

$$p_0 + \rho p_0 + \frac{\rho^2}{2!}\, p_0 + \cdots + \frac{\rho^{m-1}}{(m-1)!}\, p_0$$

$$+ \frac{\rho^m}{m!}\, p_0 + \frac{\rho^{m+1}}{m!\, m}\, p_0 + \frac{\rho^{m+2}}{m!\, m^2}\, p_0 + \cdots = 1.$$

The first m terms of this series cannot be expressed in closed form, but the remaining terms can be simplified. They are

$$\frac{\rho^m}{m!}\, p_0 + \frac{\rho^{m+1}}{m!\, m}\, p_0 + \frac{\rho^{m+2}}{m!\, m^2}\, p_0 + \cdots$$

$$= \frac{\rho^m}{m!}\, p_0\left[1 + \frac{\rho}{m} + \left(\frac{\rho}{m}\right)^2 + \left(\frac{\rho}{m}\right)^3 + \cdots\right];$$

when we use the formula for the sum of a geometric progression $[a + ar + ar^2 + \cdots = a/(1 - r)$ provided that $-1 < r < 1]$, this becomes

$$\frac{\rho^m}{m!}\, p_0\, \frac{1}{1 - \rho/m}.$$

When we substitute into the equation for p_0, we obtain

$$p_0 = \frac{1}{1 + \rho + \rho^2/2! + \cdots + \rho^{m-1}/(m-1)! + \rho^m/m!\,(1 - \rho/m)} \tag{10.22}$$

With some algebra it may also be shown that

$$\bar{n}_q = \frac{p_0 \rho^{m+1}}{m m!\,(1 - \rho/m)^2} \tag{10.23}$$

$$\bar{n} = \bar{n}_q + \rho \tag{10.24}$$

$$\bar{n}_s = \rho. \tag{10.25}$$

Other results are obtained in Exercises 1 to 6, which should be done at this point.

WAITING TIMES IN THE STEADY STATE

Very often the costs of a customer's waiting are dependent on either the amount of his waiting time or the total time that he spends in the system, including service. This is clearly the case when a company's trucks or ships are waiting for a dock or berth at which to be unloaded.

Consider the case shown in Figure 10.1, in which the customers are numbered in order of arrival and their waiting time is graphed against time. It can be seen that the area under the curve is simply $\bar{n}T$. If we look at the blocks labeled 3, we see that their total area (6 units) is the time that the third

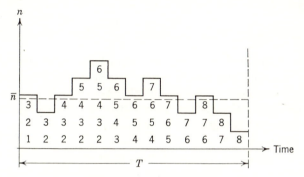

Figure 10.1   Waiting times.

man to be served waits during T. The same is true for 4, 5, and 6. Thus the area under the curve consists of the waiting time for those who arrived and were serviced during T, plus the waiting time during T for those who arrived before T started, plus the waiting time during T for those who arrived during T but were served after T. If T is large, we can expect $\bar{\lambda}T$ arrivals,[2] and all but a negligible number of them will be served during T. Also, the contribution to the area under the curve of those who arrived before T or left after T will be very small. Thus for large T the area under the curve will be the total waiting time for the $\bar{\lambda}T$ arrivals, which is $\bar{\lambda}T\overline{W}$, where $\overline{W}$ is the average waiting time. Thus

$$\bar{\lambda}T\overline{W} = \bar{n}T$$

where $\bar{n}$ is the average queue length; on dividing by T, we obtain

$$\bar{\lambda}\overline{W} = \bar{n}. \tag{10.26}$$

---

[2] Notice that $\bar{\lambda}$ is the *actual* average arrival rate over time T. If the arrival rates vary (as, for example, when they depend on the number present), they must be averaged, taking into account the fraction of time in which each applies, before this argument can be used.

Equation (10.26) permits us to obtain the average waiting time as soon as we have the distribution of the number present; unfortunately, the distribution of waiting time is not so simple. For one thing, it depends on the order of selecting from among waiting customers, whereas the average and the distributions of queue length do not.

Equation (10.26) can be shown to hold for any number of service counters and for any arrival or service pattern. If $\bar{n}$ refers to the number in the queue, $\overline{W}$ refers to waiting in the queue. If $\bar{n}$ refers to the number in the system, including any in service, $\overline{W}$ refers to total time in the system, including service time.

(Exercise 7 should be done at this point.)

SINGLE CHANNEL WITH ARBITRARY SERVICE TIMES

The preceding methods enable us to compute most of the results that enter into cost calculations, provided that we are dealing with Poisson-exponential systems. The mathematical analysis of other systems is much more difficult, but in this section we give one result for a single channel that is quite general. We retain the assumption of Poisson arrivals at a rate λ, but we permit any arbitrary distribution of service times. For such a system it can be shown that, in the steady state, the average number in the system, $\bar{n}$, is given by

$$\bar{n} = \frac{\lambda \bar{t} + \lambda^2[\bar{t}^2 + V(t)]}{2(1 - \lambda \bar{t})} , \tag{10.27}$$

where

$\bar{t} =$ average service time
$V(t) =$ variance of the service time.

From this several interesting results follow. If λ and $\bar{t}$ are fixed, the average queue length depends on $V(t)$ and can be minimized by making $V(t) = 0$. In this case the service time is constant and equal to $\bar{t}$. If we write $\rho = \lambda \bar{t}$, (10.27) becomes

$$\bar{n}_{\text{constant}} = \rho + \frac{1}{2}\frac{\rho^2}{1 - \rho} . \tag{10.28}$$

On the other hand, $\bar{n}$ can be increased indefinitely by increasing the variance of the service time. It is clear that if we wish to reduce queue lengths and if we cannot alter λ or $\bar{t}$, we should consider reducing the variance of t. In view of (10.26), this will also reduce the average waiting time.

In order to use (10.27) it is necessary to be able to compute means and variances. In general, this requires the use of integral calculus, but in some cases other techniques are possible. Calculus can be used to show that if we have exponential service times, the mean service time is $1/\mu$ and the variance is $1/\mu^2$.

Results for two other systems can now be obtained. Suppose that a service consists of k separate tasks that are performed in sequence and that at any one time the service channel can perform one of these tasks. Let each task have an exponential service time, with mean $1/k\mu$. Then the average time to complete all k tasks is k times as much as for one task, or $1/\mu$. Now, provided that the times are mutually independent, the variance of the sum of k times may be found by adding their separate variances. Because each task has an exponential time of mean $1/k\mu$, its variance is $1/k^2\mu^2$, and the variance of all k tasks is $1/k\mu^2$. Channels whose total service time is distributed in this way are called *k-Erlang*. They were discussed by a Danish telephone engineer, A. K. Erlang, about fifty years ago. Because k is an integer, the Erlang distribution has a smaller variance than the corresponding exponential distribution. It is often used as an approximation to any distribution in which the standard deviation is less than the mean, even though the separate tasks have no physical existence.

If we substitute $\bar{t} = 1/\mu$, $V(t) = 1/k\mu^2$ in (10.27), we obtain, after putting $\lambda/\mu = \rho$,

$$\bar{n}_{\text{Erlang}} = \rho + \frac{\rho(1 + 1/k)}{2(1 - \rho)} \ . \tag{10.29}$$

Notice that when k approaches infinity, the variance becomes zero and we have the constant service-time formula.

The fact that it is relatively easy to compute the variance of the k-Erlang distribution is not the main reason that such distributions are of interest. Until recently, almost the only method available for analyzing queuing systems involved the use of balance equations similar to (10.5). Such equations are reasonably simple to handle, provided that we can define states in such a way that the probability of passing from one to another does not depend on the time that the system has been in the first state. For Erlang service times, the state of the system may be defined as the number of tasks to be performed before the queue is cleared. Thus, if the man in service has r tasks still to be completed and if there are $(n - 1)$ persons in the queue, there are $k(n - 1) + r$ tasks to be completed. This number jumps by k each time there is an arrival and drops by one each time a task is completed. The interested reader can pursue the details in Morse (1958).

In an attempt to analyze systems in which the service-time variance is greater than that of the corresponding exponential distribution, Morse (1958) suggested the following model of what he called the *hyperexponential* channel. Imagine that a service channel has two counters, only one of which can be used at a time. Arrivals are Poisson at a rate λ; with probability σ they go to the first counter and with probability $1 - \sigma$ they go to the second counter. Each counter has an exponential service time; the first operates at a rate $2\sigma\mu$, and the second operates at a rate $2(1 - \sigma)\mu$. The average service times thus are $1/2\sigma\mu$ and $1/2(1 - \sigma)\mu$, and the overall average time is

$$\sigma \frac{1}{2\sigma\mu} + (1 - \sigma) \frac{1}{2(1 - \sigma)\mu} = \frac{1}{\mu}.$$

The reader should show that the service-time variance, overall, is

$$V(t) = \frac{1 - 2\sigma(1 - \sigma)}{2\mu^2\sigma(1 - \sigma)}.$$ (10.30)

When $\sigma = \frac{1}{2}$, the two counters are obviously identical and the system operates as if it were one exponential channel. For all other values of σ, in the range between zero and one, the variance is greater than that of the exponential systems. Apart from inserting (10.30) into (10.27) to give the average number in the system, it is possible to obtain balance equations by defining the states as the number in the system together with the counter (first or second) at which the service is taking place.

OTHER QUEUING MODELS

Many special queuing situations have been discussed in the literature, only a few of which can be mentioned here. It should be realized that as long as we can describe the situation with a set of states such that the rates of transition between states do not depend on the elapsed time since entering a state, we can obtain a set of homogeneous linear equations for the steady-state probabilities of being in the various states. If we require the time-dependent or transient solutions, we have a set of linear differential equations. When there is a finite number of states, numerical solutions of either set may be obtained fairly easily. If the number of states is infinite, even numerical solutions for the steady state may require some ingenuity. However, if such solutions exist, it is usually possible to approximate them by setting a finite limit to the number of states. This can be done by assuming that no arrivals can occur when there are N in the system. If the probability of N occurring then turns out to be negligible, the approximation is good enough.

Sometimes it is possible, by adding hypothetical states, to convert to a system with transition probabilities that do not depend on elapsed time in the state. We have referred briefly to the Erlang and hyperexponential distributions that can be modeled in this way.

Among the systems that have been analyzed by means of state balance equations are the following:

Single and multicounters with finite and infinite queues.

Priority systems such as exist, for example, in a military telephone network in which the general's calls take precedence over all others, or in a hospital where surgical emergencies are admitted immediately while the other patients have to wait their turn.

Queues in tandem where the output from one queue becomes the input of another.

Circular queues where customers completing service return to the back of the queue.

Multicounter problems with different service rates at each counter and various rules for customers to choose the counter at which they line up.

Impatient customer who leaves without waiting for service.

Some writers have attacked queuing problems by studying the distribution of waiting times directly, which leads to a set of integrodifferential equations; these can either be solved directly or used to infer necessary and sufficient conditions for the existence of steady-state solutions.

Despite the great ingenuity and powerful mathematical techniques employed in analysis of queues, explicit solutions have only been obtained in relatively simple situations. In many practical problems the choice is either to assume independent exponential distributions for service and interarrival times and use analytical techniques, or to use simulation.

SIMULATION OF QUEUES

Any queuing system that can be described and for which data on arrival and service times can be obtained, can be simulated. Because most queuing problems involve determination of the number of facilities that must be made available, and because we generally can estimate fairly closely what the optimal number is, it is usually not necessary to simulate very many different numbers of facilities to find the optimum.

The availability of computers has greatly reduced the time required to solve large queuing problems by simulation. Running time is often very short. Programming, which once required a great deal of time, can now be reduced by use of such special simulation languages as SIMSCRIPT. Many smaller queuing systems can be simulated by hand, as in the case that is described below.

The use of simulation in queuing problems is particularly useful when either the process never reaches stability (as when a service facility is open for only a short time) or the transient states are critical (as in the opening of a department store on the day of a big sale). It is usually very difficult to study nonsteady states of queues by analytic procedures, but it is quite easy to do so by use of simulation.

Simulating a Barbershop

The essential characteristics of a queuing process can usually be shown in a flow chart, as is done in Figure 10.2, which shows a queuing process that might occur at a barbershop. In this diagram the circles represent points of decision for customers. The probability of their selecting each alternative must be determined. In some cases these may be conditional probabilities. For example, the decision of a customer in the waiting line about whether to continue waiting or not may depend on (1) how long he has been waiting and (2) how many other customers remain in front of him in the queue.

Let us suppose that there are three barbers and that the time during which a customer is in the chair averages 20 minutes and is normally distributed with a standard deviation of 5 minutes. During the peak lunch-hour period from midday to 1:45 P.M. customers arrive at the shop in a Poisson stream with an average of 12 per hour. There are 3 chairs for waiting customers; when they are full (6 customers in the shop in all), further arrivals leave immediately. If all barbers are busy and if there are 0, 1, 2 waiting customers, the probabilities that an arrival leaves without waiting are 0.1, 0.3, and 0.5. Customers who have waited 15 minutes and are not about to receive service have an even chance of leaving without waiting further.

From the opening of the shop (10 A.M.) to noon and from 1:45 P.M. to closing time (5 P.M.), customer arrival is at the rate of 6 per hour. One barber goes to lunch[3] from 11 to 11:30, and on his return a second man goes from 11:30 to 12. The third man takes lunch from 2 to 2:30. On the average, how many customers leave without receiving a haircut?

The reader is advised to review the section on simulation, Chapter 4, before proceeding.

The first step in simulating such a problem is to decide on the minimum time interval to be considered. To keep the arithmetic within bounds, we shall use 5 minutes and assume that all events occur at the end of an integral number of 5-minute intervals. We shall number customers in order of arrival and start by finding the number of arrivals in each interval. For the lunch period, the rate of arrival is one per 5 minutes; thus the distribution is Poisson

---

[3] We assume that each barber completes the service for the customer in his chair when his lunch period starts and then takes his full half hour. The second man will not leave for lunch until the first man has returned.

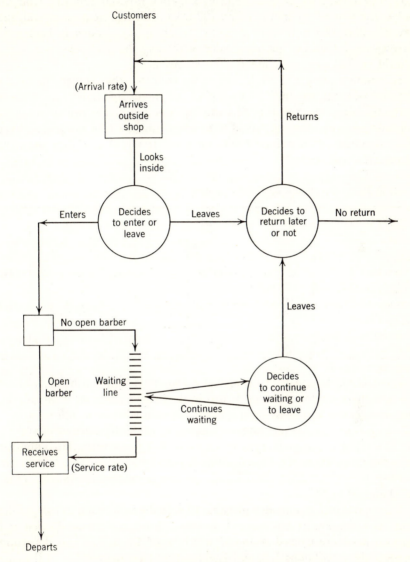

Figure 10.2 Diagram of barbershop queue.

with parameter one, and the probabilities of 0, 1, 2, 3, 4 arrivals are 0.37, 0.37, 0.19, 0.06, 0.01. We will be using two-digit random numbers, from 00 to 99. The first 37 random numbers (00 to 36) will represent no arrival, the next 37 will represent one arrival (37 to 73) and so on, as shown in Table 10.3 (arrivals, $\lambda = 1.0$). For the remainder of the day the parameter is $\lambda = 0.5$ and the critical random numbers are also given.

To obtain a sample of service times, we note that the standard deviation is 5 and we treat any time between plus and minus one half of a standard deviation of the mean as if it were exactly 20 minutes. The probability of a normal variate in this range is 0.38. We obtain Table 10.2. (A random number 00 yields a time of 5 minutes; 01 to 06 inclusive, 10 minutes; 07 to 30 inclusive 15 minutes; and so on.)

TABLE 10.2 *Derivation of Service Times*

Assumed service time (minutes)	5	10	15	20	25	30	35
Interval (minutes)	$<7\frac{1}{2}$	$(7\frac{1}{2}, 12\frac{1}{2})$	$(12\frac{1}{2}, 17\frac{1}{2})$	$(17\frac{1}{2}, 22\frac{1}{2})$	$(22\frac{1}{2}, 27\frac{1}{2})$	$(27\frac{1}{2}, 32\frac{1}{2})$	$>32\frac{1}{2}$
Interval (standard deviations)	$<-2\frac{1}{2}$	$(-2\frac{1}{2}, -1\frac{1}{2})$	$(-1\frac{1}{2}, -\frac{1}{2})$	$(-\frac{1}{2}, \frac{1}{2})$	$(\frac{1}{2}, 1\frac{1}{2})$	$(1\frac{1}{2}, 2\frac{1}{2})$	$(>2\frac{1}{2})$
Probability	0.1	0.6	0.24	0.38	0.24	0.06	0.01
Critical random number	00	06	30	68	92	98	99

The decision to depart at the end of a 15-minute wait will be determined by choosing a random number. If it is in the interval 00 to 49 inclusive, the customer leaves; otherwise he stays. The decision whether or not to wait at all depends on the number already waiting. If all barbers are busy and no one is waiting, the probability of leaving is 0.10. Thus, if the random number is in the range 00 to 09, the customer leaves. When 1 or 2 customers are waiting, the probabilities are 0.3 and 0.5. The corresponding ranges are 00 to 29 and 00 to 49.

A complete day is simulated in Table 10.3. In the table, column 1 shows the times at which events can occur. Columns 2 through 8 are subdivided and the two parts are labeled A and D which stand for arrival and departure respectively. In columns 2, 3, and 4 under A we have the number of the customer who is present in each barber chair. Under D the number of the departing customer is shown. Columns 5 through 7 refer to the chairs for waiting customers. Under D are shown customers who leave at the end of a 15-minute wait. Column 8, under A, shows the reference numbers of the customers arriving; under D are shown any who leave immediately on arrival.

Column 9 shows the random numbers used to determine the number of arrivals. The first 3 entries 10, 37, 08 are below the critical number (60) for one arrival; thus there are no corresponding entries in column 8. The fourth entry (99) corresponds to 2 arrivals, and their numbers 1 and 2 are shown under A in column 8. Both enter the barbers' chairs immediately as shown under A in columns 2 and 3. The random numbers (09, 54) for determining their service times are shown in column 10 and the corresponding times (15, 20) are shown in column 11. Their presence in barber chairs 1 and 2 is shown in columns 2 and 3 under A and their departures at 10:30 and 10:35 are shown under D in columns 2 and 3. If an arriving customer finds all barbers busy, a random number is drawn to determine whether he leaves immediately. These numbers are shown in column 12. (See, for example, customer 8 who waits or customer 12 who leaves). The random numbers to determine if customers wait more than 15 minutes are in column 13. (See, for example, customer 33 who stays and customers 13 and 14 who leave.)

Once Table 10.3 is complete, it is easy to count the customers who leave without receiving service: customers 12, 13, 16, 17, 22, 32, 34, 35, 38, and 41 leave immediately, and 14, 15, and 40 leave after 15 minutes. Thus 13 customers are lost out of a total of 58.

The objective of a simulation such as this might be to determine the profit that could be obtained by having a fourth barber, but conclusions could not be made on the basis of a single day. In any case, it is as well to check the total number of arrivals (58) against the expected number, which is 6 per hour from 10 to noon and from 1:45 to 5, and 12 per hour from noon to 1:45. That is, $6(2 + 3\frac{1}{4}) + 12 \times 1\frac{3}{4} = 52\frac{1}{2}$. Now, we observed the following frequencies of service times:

Service time (minutes)	5	10	15	20	25	30	35	Total
Frequency	1	4	7	24	7	2	—	45

The average service time, which should have been 20, was

$$\frac{5 \times 1 + 10 \times 4 + 15 \times 7 + 20 \times 24 + 25 \times 7 + 2 \times 30}{45} = 19.2.$$

Thus the number of arrivals and average service time have errors in opposite directions, the arrival rate increasing the number of customers who depart without service and the service rate decreasing it. However, the error in arrival rate is the larger, and we might guess that the 13 lost customers is an overestimate of the true average loss per day.

In Chapter 4 we discussed several methods of reducing the amount of calculation required in simulations. We know that an important factor in

TABLE 10.3 Simulation of a Barbershop

(1) Time	Barber 1 (2) A	Barber 1 (2) D	Barber 2 (3) A	Barber 2 (3) D	Barber 3 (4) A	Barber 3 (4) D	Chair 1 (5) A	Chair 1 (5) D	Chair 2 (6) A	Chair 2 (6) D	Chair 3 (7) A	Chair 3 (7) D	Cust (8) A	Cust (8) D	Arrival Random Numbers (9)	Service Random Numbers (10)	Service Time (11)	Arrival RN Initially (12)	Staying RN After 15 Minutes (13)
10:00															10				
05	1														37				
10	1														08				
15	1		2										1, 2		99	09, 54	15, 20		
20			2												12				
25			2		3								3		66	42	20		30
30		1	2		3										31				35
35	4			2	3								4		85	01	10		
40	4		5		3								5		63	80	25		
45	6		5			3							6		73	06	10		
50	6		5		7								7		98	26	15		
55		6	5		7										11				
11:00	Lunch			5	7		8						8		83	79	25	57	
05	Lunch					7	10						9		88	52	20		
10	Lunch				9		10		11				10, 11		99	76, 64	25, 20	80, 45	
15			8		9		10		11				12	12	65			19	
20			8		9		14		11				13	13	80			09	
25			8		9		14		11				14		74			34	
30	11		8		10		14		15				15		69			45	
35	11			Lunch	10			14	15						09				
40	11			Lunch	10				15				16	16	91			05	
45	11			Lunch	10					15			17	17	80			03	
50						10									44				
55		11													12				

Critical Random Number

Arrivals

λ = 0.5	
n	RN
0	60
1	90
2	90

λ = 1.0	
n	RN
0	36
1	73
2	92
3	98
4	99

Service

t	RN
5	00
10	06
15	30
20	68
25	92
30	98
35	99

Legend

Arrival remains initially

n	RN
0	09
1	29
2	49

Arrival remains after 15 minutes

RN = 49

Table

Time									Arrivals		RN				
12:00	18	18	19	19					18, 19	22	65	33, 67	20, 20	—, 34, 00, 74	
05	18	21	19	19	20				20, 21, 22		61	31, 48, —, 35	20, 20, 20		
10	18		19	19	20						15		—, 20		
15	18	21	19	19	20	21			23		94				
20	21		23	20	20	23			24		42	17	15		
25	21		23	20	20	26			25		23	03	10		
30	21		23	20	20	26					04				
35	21		23						26		00	05	10		
40	24		25	26	26	29			27, 28, 29, 30	32	35	23	15	—, —, 42	—, —, 53
45	24	21	25	26	26	29			31, 32, 33		59	98, 49, 29	30, 20, 15	76, 37, 60	
50	24		25	29	29	30	31	33	34, 35	34, 35	46	65, —, 70	20, —, 25	14, 18	—, 58
55	24			29	29	30	31	33	36, 37		32	58, 48	20, 20	48, 82	—, 74
1:00	27	24	28	29	29	36	37	39	38, 39	38	69	—, 49	—, 20	28, 74	10
05	27		28	31	31	36	37	39	40		19			74	
10	25		28	31	31	40	37	39	41	41	45	36	20	16	
15	25		28	31	31	40	37	39	42, 43		94	68	20	76	
20	27			37	37	40	37	39			98				
25	30	27	28	37	37			39			33				
30	30		28					39			80				
35	30	30	28					39			79				
40	33		36								78				
45	33		36								51				
1:50	33	33	36								03				
55	33		36								88				
2:00	33										51				
05	39	36	42								35				
10	39		42								75				
15	39		42								97				

TABLE 10.3 *Simulation of a Barbershop (Continued).*

Time	Barbers						Waiting Chairs						Customer		Arrival Random Numbers	Service Random Numbers	Service Time	Arrival Random Number Initially	Staying Random Number After 15 Minutes	Critical Random Number
	1		2		3		1		2		3									
	A	D	A	D	A	D	A	D	A	D	A	D	A	D						
(1)	(2)		(3)		(4)		(5)		(6)		(7)		(8)		(9)	(10)	(11)	(12)	(13)	
20	39				←		43		44				44		63	97	30	91		
25	43	39	42												29					
30	43		42	42	Lunch										48					
35	43		44												31					
40	43		44										45		67	56	20			
45	45	43	44		→		45								16			85		
50	45		44										46		25	84	25			
55	45		44	44	46								47		96	39	20			
3:00	45		44		46										62					
05	48	45	47		46										00					
10	48		47		46								48		77	78	25			
15	48		47		46										07					
20	48			47		46									00					
25	48		49										49		85	78	25			

Time											
30	48						49				
35	48				48		49				
40	50				50		49	49	51		
45	50						49		51		
50	50						52		51		
55	53				53		52	52	51		
4:00	53						52		51		
05	53						52				
10	55				55		54			51	
15	55						54				54
20							54	54			54
25							54				55
30										56	
35	57				57		58		56		
40	57						58		56		
45	57						58		56		
50	57						58				
55											
5:00					58						
05											
10											
15											

50	43 53	10	15	
51	96 81	41	20	
52	87 91	65	20	
53	74 19	37	20	
54	69 39	64	20	26
55	70 01	00	5	45
56	45 65	23	15	
57	06 59	64	20	
58	33 70 32	58	20	

this problem is the ratio

$$R = \frac{\text{average service time}}{\text{average interval between arrivals}}.$$

This suggests that as successive days are simulated, we should plot the number of lost customers, L, against R. For the first day, $L = 13$ and the average interval between arrivals is

$$\frac{7 \times 60}{58} = 7.24 \text{ minutes.}$$

Average service time $= 19.2$ minutes. Thus

$$R = \frac{19.2}{7.24} = 2.65.$$

For the data given, R should be

$$R = \frac{52.5 \times 20}{7 \times 60} = 2.50.$$

From a plot of observed L against R, we can form an estimate of the value of L corresponding to $R = 2.50$, which is likely to have a lower sampling variance than a simple average of the observed values of L.

The reader should now simulate a second day for this problem; if further practice is wanted, the same shop under some alternative assumptions should be simulated. For example, consider the effect of moving lunch breaks to different times, or of adding a fourth barber.

EXERCISES

1. Suppose that the arrival rate is a constant λ until the number in the system is N. When N customers are present, further arrivals leave immediately without waiting for service. This is called a *finite queue*. It can be shown to reach a steady state no matter what the relative values of λ and the mean service time. Let the service-time distribution be exponential at a rate μ independent of n. Show that

$$p_n = \left(\frac{1 - \rho}{1 - \rho^{N+1}} \right) \rho^n \quad \text{where} \quad \rho = \lambda / \mu.$$

2. Suppose that we have N machines, each of which, when running, suffers breakdowns at an average rate of λ per hour. There are M servicemen, and only one man can work on a machine at a time. If $n > M$ machines are out of action, $n - M$ of them wait until a serviceman is free. Once a serviceman starts work on a machine, the time to complete the repair has an exponential distribution with parameter μ.

Show that when n machines have broken down, the rate of further breakdowns is $(N - n)\lambda$, and that the rate of completing services is $n\mu$ if $n \leq M$ and $M\mu$ if $n > M$. Hence find the distribution of the number of machines out of action at a given time.

3. Suppose that the cost of a repairman is c per hour and the gross profit on a machine that is running is p per hour. With the data of Exercise 2, how would you find the number of servicemen to maximize net profit if we have N machines?

4. A supermarket has m check-out lanes, and customers can be assumed to choose a lane at random and remain there until served. If the service time is exponential with parameter μ and the arrivals at the check-out area are Poisson at a rate λ, what is the steady-state average queue at each lane. What is the average number of customers in all lanes?

5. In the circumstances of Exercise 5, we might assign a number to each customer arriving at the check-out area and allow customers to proceed to the first free lane in the order of arrival. Assuming that this procedure does not alter the arrival rates or check-out times, what is the average number of customers who are waiting?

6. Compare the numerical results in Exercises 4 and 5 when $\lambda/\mu = 3$ and there are five check-out lanes.

7. In each of the following cases, find expressions for the average waiting time (1) in the system, (2) in the queue.

   (a) Single channel with Poisson arrivals at rate λ and exponential services at a rate μ.

   (b) m-channels each with exponential service times at a rate μ, and Poisson arrivals to the system at rate λ.

   (c) The finite queue of Exercise 1. (*Hint:* use the average arrival rate. This is not λ, because arrivals are at a rate zero when there are N persons in the system. The average arrival rate is $\lambda(1 - p_N)$.)

   (d) The situations of Exercise 2.

   (e) The situations in Exercises 4 to 6.

   assume $\lambda = 3$, $\mu = 1$

8. Prove that if we have Poisson arrivals and a single service counter with exponential service times, then with the usual notation, the probability of r arrivals during the service time of any given customer is

$$k_r = \left(\frac{\lambda}{\mu + \lambda}\right)^r \frac{\mu}{\lambda + \mu}$$

(This requires a knowledge of integration.)

Suppose that a departing customer leaves n persons in the system, and that a time u_n later the service facility is idle for the first time. Let $\bar{u}_n$ be the average value of u_n. Show that

$$\bar{u}_1 = \bar{t} + k_1\bar{u}_1 + k_2\bar{u}_2 + k_3\bar{u}_3 + \cdots$$

and

$$\bar{u}_n = \bar{t} + k_0\bar{u}_{n-1} + k_1\bar{u}_n + k_2\bar{u}_{n+1} + k_3\bar{u}_{n+2} + \cdots .$$

Show that the solution to these equations is

$$\bar{u}_n = \frac{n\bar{t}}{1 - \rho}$$

where $\bar{t}$ = average service time = $1/\mu$ and $\rho = \lambda/\mu$. (This result shows that the average length of a busy period is $\bar{u}_1 = \bar{t}/(1 - \rho)$. Busy periods would be of interest if problems of worker fatigue arose or if we were trying to schedule other activities such as maintenance between busy periods.)

Suggested Readings

It should be clear that the analysis of most queuing systems requires a considerable amount of mathematical sophistication. However, a relatively simple and short introduction to queuing theory is provided by Cox and Smith (1961). For those who have the ability to manipulate involved algebraic expressions we recommend Morse (1958) who takes the subject as far as possible without the use of advanced mathematical tools. Saaty (1961) goes much further, and his book contains many excellent references. However, Saaty cannot be read by those who have not had several semesters of college mathematics.

Bibliography

Cox, D. R., and W. Smith, *Queues*, Methuen & Co., London, and John Wiley and Sons, New York, 1961.

Morse, P. M., *Queues, Inventories and Maintenance*, John Wiley and Sons, New York, 1958.

Prabhu, N. U., *Queues and Inventories*, John Wiley and Sons, New York, 1965.

Riordan, J., *Stochastic Service Systems*, John Wiley and Sons, New York, 1962.

Saaty, T. L., *Elements of Queuing Theory*, McGraw-Hill Book Co., New York, 1961.

Takacs, L., *Introduction to the Theory of Queues*, Oxford University Press, London, 1962.

CHAPTER **11**

Sequencing and Coordination (Pert and Critical Path) Problems

INTRODUCTION

In this chapter we discuss two types of problems. The first type concerns the selection of a queue discipline, which, in queuing problems, is taken as given or fixed. The selection of an appropriate order in which to service waiting customers is called *sequencing*.

The second type of problem entails projects or jobs that consist of tasks that must be performed in a specified sequence. These problems involve determining how much effort should be put into the performance of each task and when to schedule it so as to optimize some measure of overall project performance. These may be called *coordination* problems, but are frequently referred to by the names of the techniques applied to their solution: *PERT* and *critical path*.

SEQUENCING PROBLEMS

Sequencing problems can be represented by a matrix such as is shown in Table 11.1.

There is a set of either two or more customers to be serviced or two or more jobs to be done and a set of one or more facilities on which to do them. We need to know when each job is ready to begin and what its due date is. We also need to know which facilities are required to do each job, in what order these facilities are required, and how long each operation will take.

The most common context of such problems is a "job shop," a production facility that processes many different products over a variety of combinations of machines. In such a context, a sequencing problem is sometimes called a *scheduling* problem; we do not use this term here to avoid confusion with the queuing type of scheduling problem.

275

TABLE 11.1 *General Representation of a Sequencing Problem*

Customers (or Jobs)	Service Facilities						Ready-to-Start Time	Time Due
	S_1	S_2	$\cdots$	S_j	$\cdots$	S_m		
J_1								
J_2								
$\vdots$								
J_i								
$\vdots$								
J_n								

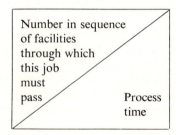

Number in sequence of facilities through which this job must pass

Process time

It should be noted that sequencing problems can arise even if only one service facility is involved. For example, if each of the jobs to be done has a due date and an associated cost of lateness, minimization of the total cost of lateness may not be easy to obtain. Such problems are quite common, for example, when there are a number of problems waiting to get on a computer or a number of emergencies waiting for a doctor.

Sequencing problems may be complicated by a number of conditions, among the more important of which are the following:

1. *Overlap.* If a job consists of making a number of similar items (a *lot*), the first items coming out of one operation may be processed in a succeeding operation before some items in the lot have had the first operation applied to them.

2. *Transportation time.* It may take a significant amount of time to transport items from one facility to another. The facilities may even be in different plants.

3. *Rework.* If one of the operations in a sequence consists of an inspection, defective items may have to be sent back to a previous operation for reworking, causing either a delay to the acceptable items or a splitting of the job into two lots. If the defective items cannot be reworked, a new job may have to be started.

4. *Expediting.* Because of the pressure from a customer or someone else, a job may be moved out of sequence and speeded up, that is, moved up in the waiting line.

5. *Machine breakdowns.* A service facility may break down or its operator may fail to appear, thereby causing an unexpected delay.

6. *Material shortages.* The material required for performance of an operation may run out.

7. *Variable processing time.* In a multishift operation, for example, the time required to perform an operation may vary from shift to shift, as it frequently does. Even the same shift may require different operating times for different lots of the same item.

The measures of performance in a sequencing problem may take a number of different forms, some of the more common of which are the following:

1. *Minimizing total elapsed time,* that is, when all the jobs are waiting to be done, the time between starting the first job and completing the last one. (This is not an appropriate criterion when jobs arrive continually at the service facility.)

2. *Minimizing total tardiness.* Tardiness is defined as "time of completion" minus "due time" when this is a positive quantity. Total tardiness is the sum of tardiness over all the jobs in the set.

3. *Minimizing maximum tardiness*, that is, minimizing the magnitude of the tardiest job in the set.

4. *Minimizing in-process inventory cost.*

5. *Minimizing the cost of being late.*

Ideally, the measure of performance should reflect three types of cost: (1) the cost of being late, (2) the cost of the operations, and (3) the cost of in-process inventory. Because lateness frequently involves customer's reactions, which are difficult to assess, a less-than-ideal measure is commonly used together with a satisficing criterion on lateness (e.g., no more than a specified percentage of the orders may be late or an upper limit on lateness is imposed).

Very simple sequencing problems have been solved for some time by use of the Gantt chart. For example, suppose that there are two jobs, J_1 and J_2, each requiring work on two machines, M_1 and M_3, in this order, with the required processing times shown in Table 11.2.

TABLE 11.2   *A Two-Job, Two-Machine Problem*

	M_1	M_2
J_1	2	7
J_2	5	4

There are two possible sequences, $J_1 - J_2$ and $J_2 - J_1$, which are evaluated graphically in Figure 11.1. From this figure it is apparent that the sequence $J_1 - J_2$, which takes 13 hours, is better than $J_2 - J_1$, which requires 16 hours. When there are n jobs, however, even if only two machines exist and all jobs go over them in the same order, there are $n!$ possible sequences. Consequently, even if n is small, use of the Gantt chart is not very practical.

Analytic methods have been developed only for solving very simple sequencing problems. Johnson (1954) and Bellman (1955) have found the optimal decision rule for n jobs going over two facilities in the same order, where optimality is defined as the minimum total elapsed time and the order of the completion of the jobs has no significance. It may be shown that the shortest elapsed time occurs when all jobs go through both machines in the same order. It is also assumed that in-process storage space is available and that the cost of in-process inventory either is the same for each job or is too small to be taken into account. For processes that are short in duration this is usually the case, but for extended processes the assumption may not be justified.

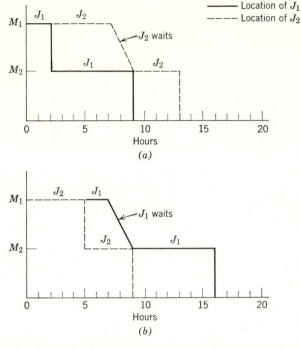

Figure 11.1 Gantt charts of a two-job, two-machine problem.

To illustrate the analytical procedure, consider the problem shown in Table 11.3. The steps in the procedure are as follows:

1. Find the lowest entry (hours) in the table. (In this case it is 2 for job 4 on machine 2.)

2. If this value falls in the first column, place the job first; otherwise place it last. (In this case job 4 is placed last in the sequence.) If there are equal

TABLE 11.3 *Machine Times (in Hours) for Six Jobs and Two Machines*

Job	Machine 1	Machine 2
1	4	6
2	8	3
3	3	7
4	6	2
5	7	8
6	5	4

TABLE 11.4   *Machine Time (in Hours) for Five Jobs and Three Machines*

Job	Machine 1	Machine 2	Machine 3
1	7	4	3
2	9	5	8
3	5	1	7
4	6	2	5
5	10	3	4

minimal entries, one in each column, place the one in the first column first, and the one in the second column last. If the equal values are both in the first column, select the one with the lowest entry in column 2 first. If the equal values are in the second column, select the one with the least entry in the first column.

3. Cross out the job assigned and continue the process, placing the jobs next to first or next to last, and so on. (In this case we obtain the following sequence: 3-1-5-6-2-4.)

Johnson (1954) also found a procedure for obtaining an optimal sequence for n jobs over three machines, with no passing of jobs permitted (i.e., maintaining the same order over each machine), if either one of the two following conditions is satisfied:

1. The minimum time on machine 1 is greater than or equal to the maximum time on machine 2.
2. The minimum time on machine 3 is greater than or equal to the maximum time on machine 2.

The first of these conditions is satisfied in the problem shown in Table 11.4. To solve this problem, two columns are formed, one consisting of the sum of the first two columns and the other consisting of the sum of the last two columns. The results are shown in Table 11.5.

TABLE 11.5   *Consolidation of Table* 11.4

Job	Machine 1 + Machine 2	Machine 2 + Machine 3
1	11	7
2	14	13
3	6	8
4	8	7
5	13	7

The problem shown in Table 11.5 is now solvable by the procedure described for two machines. Among the equivalent optimal sequences are 3-2-1-4-5, 3-2-4-5-1, and 3-2-4-1-5.

(Exercises 1 and 2 should be done at this point.)

There is a graphic technique for finding a minimal elapsed-time sequence for two jobs over *m* facilities. Suppose, for example, that we have the problem shown in Table 11.6. The problem can be displayed graphically, as is done in Figure 11.2. The crosshatched rectangular blocks represent overlaps that must be avoided. A horizontal line in the graph represents work on job 1 while job 2 remains idle. A vertical line represents work on job 2 while job 1

TABLE 11.6   *Two-Job, Four-Machine Problem*

		Machines			
Job 1	Sequence	*A*	*B*	*C*	*D*
	Time	2	4	5	1
Job 2	Sequence	*D*	*B*	*A*	*C*
Time	Time	6	4	2	3

remains idle. A 45° line to the base represents simultaneous work on both jobs. Consequently, the shortest line consisting of combinations of horizontal, vertical, and 45° lines from the origin to the goal represents an optimal sequence. Such a line is shown in Figure 11.2. It shows that both jobs can be worked on simultaneously until job 1 is completed, and then job 2 is completed. The total elapsed time is 15 hours.

(Exercise 3 should be done at this point.)

Bellman and Johnson have shown that the optimal sequence of *n* jobs with identical routing over three facilities necessarily involves the same ordering of jobs over each facility. This result, however, does not necessarily hold if more than three facilities are involved.

The procedures that we have considered are all restricted to small *deterministic* sequencing problems, that is, problems in which processing times are assumed to be known without error. This condition, of course, is seldom met. Attempts to solve analytically large stochastic sequencing problems have resulted in only limited success in special cases; for example, Jackson (1959) and Reinitz (1961). Queuing theory has been the principal method of attack on such problems. Another type of probabilistic approach has been taken by Heller (1959 and 1960).

Efforts have been made to solve sequencing problems by using integer linear programming. Most of this effort is due to Wagner (1959), Bowman (1959), and Manne (1959). This approach has not so far led to computationally practical methods of solution, but it may do so with further development of computers and computational procedures.

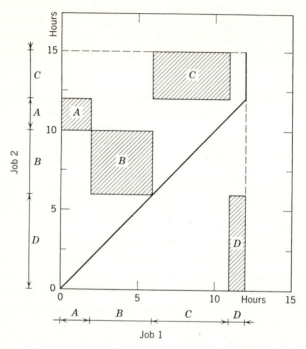

Figure 11.2 Representation of problem shown in Table 11.6.

At present, solutions to most large sequencing problems have to be sought through simulation. The amount of computation required by simulation may be very great. Hence a good deal of attention has been directed to reducing the number of sequences that have to be tested and the number of trials that are required to test each sequence. For a review of these and other approaches to sequencing problems, see Sisson (1961). The Las Vegas technique, discussed earlier (Chapter 4) was developed in this context. In this procedure, the time required to reach the point at which expected future improvements no longer exceed the cost of computation, depends on the effectiveness of the rule for modifying successive sequences. Much research remains to be done in this area.

In large sequencing problems, which involve many facilities and uncertain processing times, there are two types of approach. In the first approach, a sequence of jobs for each facility is sought in advance. In the second, rules are sought that can be applied at each facility to determine which of the waiting jobs should be handled next. In general, the second approach appears to be more practical, because it is less sensitive to errors of estimation and unanticipated events. In effect, it is a more *adaptive* type of procedure. A large number of local sequencing rules have been studied in experimental simulations (e.g., Jackson and Kuratani, 1957, and Conway, 1960). One rule that is particularly appealing intuitively and appears to work well in many situations consists of selecting that job to work on next for which π is minimum, where

$$\pi = \text{due time} - \text{expected time needed for future transport} - kx,$$

and

$$x = \text{expected time for future processing}$$

$$k = \text{a constant.}$$

The experiments have been directed to finding values of k that minimize either (*a*) the sum of positive tardiness, (*b*) the sum of the squares of positive tardiness, or (*c*) the maximum tardiness. The results, however, apply only to the specific conditions that have been simulated in the experiment.

The status of research on sequencing problems was recently summarized by Sisson (1961) in two tables that are reproduced here as Tables 11.7*a* and 11.7*b*. Very few applications of sequencing theory to actual problems have been reported in the literature, but more have been carried out than have been reported. At least two companies, Hughes Aircraft and Westinghouse, have used simulation on a routine daily basis to improve sequences in real shops. A very good data-processing system is needed to implement such "real-time" use of simulation. It is apparent, however, that a great deal more development of techniques for handling such problems is required.

COORDINATION PROBLEMS

In the past few years a class of problems that involve the relationship between the completion date of a large project and the times of starting each of the tasks of which it is composed have been extensively analyzed. The following conditions are necessary for the existence of this type of problem:

1. A well-defined collection of tasks that are to be completed before the project of which they are a part is completed.

2. The tasks can be started and completed independently within a specified sequence. (It is generally assumed that sufficient resources are available to do

TABLE 11.7a *Summary of Sequencing Research*[a]

		Assumptions												
	M No. of Machs.	1 One Job per Mach.	2 No Interrupted Opns.	3 No Split Lots	4 Well-Defined Opn. Times	5 Time Independent of Sequence	6 Routing Given	7 One Mach. per Type	8 Process Opn. as Soon as Possible	9 All Jobs Ready	10 Neglect Transportation Times	$N(\mathscr{J})$ (if = 1, all jobs have same routing)	$N(\mathscr{M})$ (if = 1, jobs in same order on all M)	Objective Function
I	1	✓	✓	✓	✓	✓	✓	✓	✓	no	✓	1	1	meet due date
II	2	✓	✓	✓	✓	✓	✓	✓	no (3)	✓	✓	1	1	min T (4)
	2	✓	✓	✓	✓	✓	✓	✓	no (3)	✓	✓	1	any	min T
III	3	✓	✓	✓	✓	✓	✓	✓	not explicit	✓	✓	1	1 (1)	min T
IV	many	✓.	✓	✓	✓	✓	✓	✓	✓	✓	✓	1	many	min T
	many	✓	✓	✓	✓	✓	✓	✓	not explicit	✓	✓	1	many (2)	min T
V	many	✓	✓	✓	✓	✓	partial	no	not explicit	✓	✓	many	many	min T
	many	✓	✓	✓	✓	✓	partial	✓	✓	✓	✓	many	many	min T
	many	✓	✓	✓	✓	✓	partial	✓	no (3)	✓	✓	many	many	min T or meet due date
VI	many	✓	✓	✓	✓	✓	✓	no	not explicit	no	✓	many	many	various
VII	many usually	usually	no	no	stochastic	no	partial	no	no (3)	no	✓	many	many	complex

(1) For m = 2, 3 it can be shown that this causes no loss of optimality (under assumption 8) (Johnson, 1954).
(2) The case of $N(\mathscr{M}) = 1$ is also explicitly considered.
(3) In these cases, specific interoperation delays can be included.
(4) T = total elapsed time.

[a] Reprinted from *Progress in Operations Research, Vol. 1*, R. L. Ackoff (ed.), John Wiley and Sons, New York, 1961.

TABLE 11.7*b*   *Summary of Sequencing Research*[a]

Researcher	Method of Arriving at Optimizing Procedures	Method of Executing the Procedure to Obtain Specific Solution
I Jackson	statistical analysis (queuing)	none yet
II Johnson (1959), Mitten	combinatorial analysis	solve algorithm on paper
Johnson (1959)	combinatorial analysis	solve algorithm on paper
III Wagner, Part IV	integer linear programming	paper or computer for small problems, $J < 25$
IV Wagner, Part III	integer linear programming	computer may be feasible for small problems
Heller	combinatorial + statistical analysis	computer—Monte Carlo
Smith	statistical analysis	computer—Monte Carlo
V Wagner	integer linear programming	numerical analysis to judge economics not reported
Giffler and Thompson	combinatorial analysis	computer-algorithm + enumeration or Monte Carlo
Manne	integer linear programming	numerical analysis not reported
VI Rowe	empirical rules	computer-simulated trials
Conway, Nelson	queuing approach	computer-simulated trials
Giffler and Thompson		computer-simulated trials
VII typical actual situation		computer-simulated trials

[a] Reprinted from *Progress in Operations Research, Vol. 1*, R. L. Ackoff (ed.), John Wiley and Sons, New York, 1961.

the necessary work. If this is not so, the problem is complicated but is not made impossible.)

3. The tasks are ordered in the sense that for each task we know which tasks precede it and which must await its completion.

These conditions are characteristic of most construction projects, many systems-development and product-development projects, large maintenance and overhaul projects, manufacturing and assembly of large products (e.g., airplanes, tractors, ships, and spacecraft), and spring housecleaning in the home.

For the most part analysts have been concerned with two questions about such systems:

1. How to identify the tasks that must be completed on schedule if the entire project is to be completed on schedule, and how to review progress of the project as time passes?

2. If it is possible to reduce the time taken on some or all of the tasks at an increased cost, how should tasks be scheduled so as to minimize the project completion time for a specified total cost?

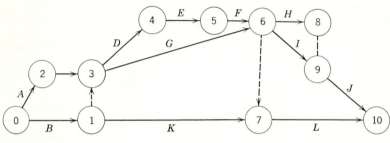

Figure 11.3

The first problem is handled by *PERT* (project evaluation and review technique). The second problem is handled by *CPM* (critical path method). The reason for the latter term will become apparent as we proceed.

Progress in analysis of large projects was accelerated when it was realized that the component tasks lend themselves to a graphical representation. Consider, for example, a project consisting of 12 tasks ($A, B, \ldots, L$), in which the following precedence relationships must hold ($X \angle Y$ means X must be completed before Y can start): $A \angle C$; $\cancel{A \angle B}$; $B \angle D$; $B \angle G$; $B \angle K$; $C \angle D$; $C \angle G$; $D \angle E$; $E \angle F$; $F \angle H$; $F \angle I$; $F \angle L$; $G \angle I$; $G \angle L$; $H \angle J$; $I \angle J$; and $K \angle L$. $\quad G \angle H$

The project can be represented by a network diagram (Figure 11.3) consisting of nodes and directed links, if we adopt the following conventions:

1. Tasks are represented by links.

2. The links directed toward a node represent tasks that must be completed before the tasks represented by links directed away from the node can start.

3. The start is represented by a node labeled zero, and the remaining nodes are numbered in such a way that if there is a link directed from i to j, then $i \angle j$.

4. The task (i, j) can start as soon as all the tasks directed toward i have been completed.

BLE 11.8 *Task Times*

k	A	B	C	D	E	F	G	H	I	J	K	L
ıe (days)	30	7	10	14	10	7	21	7	12	15	30	15

. In order that (i,j) can represent a unique task, if two or more tasks start
l end at the same nodes, we introduce a dummy node, say x, and a dummy
(x,j); the two real tasks are labeled (i,j) and (i,x).

Ve have introduced the dummy tasks $(1,3)$, $(6,7)$, and $(8,9)$ in Figure 11.3.
first $(1,3)$ is necessary because both B and C must precede D and G, but
/ B precedes K. The second $(6,7)$ is needed because G, F, and K precede
ut only F and G precede H and I. The reason for $(8,9)$ is different. We
ı to avoid two or more tasks that start at the same node and end at the
e node; because the node at which F and G end is the start of H and I,
H and I precede J, we need a dummy. If we did not use this convention,
ould not refer to a task by the nodes at which it starts and ends without
iguity.

we are given the times in which to complete each task, a diagram such
shown in Figure 11.3 may be used to determine the minimum time in
h the project can be completed. It will also identify critical tasks whose
/ will delay the entire project. Suppose that we have the data given in
ı.ı.e 11.8.

The first step is to compute the earliest times at which we can reach each
node, that is, the earliest time at which each task can be completed. Let t_i be
the earliest time for node i. We assume that we may start immediately, so
that $t_0 = 0$. Let t_{ij} be the time required for task (i,j); for dummy tasks $t_{ij} = 0$.
Table 11.9 shows t_{ij} for each task; it is essentially the same as Table 11.8.

The reader is advised to copy Figure 11.3 and insert the times from the
table on the links in the figure. The node times, t_i, can be inserted as they are
computed.

Clearly $t_1 = t_0 + t_{01} = 7$ and $t_2 = t_0 + t_{02} = 30$. We can reach node 3
by two routes—0, 1, 3 or 0, 2, 3—and the earliest time t_3 is the *longer* of the
times for these routes. That is,

$$t_3 = \max\{t_1 + t_{13}; t_2 + t_{23}\} = \max(7 + 0; 30 + 10) = 40.$$

We continue:
$$t_4 = t_3 + t_{34} = 40 + 14 = 54$$
$$t_5 = t_4 + t_{45} = 54 + 10 = 64.$$

TABLE 11.9 *Task Times*

Task (i,j)	0,1	0,2	1,3	1,7	2,3	3,4	3,6	4,5	5,6	6,7	6,8	6,9	7,10	8,9	9,10
t_{ij}	7	30	0	30	10	14	21	10	7	0	7	12	15	0	15

For t_6 there is a choice: either we reach 6 via 5 or directly from 3. Thus

$$t_6 = \max \{t_3 + t_{36}; t_5 + t_{56}\} = \max \{40 + 21; 64 + 7\} = 71$$

$$t_7 = \max \{t_6 + t_{67}; t_1 + t_{17}\} = \max \{71 + 0; 7 + 30\} = 71$$

$$t_8 = t_6 + t_{68} = 71 + 7 = 78$$

$$t_9 = \max \{t_6 + t_{69}; t_8 + t_{89}\} = \max \{71 + 12; 78 + 0\} = 83$$

$$t_{10} = \max \{t_9 + t_{9,10}; t_7 + t_{7,10}\} = \max \{83 + 15; 71 + 15\} = 98.$$

Thus the entire project can be completed in 98 days.

The rules for computing t_i may be formalized as follows:

1. $t_0 = 0$.
2. $t_i = \max \{t_k + t_{ki}\}$, where k ranges over all nodes for which tasks ki exist.

Next we wish to find the critical tasks. We compute the latest time at which each node could be reached without delaying node 10. If a node has an earliest time equal to its latest time, any delay in reaching it will delay the entire project. Let the latest times be represented by $\{T_i\}$.

If 10 is not delayed, it must be completed at time $T_{10} = 98$. So long as we reach node 9 before $T_{10} - t_{9,10} = 98 - 15 = 83$, there need be no delay in 10. In general, the latest time for node i is given by

$$T_i = \min_j \{T_j - t_{ij}\},$$

where j ranges over all nodes for which tasks (i, j) exist. We obtain Table 11.10, which shows also t_i for comparisons and the slack times $T_i - t_j$.

For management purposes it is usually more convenient to express the information in Table 11.10 in terms of the times at which the tasks are completed. This is easily done because the latest time for completion of task (i, j) is T_j. If we use E_{ij} to denote the earliest time, then because (i, j) cannot start before t_i, we see that $E_{ij} = t_i + t_{ij}$. The difference $T_j - E_{ij}$ is called the *slack time* for (i, j). Any task that has a zero slack time is critical to the completion of the entire project, because if it is completed at time $T_j + t$, the entire project will not be completed until time $T_n + t$. It will be found that the critical tasks form a path linking the nodes with zero slack time, $T_i - t_i = 0$. See Tables 11.10 and 11.11.

TABLE 11.10   *Earliest and Latest Times*

Node i	0	1	2	3	4	5	6	7	8	9	10
T_i	0	30	30	40	54	64	71	83	83	83	98
t_i	0	7	30	40	54	64	71	71	78	83	98
Slack	0	23	0	0	0	0	0	8	5	0	0

TABLE 11.11 *Results of PERT Analysis*

Task		Earliest Time of Completion	Latest Time of Completion	Slack
A	0, 2	30	30	0
B	0, 1	7	30	23
C	2, 3	40	40	0
D	3, 4	54	54	0
E	4, 5	64	64	0
F	5, 6	71	71	0
G	3, 6	61	71	10
H	6, 8	78	83	5
I	6, 9	83	83	0
J	9, 10	98	98	0
K	1, 7	37	83	46
L	7, 10	86	98	12

It is clear that attention should be given to critical tasks in managing a large project.

The procedure that has been described does not optimize anything. *Simplified* PERT, as it is called, yields information that may be useful for control purposes, but it does not specify how decisions that lead to control should be made. Nor does simplified PERT take account of chance variations in task times. *Full* PERT attempts to correct for this shortcoming.

(Exercises 4 and 5 should be done at this point.)

Full PERT

We assume that for each task there is a unimodal distribution of completion time and that we can estimate the most likely time, m. We also assume that we have an optimistic estimate, a, and a pessimistic estimate, b, such that the probability of the task time falling outside the range a to b is very small. In order to discuss the distribution of times, some further assumptions are necessary:

1. The standard deviation of the task time t is $\sigma_t = (b - a)/6$.
2. The task time has a *beta* distribution with density function

$$K(t - a)^\alpha (b - t)^\beta.$$

No assumption need be made about the relative values of a, b, and m, except that $a \leq m \leq b$. It may be shown that the expected time t_e is given by

$$t_e = \tfrac{1}{3}[2m + \tfrac{1}{2}(a + b)].$$

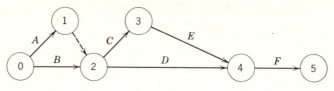

Figure 11.4

Full PERT calculates the expected project-completion time by using expected task times; it identifies critical tasks and also permits us to estimate the probabilities of various delays, not only at the outset, but at each point during the project.

As an example we shall consider the project represented by Figure 11.4. Notice that task $(1, 2)$ is a dummy, which is inserted so that each pair (i, j) refers to a unique task. Suppose that we have the data shown in Table 11.12. The first step is to compute the means and variances of the task times. The next step in the analysis is to compute the expected earliest and latest times[1] for each node, using the expected task times. The formulas are the same as in simplified PERT.

Earliest time $t_0 = 0$

$$t_i = \max_k \{t_k + t_{ki}\},$$

where k is any node such that (k, i) is a task. It is necessary to record the value k, say k', that maximizes, because we shall need it in computing variances.

Latest time $T_n = t_n$

$$T_i = \min_j \{T_j - t_{ij}\},$$

where j is any node such that (i, j) is a task. We also compute the variances, σ_i^2, of t_i by the formula $\sigma_0^2 = 0$

$$\sigma_i^2 = \sigma_{k'}^2 + \sigma_{k'i}^2,$$

TABLE 11.12   *PERT Data*

Task	a	b	m	$t_e = \frac{1}{3}[2m + \frac{1}{2}(a + b)]$	$\sigma^2 = [\frac{1}{6}(b - a)]^2$
01, A	8	14	10	10.33	1
02, B	14	26	20	20.00	4
12	0	0	0	0	0
23, C	16	22	20	19.67	1
24, D	24	36	30	30.00	4
34, E	28	46	36	36.33	9
45, F	18.5	21.5	20	20.00	0.25

[1] It is assumed that the expectation of the maximum of several random variables is approximately the maximum of their expectations.

where σ_{rs}^2 is the variance of task time for task (r, s) and k' is the node that maximizes in computing t_i. If there are equal maxima in computing t_i, choose the k that yields the largest σ_i^2.

These computations are entered in Table 11.13, which also shows the scheduled dates, θ_i, for each node. These dates are expressed as a number of time units from the present time. Initially they may be the latest times, T_i, for each node, but after a project is started we shall know how far it has progressed at any given date, and the scheduled times will be the latest times if the project is to be completed on its original schedule.

TABLE 11.13 *Earliest, Latest, and Scheduled Times*

Node i	Earliest Time t_i	Variance σ_i^2	Latest Time T_i	Scheduled Time θ_i	Slack $T_i - y_i$	Probability of Meeting Schedule
0	0	0	0	0	0	1.00
1	10.33	1	20	20	9.67	1.00$^-$
2	20	4	20	20	0	0.50
3	39.67	5	39.67	40	0	0.56
4	76	14	76	80	0	0.61
5	96	14.25	96	100	0	0.61

The last column is an estimate of the probability that each node will be reached at the scheduled time. We assume that the actual completion time is normally distributed about t_i with a variance σ_i^2. Thus we compute $z_i = (\theta_i - t_i)/\sigma_i$ and use tables to find the probability that a standard normal variate will exceed z_i. This procedure is subject to serious theoretical objections (see, for example, Grubbs, 1962), but in practice the computed probabilities are found to be a useful guide for determining which tasks need expediting. From Table 11.13 we see that unless something is done, there is about an even chance that nodes 2 and 3 will not be reached on schedule.

For management purposes it is better to present results in terms of tasks rather than nodes; this is done in Table 11.14, which shows for each task (i, j)

(1) the expected earliest time for completion, E_{ij},

$$E_{ij} = t_i + t_{ij};$$

(2) the variance of the earliest time to completion, S_{ij}^2,

$$S_{ij}^2 = \sigma_i^2 + v_{ij}^2,$$

where $v_{ij}^2 = $ variance of task time (i, j);

TABLE 11.14 *Outputs from PERT Analysis*

Task	Expected Time E_{ij}	Variance $S_{ij}{}^2$	Latest Time T_j	Scheduled Time θ_j	Slack $T_j - E_{ij}$	Probability of Meeting Schedule
01, A	10.33	1	20	20	9.67	1.00⁻
02, B	20	4	20	20	0	0.50
23, C	39.67	5	39.67	40	0	0.56
24, D	50	8	76	80	26	1.00⁻
34, E	76	14	76	80	0	0.61
45, F	96	14.25	96	100	0	0.61

(3) the expected latest times of completion, which are T_j;

(4) the scheduled time of task (i, j), which is θ_j;

(5) the probability of meeting the scheduled date, which is found by computing z_{ij},

$$z_{ij} = \frac{\theta_j - E_{ij}}{S_{ij}},$$

and by using normal tables.

(Exercise 6 should be done at this point.)

Critical Path Method, CPM

Full PERT assumes that the task times $\{t_{ij}\}$ are not subject to control, and merely reviews progress as the project proceeds. It may often be the case, however, that the cost of performing a task (i, j) depends on the scheduled time, and various times may be obtained for different costs. Usually, the more rapidly a task is performed, the higher is the cost. We shall now assume that if a task (i, j) is completed in time t_{ij}, the cost c_{ij} is given by

$$c_{ij} = k_{ij} - t_{ij}h_{ij}, \qquad a_{ij} \leq t_{ij} \leq b_{ij}, \tag{11.1}$$

where h_{ij} and k_{ij} are positive constants, $a_{ij} \geq 0$ is the shortest possible time, and $b_{ij} \geq a_{ij}$ is the longest time. (See Figure 11.5.) The total cost of such a project is

$$K = \sum_{ij}(k_{ij} - t_{ij}h_{ij}) = \sum_{ij} k_{ij} - \sum_{ij} t_{ij}h_{ij}. \tag{11.2}$$

At first sight we might suppose that we should choose the task times so as to minimize K. Reflection will show that when all task times are set at their maximum (i.e., $t_{ij} = b_{ij}$), no further cost reduction is possible. Suppose that when $t_{ij} = b_{ij}$, the project will be completed at time λ_M. If we cannot afford to wait so long, earlier completion is possible at an increased cost. In fact, if we allow $\lambda < \lambda_M$, the problem is to find a set of times t_{ij} that minimize the cost K, subject to the completion time being equal to λ. The minimum cost is a function of λ and will decrease as λ increases. The computation of the values of t_{ij} and the cost function is the problem that the critical path method (CPM) solves.

Notice that the values of the $\{k_{ij}\}$ are not relevant, because these costs will always occur. Hence our problem is to maximize Z (which is equivalent to minimizing $-t_{ij}h_{ij}$), where

$$Z = \sum_{ij} t_{ij}h_{ij} \tag{11.3}$$

subject to the project-completion time equaling λ.

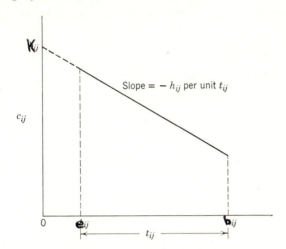

Figure 11.5 Plot of Equation 11.1.

Not all values of λ are of interest because, if we set all task times equal to their minima, the resulting project time will be the least possible. If we set all the task times at their maxima, the resulting costs cannot be reduced further by increases in the project time. Therefore, we shall only be interested in λ in some range

$$\lambda_m \leq \lambda \leq \lambda_M, \tag{11.4}$$

where λ_m = project time, when for all (i, j) we have $t_{ij} = a_{ij}$
λ_M = project time, when for all (i, j) we have $t_{ij} = b_{ij}$.
Notice that setting $t_{ij} = a_{ij}$ will usually result in high costs, although it will assure the minimum project-completion time.

The equation for Z is a linear function, and if we could express the constraints as linear functions, the problem would be solvable by methods discussed in Chapter 6. Kelley (1961) has shown that this can be done in the following way.

Using the notation of the previous section, we have

$$t_0 = 0$$

$$t_i = \max_k \{t_k + t_{ki}\}. \tag{11.5}$$

where t_i is the minimum time to reach node i. Thus

$$t_i \geq t_k + t_{ki}, \qquad i = 1, 2, \ldots, n. \tag{11.6}$$

This inequality must be understood as applying to all k for which there is a task (k, i). In addition, there are the constraints on maximum and minimum task times. Consequently, for all tasks (i, j)

$$a_{ij} \leq t_{ij} \leq b_{ij}. \tag{11.7}$$

Finally, we have the constraint that the project-completion time must equal λ; that is,

$$t_n = \lambda. \tag{11.8}$$

We also wish to make certain that while t_i satisfies (11.6) it is as small as possible and yet satisfies (11.5). This can be done by defining the expression

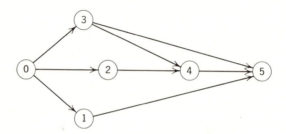

Figure 11.6

to be maximized as

$$Z' = \sum_{ij} t_{ij} h_{ij} - \sum_i t_i M_i, \tag{11.9}$$

where the M_i are very large positive constants. If we maximize (11.9) over all positive $\{t_{ij}\}$, $\{t_i\}$ that satisfy (11.6), (11.7), and (11.8), we find that in the optimal solution the $\{t_i\}$ are as small as possible, which means that they also satisfy (11.5).

Kelley developed an algorithm, suitable for machine computation, for solving this problem. Because of certain special features of the problem, Kelley's algorithm is more efficient than the simplex method. However, the number of variables, even in a small problem, is quite large and the method is rather tedious for hand computation.[2] The interested reader is referred to Kelley's original paper for details of his method.

Many small problems can be solved by simple heuristic reasoning. Consider the project represented by Figure 11.6 and the data in Table 11.15 We start by computing the total time for the entire project when $t_{ij} = b_{ij}$.

[2] In the example used earlier, there were 15 tasks (including 3 dummies) and 9 nodes (excluding the start, 0). Consequently there would be 24 variables. Condition (11.6) provides 15 constraints, condition (11.7) provides 30 constraints, and condition (11.8) provides one further constraint, which make a total of 46 constraints.

TABLE 11.15 *Data for Project Shown in Figure* 11.5

Task (i,j)	a_{ij}	b_{ij}	h_{ij}
0,1	4	7	2
0,2	5	10	4
0,3	3	6	5
1,2	5	8	3
1,5	11	15	4
2,4	3	7	6
3,4	6	8	5
3,5	13	15	3
4,5	4	9	6

The result is $\lambda_M = 31$. We also compute the project time when $t_{ij} = a_{ij}$, and we find that $\lambda_m = 16$. The objective of the remaining calculations is to express the cost as a function of λ for $\lambda_m = \lambda = \lambda_M$. When $\lambda = \lambda_M$, the total cost is K_M, where

$$K_M = \sum_{ij} k_{ij} - \sum_{ij} b_{ij} h_{ij},$$

For any value of $\lambda \leq \lambda_M$, let the minimum cost be $K_M + f(\lambda)$. We know that $f(\lambda_M) = 0$, and we proceed as follows:

1. Find all the distinct routes from 0 to 5. These are 0245, 01245, 015, 035, and 0345.

2. Set up a table (Table 11.16) showing tasks along the top row and the five routes in the first column. Under each task insert the cost h_{ij}, if the task is part of the route represented by the row. If the route does not include the task, leave the space blank. Insert a final row (labeled 1) showing the possible reductions in task times $b_{ij} - a_{ij}$.

TABLE 11.16

	01	02	03	12	15	24	34	35	45	1	2	3	4	5	6	7
A: 0245		4				6			6	26	26	26	21	19	17	16
B: 01245	2			3		6			6	31	28	26	21	19	17	16
C: 015	2				4					22	19	19	19	19	17	16
D: 035			5					3		21	21	21	21	19	17	16
E: 0345			5				5		6	23	23	23	19	18	16	15
1: $b_{ij} - a_{ij}$	3	5	3	3	4	4	2	2	5							
2	0	5	3	3	4	4	2	2	5							
3	0	5	3	1	4	4	2	2	5							
4	0	5	3	1	4	4	2	2	0							
5:	0	5	3	1	4	2	2	0	0							
6	0	5	1	1	2	0	2	0	0							
7:	0	4	0	0	1	0	2	0	0							

3. In the first column to the right (labeled 1) insert the total times for the tasks along each route. At least one of these will be λ_M. Any reduction of the total time λ must come about by reducing the times of the longest routes. In the example route B can be reduced by up to 5 units, until it equals route A. Further reductions in λ must reduce the times for both routes A and B. We see that the least cost of reducing a task time is 2 per unit for task 01, and that task 01 may be reduced by up to 3 units. Thus, if $28 \leq \lambda \leq 31$, the reduction of time $\lambda_M - \lambda$ will come from task 01 at a cost of $2(\lambda_M - \lambda)$. We have

$$f(\lambda) = 2(\lambda_M - \lambda) = 2(31 - \lambda), \qquad 28 \leq \lambda \leq 31.$$

This is shown in column 2 by inserting the new path times when the maximum reduction is made in t_{01}. Of course, only the paths that include 01 are affected. We also insert a new row (labeled 2) to show the amount of reductions still possible in task times.

4. Path B can be reduced by another 2 units, at which point it will be equal to path A. The cheapest reduction is now in task $(1, 2)$, which costs 3 per unit. We see that 3 units of $(1, 2)$ are available and we may reduce t_{12} by up to 2 units. In the range $26 \leq \lambda \leq 28$ we see that

$$f(\lambda) = 6 + 3(28 - \lambda).$$

This result is summarized in column 3 by showing the effects on the path times when t_{12} has been reduced by 2 units. Further possible reductions in task times are shown in row 3.

5. Any further reduction in λ must reduce routes A and B. This may be done at a cost of 6 per unit by changing t_{24} or t_{25}. (It can also be done by changing t_{12} and t_{24}, but this costs 7 per unit.) We see that if we choose t_{24}, we can reduce λ to 23, at which point the time for E must also be reduced. However, if we reduce t_{45}, we reduce the times for routes A, B, and E. We choose t_{45}, of which 5 units are available; we use all 5 of them, at which point λ is reduced to 21 and route D becomes critical. Thus for $21 \leq \lambda \leq 26$ we have

$$f(\lambda) = 12 + 6(26 - \lambda).$$

The new route times appear in column 4, and the possible further reductions in task times appear in row 4.

6. The next reductions must be chosen so as to reduce the times on paths A, B, and D. The least expensive way of doing this is by manipulating tasks $(2, 4)$ and $(3, 5)$ at a cost of $6 + 3 = 9$ per unit. Reductions of up to 2 units are possible, at which point route C is affected and t_{35} reaches its minimum. Thus for $19 \leq \lambda \leq 21$ we have

$$f(\lambda) = 42 + 9(21 - \lambda).$$

The results appear in column 5 and row 5.

7. Now we must reduce A, B, C, and D. The least expensive way involves changing (0, 3), (1, 5), and (2, 4) at a cost of $5 + 4 + 6 = 15$. These will also reduce the time for E, and the available reductions are 3 for (0, 3), 4 for (1, 5), and 2 for (2, 4). Hence for $17 \leq \lambda \leq 19$ we see that

$$f(\lambda) = 60 + 15(19 - \lambda).$$

The results appear in column 6 and row 6.

8. Any further reductions in λ must affect all five routes. The only possibility that remains is to reduce times for (0, 2), (1, 2), (1, 5), and (0, 3). The maximum available reduction is 1—because of (0, 3)—and we finally obtain

$$f(\lambda) = 98 + 16(17 - \lambda), \qquad 16 \leq \lambda \leq 17.$$

The final results appear in column 7 and row 7.

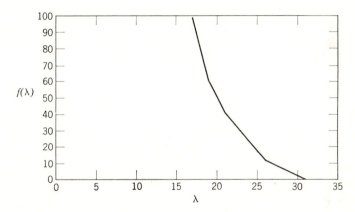

Figure 11.7 Graph of $f(\lambda)$.

The graph of $f(\lambda)$ versus λ is shown in Figure 11.7. It will be noticed that $f(\lambda)$ consists of straight-line segments and is a decreasing function of λ; the rate of decrease is nonincreasing. These properties will always occur, as Kelley has shown in his paper.

The procedure just described works fairly well for small problems, but can run into difficulties for large projects. If the number of routes through the network is large, it is easy to miss some routes and to pick task times for reduction that do not yield the least cost. Worse still, it is possible to construct examples in which one or more task times should be increased when λ decreases. Figure 11.8 and the data of Table 11.17 provide such an example.

We easily find that $\lambda_M = 11$ and $\lambda_m = 3$; the remaining calculations are shown in Table 11.18. The steps in obtaining Table 11.18 are summarized in Table 11.19. Notice that following column 6 all three routes must be

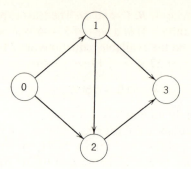

Figure 11.8

TABLE 11.17

Task (i,j)	a_{ij}	b_{ij}	h_{ij}
01	1	3	3
02	2	4	1
12	0	2	1
13	2	5	1
23	1	6	3

TABLE 11.18

	01	02	12	13	23	1	2	3	4	6	6	7
013	3			1		8	8	8	8	5	4	3
0123	3		1		3	11	10	9	8	5	4	3
023		1			3	10	10	9	8	5	4	3
1: $b_{ij} - a_{ij}$	2	2	2	3	5							
2	2	2	1	3	5							
3	2	1	0	3	5							
4	2	1	0	3	4							
5	2	1	0	0	1							
6	1	0	0	0	1							
7	0	0	1	0	0							

298

reduced. The only way of doing this is to reduce t_{01} and t_{23}, which produces a double reduction in route 0123. Because an increase in t_{12} affects only this route, we may save money by increasing t_{12}, which has been done in row and column 7.

If we decrease two or more task times, there is the possibility of some route receiving a double reduction. If there is a task (i, j) on that route which has $t_{ij} < b_{ij}$ and such that an increase in t_{ij} does not affect routes whose times must be decreased, it will pay to increase t_{ij}.

The system of tabular computation given above works well for problems that are small enough for hand calculations. It is even possible to extend the reasoning to take care of certain types of nonlinear problems. It will be realized that hand calculations require great care, because arithmetical errors arise readily in the search procedure described. For larger problems a digital computer is essential, and when a computer is used, Kelley's algorithm is probably the most efficient. Interested readers should consult the original paper.

(Exercise 7 should be done at this point.)

TABLE 11.19

Row and Column	Action Taken
2	Reduce t_{12} from 2 to 1; cost $1 \times 1 = 1$.
3	Reduce to t_{02} and t_{12} by 1; cost $1 \times (1 + 1) = 2$.
4	Reduce t_{23} by 1; cost $1 \times 3 = 3$.
5	Reduce t_{13} and t_{23} by 3; cost $3 \times (1 + 3) = 12$.
6	Reduce t_{01} and t_{02} by 1; cost $1 \times (3 + 1) = 3$.
7	Reduce t_{01} and t_{23} by 1 and increase t_{12} by 1; cost $1 \times (3 + 3 - 1) = 5$.

SUMMARY

In this chapter we have considered two types of problems that involve the order in which tasks are done. In the first—the sequencing problem—the objective is to find an order in which to perform independent tasks that use common facilities so that some measure of performance that covers the entire set of tasks is optimized. In the second—the coordination problem—the order of interdependent tasks is given and the objectives are to find the critical tasks that control the time required to complete the set and how much to spend on getting the critical tasks done so as to meet a desired completion data at least cost.

Only the simplest of sequencing problems can be solved exactly. Others generally require simulation, which does not assure an optimal solution, but it can yield better solutions in most cases than can be obtained by intuition and experience. In sequencing problems that involve large numbers of servicing facilities, particularly when there is some uncertainty concerning task times, it has been found preferable to apply a rule for ordering jobs waiting at each work center rather than attempt a complete a priori ordering.

Sequencing problems are most acute in job shops. Hence most sequencing research has been directed to this type of problem. Little progress has been made, however, in developing principles that can guide sequencing research even over a range of job-shop problems. Most sequencing problems that arise, therefore, require individual treatment.

Coordination problems, on the other hand, can be treated by PERT and the critical path method. The former can take account of uncertainties in task times under special conditions, but does not concern itself with direct control of task times by allocation of resources to tasks. The CPM does this, but only in a deterministic context. Despite the limitations, these techniques are widely used and are reported as being very helpful in a wide variety of problems. Because of their limitations, however, the output of these methods should not be interpreted too literally.

EXERCISES

1. Find the sequence that minimizes the total elapsed time required to complete the following tasks:

Task	A	B	C	D	E	F	G	H	I
Time on 1st machine	2	5	4	9	6	8	7	5	4
Time on 2nd machine	6	8	7	4	3	9	3	8	11

2. Find the sequence that minimize the total elapsed time required to complete the following tasks:

Task	A	B	C	D	E	F	G
Time on 1st machine	3	8	7	4	9	8	7
Time on 2nd machine	4	3	2	5	1	4	3
Time on 3rd machine	6	7	5	11	5	6	12

3. Use the graphical method to minimize the time needed to process the following jobs on the machines shown:

			Machines		
Job 1 Sequence	A	B	C	D	E
Time	2	3	4	6	2
Job 2 Sequence	C	A	D	E	B
Time	4	5	3	2	6

4. A project consists of a series of tasks labeled $A, B, \ldots, T$, with the following relationships ($X, Y > W$ means X and Y cannot start until W is complete;

$W > X$, Y means W cannot start until both X and Y are complete): A, B, C can start immediately; $D, E > A$; $F > B$; $G, H > D$; $I > F, G$; $J, K > C$; M, $L > J$; $N > K, L$; $O > M, N$; $P > H, I, O$; $R, Q > P$; $S > Q$; $T > R, S$. Draw the network diagram for this project and label the nodes in such a way that if (i, j) is a task, $i < j$.

5. For the project of Exercise 4 find the earliest and latest times to reach each node, given the following task times:

Task	A	B	C	D	E	F	G	H	I	J	K	L	M	N	O	P	Q	R	S	T
Time	5	9	14	4	3	10	6	12	10	3	4	5	5	8	18	3	6	13	5	7

Find also the earliest and latest times to complete each task.

6. Given the data below find the following:
   (a) The expected task times and their variance.
   (b) The earliest and latest expected times to reach each node.
   (c) The variances of the earliest node times.
   (d) The earliest and latest expected times to complete each task and the variances of the earliest times.
   (e) The probabilities that each task will be completed on schedule.

Task	A	B	C	D	E	F	G	H	I	J	K
Least time	4	5	8	2	4	6	8	5	3	5	6
Greatest time	8	10	12	7	10	15	16	9	7	11	13
Most likely time	5	7	11	3	7	9	12	6	5	8	9
Scheduled completion date	7	18	16	6	26	20	25	30	30	48	50

Precedence relationships: A, C, D can start immediately; $E > B, C$; $F, G > D$; $H, I > E, F$; $J > I, G$; $K > H$; $B > A$.

7. Let t be the project completion time for the data below and let $f(t)$ be the increased cost when t is less than its maximum value. Find the function $f(t)$.

Task	A	B	C	D	E	F	G	H
a	3	8	2	4	3	4	6	5
b	8	15	9	8	6	9	11	12
h	3	2	6	5	4	7	3	8

Precedence relationships: A, D, E can start immediately; $B, C > A$; $G, F > D$; C; $H > E, F$.

Suggested Readings

For the most complete summary and evaluation of the state of sequencing, see Sisson (1961). For a review of efforts to find principles to guide sequencing, efforts that are based on simulation, see Jackson, Nelson, and Grindlay (1962). One of the most comprehensive attempts to handle such problems analytically can be found in Reinitz (1961).

The papers by Malcolm et al. (1959), Kelley and Walker (1959), and Kelley (1961) provide detailed expositions on PERT and CPM. A critique of PERT can be found in Healy (1961).

Bibliography

Akers, S. B., and J. Friedman, "A Non-Numerical Approach to Production Scheduling Problems," *Operations Research*, 3 (1955), 429–442.

Bellman, R., "Some Mathematical Aspects of Scheduling Theory," *Journal of the Society of Industrial and Applied Mathematics*, 4 (1956), 168–205.

Blake, K. R., and W. S. Stopakis, *Some Theoretical Results on the Job Shop Scheduling Problem*, Report M-1533-1, United Aircraft Corp., Research Dept., East Hartford, Conn. (July 1, 1959).

Freeman, R. J., "A Generalized PERT," *Operations Research*, 8 (1960), 281.

Fulkerson, D. R., "An Out-of-Kilter Method or Minimal Cost Flow Problems," RAND Paper P-1825, January 18, 1960.

——, "A Network Flow Computation for Project Cost Curves," RAND Paper P-1947, March 18, 1960.

Giffler, B., *Mathematical Solution of Explosion and Scheduling Problems*, IBM Research Report RC-118, IBM Research Center, Business Systems Research, Yorktown Heights, N.Y. (June 18, 1959).

——, and G. L. Thompson, *Algorithms for Solving Production Scheduling Problems*, IBM Research Report RC-118 (June 18, 1959).

Grubbs, F. E., "Attempts to Validate Certain PERT Statistics or 'Picking a PERT'," *Operations Research*, 10 (1962), 912–915.

Healy, T. L., "Activity Subdivision and PERT Probability Statements," *Operations Research*, 9 (1961), 341–348.

Heller, J., *Combinatorial, Probabilistic and Statistical Aspects of an MxJ Scheduling Problem*, Report NYO-2540, AEC Computing and Applied Mathematics Center, Institute of Mathematical Science, New York University, New York (February 1, 1959).

Jackson, J. R., "An Extension of Johnson's Result on Job Lot Scheduling," *Naval Research Logistics Quarterly*, 3 (1956), 201–203.

——, *Some Problems in Queueing with Dynamic Priorities*, Management Sciences Research Project, UCLA, Research Report 62 (November 1959).

——, and Y. Kuratani, *Production Scheduling Research; A Monte Carlo Approach*, Management Sciences Research Project, UCLA, Discussion Paper No. 61 (May 20, 1957).

——, R. T. Nelson, and A. A. Grindlay, *Research on Job-shop-Like Models: A Progress Report*, Western Management Science Institute, UCLA, Working Paper No. 12 (July 18, 1962).

Johnson, S. M., "Optimal Two and Three Stage Production Schedules with Setup Times Included," *Naval Research Logistics Quarterly*, 1(1954), 61–68.

——, "Discussion," *Management Science*, 5 (1959), 299–303.

Kelley, J. E., Jr., "Critical-Path Planning and Scheduling: Mathematical Basis," *Operations Research*, 9 (1961), 296–320.

——, and M. R. Walker, "Critical-Path Planning and Scheduling," *Proceedings, Eastern Joint Computer Conference*, Boston, December 1–3, 1959, 160–173.

Kuratani, Y., and R. T. Nelson, *A Pre-Computational Report on Job-Shop Simulation Research*, Management Sciences Research Project, UCLA (October 1959).

Levy, F. K., G. L. Thompson, and J. D. Wiest, "Critical Path Method: A New Tool for Management," O.N.R. Research Memorandum, No. 97. Carnegie Institute of Technology, Pittsburgh, May 25, 1962.

Malcolm, D. G., J. H. Roseboom, C. E. Clark, and W. Fazar, "Applications of a Technique for Research and Development Evaluation," *Operations Research*, 7 (1959) 646–669.

Manne, A. S., *On the Job-Shop Scheduling Problem*, Cowles Foundation Discussion Paper No. 73 (May 8, 1959).

McNaughton, R., "Scheduling with Deadlines and Loss Functions," *Management Science*, 6 (1959), 1–12.

Miller, R. W., *Schedule, Cost, and Profit Control with PERT*, McGraw-Hill Book Co., New York, 1963.

Mitten, L. G., "A Scheduling Problem," *Journal of Industrial Engineering*, 10 (1959), 131–134.

———, "Sequencing in Jobs on Two Machines with Arbitrary Time Lags," *Management Science*, 5 (1959), 293–298.

Reinitz, R. C., *An Integrated Job Shop Scheduling Problem*, Ph.D. Thesis, Case Institute of Technology, Cleveland, Ohio, 1961.

Rowe, A. J., *Toward a Theory of Scheduling*, Report SP-61, System Development Corp., Santa Monica, Calif. (April 1, 1959).

Sisson, R. L., "Sequencing Theory," in *Progress in Operations Research*, Vol. I, R. L. Ackoff (ed.), John Wiley and Sons, New York, 1961, pp. 293–326.

Smith, W. E., "Various Optimizers for Single Stage Production," *Naval Reseach Logistics Quarterly*, 3 (1956), 59–66.

———, *Applications of A Probability*, Research Report No. 56, UCLA, Management Science Research Project (Sept. 19, 1958).

Wagner, H. M., "An Integer Linear-Programming Model for Machine Scheduling," *Naval Research Logistics Quarterly*, 6 (1959), 131–140.

CHAPTER 12

Routing Problems in Networks

INTRODUCTION

Network problems may occur in many areas, but they are most commonly found in transportation and communication processes. A typical network problem consists of finding a route from city A (the origin) to city B (the destination), between which alternative paths are available at various stages of the journey. The cost of the journey—which may be measured in terms of time, money, or total distance—depends on the route that is chosen. The problem is to find the least costly route. In principle this problem can be solved by trying all the possibilities and selecting the best one. In practice the number of alternative routes usually is too large to permit exhaustive trials. In most cases it is therefore necessary to find a more efficient way of determining the "best" route.

A network can be defined by a set of points or *nodes* that are connected by lines or *links*. A way of going from one node (the *origin*) to another (the *destination* or *terminus*) is called a *route* or *path*. The links in a network may be one-way (in either direction) or two-way. They are usually characterized by the time, cost, or distance involved in traversing them.

A routing problem consists of finding a route between two or more nodes which minimizes (or maximizes) some measure of performance that is a function (usually the sum) of the link measures. A number of different constraints may be placed on acceptable routes; for example, no returning to the node already passed through or passing through every node once and only once.

Delays may occur at nodes (e.g., at highway intersections or telephone switchboards). These may be probabilistic, depending on the load at the node or occupancy of the links that emanate from the node (e.g., highways or telephone lines). The links may have limited capacity (as low as one unit at a time) or may be unconstrained. In some cases either the nodes or links may break down or may be closed completely or in part (e.g., for repair).

A large variety of problems other than routing may develop in connection with the construction and utilization of networks. Here, however, we shall consider only two types of routing problem, which occur most frequently in OR: the *traveling salesman* and *minimal path* problems.

THE TRAVELING SALESMAN PROBLEM

Mathematicians have long amused themselves with very difficult problems that are treated as puzzles. One of the more recent of these is the traveling salesman problem. It is usually formulated as follows. A salesman has a certain number of cities that he must visit. He knows the distances (or time, or cost) of travel between every pair of cities. His problem is to select a route that starts at his home city, passes through each city once and only once, and returns to his home city in the shortest possible distance (or in least time, or at the least cost).

If the distance (or time, or cost) between every pair of cities is independent of the direction of travel, the problem is said to be *symmetrical*. If for one or more pairs of cities the distance (or time, or cost) varies depending on direction, the problem is *asymmetrical*. For example, it may take more time to go uphill from A to B than downhill from B to A; when flying, because of prevailing winds, travel usually takes longer when going from east to west, than from west to east.

If only two cities are involved, there is, of course, no choice. If three cities are involved, one of which (A) is the home base, there are two possible routes: ABC and ACB. For four cities there are six possible routes. But for eleven cities there are more than three and a half million possible routes. In general, if there are n cities, there are $(n - 1)!$ possible routes.

Clearly, the problem is to find the best route without trying each one. Although there have been many efforts to solve the problem analytically, no satisfactory general method exists. However, several computational techniques for solving the problem have been suggested. Competition among them has been in terms of the amount of computational time required.

The problem obviously arises in routing pickup and delivery services, but in many of these return to a visited point is not prohibited. Much less obvious contexts of the problem have been discussed, the most common of which involves the order in which different products are processed over a production facility, such as an assembly line.

For example, a manufacturer of kitchen sinks makes about twenty different models of sinks on one continuous assembly line. Some of the models are very much like others; some are quite different. The cost of a "changeover" on the assembly line from one model to another depends on the characteristics of these models.

In some cases, changeovers (setups) can be done quickly and at low cost; in others a good deal of time and labor is required. Furthermore, it may take more time to change from model A to model B than from B to A. One direction of change may eliminate some operations; the other may involve adding some, such as increasing the number of shelves in the cabinet under the sink.

To find an order in which to produce the models so that the setup costs are minimized is an asymmetrical traveling salesman problem. The changeover costs between models are analogous to distances between points. Each model must be produced once and only once and production must return to the first model.

This type of minimal setup problem arises in a wide variety of contexts, wherever work of any kind is done by a single facility and whenever unequal setup costs are involved.

The traveling salesman problem is similar to the assignment problem, except that there is an additional restraint. Let c_{ij} be the cost of going from city i to city j and let $x_{ij} = 1$ if we go directly from i to j and zero otherwise. Then we wish to minimize $\sum_{i,j} x_{ij} c_{ij}$. However the x_{ij} must be so chosen that no city is visited twice before the tour of all cities is completed. In particular, we cannot go from i directly to i. This may be avoided in the minimization process by setting $c_{ii} = \infty$. Notice that only one $x_{ij} = 1$ for each value of i and for each value of j. Thus we could solve the assignment problem and hope that the solution satisfies the additional constraint.

If solution to the assignment problem does not satisfy the additional constraint, we can often adjust the solution by inspection. This is frequently a satisfactory procedure for small problems, and the reader will easily be able to devise his own empirical rules. For larger problems, we require a more systematic approach such as that due to J. D. C. Little and his colleagues, which we now consider.

The Procedure of Little et al.

This iterative procedure was developed by Little, Murty, Sweeney, and Karel (1963). It is generally considered to be the most efficient procedure published to date, although the computational time (by hand or computer) rises very rapidly as the size of the problem increases.

First we describe the procedure abstractly and then illustrate it by use of a numerical example.

Let $S(0)$ be the set of all feasible tours to an $n \times n$ traveling salesman problem with a cost matrix $[c_{ij}]$. There are $(n - 1)!$ tours in $S(0)$. As in the assignment problem, we reduce the matrix $[c_{ij}]$ so that every row and column contains at least one zero element. If we could find a tour among the zeros, it would be optimal, and in terms of the original matrix the cost would be equal to the amount of the reduction. Let $[c_{ij}{}']$ be the reduced matrix and let r be the reduction from $[c_{ij}]$. Thus *every* tour in $S(0)$ will cost at least r. We say that r is a lower bound on the tours contained in $S(0)$. The method of Little et al. proceeds by partitioning $S(0)$ into two mutually exclusive subsets and by computing lower bounds for each. We then partition the subset with the smaller lower bound and compute two more lower bounds. At each stage we select the subset with the smallest lower bound obtained so far and partition it again. Eventually we obtain a subset that contains a single tour whose cost equals the lower bound; this tour is optimal. (All other tours have lower bounds that are greater.)

We illustrate the details by reference to the ten-city problem originally used by Murty. The entries were random numbers; the initial reduced matrix is shown in Table 12.1. Notice that the diagonal entries, c_{ii}, are all infinite because we cannot go from a city to itself in one step.

TABLE 12.1 *A Ten-City Asymmetrical Traveling Salesman Problem*

					To					
From	1	2	3	4	5	6	7	8	9	10
1	∞	51	55	90	41	63	77	69	0	23
2	50	∞	0	64	8	53	0	46	73	72
3	30	77	∞	21	25	51	47	16	0	60
4	65	0	6	∞	2	9	17	5	26	42
5	0	94	0	5	∞	0	41	31	59	48
6	79	65	0	0	15	∞	17	47	32	43
7	76	96	48	27	34	0	∞	0	25	0
8	0	17	9	27	46	15	84	∞	0	24
9	56	7	45	39	0	93	67	79	∞	38
10	30	0	42	56	49	77	76	49	23	∞

The Algorithm

1. Reduce the cost matrix until there is a zero in every row and column. This is done by subtracting the smallest element in each row from every element in the row, and then subtracting the smallest element in each column of the remaining matrix from each element in the column. The total reduction, r, is the sum of the amounts subtracted. Call the resulting matrix $[c_{ij}']$. A reduced matrix is shown in Table 12.1. Therefore, for this problem $r = 0$.

2. For each zero element in $[c_{ij}']$ record the penalty (p_{hk}) for nonuse. We argue that if we do not use the link (h, k), we must use some element in row h and some element in column k. Thus the cost of not using (h, k) is at least the sum of the smallest elements in row h and in column k (excluding c_{hk}' itself). Thus

$$p_{hk} = \min_{j \neq k} \{c_{hj}'\} + \min_{i \neq h} \{c_{ik}'\}.$$

Record the result in the upper left-hand corner of each zero-entry cell. For example, consider the zero in $(1, 9)$. The sum of the minima in row 1 and column 9 [excluding the zero in $(1, 9)$] is $23 + 0 = 23$. For $(10, 2)$ the sum is also $23 + 0 = 23$ and for $(2, 7)$ it is $0 + 17 = 17$. The results of these calculations are shown in Table 12.2. In the first cycle go to step 3; in subsequent cycles go to step 6.

TABLE 12.2

To

From	1	2	3	4	5	6	7	8	9	10
1	∞	51	55	90	41	63	77	69	23 0	23
2	50	∞	0 0	64	8	53	17 0	46	73	72
3	30	77	∞	21	25	51	47	16	16 0	60
4	65	2 0	6	∞	2	9	17	5	26	42
5	0 0	94	0 0	5	∞	0 0	41	31	59	48
6	79	65	0 0	5 0	15	∞	17	47	32	43
7	76	96	48	27	34	0 0	∞	5 0	25	23 0
8	0 0	17	9	27	46	15	84	∞	0 0	24
9	56	7	45	39	9 0	93	67	79	∞	38
10	30	23 0	42	56	49	77	76	49	23	∞

3. Let (h, k) be the zero entry with the largest penalty. In the case of a tie, select arbitrarily. We now partition the set $S(0)$ of all possible routes into those that contain the link (h, k) and those that do not. Call these subsets $S(h, k)$ and $S(\overline{h, k})$.

4. We next compute lower bounds on the costs of all routes in each subset.

4.1. We have seen that if (h, k) is not used, in addition to the reduction, r, there will be a cost of at least p_{hk} (step 1). Thus the lower bound $\theta(\overline{h, k})$ is given by

$$\theta(\overline{h, k}) = r + p_{hk}.$$

In the example $r = 0$ and $p_{1,9} = 23$, so that

$$\theta(\overline{1, 9}) = 0 + 23 = 23.$$

4.2. To compute a lower bound for $S(h, k)$, we observe that if we use the link (h, k), we cannot use the link (k, h); if we did use (h, k) and (k, h), we would go from h to k and back again to h without visiting the other cities. To avoid using (k, h), we set the cost $c_{kh}' = \infty$. Once we have used (h, k), we will not use any other link in row h or column k. We delete row h and column k. In the remaining matrix we must select an element from each row and column so that the cost will be at least the amount by which the remaining matrix can be reduced. Let this be

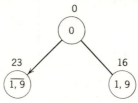

Figure 12.1

r_{hk}. Then the lower bound $\theta(h, k)$ for $S(h, k)$ is given by

$$\theta(h, k) = r + r_{hk}.$$

In the example we set $c_{9,1}' = \infty$ and delete row 1 and column 9. The resulting matrix can be reduced by 16 in row 3, and $\theta(1, 9) = 0 + 16 = 16$. The results that we have obtained so far are recorded in Figure 12.1.

5. Select $S(h, k)$ or $S(\overline{h, k})$ for further partitioning according as $\theta(h, k)$ or $\theta(\overline{h, k})$ is smaller. If $S(h, k)$ is selected, return to step 2, using the reduced matrix obtained in step 4.2. If $S(\overline{h, k})$ is selected, return to the matrix $[c_{ij}']$, set $c_{hk}' = \infty$, and reduce the resulting matrix. Return to step 2, using the matrix obtained.

In the example $\theta(1, 9) = 16$ and $\theta(\overline{1, 9}) = 23$. We next partition $S(1, 9)$. The matrix obtained at step 4.2 is shown in Table 12.3.

6. Let (u, v) be the cell that has the largest penalty p_{uv}. Partition again into sets that contain (u, v) and those that do not.

In our example the penalties are shown in the upper left-hand corners of Table 12.3. We select $(10, 2)$ with the penalty 30.

7. Compute the lower bounds on the new sets. Let θ' be the lower bound on the set to be partitioned.

7.1. For the set excluding (u, v) the lower bound is θ, where $\theta = \theta' + p_{uv}$.

7.2. For the set including (u, v) delete row u and column v. Find the element (α, β) that together with (u, v) and the elements previously included would make a subtour.[1] Set the cost in (α, β) equal to infinity. Reduce the resulting matrix. Let r_{uv} be the reduction; then $\theta = \theta' + r_{uv}$.

TABLE 12.3

	1	2	3	4	5	6	7	8	9	10
1										
2	50	∞	$^{0}0$	64	8	53	$^{17}0$	46		72
3	14	61	∞	5	9	35	31	$^{5}0$		44
4	65	$^{2}0$	6	∞	2	9	17	5		42
5	$^{0}0$	94	$^{0}0$	5	∞	$^{0}0$	41	31		48
6	79	65	$^{0}0$	$^{5}0$	15	∞	17	47		43
7	76	95	48	27	34	$^{0}0$	∞	$^{0}0$		$^{24}0$
8	$^{9}0$	17	9	27	46	15	84	∞		24
9	∞	7	45	39	$^{9}0$	93	67	79		38
10	30	$^{30}0$	42	56	49	77	72	49		∞

In the example we selected $(10, 2)$; we delete row 10 and column 2. The set to be partitioned is all tours that include $(1, 9)$. When we partition into sets containing $(1, 9)$ and $(10, 2)$, we must exclude $(2, 10)$ to avoid a subtour. We set $c'_{2,10} = \infty$ in Table 12.3. The resulting matrix can be reduced by 2 (in row 4). The reduced matrix is shown in Table 12.4. We extend Figure 12.1 to show our new results, as in Figure 12.2.

[1] To find the link that would complete a subtour, it is useful to introduce the concept of a *chain*. A single link is a chain of length 1; we have a chain of length k when we have links of the form (a, b), (b, c), (c, d), . . . , (g, h), (h, j) comprising k links. When we add an additional link (j, l), we must exclude (l, a) to avoid a subtour. We might add a link that joins two chains, for example, add (h, u) to the chains (a, b), (b, c), . . . , (g, h) and (u, v), (v, w), . . . (y, z). In this case we must exclude (z, a).

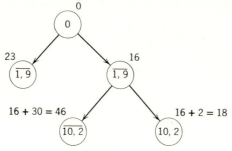

Figure 12.2

The lowest cost (Figure 12.2) is 18 at (10, 2), and we partition the set that includes (1, 9) and (10, 2). Compute the penalties for the zero elements in Table 12.4, as shown in the upper left-hand corners. The highest penalty is 38 for (9, 5). If (9, 5) is included, we have the chain (1, 9), (9, 5); therefore, we must exclude (5, 1). We put $c_{5,1} = \infty$, delete row 9 and column 5 from Table 12.4, and compute the reduction; that is 3 in row 4. We extend Figure 12.2 to form Figure 12.3. Because the set containing (9, 5) has the lowest $\theta = 21$, we split it again. We reduce Table 12.4 and obtain Table 12.5; we

TABLE 12.4

	1	2	3	4	5	6	7	8	9	10
1										
2			0 \ 0	64	8	53	15 \ 0	46		72
3	14		∞	5	9	35	31	5 \ 0		44
4	63		4	∞	4 \ 0	7	15	3		40
5	0 \ 0		0 \ 0	5	∞	0 \ 0	41	31		48
6	79		0 \ 0	5 \ 0	15	∞	17	47		43
7	76		48	27	34	0 \ 0	∞	0 \ 0		24 \ 0
8	9 \ 0		9	27	46	15	84	∞		24
9	56		45	39	38 \ 0	93	67	79		38
10										

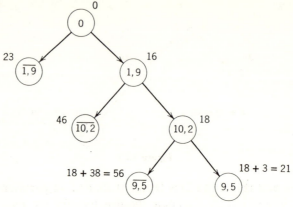

Figure 12.3

find that the highest penalty is 24 at (7, 10). We delete row 7 and column 10.

We now have the chain (7, 10), (10, 2); therefore we put $c_{2,7} = \infty$. We obtain a reduction of 12 (in column 7) and extend Figure 12.3 to obtain Figure 12.4.

The cost of the sets including (7, 10) is 33, which is higher than for those that exclude (1, 9), for which the cost is 23. We now start to partition the set of all tours that exclude (1, 9). To do so we return to Table 12.1, put $c_{1,9} = \infty$, and reduce the matrix. The result is Table 12.6, which also shows the penalties. The highest is 30 at (10, 2). We delete row 10 and column 2, put $c_{2,10} = \infty$, and reduce the resulting matrix. The reduction is 2 in row 4. We extend

TABLE 12.5

	1	3	4	6	7	8	10
2	50	0 0	64	53	12 0	46	∞
3	14	∞	5	35	31	5 0	44
4	60	1	∞	4	12	1 0	37
5	∞	0 0	5	0 0	41	31	48
6	79	0 0	5 0	∞	17	47	43
7	76	48	27	0 0	∞	0 0	24 0
8	23 0	9	27	15	84	∞	24

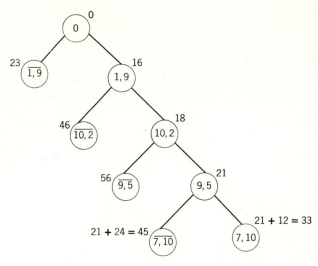

Figure 12.4

TABLE 12.6

	1	2	3	4	5	6	7	8	9	10
1	∞	29	32	67	18	40	54	46	∞	$\overset{18}{0}$
2	50	∞	$\overset{0}{0}$	64	8	53	$\overset{17}{0}$	46	73	72
3	30	77	∞	21	25	51	47	16	$\overset{16}{0}$	60
4	65	$\overset{2}{0}$	6	∞	2	9	17	5	26	42
5	$\overset{0}{0}$	94	$\overset{0}{0}$	5	∞	$\overset{0}{0}$	41	31	59	48
6	79	65	$\overset{0}{0}$	$\overset{5}{0}$	15	∞	17	47	32	43
7	76	96	48	27	34	$\overset{0}{0}$	∞	$\overset{5}{0}$	25	$\overset{0}{0}$
8	$\overset{0}{0}$	17	9	27	46	15	84	∞	$\overset{0}{0}$	24
9	56	7	45	39	90	93	67	79	∞	38
10	30	$\overset{30}{0}$	42	56	49	77	76	49	23	∞

Figure 12.4 and obtain Figure 12.5. Continuing in this way we obtain the final result that is shown in Figure 12.6.

Notice in Figure 12.6 that when we reach a solution at (6, 3), we obtain a cost of 33. This is the same as the cost of the branch that we abandon at (7, 10). We are able to go back to this branch and obtain an alternative solution. The method will always reveal alternative solutions in this way.

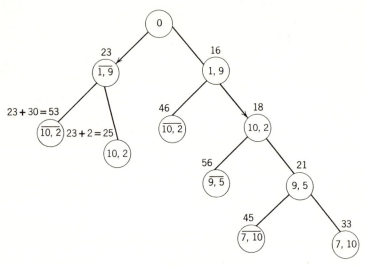

Figure 12.5

The final results are the tours

$$1—10—2—7—6—3—9—5—4—8—1$$

and

$$1—9—5—6—4—7—10—2—3—8—1$$

Both of these cost 33.

The reader may wonder why this procedure works. We have arrived at one (or more) subsets that have the same lower bounds. Each of these subsets contains a single tour whose cost equals the lower bound, and all other tours belong to subsets whose lower bounds are greater. Hence we must have the tours with minimum costs.

The procedure that we have described for solving the traveling salesman problem is one example of a general technique called *branch and bound*.

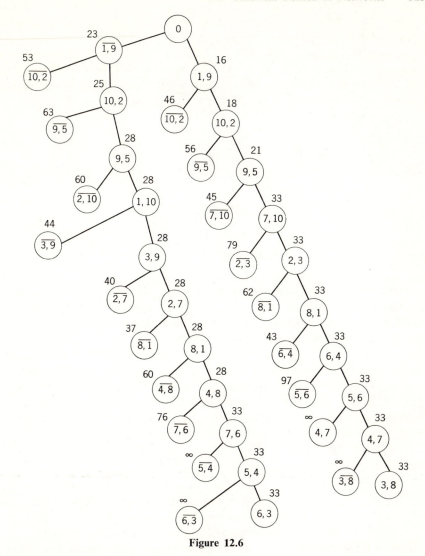

Figure 12.6

MINIMAL ROUTES IN NETWORKS

The traveling salesman problem is a routing problem that is subject to rather severe constraints. A more typical routing problem is one in which we wish to go from one place to another, or to several others, and to get there we must select among several routes involving different stopping places along the way. Suppose, for example, that we wish to go from *a* to *k* in the network shown in Figure 12.7. Links work in both directions unless marked otherwise.

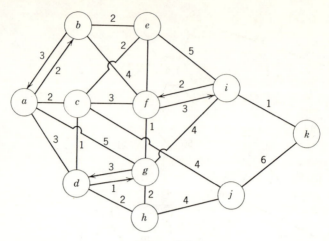

Figure 12.7

There are many different routes between *a* and *k*, but we wish to select the one that involves the least time, cost, or distance. The numbers on the links in the network may represent any of these measures or others, the sum of which are to be minimized. Assume that the way in which we enter a node has no effect on the way of leaving it—an assumption that does not hold in the traveling salesman problem.

It will turn out that in finding the shortest route between *a* and *k*, we must find the shortest route from *a* to every other point in the network, which may be very useful in real cases. There are several ways in which this can be done. First, we consider a graphic procedure.

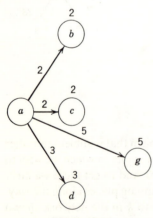

Figure 12.8

Graphic Procedure

1. Starting at the origin, *a*, draw all links by which one can go from *a* to another node and insert the direct distance from *a* on each of these nodes. (See Figure 12.8.)

2. If there are any links between any of the nodes obtained in step 1, determine for each link whether the indirect route from *a* is shorter than the direct route. Draw the shorter route as a solid line and use a broken line for the longer route; insert the shortest distance found alongside each node.

For example, in Figure 12.9 it is seen that one can go from *a* to *g* through *d* at a lower "cost" than going directly. In addition, one may go to *d* directly or through *c*. In case of a tie, draw both routes as solid lines.

3. Add any nodes to which one can go from any of the nodes considered in step 2 and repeat step 2 with respect to them; insert the distances. This is done in Figure 12.10.

4. Continue until completed. The completed diagram is shown in Figure 12.11. The solid lines in Figure 12.11 show the routes that can be taken from *a* to every other point. Note that there are alternatives. For example, one can go from *a* to *e* through *b* or *c*.

One can easily solve this problem subject to an additional constraint: the number of nodes is to be minimized among equally short alter-

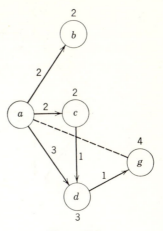

Figure 12.9

native routes. If this constraint were imposed on the problem just solved, we would eliminate the following links: *cd, ef, qf*, and *qh*.

A Matrix Procedure

A second method of solving the problem just considered involves the use of a "dispersion matrix," which was developed by Shimbel (1954). It does not tell us directly what the shortest route is, but it gives its length. It also gives the length of the shortest route between *any* two points in the network.

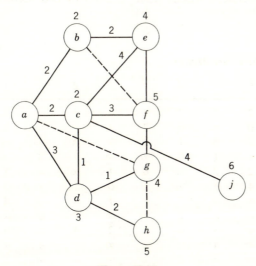

Figure 12.10

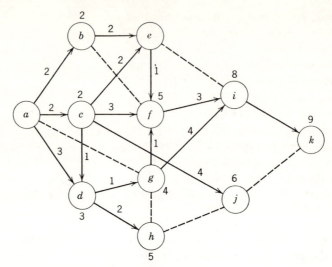

Figure 12.11

The procedure involves the following steps:

1. Translate the network into a $k \times k$ structure matrix $S = [s_{ij}]$, where k is the number of cities. This is done by choosing s_{ij} equal to the distance from i to j if there is a direct link, and $s_{ij} = \infty$ if not. The diagonal entries s_{ii} are all zero. Such a matrix is shown in Table 12.7.

2. We now define a special multiplication of two matrices S and T as follows:

$$ST = U$$

TABLE 12.7   *Structure Matrix*

From	a	b	c	d	e	f	g	h	i	j	k
a	0	2	2	3	∞	∞	5	∞	∞	∞	∞
b	3	0	∞	∞	2	4	∞	∞	∞	∞	∞
c	2	∞	0	1	2	3	∞	∞	∞	4	∞
d	3	∞	1	0	∞	∞	1	2	∞	∞	∞
e	∞	2	2	∞	0	1	∞	∞	5	∞	∞
f	∞	4	3	∞	1	0	1	∞	3	∞	∞
g	5	∞	∞	3	∞	1	0	2	4	∞	∞
h	∞	∞	∞	2	∞	∞	2	0	∞	4	∞
i	∞	∞	∞	∞	5	2	4	∞	0	∞	1
j	∞	∞	4	∞	∞	∞	∞	4	∞	0	6
k	∞	∞	∞	∞	∞	∞	∞	∞	1	6	0

where

$$S = [s_{ij}], \qquad T = [t_{ij}], \qquad U = [u_{ij}]$$

and

$$u_{ij} = \min \{s_{i1} + t_{1j}; s_{i2} + t_{2j}; s_{i3} + t_{3j}; \ldots; s_{ik} + t_{kj}\}$$

$$= \min_k \{s_{ik} + t_{kj}\}.$$

Using this rule, we multiply S by itself and obtain a dispersion matrix $C = S^2$. It should be clear that the elements of D are the shortest distances from i to j in two or fewer steps. The result of this calculation is shown in Table 12.8.

3. Powers of S obey the usual rules of indices, that is, $S^a \times S^b = S^{a+b}$, and S^n contains the shortest distances from i to j in n steps or fewer. At most, the shortest route from i to j can contain $k - 1$ steps; any route containing

TABLE 12.8 *Dispersion Matrix*

From	a	b	c	d	e	f	g	h	i	j	k
a	0	2	2	3	4	5	4	5	9	6	∞
b	3	0	4	6	2	3	5	∞	7	∞	∞
c	2	4	0	1	2	3	2	3	6	4	10
d	3	5	1	0	3	2	1	2	5	5	∞
e	4	2	2	3	0	1	2	∞	4	6	6
f	5	3	3	4	1	0	1	3	3	7	4
g	5	5	4	3	2	1	0	2	4	6	5
h	5	∞	3	2	∞	3	2	0	6	4	10
i	9	6	5	7	3	2	3	6	0	7	1
j	6	∞	4	5	6	7	6	4	7	0	6
k	∞	∞	10	∞	6	6	5	10	1	6	0

k steps must contain a loop and could be shortened. Thus the elements of S^{k-1} must be the shortest routes. However if $S^n = S^{n-1}$, $n < k - 1$, then S^n comprises the shortest routes. Instead of computing powers by successive multiplication by S, it is quicker to use successive squaring and compute $S, S^2, S^4, S^8, \ldots$. The shortest routes have been found at the rth step when $S^{2^r} = S^{2^{(r-1)}}$ or when $2^r \geq k - 1$ for the first time. In our example $S^8 = S^{16}$; the solution is shown in Table 12.9. If we wish to identify the shortest routes, we may do so by comparing Tables 12.7 and 12.9. Any elements that are the same in both constitute one-step shortest paths, and all other shortest paths must be made up of these. In fact, no shortest route would be increased if all but the one-step shortest links were deleted. In Table 12.9 we have starred elements that are the same as the corresponding elements in Table 12.7. The unstarred elements must be the sum of two or more starred elements.

For example, the shortest distance from *a* to *e*, which is 4, must pass through *b*, *c*, or *d*. Thus it might be either *abe* or *ace*. In this way we can discover all the two-step shortest distances. From these we may construct the three-step shortest distances and so on, until all paths have been identified.

TABLE 12.9 *Solution Matrix*

	To										
From	*a*	*b*	*c*	*d*	*e*	*f*	*g*	*h*	*i*	*j*	*k*
a	0	2*	2*	3*	4	5	4	5	8	6	9
b	3*	0	4	5	2*	3	4	6	6	8	7
c	2*	4	0	1*	2*	3*	2	3	6	4*	7
d	3*	5	1*	0	3	2	1*	2*	5	5	6
e	4	2*	2*	3	0	1*	2	4	4	6	5
f	5	3	3*	4	1*	0	1*	3	3*	7	4
g	5*	4	4	3*	2	1*	0	2*	4*	6	5
h	5	6	3	2*	4	3	2*	0	6	4*	7
i	7	5	5	6	3	2*	3	5	0	7	1*
j	6	8	4*	5	6	7	6	4*	7	0	6*
k	8	6	6	7	4	3	4	6	1*	6*	0

* The star denotes elements that are the same as the corresponding elements in Table 12.7. Such elements are one-step shortest paths.

SUMMARY

Routing problems involve finding a path through a network—a system of points and the links that connect the points—which minimizes (or maximizes) some function of a property of the links in the path selected. Routing problems are pervasive in transportation and communication systems, but also occur in a wide variety of other contexts; for example, (1) in determining the order in which to produce a variety of products on a common production facility so as to minimize the sum of the setup costs and (2) in determining the subset of tasks in a set of interrelated tasks whose time of completion fixes the total minimum time to completion of the set. The latter was shown in Chapter 11 to be a "longest-route" problem.

More complex routing problems than we have considered here do arise. For example:

> . . . when a number of "salesmen" from given "home" locations are to visit all locations of a network, each location to be visited a specified number of times by any one of the salesmen (*not predetermined*), so as to minimize the total mileage or cost involved. Closely related are problems concerning the optimal locations of terminals ("home" locations), the optimal number of vehicles (salesmen) and

composition, for example with respect to carrying capacity, of vehicle fleets. Further extensions would obviously include machine sequencing problems, the determination of optimal bus lines, etc. (Loubal, 1964, p. 1).

Here we considered only two problems in any detail—the traveling salesman problem and the minimal path problem. Methods of solving them were presented, but it should be clear to the reader that further improvements (e.g., simplifications) in currently available algorithms, particularly for the traveling salesman problem, are desirable.

EXERCISES

1. Solve the traveling salesman problem in the matrix shown in Table 12.10.

TABLE 12.10

				To			
From	1	2	3	4	5	6	7
1	∞	6	12	6	4	8	1
2	6	∞	10	5	4	3	3
3	8	7	∞	11	3	11	8
4	5	4	11	∞	5	8	6
5	5	2	7	8	∞	4	7
6	6	3	11	5	4	∞	2
7	2	3	9	7	4	3	∞

2. Find the shortest path from a to i in Figure 12.12 by using the graphic method and then find the shortest path between every pair of points by using Shimbel's procedure. Assume all links are two-way, except where shown.

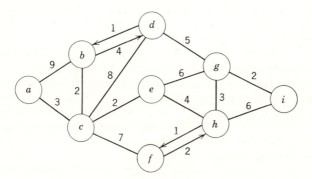

Figure 12.12

Suggested Readings

There is no comprehensive text on networks at an elementary level; the mathematically knowledgeable reader will find a complete and authoritative treatment of the subject in Ford and Fulkerson (1962).

Bibliography

Bock, F., "Mathematical Programming Solution of Traveling Salesman Examples," in *Recent Advances in Mathematical Programming*, R. L. Graves and P. Wolfe (eds), McGraw-Hill Book Co., New York, 1963.

Croes, G. A., "A Method for Solving Traveling Salesman Problems," *Operations Research*, 6 (1958), 791–814.

Dantzig, G. B., D. R. Fulkerson, and S. M. Johnson, "Solution of a Large Scale Traveling Salesman Problem," *Operations Research*, 2 (1954), 393–410.

Ford, L. R., Jr., and D. R. Fulkerson, *Flows in Networks*. Princeton University Press, Princeton, N.J., 1962.

Flood, M. M., "The Traveling Salesman Problem," *Operations Research*, 4 (1956), 61–75.

Gilmore, P. C., and R. E. Gomory, "Sequencing a One State Variable Machine. A Solvable Case of the Traveling Salesman Problem," I.B.M. Research Paper, RC-1103 (1964).

Gonzalez, R. H., "Solution of the Traveling Salesman Problem by Dynamic Programming of the Hypercube," Interim Technical Report No. 18, O.R. Center, M.I.T. (1962).

Hardgrove, W. W., and G. L. Nemhauser, "On the Relation Between the Traveling Salesman and the Longest Path Problems," *Operations Research*, 10 (1962), 647–657.

Lawler, E. L., and D. E. Wood, "Branch and Bound Methods: A Survey," *Operations Research*, 14 (1966), 699–719.

Leyzorek, M. *et al.*, *A Study of Model Techniques for Communication Systems*, First Annual Report, Contract No. DA-36-039-SC-67848, Case Institute of Technology, Cleveland, Ohio, 1957.

Little, J. D. C., K. G. Murty, D. W. Sweeney, and C. Karel, "An Algorithm for the Traveling Salesman Problem," *Operations Research*, 11 (1963), 972–989.

Loubal, P. S., "A Traveling Salesman Algorithm Suitable for Vehicle Routing Problems," Interdepartmental Working Paper No. 3, Institute of Transportation and Traffic Engineering, University of California, Berkeley, July 1964.

Miller, C. E., A. W. Tucker, and R. A. Zemlin, "Integer Programming Formulation of Traveling Salesman Problems," *Journal of the Association of Computing Machines*, 7 (1960), 326–329.

Pandit, S. N. N., "Some Observations on the Routing Problem," *Operations Research*, 10 (1962), 726–727.

Robacker, J. T., *On Network Theory*, RM-1498, The RAND Corp., May 1955.

Shimbel, A., "Structure in Communication Nets," *Proceedings of the Symposium on Information Neworks*, Polytechnic Institute of Brooklyn, New York, April 1954.

CHAPTER 13

Competitive Problems

INTRODUCTION

We have seen that the decision-making process requires that an individual (or a group of individuals) choose the value of a controlled variable X; depending on the value chosen and the values of the uncontrolled variables Y, there is a payoff U to the individual and

$$U = f(X, Y). \tag{13.1}$$

We have assumed either one or the other of the following two situations:

(a) The value of Y can be measured before the value of X is determined and that it will not change until the decision has been made and the payoff received. In this case, we choose $X = X_0$, where X_0 maximizes the payoff; that is, for all X

$$f(X_0, Y) \geq f(X, Y). \tag{13.2}$$

(b) The value of Y cannot be known in advance of our decision, but we know the distribution of Y. If $\phi(Y)$ is the probability density function for Y, we choose X to maximize the expected payoff; that is, we choose $X = X_0$, where for all X

$$\int f(X_0, Y)\phi(Y)\,dY \geq \int f(X, Y)\phi(Y)\,dY. \tag{13.3}$$

Most of our work so far has been concerned with three problems implied by these situations: the determination of the function $f(X, Y)$, the computation of its expected value, and the calculation of X_0. Problems in which the calculation of X_0 is the major difficulty are called *mathematical programming*, and the techniques are quite general inasmuch as they can be applied to any problem situation once a model has been derived. Model building, on the other hand, is usually quite specific, and most models apply to particular situations.

324

Unfortunately, (a) and (b) do not exhaust the possible situations. We may have to make a decision in circumstances in which neither Y nor the distribution of Y is known. Of course, if we know *nothing* at all about Y, it is hardly possible to make a rational decision about X. We can conceive problems of this type, but they occur very rarely in practice. It almost always happens that we have some prior information. For example, a military commander does not normally know the defensive tactics that his opponent will adopt. However, if it is known who the opposing commander is, or the campaign philosophies of the army that trained him, something can be inferred about his probable behavior. Even in the absence of such information we can often infer something if we know the objectives of our opponent and how they are affected by his decisions and ours. A pessimistic but realistic approach is to make our decision so as to obtain the best possible payoff even if the unknown variable Y takes the worst possible value from our point of view. Such an approach is the best that we can have if Y is chosen by a rational opponent who is "out to get" us, but it may be unduly pessimistic if Y is chosen by "nature," which may be assumed to be indifferent to our own problems. If we do not wish to be unduly pessimistic, we may prefer the generalized maximum or the minimax-regret approaches discussed in Chapter 2.

In this chapter we are concerned with situations in which certain of the variables are controlled by individuals other than ourselves, whose interests may conflict with our own.

FORMAL STRUCTURE OF COMPETITIVE SITUATIONS

For simplicity we limit the discussion in this section to situations that involve two competitors and in which the decision variables can only take a finite number of values. Suppose that in a given environment an individual I_1 may choose the value of X. It is convenient to designate the possible values of X as $1, 2, \ldots, m$. If I_1 chooses $X = x$, the payoff to I_1 is $f_1(x, y)$, where y is the value of a variable Y that I_1 cannot control. We assume that the value of Y cannot be observed until the value of X is chosen. We now imagine a second individual who chooses the value of Y. Let q_y be the probability that I_2 chooses $Y = y$, where $y = 1, 2, \ldots, n$, and let p_x be the probability that I_1 chooses $X = x$. Then the expected payoff to I_1 is V_1, where

$$V_1 = \sum_{x=1}^{m} \sum_{y=1}^{n} f_1(x, y) p_x q_x. \tag{13.4}$$

On the other hand, if I_2 is not present, perhaps Y takes the value y with probability $\bar{q}_y$; then I_1 may change his choice of probabilities such that the probability that $X = x$ is $\bar{p}_x$. Thus in the absence of I_2 the expected payoff to I_1 is $\bar{V}_1$, where

$$\bar{V}_1 = \sum_{x=1}^{m} \sum_{y=1}^{n} f_1(x, y) \bar{p}_x \bar{q}_y. \tag{13.5}$$

If $V_1 = \bar{V}_1$, the presence or absence of I_2 makes no difference to I_1; otherwise it does. If $V_1 > \bar{V}_1$, I_2's presence adds to I_1's expectation and I_2 can be said to *cooperate* with I_1 (whether he intends to do so or not). The difference $D_{12} = V_1 - \bar{V}_1$ is a measure of the degree of cooperation of I_2 with I_1. This measure may be negative, in which case we have a *conflict*. Thus if I_2's presence decreases I_1's expectation, we say that I_2 is in conflict with I_1.

If there is also a payoff function $f_2(x, y)$ for I_2, we can define expectations V_2 and $\bar{V}_2$ for I_2 in the presence or absence of I_1. The difference $D_{21} = V_2 - \bar{V}_2$ is the degree of cooperation of I_1 with I_2. Notice that D_{21} is not necessarily the same as D_{12}. If they are different, one of I_1 and I_2 may be said to be *exploiting* the other, according as D_{12} or D_{21} is larger. If $D_{12} > D_{21} > 0$, we would say that I_1 is exploiting I_2 and that the exploitation is *benevolent* because I_2 is benefiting from I_1's presence, but by less than I_1 is benefiting from I_2's presence. On the other hand, if $D_{12} > 0 > D_{21}$, the exploitation is malevolent. We might regard the difference as the degree of exploitation, $(DE)_{12}$:

$$(DE)_{12} = D_{12} - D_{21}.$$

Notice that

$$(DE)_{21} = -(DE)_{12}.$$

The *intensity* of conflict can be measured in two ways: it increases as $D_{12} + D_{21}$ decreases and as $|D_{12} - D_{21}|$ decreases. Conflict intensifies as each party conflicts more with the other and as exploitation decreases.

Competition is often loosely treated as though it were synonymous with conflict. On reflection, however, it is clear that in some sense competition is a regulated or constrained conflict. With further reflection it becomes apparent that competition involves both conflict and cooperation.

Consider a situation in which I_1 and I_2 are in conflict about their respective objectives (desired outcomes) O_1 and O_2. That is, as I_1's chances of obtaining O_1 increase, I_2's chances of obtaining O_2 decrease. Now suppose that I_1 and I_2 also have a common objective O_3. For example, if I_1 and I_2 are opponents in tennis, I_1 wants to win (O_1) and so does $I_2(O_2)$; hence they are in conflict relative to O_1 and O_2. But they both also want recreation (O_3), and the conflict relative to O_1 and O_2 is efficient relative to O_3. Then I_1 and I_2 can be said to be *competing*. Their conflict is regulated (constrained by rules), which is intended to assure the efficiency of the conflict for their "cooperative" objective.

Now suppose that the objective O_3 is not held by I_1 and I_2 but by I_3, which is a third party or group. For example, I_3 may be an audience and O_3 its entertainment objective. In such a case the conflict of I_1 and I_2 is imbedded in *extrinsic* (in contrast to *intrinsic*) competition. Hence economic competition in business is usually extrinsic, involving the consumer as the "third party."

Conflict, and the conflict component of competition, have received considerable research attention, but cooperation has been seriously neglected so far. Most of the research to date has been related to ways of waging conflict. In this connection it is useful to keep in mind the three modes of conflict identified by Rapoport (1960, 1961).

1. *Fights*, in which the objective is to eliminate the opponent.
2. *Games*, in which the objective is to outwit the opponent.
3. *Debates*, in which the objective is to convince the opponent.

Competitive theory has been preoccupied with fights and games, but not with debates. (For a discussion of debates, see Rapoport, 1960.) It is perhaps characteristic of our culture that we are more interested in increasing our ability to wage conflict than we are in increasing our ability to cooperate.

A significant advance in our understanding of the competitive process resulted from the now classic work of von Neumann and Morgenstern, *The Theory of Games and Economic Behavior*. But this theory has done little to increase directly our ability to solve competitive problems. There are a number of reasons for this, which need not occupy us here [see Ackoff (1962) and Rapoport (1959)]; we shall discuss a few of them later. Nevertheless, the theory is very important. First, it has provided a set of concepts that enable us to formulate competitive problems in precise and quantitative ways. Second, it has highlighted some of the gaps in our knowledge. If these gaps are filled, our ability to eliminate or control conflict as well as to wage it effectively where doing so constructively serves society's interests will be increased. In evaluating the theory, Rapoport (1959) has observed that there have been

... 15 years of rich theoretical developments of the theory unaccompanied by anything comparable in applications to behavior.
... its significance was seen in that it broke away from a conceptual framework which had been unable to cope with certain aspects of human behavior. It offered a new one which did appear to capture the "essence" of that behavior. True, the present tools of game theory are still not powerful enough or not refined enough to deal with the subject matter for which it was meant ... (p. 50).
As much as anything else, then, the achievement was in focusing attention on the nature of reasoning involved in the logic of events where conflict ... of interest enters ... perhaps for the first time the difficulties of reasoning about typically human affairs have been pointed out and made explicit (p. 52).

Consequently, in the discussion that follows the emphasis is on the conceptual aspects of game theory rather than on the mathematical techniques for solving games.

GAME THEORY

A game is a situation in which two or more decision makers (or players) choose courses of action and in which the outcome is affected by the combination of choices taken collectively. More specifically:

1. There are n decision makers, $n \geq 2$. Where $n = 2$, it is called a *two-person game*. Where $n > 2$, it is referred to as an *n-person game*.

2. There is a set of rules that specify what courses of action can be chosen (i.e., what plays can be made) and these are known by the players.

3. There is a well-defined set of end states that terminate the competition (e.g., win, lose, or draw).

4. The payoffs associated with each possible end state are specified in advance and are known by each player.

TABLE 13.1   *A Payoff Matrix for a Two-Person Zero-Sum Game*

		Player B	
		1	2
Player A	1	$1	$3
	2	$2	$4

Payoffs to A

It will be noted immediately that only a portion of competitive situations can be modeled as games, because in reality conditions 2, 3, and 4 frequently are not satisfied.

When each decision maker selects his own course of action, we say that a *play* has occurred. A strategy for a given player is a set of rules (or program) that specify which of the available choices he should make at each play. Game theory seeks strategies that maximize or minimize some objective function (i.e., some function of the utilities of the payoffs to the decision maker).

A zero-sum game is one in which the losses of one player (or players) are equivalent to the gains of another player (or a set of players). For example, the payoffs in a zero-sum two-person game can be indicated in a payoff matrix such as is shown in Table 13.1, where the payoffs to player B are equal to "minus the payoffs to player A." If both players select choice "1," A receives $1 and B loses $1, and so on. In a nonzero-sum game, a third party (e.g., the "house" or a "kitty") receives or makes some payment. A payoff matrix for such a game is shown in Table 13.2. The left-hand entry in each

TABLE 13.2 *A Payoff Matrix for a Two-Person Nonzero-Sum Game*

		B	
		1	2
A	1	1, 1	−5, 5
	2	5, −5	−1, −1

cell is the payoff to *A*, and the right-hand entry is the payoff to *B*. Note that for play combinations (1, 1) and (2, 2) the sums of the payoffs are not equal to zero.

A solution to a game is obtained when the "best" strategy for each player is determined. "Best" is defined in terms of a specified objective function. The "appropriate" objective function depends on the kind of prior knowledge that the players have about each other's choices. If each player knows exactly what the other is going to do, we have a deterministic situation and the objective function is to maximize utility. If the probabilities of each choice are known, the objective is to maximize expected utility. If the probabilities are not known, we have an uncertainty situation, for which a variety of objective functions have been suggested, the three most important of which we considered in Chapter 2: minimax (and maximin), generalized minimax, and minimax regret.

Game theory is preoccupied with the uncertainty type of situation. Its objective, in effect, has been to convert the uncertainty type of situation into a certainty type of situation by use of certain "rationality assumptions" about the players. Each player is assumed to act so as to maximize his expected utility. From this assumption it is argued that each player will act so as to maximize his minimum gain or minimize his maximum loss. Therefore, if player *A* in Table 13.1 assumes that *B* is rational, he argues that *B* will select choice 1 because its maximum loss (2) is less than (3) the maximum loss for choice 2. On the basis of this conclusion, that *B* will play 1, *A* selects his choice 2 to maximize his utility. By this type of reasoning the uncertainty is removed.

The difficulty lies in the deduction from the assumption of "rationality" that the other player will maximize his minimum gain. There is no agreement even among game theorists that rational players should so act, and there is abundant evidence that apparently rational players do not, in fact, act in this way, or in any one consistent way. Therefore, game theory is generally interpreted as an "as if" theory, that is, as if rational decision makers behaved in some well-defined (but arbitrarily selected) way, such as maximizing minimum gains.

The Zero-Sum Two-Person Game

Suppose that player A must choose a number from $1, 2, \ldots, m$ and player B must choose from $1, 2, \ldots, n$. Each chooses in ignorance of the other's choice. If A chooses i and B chooses j, A will receive α_{ij} from B. Thus B will gain $-\alpha_{ij}$, and we have a zero-sum game.

Let x_i be the probability that A chooses i and y_j the probability that B chooses j. The expected payoff to A is

$$E = \sum_{i=1}^{m} \sum_{j=1}^{n} x_i y_j \alpha_{ij}.$$

Game theory now assumes that A will choose $x_1, x_2, \ldots, x_m$ in such a way that

(*a*) no matter how B chooses $y_1, y_2, \ldots, y_m$, the gain to A will be at least v, and

(*b*) the amount v is as large as possible.

Now

$$E = \sum_{j=1}^{m} y_j \sum_{i=1}^{n} x_i \alpha_{ij} = \sum_{j=1}^{m} y_j v_j, \qquad (13.6)$$

where

$$v_j = \sum_{i=1}^{n} x_i \alpha_{ij}. \qquad (13.7)$$

Let us divide the v_j into two subsets S and $\bar{S}$. In the set S we place all $\{v_j\}$ such that

(*a*) all v_j in S are equal,
(*b*) all v_j in S are smaller than any v_j not in S (in $\bar{S}$), and
(*c*) every v_j is either in S or $\bar{S}$.

Because B wishes to minimize A's gains, it is clear that he will choose $y_j = 0$ if v_j is in $\bar{S}$. Thus A should choose $x_1, \ldots, x_n$ such that

$$v_j = \sum_{i=1}^{m} x_i \alpha_{ij} \geq v$$

and v is as large as possible. However, $x_1, x_2, \ldots, x_n$ are a probability distribution; hence they are nonnegative and sum to unity. Thus A's problem is to find $x_1, \ldots, x_n$ to maximize v subject to

$$v - \sum_{i=1}^{m} x_i \alpha_{ij} \leq 0 \qquad j = 1, 2, \ldots, n, \qquad (13.8)$$

$$\sum_{i=1}^{m} x_i = 1, \qquad (13.9)$$

and

$$x_i \geq 0 \qquad i = 1, 2, \ldots, m. \qquad (13.10)$$

Because v is a linear function of v and $x_1, \ldots, x_n$ and the constraints are obviously linear, this is a linear programming problem.

Let us now consider the problem from B's point of view. The main difference is that B's payoff is $-\alpha_{ij}$. B will arrive at the following formulation.

Maximize u subject to

$$u - \sum_{j=1}^{n} y_j(-\alpha_{ij}) \leq 0 \qquad i = 1, 2, \ldots, m, \qquad (13.11)$$

$$\sum_{j=1}^{n} y_j = 1, \qquad (13.12)$$

and

$$y_j \geq 0 \qquad j = 1, 2, \ldots, n. \qquad (13.13)$$

We now use the principle of duality to show that the maximum gain that A can guarantee is equal to the least loss that B can guarantee. B's loss is $-u$, which we denote by u'. Thus we can reformulate B's problem.

Minimize u' subject to

$$u' - \sum_{j=1}^{m} y_j \alpha_{ij} \geq 0 \qquad i = 1, 2, \ldots, m, \qquad (13.11a)$$

$$\sum_{j=1}^{m} y_j = 1, \qquad (13.12a)$$

and

$$y_j \geq 0 \qquad j = 1, 2, \ldots, n. \qquad (13.13a)$$

In this form B's problem is the dual of A's, and it follows that

$$\min u' = \max v.$$

The common value is called the *value of the game* to A.

To see the duality of the two problems it is necessary to recall that if the primal problem has a variable that is unconstrained in sign (in this case v), the corresponding dual constraint is a strict equality, and if the primal problem has a strict equality constraint, the corresponding dual variable is unconstrained in sign.

The primal problem may be written: maximize v subject to

$$v - \alpha_{11}x_1 - \alpha_{21}x_2 - \cdots - \alpha_{m1}x_m \geq 0$$

$$v - \alpha_{12}x_1 - \alpha_{22}x_2 - \cdots - \alpha_{m2}x_m \geq 0$$

$$\vdots$$

$$v - \alpha_{1n}x_1 - \alpha_{2n}x_2 - \cdots - \alpha_{mn}x_m \geq 0$$

$$x_1 + x_2 + \cdots + x_m = 1$$

and

$$x_1 \geq 0, x_2 \geq 0, \ldots, x_n \geq 0.$$

Let $y_1, y_2, \ldots, y_m$ and u' be the dual variables corresponding to the 1st, 2nd, ... nth and last constraint.

From the right-hand column of the primal constraints, the function to be minimized in the dual problem is simply u', which from the strict equality is a variable unconstrained in sign.

From the coefficients of v in the primal constraints and the primal objective function, we have

$$\sum_{j=1}^{m} y_j = 1$$

from the coefficients of x_i, we have

$$u' - \sum_{j=1}^{m} y_j \alpha_{ij} \geq 0.$$

Also, because the first n primal constraints are inequalities, the y_j's must be nonnegative.

The principle of duality ensures that if any solution of A's problem yields a value of v equal to the value of u' corresponding to some solution to B's problem, the common value is the largest possible v and the smallest possible u'. Thus we solve both problems if we can find $x_1, x_2, \ldots, x_n$ and $y_1, y_2, \ldots, y_m$ and v such that all x's and y's are nonnegative and

$$\sum_{i=1}^{m} x_i = 1 \tag{13.9}$$

$$\sum_{j=1}^{n} y_j = 1 \tag{13.12}$$

$$\sum_{i=1}^{m} x_i \alpha_{ij} \geq v \qquad j = 1, 2, \ldots, n \qquad \text{[cf. (13.8)]} \quad (13.8a)$$

$$\sum_{j=1}^{n} y_j \alpha_{ij} \leq v \qquad i = 1, 2, \ldots, m \qquad \text{[cf. (13.11a)]} \quad (13.11b)$$

The computation of $(x_1, \ldots, x_m)$, $(y_1, \ldots, y_n)$, and v is called "solving the game." Most numerical game solutions rely on trial-and-error methods of solving these inequalities. It should be mentioned that if some $x_i = 1$ (and the others are all zero), A is said to use a *pure strategy*. If A uses two or more pure strategies, each with probability less than 1, he is said to use a *mixed strategy*.

The following results are also helpful in finding numerical solutions. If A's optimal policy is a mixed strategy in which exactly r pure strategies have nonzero probabilities, B's optimal strategy also uses r pure strategies. This follows from the way in which the solution to a dual problem is constructed from that of the primal.

It should also be clear that if for any j we have

$$\sum_{i=1}^{m} x_i \alpha_{ij} > v,$$

then $y_j = 0$, and if for any i we have

$$\sum_{j=1}^{n} y_j \alpha_{ij} < v,$$

then $x_i = 0$.

The Numerical Solution of Two-Person Zero-Sum Games.   In practice it is seldom necessary to use a linear programming algorithm to solve a game; the following methods should be tried first.

Saddle-point games. An element in the matrix $[\alpha_{ij}]$ is called a saddle point if it has the following properties:

(*a*) it is the lowest in its row, and
(*b*) it is the highest in its column.

If a game has a saddle point, say, at (h, k), A should choose h and B should choose k. The value of the game is α_{hk}. The result is justified as follows. Assume for the moment that there is only one saddle point. If A chooses h, he must gain at least α_{hk} (all other entries in row h exceed α_{hk}). If A chooses a row other than h, he cannot be certain of as much as α_{hk}, because B can choose k and $\alpha_{rk} < \alpha_{hk}$ for all $r \neq h$. Thus A will choose h. Similarly B will choose k.

If there are two or more saddle points, they must be equal. Moreover, if (h, k) and (h', k') are both saddle points with $h \neq h'$, $k \neq k'$; then so are (h, k') and (h', k). The reader should be able to verify these statements directly from the definition of a saddle point.

Dominance. If no element in one row of $[\alpha_{ij}]$ is less than the corresponding element in another row, A will never choose the second row. That is, if for all $j = 1, 2, \ldots, n$ we have

$$\alpha_{rj} \geq \alpha_{sj},$$

then

$$x_s = 0.$$

The value of the game and the nonzero choice probabilities are unaltered if row s is deleted. We say row r *dominates* row s. Similarly, if no element in one column is more than the corresponding element in a second column, B will never choose the second column, and it may be deleted.

Two-by-two games. If both players have only two choices and *if the game has no saddle point*, the game may be solved as follows.

If the payoff matrix to A is

$$\begin{bmatrix} \alpha_{11} & \alpha_{12} \\ \alpha_{21} & \alpha_{22} \end{bmatrix}$$

then

$$\frac{x_1}{x_2} = \frac{\alpha_{22} - \alpha_{21}}{\alpha_{11} - \alpha_{12}}; \quad \frac{y_1}{y_2} = \frac{\alpha_{22} - \alpha_{12}}{\alpha_{11} - \alpha_{21}},$$

and the value of the game is

$$v = \frac{\alpha_{11}\alpha_{22} - \alpha_{12}\alpha_{21}}{\alpha_{11} + \alpha_{22} - (\alpha_{12} + \alpha_{21})}.$$

Proof: We wish to find $x_1 \geq 0$, $x_2 \geq 0$, $y_1 \geq 0$, $y_2 \geq 0$, and v to satisfy

$$x_1 + x_2 = 1$$
$$y_1 + y_2 = 1$$
$$\alpha_{11}x_1 + \alpha_{21}x_2 \geq v$$
$$\alpha_{12}x_1 + \alpha_{22}x_2 \geq v$$
$$\alpha_{11}y_1 + \alpha_{12}y_2 \leq v$$
$$\alpha_{21}y + \alpha_{22}y_2 \leq v.$$

We assume that all constraints are strict equalities and obtain

$$\frac{x_1}{x_2} = \frac{\alpha_{22} - \alpha_{21}}{\alpha_{11} - \alpha_{12}} \quad \text{and} \quad \frac{y_1}{y_2} = \frac{\alpha_{22} - \alpha_{12}}{\alpha_{11} - \alpha_{21}}.$$

These lead to

$$v = \frac{\alpha_{11}\alpha_{22} - \alpha_{12}\alpha_{21}}{\alpha_{11} + \alpha_{22} - (\alpha_{12} + \alpha_{21})}.$$

If the ratios x_1/x_2 and y_1/y_2 are both positive, they will lead to acceptable values of x_1, x_2, y_1, and y_2, and we will have found a solution satisfying all constraints including nonnegativity. It must be *the* solution.

If, in fact, there is no saddle point, the largest and second largest elements of $[\alpha_{ij}]$ must lie on a diagonal. Thus the only possible orderings without a saddle point are

$$a_{11} \geq a_{22} \geq a_{12} \geq a_{21}$$
$$a_{11} \geq a_{22} \geq a_{21} \geq a_{12}$$
$$a_{22} \geq a_{11} \geq a_{12} \geq a_{21}$$
$$a_{22} \geq a_{11} \geq a_{21} \geq a_{12}$$
$$a_{12} \geq a_{21} \geq a_{11} \geq a_{22}$$
$$a_{12} \geq a_{21} \geq a_{22} \geq a_{11}$$
$$a_{21} \geq a_{12} \geq a_{11} \geq a_{22}$$
$$a_{21} \geq a_{12} \geq a_{22} \geq a_{11}.$$

It is easy to verify that with all of these orderings the ratios x_1/x_2 and y_1/y_2 are nonnegative, which completes the proof.

It should be noted that the reasoning fails if there is a saddle point.

The formulas are very easy to apply. As an example consider the following matrix of payoffs to A, which has no saddle point.

$$\begin{bmatrix} 1 & 3 \\ 2 & -1 \end{bmatrix}$$

Alongside the top row we write the numerical value of the difference between the elements of the second row, and alongside the second row we write the numerical value of the difference between the elements of the top row. Beneath the first column we write the numerical value of the difference between elements of the second column, and finally beneath the second column we write the numerical value of the difference between elements of the first column. Thus

$$\begin{bmatrix} 1 & 3 \\ 2 & -1 \end{bmatrix} \quad \begin{matrix} 2-(-1)=3 \\ 3-1=2 \end{matrix}$$

$$3-(-1)=4 \quad 2-1=1$$

The numbers by each row (or column) are the relative frequencies with which they are chosen. Thus $x_1 = \frac{3}{5}$, $x_2 = \frac{2}{5}$, $y_1 = \frac{4}{5}$, $y_2 = \frac{1}{5}$. The value of the game to A is

$$\tfrac{3}{5} \times 1 + \tfrac{2}{5} \times 2 = \tfrac{7}{5} = \tfrac{3}{5} \times 3 - 1 \times \tfrac{2}{5} = \tfrac{4}{5} \times 1 + \tfrac{1}{5} \times 3 = \tfrac{4}{5} \times 2 - \tfrac{1}{5} \times 1.$$

Two-by-n games. Because the optimal strategies for both players assign nonzero probabilities to the same number of pure strategies, it is clear that if one player has only two strategies, the other player will only use two strategies. If we could find which two strategies will be used, we would have reduced the game to a 2×2 game, which we know how to solve. There is a simple graphical method for discovering which strategies are used. We illustrate with a numerical example.

Consider the following payoff matrix to A

$$\begin{array}{c} \\ 1 \\ 2 \end{array} \begin{array}{ccccc} 1 & 2 & 3 & 4 & 5 \\ \begin{bmatrix} 1 & 4 & -1 & -5 & 6 \\ 3 & 2 & 6 & 4 & -3 \end{bmatrix} \end{array}$$

Draw two parallel lines one unit apart and mark a scale on each. They represent the two strategies available to A. (See Figure 13.1.) We then draw lines to represent each of B's strategies. For example, to represent B's first strategy, join 1 on scale 1 to 3 on scale 2; to represent B's second strategy, join 4 on scale 1 to 2 on scale 2; and so on. Suppose that B plays a strategy that joins a on scale 1 to b on scale 2, and A plays his first strategy with probability p. The A's expectation is PN, where N is distance $1 - p$ from the scale representing A's first strategy. (See Figure 13.2.) Now, if the line through N meets the lines representing B's strategies at $P_1, P_2, \ldots, P_n$, B will choose the strategy j^* such that $P_j * N$ is as small as possible. Thus A will choose N such that $P_j * N$ is as large as possible. This means that N will be chosen as in Figure 13.1, where P is the highest point on the lower boundary of the figure

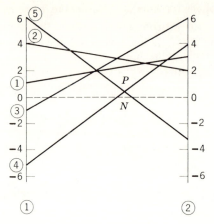

Figure 13.1   Graphical solution of a 2 × *n* game.

made by *B*'s strategies. To guarantee that *A* does not gain more than *PN*, *B* must use only strategies 4 and 5. Thus the game reduces to:

$$\begin{bmatrix} -5 & 6 \\ 4 & -3 \end{bmatrix}$$

From this matrix we obtain

$$x_1 = \tfrac{7}{18}, \quad x_2 = \tfrac{11}{18}, \quad y_1 = y_2 = y_3 = 0, \quad y_4 = y_5 = \tfrac{1}{2}, \quad \text{and} \quad v = \tfrac{1}{2}.$$

In general, we identify *A*'s mixed strategy by finding the highest point on the lower boundary of the figure. *B*'s best strategies are those that pass through this point. If *A* has *n* strategies and *B* has only 2, *A*'s best strategies are those that pass through the lowest point on the upper boundary.

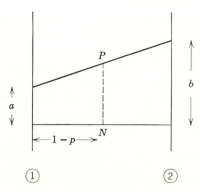

Figure 13.2

Summary of Methods for Solving Two-Person Zero-Sum Games. Use the following methods in the order given:

1. Search for a saddle point.
2. Use the concept of dominance to reduce the size of the game.
3. For $2 \times n$ games, use a graphical method to reduce to 2×2 games.
4. For 2×2 games, use the formula.
5. If these methods fail, try to guess which constraints become equalities, solve the resulting equations, and check the remaining constraints.
6. If all else fails, use a linear programming algorithm.

NONZERO-SUM GAMES

Until recently there was no satisfactory theory either to explain how people should play nonzero-sum games or to describe how they actually play such games. In zero-sum two-person games such as we have just examined we at least have a theory that prescribes how people should play if they wish to maximize their minimum gain. Recently, however, Nigel Howard (1966) has developed an extension of game theory, the *theory of metagames*, which appears to describe how most people play nonzero-sum games involving any number of persons. It also promises to be capable of being developed so that it prescribes how people should play such games. The basic characteristics of this new theory are presented here.

Consider one of the most common nonzero-sum two-person games—the prisoner's dilemma.[1] Table 13.2 shows a payoff matrix for such a dilemma. However, it may be formulated more generally, as is done in Table 13.3, where the entries in the payoff matrix indicate the *order* of preferences of the two players. The absolute values of the payoffs are not relevant in the development of the theory of metagames.

The nature of this dilemma becomes apparent on examining Table 10.3. We may suppose that if both players study the situation, they will both decide to play 1, which gives each a payoff of 3 per play. However, with further reflection A may reason as follows: if B plays 1, then I should play 2 because it will increase my gain to 4. But B can use the same reasoning and also decide to play 2. If both players play 2, each receives a payoff of only 2. The pair of plays (2, 2) forms an *equilibrium point*, because if either party departs from it without the other doing so, he will be worse off than he was before he departed

---

[1] The game derives its name from the following story. The district attorney has two bank robbers in separate cells and offers each the chance of confessing. If one confesses and the other does not, then the confessor will get 2 years and the other 10. If both confess they will get 8 years and if neither confess there is only evidence to ensure conviction on a lesser charge and each will receive 5 years.

TABLE 13.3   *A Prisoner's Dilemma*

B

		1	2
A	1	3, 3	1, 4
	2	4, 1	(2, 2)

from it. Game theory seems to indicate that they should play (2, 2) because it is an equilibrium point, but this is not intuitively satisfying. On the other hand, (1, 1) is intuitively satisfying but does not appear to provide stability. Hence the dilemma.

Consider a case in which two large corporations have the same price for their principal competing products. Each considers cutting their price to gain market share and profit. The situation is shown in Table 13.4. It can be seen that this is a prisoner's dilemma.

There are many practical examples of this kind of dilemma. For example, consider the problem facing the agricultural industry. Each individual farmer can maximize his own income by maximizing the amount of crops that he produces. When all farmers follow this policy, however, the supply exceeds demand and prices fall. Thus collectively farmers can increase their income by reducing their production. In practice, the Federal Government has to intervene with a complex system of controls designed to provide assurance that the total production that reaches the market is low enough to maintain prices.

In an attempt to extend the theory of games so that it would better identify points at which players actually tend to stabilize their play in nonzero-sum games, Howard argued as follows.

TABLE 13.4   *Another Prisoner's Dilemma*

B

		Maintain prices	Decrease prices
A	Maintain prices	3, 3 *Status quo*	1, 4 B gains market share and profit
	Decrease prices	4, 1 A gains market share and profit	2, 2 Both retain market shares but lose profit

TABLE 13.5 *B's Policies with Knowledge of A*
B's Possible Policies

		1 Regardless	2 Regardless	Tit-for-Tat	Tat-for-Tit
A	1	(1) = 3, 3	(2) = 1, 4	(1) = 3, 3	(2) = 1, 4
	2	(1) = 4, 1	(2) = (2, 2)	(2) = 2, 2	(1) = 4, 1

Referring to Table 13.3, suppose that *B* knew, or believed that he could accurately predict, what *A* was going to do. Then *B* could formulate 4 different policies, which are shown in Table 13.5. It will be observed that in this extended matrix there is still only one equilibrium point (2, 2), which is the same one that appeared in the original matrix.

Now suppose that *A* knows, or believes that he can accurately predict, which of the four policies *B* will pursue. Then *A* can formulate 16 possible policies. These are shown in Table 13.6. *A*'s first policy consists of playing 1 no matter what policy *B* selects. His second policy consists of playing 1 unless *B* plays tit-for-tat, in which case he plays 2; and so on. It will be observed

TABLE 13.6 *A Metagame Payoff Matrix*

A's Possible Policies	B's Possible Policies			
	1 Regardless	2 Regardless	Tit-for-Tat	Tat-for-Tit
1. 1, 1, 1, 1	3, 3	1, 4	3, 3	1, 4
2. 1, 1, 1, 2	3, 3	1, 4	3, 3	4, 1
3. 1, 1, 2, 1	3, 3	1, 4	2, 2	1, 4
4. 1, 2, 1, 1	3, 3	2, 2	3, 3	1, 4
5. 2, 1, 1, 1	4, 1	1, 4	3, 3	1, 4
6. 1, 1, 2, 2	3, 3	1, 4	2, 2	4, 1
7. 1, 2, 1, 2	3, 3	2, 2	(3, 3)	4, 1
8. 2, 1, 1, 2	4, 1	1, 4	3, 3	4, 1
9. 1, 2, 2, 1	3, 3	2, 2	2, 2	1, 4
10. 2, 1, 2, 1	4, 1	1, 4	2, 2	1, 4
11. 2, 2, 1, 1	4, 1	2, 2	3, 3	1, 4
12. 1, 2, 2, 2	3, 3	2, 2	2, 2	4, 1
13. 2, 1, 2, 2	4, 1	1, 4	2, 2	4, 1
14. 2, 2, 1, 2	4, 1	2, 2	(3, 3)	4, 1
15. 2, 2, 2, 1	4, 1	2, 2	2, 2	1, 4
16. 2, 2, 2, 2	4, 1	(2, 2)	2, 2	4, 1

that in this matrix 3 equilibrium points appear including (1, 1), which clearly dominates (2, 2). Note that A's policy 14 (2, 2, 1, 2) is the *rational* policy, because it maximizes A's gain for each of B's policies.

It is natural to wonder what would happen if B were now to formulate a further matrix based on knowledge of A's 16 strategies. Howard has shown, however, that further explosion of the matrix beyond n levels (where n is the number of players) will not reveal any additional equilibrium points.

Note that if A plays policy 14 and B plays tit-for-tat, he cannot be certain whether A is playing policy 14 or policy 5. If B thinks A is playing 5, he will be tempted to shift to "2 regardless" and increase his gain to 4. This would

TABLE 13.7

		B	
		1	2
A	1	4, 3	1, 4
	2	3, 2	2, 1

in turn drive A to policy 16 and a (2, 2) payoff for both. The role of communication in avoiding such misinterpretations is apparent. In experimental plays of nonzero-sum games with and without communication between the players, games with communication have been found to have a higher probability of reaching stability and of reaching it sooner.

The theory of metagames not only identifies equilibrium points missed by traditional game theory in games that have one or more such points, but it also does so in games in which the traditional theory finds no such points. For example, consider the game shown in Table 13.7. This game has no "traditional" equilibrium point, but in the metagame matrix derived from it (1, 1) it appears as an equilibrium point.

An equilibrium point that dominates all others in the metagame matrix appears to be one that most players in experimental and real conflict situations seem to select. Extension of the theory to explain the departures from the dominant equilibrium point is in process.

Of particular importance in the theory of metagames is what can be called an *altruistic* equilibrium point. It is a dominant equilibrium point that has an additional characteristic: it results from each player's trying to maximize the minimum gain of his opponent. According to Howard, only an altruistic equilibrium point, if it exists, will be fully acceptable to all the players; hence it will be capable of producing long-run stability.

(Excercises 1 to 7 should be done at this point.)

BIDDING PROBLEMS

One of the more common competitive business problems involves bidding for contracts. Two types of bids are possible. In the first type the bidders announce prices at which they are prepared to perform a service. For example, a city wishes to buy police cars and invites automobile dealers to quote prices. The other type of bid is an offer to pay in order to obtain some privilege. A good example is the bidding of companies for the right to obtain offshore oil leases. Bidding situations may also be classified as open or closed. In the former, bids are announced as they are made, and a bidder is free to improve on the best existing bid at any time. In closed bidding, the bids are submitted in sealed envelopes and all bids are opened simultaneously. Usually, the lowest (or highest depending on the nature of the situation) bid is accepted, but there are occasions when this is not so. For example, all bids may be too high or the low bidder may not be thought technically competent.

Attempts to model bidding situations fall into two classes. On the one hand, we may suppose that the strategy of a single bidder will not, in the short run, influence his competitors, and that their behavior is statistically stable. Models of this type treat competitive bids as uncontrolled variables whose distribution is known. On the other hand, models have been made that endeavor to use the concepts of game theory to explain how bids should be made. We now turn to some examples.

Sealed Bids for a Contract to Perform a Service

The first step in submitting such a bid is to estimate our costs of performing the service. Normally we bid a higher figure, and if our bid is accepted, the difference is our profit. If the bidding is sealed, the winning price is often the only one that is made public. Thus we might have acquired a list of our cost estimates and the lowest bid submitted in those cases in which we did not obtain the contract. Suppose that we have found that the ratio

$$x = \frac{\text{lowest bid}}{\text{our cost estimate}}$$

has, in the past, been normally distributed about a mean of μ with a variance σ^2. Our problem is to choose our own bid so as to maximize our expected profit.

Suppose that we estimate the cost of a contract as c and bid a price p. Then our profit is

$p - c$ if we have the lowest bid

0 if our bid is not the lowest.

The probability that we have the lowest bid is the probability that p/c is less than a random variable that is normally distributed about μ with variance σ^2. This probability is $f(p/c)$, where

$$f(z) = \int_z^\infty \frac{1}{\sqrt{2\pi}\sigma} \exp -\frac{(x-\mu)^2}{2\sigma^2}\, dx.$$

Thus our expected profit is

$$p = (p - c)f\left(\frac{p}{c}\right).$$

We wish to maximize P with respect to p. We differentiate and obtain

$$\frac{dP}{dp} = f\left(\frac{p}{c}\right) + (p - c)f'\left(\frac{p}{c}\right)\frac{1}{c} = 0.$$

If we write $p/c = z$, we have

$$f(z) + (z - 1)f'(z) = 0,$$

and if $z = \mu + t\sigma$, then

$$f(z) = \int_t^\infty \frac{1}{\sqrt{2\pi}} e^{-x^2/2}\, dx,$$

and

$$f'(z) = \frac{-1}{\sqrt{2\pi}\sigma} e^{-t^2/2}.$$

Thus t satisfies

$$\int_t^\infty \frac{1}{\sqrt{2\pi}} e^{-x^2/2}\, dx = (\mu + t\sigma - 1)\frac{1}{\sqrt{2\pi}\sigma} e^{-t^2/2}.$$

Both the integral and the exponential function can be found from standard normal tables and the equation can be solved by graphical methods. (See Figure 13.3.) The optimal bid is where the two curves intersect.

Notice that implicit in our reasoning is the assumption that the distribution of the winning bids will not change in response to any change in our behavior. When the competition consists of a large number of firms, each acting independently, this is a reasonable assumption in the short run. In the earlier part of this chapter we considered competition that consists of a single individual who might well respond quickly to our changed behavior, and we had to take this into account in our own planning.

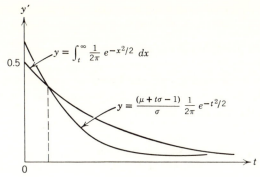

Figure 13.3 Graphical solution of equation.

Public Auctions

The situation is different at a public auction, where every bid is announced as it is made and opportunities for changing a bid exist. Suppose that two bidders are both interested in two items that are worth $75 and $125 each. Bidder A has $100 and bidder B has $140. We wish to find appropriate strategies for each bidder.

A might argue that because he has less capital than B, he cannot hope to obtain both items. From A's point of view the best outcome is to buy one item. If the $75 item is offered first, A will continue to raise the bid price until his profit will be the same whether he wins the $75 or the $125 item. If B wins the $75 item for $\$x$, B has $140 - x$ left, and A must win the $125 item for just above $140 - x$, provided that $140 - x \leq 100$. If A wins the first item for x, his profit is $75 - x$, and if B wins the first item for x, A's profit is $125 - (140 - x)$. Thus A will raise the price until

$$75 - x = 125 - (140 - x) = x - 15,$$

from which

$$x = 45.$$

B recognizes that he might obtain both items, and if he buys the first item for less than $40, he is bound to obtain the second for just over $100. Thus if B can obtain the first item for $y < 40$, his total profit is

$$75 - y + 125 - 100 = 100 - y$$

On the other hand, if the first item goes to A for y, then B wins the second for $100 - y$, so that B's profit is $125 - (100 - y) = 25 + y$.

Thus B will bid for the first item until

$$100 - y = 25 + y,$$

or

$$y = 37.5.$$

If we assume that both A and B have performed these calculations, B will realize that

(a) the highest price that B can afford for the first item if he is to pay for both is \$37.50;

(b) A will never allow B to win the first item for less than \$45, for if B wins below \$45, A's profit is less than if A increased his bid; and

(c) if A wins the first item, then the more A pays for it, the cheaper B can win the second item.

Thus B will force A to pay \$45 for the first item, and the second item will be sold to B for $100 - 45 = 55$; A makes a profit of \$30 and B makes \$70.

It is instructive to view the bidding problem as one in dynamic programming. Suppose that there is only one item for sale and that A has α to spend and B has β. Both value the item at z_1. Let $f_1(\alpha, \beta)$ be A's profit and $g_1(\alpha, \beta)$ B's profit.

If B has bid x and the minimum difference between bids is Δ, A can make a profit of $z_1 - x - \Delta$ by increasing the bid; if B wins, A makes nothing. Therefore, A will increase the bid provided that

$$x < z_1$$

and, because A has only α to spend, provided that

$$x < \alpha.$$

B will reason in a similar fashion. We conclude that

(a) if $\alpha < z_1$ and $\alpha < \beta$, B will win the item for just over α and $f_1(\alpha, \beta) = 0$; $g_1(\alpha, \beta) = z_1 - \alpha$;

(b) if $\alpha \geq z_1$ and $\beta \geq z_1$, the item will be purchased for z_1 and $f_1(\alpha, \beta) = g_1(\alpha, \beta) = 0$;

(c) if $\alpha > \beta$ and $\beta < z_1$, A will win the item for just over β and $f_1(\alpha, \beta) = z_1 - \beta$; $g_1(\alpha, \beta) = 0$.

Now suppose that there is another item to be offered and both A and B value it at z_2. Suppose also that z_2 item is offered first. Let $f_2(\alpha, \beta)$ and $g_2(\alpha, \beta)$ be the profits made by A and B.

If B has bid x for the z_2 item, A can let him have it, and A's total profit will be $f_1(\alpha, \beta - x)$; or A can increase the bid to just over x, in which case if B lets him win, A's profit is $z_2 - x + f_1(\alpha - x, \beta)$. If A has sufficient resources, he will continue to raise the bid until

$$z_2 - x + f_1(\alpha - x, \beta) = f_1(\alpha, \beta - x). \tag{13.14}$$

Similarly, B will raise his bid until

$$z_2 - x + g_1(\alpha, \beta - x) = g_1(\alpha - x, \beta). \tag{13.15}$$

Once we have tabulated f_1 and g_1, it is easy enough to compute the solutions to (13.14) and (13.15), say x_1 and x_2. Then A will bid up to min (x_1, α) and B will bid up to min (x_2, β) for the z_2 item. It will go to A, provided that

$$\text{min } (x_1, \alpha) > \text{min } (x_2, \beta).$$

Once we know who obtains the z_2 item, it is easy to find $f_2(\alpha, \beta)$ and $g_2(\alpha, \beta)$.

The method can now be extended to any number of items. Let z_n be the value of the first of n items and $f_n(\alpha, \beta)$ and $g_n(\alpha, \beta)$ the profits to A and B. Then A will bid x as long as $x < \alpha$ and

$$z_n - x + f_{n-1}(\alpha - x, \beta) \geq f_{n-1}(\alpha, \beta - x),$$

and B will bid as long as $x < \beta$ and

$$z_n - x + g_{n-1}(\alpha, \beta - x) \geq g_{n-1}(\alpha - x, \beta).$$

In practice the problem is more complicated. There is usually a reserve price for each item such that if the bidding does not reach the reserve, the item is withdrawn. It is not customary to announce the reserve either before or after the bidding. All that is ever available is the highest price bid on an item that is withdrawn. It is also usual for the auctioneer to announce a minimum incremental bid, so that our tacit assumption that if A has bid x, then B can bid slightly over x is not correct. Finally, there may be more than two bidders. Much work remains to be done, and we can only sketch the merest outline of some simple situations.

A MARKETING PROBLEM

Almost every decision made in marketing must involve competitive problems. Usually the situation cannot be modeled as a zero-sum game. Suppose that two companies dominate a market in which their combined sales total S. We assume that for each company there is an advertising-effectiveness factor such that the market is split in proportion to the money spent on advertising multiplied by the effectiveness factor. Thus if company A spends x, company B spends y, and the factors are α and β, their sales are

$$\frac{S\alpha x}{\alpha x + \beta y}$$

and

$$\frac{S\beta y}{\alpha x + \beta y}.$$

Suppose that production and distribution costs (other than advertising) are such that if company A sells S_A, its gross profit is $g_A S_A$; for company B, sales of S_B produce profits of $g_B S_B$.

The net profit, P_A, for A is

$$P_A = \frac{g_A S \alpha x}{\alpha x + \beta y} - x,$$

and the net profit for B is

$$P_B = \frac{g_B S \beta y}{\alpha x + \beta y} - y.$$

Suppose that A has determined the value of y and now wishes to choose x to maximize P_A. A sets $\partial P_A / \partial x = 0$ and obtains

$$\frac{\partial P_A}{\partial x} = \frac{g_A S \alpha \beta y}{(\alpha x + \beta y)^2} - 1 = 0,$$

or

$$(\alpha x + \beta y)^2 = g_A S \alpha \beta y.$$

In the same way B obtains

$$(\alpha x + \beta y)^2 = g_B S \alpha \beta x.$$

Thus

$$g_A y = g_B x,$$

and

$$x = \frac{S \alpha \beta g_A{}^2 g_B}{(\alpha g_A + \beta g_B)^2} \, ; \quad y = \frac{S \alpha \beta g_A g_B{}^2}{(\alpha g_A + \beta g_B)^2} \, .$$

Substituting these values for x and y in the expression for net profit, P_A, we find

$$P_A = g_A S \frac{\alpha g_A}{\alpha g_A + \beta g_B} - \frac{S \alpha \beta g_A{}^2 g_B}{(\alpha g_A + \beta g_B)^2}$$

$$= \frac{S \alpha g_A{}^2}{(\alpha g_A + \beta g_B)^2} [\alpha g_A + \beta g_B - \beta g_B]$$

$$= \frac{S \alpha^2 g_A{}^3}{(\alpha g_A + \beta g_B)^2} \, .$$

Similarly, B's net profit is

$$P_B = \frac{S \beta^2 g_B{}^3}{(\alpha g_A + \beta g_B)^2} \, .$$

The policies that lead to these values of P_A and P_B are stable in the sense that if A uses this policy and B uses any other policy, B's net profit will be reduced, and vice versa. Of course, on the assumption that the market will be divided between A and B, it is obvious that if they can reach agreement to reduce advertising while at the same time preserving the condition $g_A y = g_B x$, both will increase net profit. However, such agreement is unstable, because if A agree to limit his advertising to the sum x, the optimal expenditure for B is

$$y_0 = \sqrt{g_B S \frac{\alpha}{\beta} x} - \frac{\alpha}{\beta} x,$$

which is greater than $g_B x / g_A$ so long as x is less than the value given by the stable policy.

SUMMARY

Competitive situations exist whenever two or more persons have objectives and courses of action such that as one person increases the chances of attaining his objectives, he reduces the chances that others will attain theirs. A body of mathematical theory has been developed to describe how people should behave in such circumstances. The theory requires some assumption about the motives of the persons involved, so that each may infer the behavior of the others and thus in a sense optimize his own behavior.

For two-person zero-sum games it is assumed that each player wishes to maximize the minimum amount that he can guarantee to himself, no matter what the other player does. When each player is faced with a finite number of courses of action (pure strategies), the problems can always be solved by allowing mixed strategies in which each course of action is chosen by a chance device with predetermined probabilities. Such chance mechanisms ensure that the players are unable to take advantage of any prediction that they may make of their opponents' behavior.

We have seen in both the bidding and the marketing examples that it is possible to find stable strategies for nonzero-sum games. They are such that if $(n-1)$ out of n players use the staple strategy, the odd man out is worse off than if he goes along with the others. Unfortunately, staple strategies often result in every player's being worse off than if all had agreed to some other strategy. The difficulty with such agreements is that if $(n-1)$ out of n players keep an agreement, the odd man out may be better off than if he sticks with the crowd.

EXERCISES

In Exercises 1 to 5 find the optimal strategies and the value of the game to player A. In each matrix $[\alpha_{ij}]$ A chooses a row and B chooses a column; the payoff to A is α_{ij} and the payoff to B is $-\alpha_{ij}$.

1. $\begin{bmatrix} 3 & 5 & 4 & 9 & 6 \\ 5 & 6 & 3 & 7 & 8 \\ 8 & 7 & 9 & 8 & 7 \\ 4 & 2 & 8 & 5 & 3 \end{bmatrix}$

2. $\begin{bmatrix} 2 & 2 & 1 & -2 & -3 \\ 4 & 3 & 4 & -2 & 0 \\ 5 & 1 & 2 & 5 & 6 \end{bmatrix}$

3. $\begin{bmatrix} 2 & -1 & 5 & -2 & 6 \\ -2 & 4 & -3 & 1 & 0 \end{bmatrix}$ (*Hint:* Reduce to a 2 × 2 by a graphical method.)

4. $\begin{bmatrix} 5 & 3 & 1 \\ 2 & 4 & 5 \\ 2 & 1 & 6 \end{bmatrix}$

5. $\begin{bmatrix} 6 & 8 & 3 & 13 \\ 4 & 1 & 5 & 3 \\ 8 & 10 & 4 & 12 \\ 3 & 2 & 7 & 2 \end{bmatrix}$

6. An old childrens' game called "Scissors, Paper, Stone" is played by two children as follows.

Index and middle fingers spread apart are scissors, the entire hand with fingers together is paper, and a fist is stone. Both players simultaneously present scissors, paper, or stone. Scissors beats paper (because scissors cut paper), paper beats stone (because a stone can be wrapped in paper), and stone beats scissors (because a stone can blunt scissors). If both children present the same thing, there is a tie.

Suppose that we score one for a win, zero for a tie, and minus one for a loss. Write down the payoff matrix and determine the optimal strategies and value of the game.

7. Player A choses a number x and announces his choice to player B, who then chooses a number y. Without knowing the value of y, player A then chooses a number z. The payoff to A is $f(x, y, z)$, as shown in Table 13.8. The payoff to B is $-f(x, y, z)$.

TABLE 13.8

	$z = 1$		$z = 2$	
	$x = 1$	$x = 2$	$x = 1$	$x = 2$
$y = 1$	-2	-3	-1	1
$y = 2$	4	3	5	2

At first sight, this game does not fit the matrix form that we have discussed.

Player A has four strategies:

$$(1)\ x = 1; \qquad z = 1$$
$$(2)\ x = 1; \qquad z = 2$$
$$(3)\ x = 2; \qquad z = 1$$
$$(4)\ x = 2; \qquad z = 2$$

Player B appears to have two strategies ($y = 1$ or $y = 2$) but in fact has four, because in making a choice for y, B must consider the value that A chose for x. B's strategies are:

(1) If $x = 1$, then $y = 1$; if $x = 2$, then $y = 1$.

(2) If $x = 1$, then $y = 1$; if $x = 2$, then $y = 2$.

(3) If $x = 1$, then $y = 2$; if $x = 2$, then $y = 2$.

(4) If $x = 1$, then $y = 2$; if $x = 2$, then $y = 1$.

Write down the payoff matrix to A; find the optimal strategies and the value of the game.

8. A and B are bidding at an open auction for two items X and Y. A values X at \$100 and Y at \$150, but B values X at \$110 and Y at \$130. A is prepared to spend up to \$200 and B is prepared to spend up to \$170. What will happen in the following circumstances?

1. Both A and B know that amount of the other's resources, but each assumes that the other values X and Y as he does himself.

2. Both A and B know the amount of the other's resources, but neither is prepared to make any assumption about the other's evaluations.

3. Both A and B know the other's resources and the other's evaluations.

9. A caterer is about to submit a sealed bid to run a restaurant concession at a municipal airport for the next five years. He must state the fixed rent that he is prepared to pay annually. He estimates that gross profits, before rent is paid, will be \$100,000 the first year and will increase by 10 per cent per year. Past experience shows that if R is the annual rent offered by a winning bid and G is his own estimate of the total gross profit of a contract running n years, the ratio nR/G is normally distributed about 0.5 with a standard deviation of 0.07. What should he bid so as to maximize his expected net profit?

10. Suppose that in the circumstances of Exercise 9 the caterer wishes to bid so that on average the "money left on the table" does not exceed 10 per cent of his bid. What should the bid be? (The money left on the table is the difference between the winning and the second bid. When all bids are published, the winner does not wish to appear foolish for having bid way above his competitors. The average value is computed only over the cases in which the caterer wins the concession.)

11. A market of total volume S is shared between n competing producers. The ith producer spends x_i on marketing, sells an amount S_i, and makes a gross profit $g_i S_i$, where

$$\frac{S_i}{S} = \frac{\alpha_i x_i}{\sum_{j=1}^n \alpha_j x_j}$$

Show that a stable policy is

$$x_i = \frac{1}{\alpha_i} \frac{n-1}{\left(\sum_{j=1}^n k_j\right)^2} \left\{\sum_{j=1}^n k_j - (n-1)k_i\right\} \qquad i = 1, 2, \ldots, n$$

and the corresponding net profit P_i is given by

$$P_i = \frac{1}{\alpha_i k_i \sum_{j=1}^n k_j} \left[\sum_{j=1}^n k_j - (n-1)k_i\right]^2,$$

where $k_i = 1/\alpha_i g_i S$.

(*Note:* By "stable" we mean that if all but one producer use such a policy, the odd man out is worse off than if he had also used it. If the x_i given is less than zero for a given i, the ith producer should withdraw from the market. Thus the solution is good provided that $x_i > 0$ for all $i = 1, 2, \ldots, n$.)

Suggested Readings

Elementary and entertaining introductions to game theory can be found in McDonald (1950) and Williams (1954). McKinsey (1952) and Luce and Raiffa (1957) provide systematic and comprehensive coverage at a more advanced level. A sympathetic but critical evaluation of game theory is provided by Rapoport (1959). The relationship of game theory and linear programming is discussed in Kuhn and Tucker (1950, 1953) and Vajda (1956).

Little has been published on bidding. Friedman's thesis (1957) and Griesner and Shubik's report (1962) provide some introduction to the subject.

Bibliography

Ackoff, R. L., "Conflict, Cooperation, Competition, and Cupid," in *Essays on Econometrics and Planning*, Pergamon Press, New York, 1964, pp. 7–18.

Dresher, M., *Games of Strategy: Theory and Applications*, Prentice Hall, Englewood Cliffs, N.J., 1961.

Flood, M. M. (ed.), "A Symposium on Game Theory," *Behavioral Science*, **7** (1962), 1–102.

Friedman, L., "A Competitive Bidding Strategy," *Operations Research*, **4** (1956), 104–112.

————, *Competitive Bidding Strategies.* Ph.D. Dissertation, Case Institute of Technology, Cleveland Ohio, 1957.

Griesner, J. H., and M. Shubik, "The Theory of Bidding," *IBM Research Report*, RC-629, March 1, 1962.

Howard, Nigel, "The Theory of Meta-Games" and "The Mathematics of Meta-Games," *General Systems*, 11 (1966), 167–200.

Kuhn, H. W., and A. Tucker (eds.), *Contributions to the Theory of Games*, Vols. I and II, Princeton University Press, Princeton, N.J., 1950 and 1953.

Luce, R. D., and H. Raiffa, *Games and Decisions*, John Wiley and Sons, New York, 1957.

McDonald, J., *Strategy in Poker, Business, and War*, W. W. Norton, New York, 1950.

McKinsey, J. C. C., *Introduction to the Theory of Games*, McGraw-Hill Book Co., New York, 1952.

Rapoport, A., "Critiques of Game Theory," *Behavioral Science*, **4** (1959), 49–66.

————, *Fights, Games, and Debates*, The University of Michigan Press, Ann Arbor, Mich., 1960.

————, "Three Modes of Conflict," *Management Science*, **7** (1961), 210–218.

————, *Two-Person Game Theory*, The University of Michigan Press, Ann Arbor, Mich., 1966.

Shubik, M., "Uses of Game Theory in Management Science," *Management Science*, **2** (1955), 40–54.

————, *Strategy and Market Structure*, John Wiley and Sons, New York, 1959.

———— (ed.), *Game Theory and Related Approaches to Social Behavior*, John Wiley and Sons, New York, 1964.

Vajda, S., *The Theory of Games and Linear Programming*, John Wiley and Sons, New York, 1956.

von Neumann, J., and O. Morgenstern, *Theory of Games and Economic Behavior*, 3rd ed., Princeton University Press, Princeton, N.J., 1953.

Williams, J. D., *The Compleat Strategyst*, McGraw-Hill Book Co., New York, 1954.

CHAPTER 14

Search Problems

INTRODUCTION

In all of the problems that have been considered so far it was assumed that we have or can obtain the information that is necessary for making a decision. Hence our attention was directed at what decision to make. Now we reverse these conditions and assume that we know what we ought to do if we had certain required information, and the problem is to find the best way of obtaining it. The process involved in such problems is that of *search*.

Search is an extremely general process. It takes place in every type of problem of which the acquisition of information is a part. Search is not only involved in other problems, but in a number of problems search itself is the essential process.

Some of the more common types of search problems are the following. An audit is a search for errors. More generally, all accounting problems can be considered to be search problems, which are directed at providing information that is essential for decision making. Exploration for mineral deposits, oil, coal, and other types of raw materials, as well as gems and archeological remains, are search problems. The design of inspection and quality-control procedures are also search problems. Information storage and retrieval, screening of chemical compounds in pharmaceutical research, and the common process of shopping are problems of this type. There are also a host of military problems that involve finding potentially destructive instruments or facilities of the enemy: aircraft in the sky, submarines and ships in the sea, mines and guns on land, and many others. Finally, reconnaissance and scouting are familiar search processes.

In order to perceive the essential components of search, consider the problem of escorting a ship in time of war to detect submarines that might attack the ship. Small lighter-than-air ships were frequently used. Because they could move slowly over the water at a low altitude, they were very likely to spot a submarine, if it was actually there, and not think that they had spotted one when one was not there. The principal disadvantage of this type of aircraft derived from its low speed: it could not sweep a large portion of the sea ahead of the ship; hence, when it sighted a submarine, it usually provided little warning time. An airplane, on the other hand, could cover much more of the sea, but it was less likely to see a submarine that was there, and more likely to "see" one that was not there.

This example shows clearly the two types of error that should be taken into account in search: errors of *observation* and errors deriving from *sampling*. If fixed resources are available for search, the larger the sample that is covered, the less resources are allocated to each observation. Hence, if we try to reduce sampling error, observational error usually increases, and conversely.

Now, let us first formulate a restricted search problem more precisely and then a more general version of the problem.

There are two types of cost involved in search: the cost of error and the cost of the search itself. The error whose cost must be considered is composed of both sampling and observational error. The cost of the search has three major components: (1) the setup or design cost, (2) the cost of the observations, and (3) the cost of the analysis of the information obtained.

The controllable variables include the following:

1. The sample size: the number of observations made or the portion of an area that is examined.

2. The sample design: the way in which the observations or things to be observed are selected.

3. The way of analyzing the data: the inferential procedure.

In the restricted search problem the amount of resources available is specified and the problem is to design the search so as to minimize the expected cost of error. In the generalized problem, the amount of resources to be expended is also subject to control and the objective is to minimize the sum of this cost and the expected cost of error.

Types of Search Situations

It is convenient to classify search situations into types, which are useful even if not entirely exhaustive. Two such breakdowns are:

1. Qualitative-quantitative.
2. Distributive-collective.

The first dichotomy refers to the relevant characteristic of the individual elements of the population from which the sample is taken. In a qualitative situation, an observation consists of the assignment of an individual to a class (e.g.: to defectives or acceptables; to correct or incorrect; to red, yellow, or green). In a quantitative situation, an observation consists of a measurement along some scale (e.g., the income per household or the weight of an element).

The second dichotomy refers to the use that is to be made of the results of sampling. In a distributive situation, the action to be taken is on an individual rather than on a collective basis. For example: a defective part is sent back for repair, whereas an acceptable part is sent on; a high-income family is placed on a certain mailing list. In a collective situation, on the other hand, the action taken is on a collective basis (e.g.: the entire lot from which the sample is taken is sent on or sent back; an entire neighborhood is placed on the mailing list). In general, a collective process has as its central feature the determination of some parameter of the population; in a distributive process, such a determination does not enter the problem or enters it indirectly.

These two dichotomies are by no means the only important ones. Search processes may be classified into types that depend on whether or not the information sought (properties of elements or population) changes over the period pertinent to the problem. For example, in attempting to locate ore deposits one deals with a *stable* property. But in attempting to locate a plane in flight one deals with a dynamic property. In this discussion we shall consider only stable properties.

Quantitative search problems are more complex than qualitative problems primarily because of the complexity of calculating the cost of error.

COST OF ERROR

To calculate the cost of error in a quantitative search problem it is necessary to have a model of the decision that will use the output of the search procedure. With such a model the cost of any specified error can be defined. For example, suppose that we have the very simple decision model

$$U = XY + \frac{1}{X}, \tag{14.1}$$

where X is the controlled variable and Y is the uncontrolled variable whose value is to be sought (estimated). If we knew the true value of Y, we would proceed to find the optimal value of X and the minimum value of U that results from using it:

$$\frac{dU}{dX} = Y - \frac{1}{X^2} = 0. \tag{14.2}$$

Therefore,

$$X^0 = \frac{1}{\sqrt{Y}} \tag{14.3}$$

and

$$U^0 = \frac{Y}{\sqrt{Y}} + \sqrt{Y} = 2\sqrt{Y}. \tag{14.4}$$

Now suppose that we use an estimate of Y, y; then the estimate of X^0 is

$$x^0 = \frac{1}{\sqrt{y}},$$ (14.5)

and the estimated value of U^0 is

$$u^0 = \frac{Y}{\sqrt{y}} + \sqrt{y}.$$ (14.6)

Hence the cost of error $(y - Y)$ is given by

$$C(y - Y) = u^0 - U^0 = \frac{Y}{\sqrt{y}} + \sqrt{y} - 2\sqrt{Y}.$$ (14.7)

Unfortunately, the evaluation of this cost requires knowledge of the true value of Y, which is precisely what we do not know. Therefore, we need some prior information about the possible values that Y might assume. Let $p(Y)$ represent the distribution of possible true values of Y. Then for a specific estimate of Y, y the expected cost of error can be calculated as

$$\int_{-\infty}^{\infty} \left(\frac{Y}{\sqrt{y}} + \sqrt{y} - 2\sqrt{Y} \right) p(Y) \, dY.$$ (14.8)

For any particular sampling-estimation procedure, we do not know what specific value of y will be yielded by the observations, but we can determine for most statistical procedures the distribution of the errors of estimation. Let $f(y - Y) = f(\Delta Y)$ represent this distribution.[1] Then for a specified sampling-estimation procedure the expected cost of error is given by

$$E[C(y - Y)] = \int_{\Delta Y = -\infty}^{\infty} \int_{Y = -\infty}^{\infty} \left(\frac{1}{\sqrt{Y + \Delta Y}} + \sqrt{Y + \Delta Y} - 2\sqrt{Y} \right)$$
$$\times f(\Delta Y) p(Y) \, d\Delta Y \, dY. \quad (14.9)$$

The a priori distribution of Y, $p(Y)$ can usually be obtained from previous experience with this variable.

In some cases, but not very many, the cost of error may not depend on the true value of the variable being estimated. Then, of course, the distribution $p(Y)$ is not needed.

It is apparent that even in relatively simple quantitative search problems, estimating the expected cost of error for a particular search procedure, let alone for a variety of such procedures, can be very difficult and time-consuming. In order to make these estimates efficiently, a knowledge of Bayesian statistics is essential. (See, for example, Raiffa and Schlaifer, 1961; Chernoff and Moses, 1959; Ackoff, 1962; and Weiss, 1961.)

---

[1] We are assuming that the distribution of the error does not depend on the true value of Y.

The problem of estimation as formulated in statistical decision theory is similar to the quantitative search problem but not identical to it. In estimation theory the problem can be stated as follows. If the objective is to estimate the value of a variable Y and we have a set of observations $(y_1, y_2, \ldots, y_n)$ obtained by a specified technique of probability sampling, how can we derive an estimate y, where

$$y = \phi(y_1, y_2, \ldots, y_n),$$

such that the expected cost of error $(y - Y)$ is minimized? This problem is part of the quantitative search problem, but, as we have seen, search problems also involve designing the sampling procedure and determining the sample size, n.

There is even a further complexity in quantitative search problems that arises out of the fact that the distribution of errors, $f(y - Y)$, covers only errors caused by sampling and not by observation. Most statistical estimating procedures operate on the assumption that observational errors are insignificant, but this is frequently not the case. Let us consider the sources of such errors.

SOURCES OF OBSERVATIONAL ERROR

There are several possible sources of observational error in measurement, which may contribute to it separately or in combination: (1) the observer, (2) the instruments used, (3) the environment, and (4) the thing observed. We shall consider each of them in turn.

Error Due to the Observer

The observer may not follow the required operations either because he is neglectful or because it is not practical to do so. In this way he may bias the observations. In particular, he may not make the necessary readings as accurately as possible. He may read dials, meters, or rules incorrectly. He may not accurately record a response of a subject whom he has questioned, or he may fail to see what the respondent did. His senses as well as his powers of concentration are not perfect; hence they lead to error.

Round-robin tests, in which different observers of the same object using the same instruments obtain significantly different readings, provide strong confirmation of the fact that even in such "simple" operations as counting the observer can be a source of significant error.

Observer error first came to the serious attention of science when Bessel noted what he called the *personal equation*. In the nineteenth century it was observed that in physical measurements the distribution of an observer's errors tends to form a normal curve. The bias and spread (characterized in terms of probable error or standard deviation) differ from observer to observer and for some observers from time to time. This distribution of observer errors is usually assumed to be normal in character without any supporting evidence.

How can the nature of observer error be determined? The answer depends on the nature of the object or event observed. If the property has a constant value over a sufficiently long period of time to permit a large number of observations, multiple observations can be made and their distribution analyzed. First, it is necessary to determine the form of this distribution. This involves fitting a curve to the data. Next, the bias and dispersion of the distribution must be determined. The bias (deviation of the mean of the distribution from the "true" value) can be determined, however, only if the true value is known. Because this is never known in research, observers are usually checked by using a standard object or event under specified conditions. The standard object or event has previously been measured, by using the most highly controlled and careful observations possible. The mean of these observations is then *assumed* to be the true value and becomes the basis for computing observer bias. This assumption is important; it makes clear that observer bias itself is never measured without error.

If the thing observed is destroyed or significantly changed with respect to the relevant property by the observation process, the procedure just described cannot be used. It is still widely believed that in such situations the determination of observer error is not possible. This belief is not well founded. This type of problem arises in quality-control work, where inspection or testing of an item often involves its destruction, and in social surveys, where a respondent may be changed by the first interview. The method for determining observer error in such situations is briefly as follows. The items to be measured (or a random sample of them) are divided by a random process into groups of (approximately) equal size. Groups are then assigned to observers at random. Each observer classifies or measures the elements in the group that is assigned to him. The differences in the distributions of the observations are due to both observer error and the differences in the group assigned. The probabilities associated with differences due to the forming of the groups can usually be determined and can be made as small as desired by increasing the size of the groups. These differences can be "subtracted" from the total error, leaving the observer error for examination. The different groups can also be assigned to the same observer at different times, if we are interested in his errors rather than in those of a group of observers. For the details of such an analysis, see Hanson and Marks (1958).

A description of how observational errors of two different observers were measured in one particular situation may be helpful. The observation in this experiment was of the auditing type. Service-credit-compensation forms of a company were filled out to correspond to their normal usage, but some errors were deliberately inserted on approximately 50 per cent of the sheets.

Two auditors from the company were selected as subjects. Each auditor was given the same 120 forms, containing 61 sheets with errors, and was allowed 25 seconds per sheet to classify it as correct or erroneous. The auditors were then given 190 forms containing 90 sheets with errors and were allowed 30 seconds per sheet. Similar examinations were made of other batches of forms at 35, 40, 45, 50, 60, and 70 seconds per sheet. The performance times were

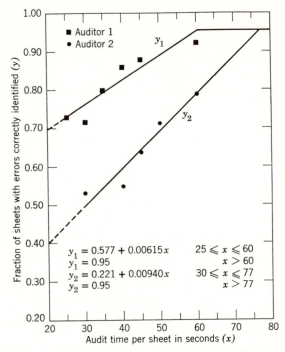

Figure 14.1 Acuity functions adjusted for cutoff points.

given to the auditors in random sequence. It took several runs for the observers to settle on an observational procedure. The early sets of observations were consequently eliminated from the analysis. The remaining data are shown in Figure 14.1.

From these data it is clear that the two observers differ significantly, and statistical tests confirmed this fact. Such data not only permit a selection of observers but also indicate how much time should be allowed for an observation in order to obtain a specified level of accuracy. This experiment should not be interpreted as having general significance for the auditing function; it is used here only to illustrate how observer error can be determined.[2]

[2] For details on this research, see Chambers and Clark (1957).

Error Due to Instruments

The instruments used in making observations, like the observer, may be biased and/or inconsistent (variable) and thus be characterized by a distribution of errors. The procedure for determining these characteristics is the same as that for an observer.

When an observation involves both an instrument and an observer, they can be considered in combination and a joint observational-instrument error can be determined. It is more difficult to obtain the error functions of each separately, because neither can be held constant with respect to the other, but it can be done by the use of designed experiments. In such situations, however, we generally wish to find the best combination of observer and instrument, which can be determined by an experiment that establishes the error function for each combination.

It is important to realize that no matter how highly developed the measuring instruments are, they still contribute to error and that a determination of the magnitude of this "contribution" is essential.

Error Due to Environment

The conditions under which the observations are made may vary so as to affect the observer, the instruments, or the thing observed, and, of course, they may fail to correspond to *standard* conditions. To determine how these differences and variations affect the accuracy of observations, it is necessary to know the laws that connect these changes to the observations. For example, we can correct for variations in observed length of a metal bar due to changing temperature, because the linear coefficient of expansion of the metal allows us to compute the resulting changes in length, hence to adjust the observations.

In many areas of inquiry such knowledge is not available, and adjustment of observations to compensate for environmental deviations and changes is not possible. It is essential then to have at least an estimate of the resulting error. This may require experimentation.

Error Due to the Observed

That which is observed may be either an active or a passive source of error. First, the process of observation may itself affect the behavior of the observed so that we cannot observe its "natural" behavior. Such an effect of the process of observation on the subject of observation has come to be characterized as the *indeterminacy principle*. In quantum mechanics, in which this principle was first formulated, it appears to be possible to reduce the error in the determination of the momentum of a particle at the cost of increasing the error in the determination of its location, and conversely.

The indeterminacy principle has been the center of a major methodological controversy in science since its formulation by Heisenberg. The question is whether this effect is inherent in nature or is a property of our state of knowledge, concepts, and observational methods. There is good reason to believe the latter.

For detailed discussions of the indeterminacy principle in physics—discussions that argue that continuous reduction of error is not precluded by the principle—see Margenau (1959) and McKnight (1959).

When the object observed is a human being, he may cause much more difficulty (and deliberately so) than does the electron, particularly when he is required to give verbal testimony. This problem has been treated at length in the literature of social-survey methodology. [See, for example, Ackoff (1953, Chapter 9).]

SAMPLE DESIGN

Present sampling theory does not provide a means for choosing the optimal procedure, in either the specialized search problem (in which the total resources are fixed) or the generalized case (in which sample size, n, and resources for observation, r, are free to vary independently). First, it assumes either that observational errors do not exist, or that they tend to cancel each other out, or that they are independent of the resources expended per observation. Second, it either minimizes sampling variability relative to fixed resources or it minimizes the resources required to yield no more than a fixed sampling variability.

Inasmuch as there is no convenient way, currently available, of representing alternative sampling plans by one or more quantitative variables, it appears necessary to determine an optimal combination (n, r) for each type of sampling plan, and to select from these that combination and plan which yield the "best" optimum. In practice, one who is familiar with sampling theory can usually select the best, or approximately best, sampling plan relative to the problem at hand. For simplicity's sake, the exploration described in this chapter involves only unrestricted random sampling, but the use of some other type of sampling plan appears to add no insuperable difficulty to the analysis.[3]

In the next chapter we survey sampling theory and indicate the minimal knowledge of this subject that should be available to an OR team. The same knowledge is necessary in the design of search procedures.

Of the few published papers on search processes, several have dealt with sampling designs. Two are mentioned here.

---

[3] For a brief introduction to the theory of sampling, see Ackoff (1962, Chapter 7).

The Optimal Distribution of Searching Effort

Suppose that an object is in an unknown position, but that the probability of its being in each of the possible positions is known. If only a limited amount of resources is available for the search, the problem is to distribute the limited amount of resources so as to maximize the chances of finding the object. For the solution to this problem in the one-dimensional case, see Houlden (1962, pp. 145–149). Observational error, in the form of a probability of detection associated with each possible location, can be taken into account. One may also take account of the fact that the value of finding the object that is being sought depends on where it is found. It is also possible to handle the situation in which observations cost more at some locations than at others.

Multistage Searches

Searches may be performed in two or more stages. In the first stage the area can be covered lightly, and in the succeeding stage the locations selected in the first stage can be examined more closely. The first stage is assumed to have observational errors, but not the second. The second stage, of course is more expensive or more time-consuming.

Given certain assumptions about signals emanating from that which is being sought, about false signals, and about the expenditure of effort, expected income can be maximized. See Houlden (1962, pp. 149–152).

MATHEMATICAL FORMULATION OF SEARCH PROBLEMS

Let us consider each of the four types of search problems identified above. It will be recalled that, in addition to the qualitative-quantitative distinction, a distributive-collective distinction also exists. A *distributive* problem is one in which we decide on a course of action for each member of the population that is observed and draw no inferences about the remainder of the population. The return associated with such a search is the sum of the returns for each member observed. A *collective* problem is one in which we make a (collective) decision for the entire population. The return then depends on all elements of the population and there is no meaning for the return associated with a single item or with a subset of the population.

Distributive Case

In this case a separate course of action is selected for each member of the sample. Because we do not know the true value of the property being observed, we base our decision on an observation that is subject to error. The likelihood or magnitude of the error depends on the amount of resources that we expend on each observation. We now have two interacting problems:

1. How much should we spend on each observation?
2. How should we select a course of action as a function of what we observe?

In practice these two problems are usually handled separately. When the answer to the second question is not obvious, we usually answer it first. Let us begin, however, by considering a very simple case in which the decision rule is obvious.

Distributive Qualitative Case. Suppose that each member of a population is to be examined to determine whether or not it is defective. If a defect is found, the item is rejected; if not, it is accepted. Hence there are four possible outcomes, which together with their associated costs are shown in Table 14.1.

TABLE 14.1 *Possible Outcomes of a Search and their Costs*

	Observation	(1) Not Defective	(2) Defective
	Decision	Accept	Reject
True state of item	(1) Not defective	$C_{11} = 0$	$C_{12} = 1.0$
	(2) Defective	$C_{21} = 3.0$	$C_{22} = 0$

Now suppose that we know that the fraction P_1 of the items are acceptable, but do not know which ones; hence $P_2 = 1 - P_1$ of the items are defective. Let $P_1 = 0.8$ and $P_2 = 0.2$ in this example. These fractions may be known because of previous inspections of similar items.

If there are N items in the population and we accept all of them without inspection, we will accept $0.2N$ defective items. The cost of so doing would be $0.2N(3.0) = 0.6N$, or 0.6 per item. If we reject all items without inspection, we reject $0.8N$ nondefectives and incur a cost of $0.8N(1.0) = 0.8N$, or 0.8 per item. Therefore, if we must do one or the other, in this case it is clearly better to accept all items than to reject them.

Now, when an item is inspected, there are two kinds of observational error that can be made: (1) to reject an acceptable (non-defective) item and (2) to accept a rejectable (defective) item. Let p_{12} be the probability of rejecting an acceptable item and p_{21} the probability of accepting a rejectable item. These probabilities will be a function of the amount of resources spent per observation (r). For example,

r	p_{12}	p_{21}
0.1	0.4	0.2
0.2	0.2	0.1
0.3	0.1	0.05
0.4	0.05	0.025
0.5	0.025	0.0125

If we spent 0.1 per observation, the expected cost per observation would be

$$\bar{C}(0.1) = P_1 p_{12} C_{12} + P_2 p_{21} C_{21} + r$$
$$= (0.8)(0.4)(1.0) + (0.2)(0.2)(3.0) + 0.1 = 0.54.$$

Similarly,

$$\bar{C}(0.2) = (0.8)(0.2)(1.0) + (0.2)(0.1)(3.0) + 0.2 = 0.42.$$
$$\bar{C}(0.3) = (0.8)(0.1)(1.0) + (0.2)(0.05)(3.0) + 0.3 = 0.41.$$
$$\bar{C}(0.4) = (0.8)(0.05)(1.0) + (0.2)(0.025)(3.0) + 0.4 = 0.455.$$
$$\bar{C}(0.5) = (0.8)(0.025)(1.0) + (0.2)(0.0125)(3.0) + 0.5 = 0.5275.$$

It is clear, therefore, that we should spend 0.3 per observation and that to do so is better than accepting or rejecting all items without inspection.

Now we can generalize as follows. Let

P_i = probability that an item is in class i.

$p_{ij}(r)$ = probability of classifying an item as j when it is an i and when r resources are expended per observation.

C_{ij} = cost of classifying an i as a j.

The expected cost of a single classification is

$$\bar{C}(r) = \sum_i \sum_j P_i p_{ij}(r) C_{ij} + r. \tag{14.10}$$

The objective is to find an r that minimizes $\bar{C}(r)$.

In some cases the resources available for classification may be limited to an amount R, and we may want to minimize the cost of classification for an expenditure of this amount. Suppose that we classify n out of N items using R/n on each. The cost of so doing would be

$$\bar{C}_n(r) = n \sum_i \sum_j P_i p_{ij} \left(\frac{R}{n}\right) C_{ij} + R. \tag{14.11}$$

If n is less than N, the remaining $(N - n)$ items must be treated as if they were in some class k, without inspection. The cost of so doing would be

$$\bar{C}(0) = (N - n) \sum_i P_i C_{ik}. \tag{14.12}$$

The total expected cost would then be

$$\bar{C}(R_n, 0_{N-n}) = n \sum_i \sum_j P_i p_{ij} \left(\frac{R}{n}\right) C_{ij} + R + (N - n) \sum_i P_i C_{ik}. \quad (14.13)$$

To solve it, we must select an n and a k to minimize this cost.

It may happen that we do not know the distribution $\{P_i\}$. We would then have to assume something about it. On the other hand, we might have some but not complete knowledge about this distribution. For example, we might know that the probability that $P_i = \pi_i$ is $F_i(\pi_i)$. In this case we would choose r to minimize the expected value of the cost. This may be done by replacing P_i by its expected value $\bar{P}_i$.

Distributive Qualitative Case. In this situation we also classify items, but to do so we must obtain an estimate y' of a continuous variable whose true value is y. The classification depends on the range in which y' lies. For example, a bolt may be classified as acceptable if its diameter lies between the "tolerance limits" $y_0 - a$ and $y_0 + b$, where y_0 is the design or intended diameter of the part. If its diameter does not lie within these limits, it is classified as unacceptable. During production of the bolt its diameter is measured to see if it meets specifications. If it does, it is sent on; otherwise it is sent back for rework. We assume that the return from a correct classification is constant, but the return (usually negative) from an incorrect classification depends on the size of the true value of y.

The items fall into two classes—acceptable (A) and rejects (R). The observations also fall into classes A' and R'. After classification we thus have four possibilities:

AA'—an acceptable item is accepted
AR'—an acceptable item is rejected
RA'—a reject is accepted
RR'—a reject is rejected

The returns of the four cases are different. We assume that with correct classification the returns do not depend on the true value of y. Let

$G_{AA'}$ = the return for correctly classified acceptable items.

$G_{RR'}$ = the return for correctly classified rejects.

However, for misclassifications the return depends on the true value of y. Let

$L_{AR'}(y)$ = the return (usually negative) if an acceptable item
$\qquad (y_0 - a \leq y \leq y_0 + b)$ is rejected.

$L_{RA'}(y)$ = the return (usually negative) if a reject
$\qquad (y < y_0 - a$ or $y > y_0 + b)$ is accepted.

We can represent the observed and true values by points on the (y, y') plane, as in Figure 14.2. The plane is divided into the four regions according to the return function. Notice that we need not reject on the obvious basis of $y' < y_0 - a$ or $y' > y_0 + b$. We could use $y' < \alpha$, $y' > \beta$ where α and β are determined so as to maximize the expected return. For the time being we assume that α and β are given.

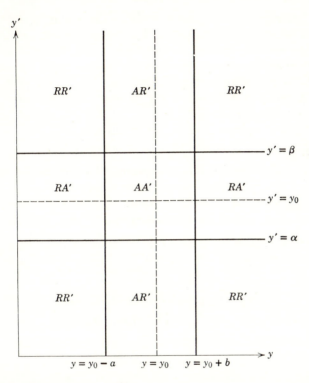

Figure 14.2   Regions of the $y - y'$ plane. $AA =$ part accepted when it should be; $AA' =$ part accepted when it should not be; $A'A' =$ part rejected when it should be; $A'A =$ part rejected when it should not be.

As in the quantitative case, the expected return is found by averaging over the four possibilities, but because returns are no longer constant in each case, the details are more involved. Suppose that we spend r on each observation and that the density functions for y and y', given y, are $p(y)$ and $p_r(y'/y)$. The joint density function of y and y' is

$$f_r(y, y') = p(y)p_r(y'/y).$$

The total expected returns is

$$\bar{C}(r) = \iint_{AA'} f_r(y, y')G_{AA'}\, dy\, dy' + \iint_{RR'} f_r(y, y')G_{RR'}\, dy\, dy'$$

$$+ \iint_{AR'} f_r(y, y')L_{AR'}(y)\, dy\, dy' + \iint_{RA'} f_r(y, y')L_{RA'}(y)\, dy\, dy' - r.$$

$$(14.14)$$

The four integrals can be expressed in forms that make them directly comparable with the quantitative case. The first two are the probabilities of correct classification multiplied by the corresponding costs. Thus if P is the probability that a randomly selected item is acceptable and $P_{AA'}(r)$ is the conditional probability of accepting an acceptable item (that is, the probability that $\alpha \leq y' \leq \beta$ given that $y_0 - a \leq y \leq y_0 + b$), then the first integral is $G_{AA'}PP_{AA'}(r)$. The second integral is $G_{RR'}(1 - P)P_{RR'}(r)$, where $P_{RR'}(r)$ is the probability of rejecting an item that should be rejected. The reader should express P, $P_{AA'}$, $P_{RR'}$ in terms of $p(y)$ and $p_r(y'|y)$. Let

$\bar{L}_{AR'}(r) =$ the conditional expected return, given that an acceptable item has been rejected.

$\bar{L}_{RA'}(r) =$ the conditional expected return, given that a reject has been accepted.

To find these functions, we need the density functions of (y, y') given that the point is in the regions AR' and RA' (see Figure 14.2). The density functions are

$$f_{AR'}(y, y') = \frac{f_r(y, y')}{\displaystyle\iint_{AR'} f_r(y, y')\, dy\, dy'}$$

$$f_{RA'}(y, y') = \frac{f_r(y, y')}{\displaystyle\iint_{RA'} f_r(y, y')\, dy\, dy'}$$

and that the denominators are the probabilities of being in the regions. Thus

$$f_{AR'}(y, y') = \frac{f_r(y, y')}{P[1 - P_{AA'}(r)]}$$

and

$$f_{RA'}(y, y') = \frac{f_r(y, y')}{(1 - P)[1 - P_{RR'}(r)]}$$

To find $L_{AR'}(r)$ and $L_{RA'}(r)$, we multiply the appropriate density functions by $L_{AR'}(y)$, $L_{RA'}(y)$ and integrate over the appropriate regions. It will be seen that $\bar{L}_{AR'}$, and $\bar{L}_{AR}$ are the third and fourth integrals of the expression for $\bar{C}(r)$ divided by the corresponding probabilities. Thus $\bar{C}(r)$ can be expressed as

$$\bar{C}(r) = G_{AA'}PP_{AA'}(r) + G_{RR'}(1 - P)P_{RA'}(r) + \bar{L}_{AR'}(r)P[1 - P_{AA'}(r)]$$
$$+ \bar{L}_{RA'}(r)(1 - P)[1 - P_{RR'}(r)] - r.$$

In this form we recognize that $\bar{C}(r)$ is similar to the return for the quantitative case, except that the losses due to errors in classification depend on r as well as on the type of error. Previously this was not so.

The numerical evaluation of the integrals in $\bar{C}(r)$ is not straightforward in most practical cases. However, it is an ideal example for the use of Monte Carlo methods. Suppose that $a = b$ and y is normally distributed about y_0 with variance σ^2. Let y' be normally distributed about y with variance s^2. Consider the two standard normal variables defined by

$$z = \frac{y - y_0}{\sigma}, \qquad z' = \frac{y' - y}{s}.$$

The conditions for an acceptable item are

$$y_0 - a \leq y \leq y_0 + a$$

or, in terms of z,

$$-\frac{a}{\sigma} \leq z \leq \frac{a}{\sigma}.$$

The conditions for an item to be accepted are

$$\alpha \leq y' \leq \beta$$

or, in terms of z and z',

$$\alpha - y_0 \leq sz' + \sigma z \leq \beta - y_0.$$

If we plot these boundary lines in the (z, z') plane (Figure 14.3), we see that they mark the regions corresponding to those of Figure 14.2. We take pairs of random normal deviates from published tables and plot the corresponding points in the (z, z') plane. It is then a simple matter to count the points in each region and obtain probabilities, or to compute the gain corresponding to each point and by addition to approximate the value of $\bar{C}(r)$.

Figure 14.3 can also be used as an aid in computing the best values of α and β. Suppose that in addition to the line $sz' + \sigma z = \beta - y_0$ we plot the parallel line $sz' + \sigma z = \beta + h - y_0$, where h is small. If we change β to $\beta + h$, all the points lying in the strip $STUV$ will be reclassified. Those in ST and UV, previously correctly classified as rejects, will now be misclassified as acceptable; those in TU, previously misclassified as rejects, will now be accepted. It is easy enough to find the net change in return for these points;

for points in *ST* and *UV* there will be a loss and for those in *TU* there will be a gain. If the net change is negative, β must be decreased, and we would consider the line $sz' + \sigma z = \beta - h - y_0$. If the net change is positive, we would increase β. When we find two adjacent strips for which the net change alters sign, we have the optimal value of β. We can find the best α in a similar fashion.

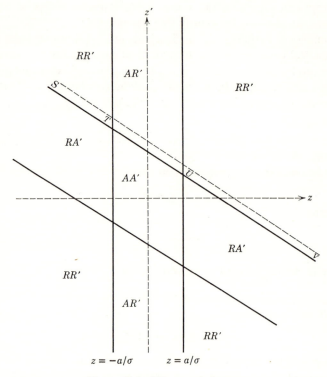

Figure 14.3 The $z - z'$ plane.

Collective Case

In the collective situation we have a sample of items whose true values are $y_1, y_2, \ldots, y_n$ and whose measured values are $y_1', y_2', \ldots, y_n'$. We wish to use this information to make a decision about the entire population. For example, in statistical quality control of a production lot of parts, a sample of items is commonly inspected, on the basis of which a decision is made to accept or reject the entire lot. Typically we have a utility function U that depends on a decision x (e.g., accept or reject) and a parameter θ (e.g., percentage defective) whose value we wish to determine. Thus $U = f(x, \theta)$, and if θ were known, we would choose $x = x_0(\theta)$, where $f[x_0(\theta), \theta] \geq f(x, \theta)$ for all x. Because we do not know θ, we form an estimate θ', which is a function of the observations. Therefore,

$$\theta = \theta'(y_1', y_2', \dots, y_n'). \tag{14.15}$$

If each observation costs r, the cost of not knowing θ is $C(\theta, \theta', r)$, where

$$C(\theta, \theta', r) = f[x_0(\theta'), \theta] - f[x_0(\theta), \theta]. \tag{14.16}$$

Typically we shall know the distribution of the estimates θ', given θ, the sample size n, and the amount spent per observation, r. Therefore, we can take the expectation of C with respect to θ'. The expected costs become a function of θ, n, and r, and the choice of (n, r) should depend on θ, which, of course, we do not know. This paradox is typical of applied statistics, and there are two ways out of it. Either we again take expectations, this time with respect to θ, or we replace θ by some a priori estimate of its value. Such an estimate permits us to design a procedure that can be used to refine it.

It should be noted that the distribution of θ' requires knowledge of the distribution of both the y's and the (y')'s. Thus we might assume that each of the y's has a density function $p(y \mid \theta)$ and the y' have a density function $p_r(y' \mid y)$. It is then possible, if we know how θ' is derived from $(y_1', y_2', \dots, y_n')$, to find the distribution. In general, the calculation will require integration in the $2n$-space, which is the Cartesian product of the n-spaces for $(y_1, y_2, \dots, y_n)$ and $(y_1', y_2', \dots, y_n')$.

Collective Qualitative Case. Let P be the proportion of the population in class 1 and $(1 - P)$ the proportion in class 2. Let $p_i(r)$ be the probability of recognizing a class i item as such $(i = 1, 2)$ and let $1 - p_i(r)$ be the probability of failing to classify correctly. Suppose that in a sample of size n we have classified z' items as class 1 and the remainder as class 2. Although we might use the information in the sample in various ways to estimate P, let us assume that we estimate P as a function of z'; that is, $P' = P'(z')$.

Suppose also that correct classification of the sample would have revealed z items in class 1, and that the cost of estimating P as P' is $H(P, P')$. Then the expected cost of the procedure is

$$\bar{C}_n(r) = \sum_{z'=0}^n \sum_{z=0}^n H[P, P'(z')]p_r(z', z) + nr, \tag{14.17}$$

where $p_r(z', z)$ is the joint probability of z and z'. Because $\sum_{z=0}^n p_r(z', z) = $ probability of $z' = p_r(z')$, we see that

$$\bar{C}_n(r) = \sum_{z'=0}^n H(P, P')p_r(z') + nr. \tag{14.18}$$

Now the probability of classifying a single item as 1 is $p(r)$, where

$$p(r) = Pp_{11}(r) + (1 - P)[1 - p_{22}(r)], \tag{14.19}$$

and, because the distribution of z' is binomial, we see that

$$p_r(z') = \binom{n}{z'} p(r)^{z'}[1 - p(r)]^{n-z'}. \tag{14.20}$$

Thus, given the "acuity functions" $p_{11}(r)$ and $p_{22}(r)$ and the return function $H(P, P')$, we can find optimal values of n and r.

Collective Quantitative Case. In this case we try to find a characteristic of the total population (θ) by measuring each of a sample of items in the population. For example, we may seek the average height of men in the army. Again we obtain an estimate θ' as a function of measurements on individuals $(y_1', y_2', \ldots, y_n')$ whose true values (e.g., heights) are $(y_1, y_2, \ldots, y_n)$. The cost-of-error function is $H(\theta, \theta')$. Let Y_n represent the (vector of) true values $(y_1, y_2, \ldots, y_n)$ and Y_n' the observations $(y_1', y_2', \ldots, y_n')$. Then the expected cost is given by

$$\bar{C}_n(r) = \int \cdots \int H(\theta, \theta') p_r(Y_n, Y_n') \, dY_n \, dY_n' + nr, \tag{14.21}$$

where $p_r(Y_n, Y_n')$ is the joint distribution of the y's and the (y')'s. In practice we would compute the density function for θ', given θ, n, and r —$f(\theta' \mid n, r, \theta)$— and write the expected cost as

$$\bar{C}_n(r) = \int H(\theta, \theta') f(\theta' \mid n, r, \theta) \, d\theta' + nr. \tag{14.22}$$

The density function can often be found without integration, as the following example shows.

Suppose that the parent population is normal with mean θ and standard deviation σ and that the distribution of an observation y' of an item whose true value is y is normal with mean y and standard deviation σ_r. We wish to estimate θ. From well-known properties of the normal distribution we see that y' is normally distributed with mean θ and variance $\sigma^2 + \sigma_r^2$. (Write y' as the sum of the two variates, $y' = (y' - y) + y$. These are each normally distributed and independent of each other.)

If our estimate of θ is

$$\theta' = \frac{1}{n} \sum_{i=1}^n y_i',$$

then θ' is normally distributed about a mean θ and with variance $(\sigma^2 + \sigma_r^2)/n$. Thus

$$f(\theta' \mid n, r, \theta) = \left[\frac{n}{2\pi(\sigma^2 + \sigma_r^2)} \right]^{\frac{1}{2}} \exp - \left[\frac{n(\theta' - \theta)^2}{2(\sigma^2 + \sigma_r^2)} \right]. \tag{14.23}$$

Because of the central limit theorem, this result will be a good approximation even if the parent population is not normal, provided that n is reasonably large.

Let us assume a cost-of-error function that is linear in $\theta' - \theta$ and symmetric; that is,

$$H(\theta', \theta) = K |\theta' - \theta|. \tag{14.24}$$

Then we have

$$\bar{C}_n(r) = K \int_{-\infty}^{\infty} |\theta' - \theta| f(\theta' \mid n, r, \theta) \, d\theta' - nr$$

$$= K \text{ (first absolute moment of } \theta' \text{ about its mean)} - nr. \tag{14.25}$$

With resources fixed at some amount R, nr is constant, and the optimal pair (n, r) will be one that (a) obeys the restriction $nr = R$ and (b) minimizes the first absolute moment of θ about its mean. Because any absolute moment of a normal distribution decreases with the variance, it is clear that $C_n(r)$ takes its minimum where $1/n(\sigma^2 + \sigma_r{}^2)$ has its minimum. Because $R = nr$, this amounts to choosing that value of r which minimizes $r(\sigma^2 + \sigma_r{}^2)$. In order to calculate this optimal r, we must know σ_r as a function of r.

If the cost of error is linear with $\theta' - \theta$ but nonsymmetric, that is, if

$$H(\theta', \theta) = K_1(\theta' - \theta) \quad \text{for} \quad \theta' > \theta$$
$$H(\theta', \theta) = K_2(\theta' - \theta) \quad \text{for} \quad \theta' < \theta,$$

it is not difficult to show that the same result applies. That is, if resources are fixed at R, the optimal r is again that value which minimizes the product $r(\sigma^2 + \sigma_r{}^2)$.

STRATEGIES AND SEARCH

In the problems considered so far the course of action associated with the output of the search has been assumed to be known. Now we consider a qualitative search problem in which the appropriate course of action must also be selected. This problem is equivalent to that of testing hypotheses. The procedure to be described is essentially Bayesian.

The Approach of Statistical Decision Theory to Hypothesis Testing

This approach may be formulated as follows.

1. Let A_1 and A_2 represent the courses of action that are available to the decision maker. Let $y_1, y_2, \ldots, y_j, \ldots$ represent the possible states of nature. There may be an infinity of such states along a continuous scale, but we consider a finite number of discrete actions and states without loss of generality because the procedure to be described can be generalized to the infinite continuous case. Finally, let $U(A_i \mid y_j)$ represent the expected value (or loss) to the decision maker of taking course of action A_i where the true state is y_j.

TABLE 14.2 *Payoff Matrix*

Possible Courses of Action	States of Nature			
	y_1	y_2	$\cdots$	y_j	$\cdots$
A_1	$U(A_1 \mid y_1)$	$U(A_1 \mid y_2)$	$\cdots$	$U(A_1 \mid y_j)$	$\cdots$
A_2	$U(A_2 \mid y_1)$	$U(A_2 \mid y_2)$	$\cdots$	$U(A_2 \mid y_j)$	$\cdots$

Now the test situation can be represented by a payoff matrix such as is shown in Table 14.2.

If the hypothesis-testing situation were to be treated as an uncertainty game against nature, it would be "solved" with only the information provided in Table 14.2. A minimax, generalized (Hurwicz) minimax, or minimax-regret solution could be selected at this point. But if observations are to be made and the resulting information is to be used, a modified approach is required. In this case we would proceed to the next step.

2. Let $y_1', y_2', \ldots, y_k', \ldots$ represent possible estimates of y (or some other computation) obtained from a sample of observations, and let $p(y_k' \mid y_j)$ represent the conditional probability of obtaining an estimate of y_k' when y_j is the true value. These conditional probabilities are usually obtained from the theory of estimation and sampling employed and (in most cases) from the knowledge or an estimate of one or more parameters of the population from which the sample is drawn. It should be noted, however, that the conditional probabilities depend on the sample size and estimating procedure, both of which must be selected.

The conditional probabilities can be displayed in the form shown in Table 14.3.

TABLE 14.3 *Conditional Probabilities*

Possible Estimates	States of Nature			
	y_1	y_2	$\cdots$	y_j	$\cdots$
y_1'	$p(y_1' \mid y_1)$	$p(y_1' \mid y_2)$	$\cdots$	$p(y_1' \mid y_j)$	$\cdots$
y_2'	$p(y_2' \mid y_1)$	$p(y_2' \mid y_2)$	$\cdots$	$p(y_2' \mid y_j)$	$\cdots$
.	.	.	$\cdots$	.	$\cdots$
.	.	.	$\cdots$	.	$\cdots$
y_k'	$p(y_k' \mid y_1)$	$p(y_k' \mid y_2)$	$\cdots$	$p(y_k' \mid y_j)$	$\cdots$
.	.	.		.	
.	.	.		.	
Sum	$\sum p(y_k' \mid y_1) = 1$	$\sum p(y_k' \mid y_2) = 1$		$\sum p(y_k' \mid y_j) = 1$	

TABLE 14.4   *Possible Strategies*

Possible Estimates	Possible Strategies			
	S_1	S_2	$\cdots$	S_h	$\cdots$
y_1'	A_1	A_1	$\cdots$	A_1	$\cdots$
y_2'	A_1	A_1	$\cdots$	A_2	$\cdots$
.	.	.		.	
.	.	.	$\cdots$	.	$\cdots$
.	.	.		.	
y_k'	A_1	A_2	$\cdots$	A_2	$\cdots$
.	.	.		.	
.	.	.	$\cdots$	.	$\cdots$
.	.	.		.	

Because the set $\{y_k\}$ exhausts all the possibilities, the sum of the probabilities in each column must equal 1.

3. Let $S_1, S_2, \ldots, S_h, \ldots$ represent the possible *strategies* available to the researcher. A strategy is a rule that dictates the course of action to be taken in the event of each possible estimate. These possible strategies are displayed in Table 14.4.

If, for example, only three estimates (y_1', y_2', and y_3') were possible, there would be eight possible strategies. These are shown in Table 14.5.

Clearly, if there are x possible estimates, there are 2^x possible strategies, which we will designate as m.

4. Now we wish to determine the probability that each course of action will be selected in each strategy for each possible true value of y_j; that is, $p(A_i \mid S_h, y_j)$. These probabilities are computed by obtaining the course of action associated with S_h from Table 14.4; then the probabilities $p(A_i \mid y_j)$ are obtained from Table 14.3 and added for each course of action. These computations yield a table of the type shown in Table 14.6. For example, using the example in Table 14.5, the action probability associated with S_2, A_1, y_1 is $p(y_1' \mid y_1) + p(y_2' \mid y_2)$ and, with S_2, A_2, y_1, it is $p(y_3' \mid y_1)$.

TABLE 14.5   *Possible Strategies for Three Possible Estimates*

	S_1	S_2	S_3	S_4	S_5	S_6	S_7	S_8
y_1'	A_1	A_1	A_1	A_2	A_1	A_2	A_2	A_2
y_2'	A_1	A_1	A_2	A_1	A_2	A_1	A_2	A_2
y_3'	A_1	A_2	A_1	A_1	A_2	A_2	A_1	A_2

TABLE 14.6   *Action Probabilities*

	S_1		S_2		S_3		S_4		S_5		S_6		S_7		S_8	
	A_1	A_2	A_1	A_2	A_1	A_2	A_1	A_2	A_1	A_2	A_1	A_2	A_1	A_2	A_1	A_2
y_1																
y_2																
.																
.																
.																
y_j																
.																
.																
.																

5. Now for each combination (S_h, y_j) the expected value, given y_j, is computed; that is,

$$U(S_h, y_j) = \sum p(A_i \mid S_h, y_j) U(A_i \mid y_j). \tag{14.29}$$

This yields values which can be displayed as in Table 14.7.

Table 14.7 is a revised payoff matrix in which *expected* gains or losses are shown. In Table 14.2 the payoffs were simply gains or losses. If the probabilities of each y_j occurring are known—that is, $p(y_j)$—then the expected value of each strategy can be determined:

$$E[U(S_h)] = \sum_j p(y_j) U(S_h, y_j). \tag{14.30}$$

One could then select the strategy that maximizes expected value (or minimizes expected cost). If the $p(y_j)$ are assumed to be unknown, we again have

TABLE 14.7   *Values Associated with Researcher's Strategies*

	S_1	S_2	$\cdots$	S_h	$\cdots$
y_1					
y_2					
.					
.					
.					
y_j				$U(S_h, y_j)$	
.					
.					

an uncertainty game against nature, and such criteria as minimax can be applied.

It is also possible to select "mixed" strategies, that is, to select one of each of a set of simple strategies according to some specified probabilities. In any particular case the number of possible mixed strategies is unlimited, because the number of mixes of probabilities is unlimited. In practice, however, it is usually possible to reduce the number of strategies that should be considered.

As indicated, if on the basis of previously available (a priori) information the probabilities of occurrence of possible states, $p(y_j)$, can be estimated, that selection of a strategy can be made which maximizes the expected value. That is, for each S_h and y_j we can compute $\sum_j p(y_j)U(S_h, y_j)$, which is the expected value of S_h, and select that S_h for which this value is maximum. If observations are made, the a priori probabilities can be adjusted to obtain a posteriori probabilities on the basis of which the expected values are adjusted. These procedures are referred to as *Bayesian strategies*.

Even if the probabilities $p(y_j)$ are not known, it is clear that we should, if possible, consider only strategies that maximize expected value for some set of possible values of $p(y_j)$. These are called *admissible* strategies.[4] In some (but relatively few) cases it is possible to identify all the admissible strategies, hence restrict attention to them.

Both the selection of admissible strategies and the calculation of a posteriori probabilities are illustrated in a very simple example of this approach given by Wagner (1957, pp. 13–17), which is reproduced here with modification of only the symbols that are employed.

Small lots of a complex assembly item are to be subjected to an acceptance sampling procedure. It is known from experience that the number of defects per item occurs according to a Poisson probability distribution; and for the sake of simplicity, it is postulated here that nature "produces" lots after selecting a Poisson distribution with an average of either 10 or 20 defects per 100 items.[5] In the former case, the lots are acceptable, and in the latter case they are unacceptable. Table 14.8 contains the payoff matrix. In this example, losses, instead of being represented as negative numbers employed in a maximizing operation, are treated as positive numbers, and strategies that minimize loss are to be investigated. It is *assumed* that these monetary outcomes are good approximations of the values involved in the decision.

---

[4] As Wagner (1957) points out, "In mathamatical statistics there is a fine distinction between the classes of admissable strategies and Bayes strategies; further, in special games no admissable strategies may exist" (p. 8, footnote). This fine distinction and limitation is not critical in this discussion.

[5] We utilize the distinction employed in quality control of defect versus defective. The latter is defined in terms of the particular number of allowable defects per item.

TABLE 14.8 *Losses*

Possible Actions	States of Nature	
	$y_1 = 10$ Defects Per 100 Items	$y_2 = 20$ Defects Per 100 Items
A_1	0	\$20
A_2	\$10	0

The minimax strategy, if no sampling is done, is to select A_1 with probability $\frac{1}{3}$ and A_2 with probability $\frac{2}{3}$. The expected value of the outcome, \$6.66, is then independent of nature's strategy. If the a priori probability $p(y_1) = \frac{3}{4}$ and $p(y_2) = \frac{1}{4}$, then A_1 is the optimal (minimax expected loss) action, giving an expected value of \$5.00.

Although the size of a sample is a variable that should be subject to economic analysis in a proposed statistical procedure, assume that for various reasons only two items drawn randomly out of the lot are to be inspected. The sample observations will be classified into three categories: $y_1' = 0$ defect, $y_2' = 1$ defect, and $y_3' = 2$ or more defects (if two defects are found in either or both items, inspection ceases). The conditional probabilities for y_k' are shown in Table 14.9.[6]

There are two possible actions and three possible observations; hence $2^3 = 8$ simple strategies exist, as shown in Table 14.10. Strategy S_4, for example, specifies selecting action A_1 if y_1' occurs, and A_2 otherwise. If y_1 is the true state of nature, y_1' occurs with probability 0.82, and consequently action A_1 is taken with probability 0.82. Table 14.11 gives the action probabilities for each strategy.[7]

TABLE 14.9 *Conditional Probabilities*

Possible Observations	States of Nature	
	y_1	y_2
$y_1' = 0$ defect in 2 items	0.82	0.67
$y_2' = 1$ defect in 2 items	0.16	0.27
$y_3' = 2$ or more defects in 2 items	0.02	0.06

[6] If the number of defects in 100 items has a Poisson distribution with an average q, it is postulated that the number of defects in two items is distributed as a Poisson with an average $2q/100$.

[7] The mathematician states that each strategy defines a "mapping" from the sample space to the action space.

TABLE 14.10 *Simple Strategies*

Observations	Strategies							
	S_1	S_2	S_3	S_4	S_5	S_6	S_7	S_8
y_1'	A_1	A_1	A_1	A_1	A_2	A_2	A_2	A_2
y_2'	A_1	A_1	A_2	A_2	A_1	A_1	A_2	A_2
y_3'	A_1	A_2	A_1	A_2	A_1	A_2	A_1	A_2

Finally, Table 14.12 combines the previous matrices to give the expected or average losses for each of the strategies. A first glance at Table 14.12 does not reveal which strategies, if any, are inadmissable. A graph aids in this process (Figure 14.4). The expected losses for each strategy are plotted on the two vertical axes and connected by a straight line. The segments of the lower boundary identify the admissable strategies: S_1, S_2, S_4, and S_8.

The minimax strategy, found at the maximum point on the lower boundary, is to select S_4 with probability 0.46 and S_8 with probability 0.54. Given a priori probabilities, the corresponding Bayes strategy is found by applying the probabilities to Table 14.12. If $p(y_1) = \frac{3}{4}$ and $p(y_2) = \frac{1}{4}$, S_1 is the optimal strategy.

If a minimax procedure is to be employed, it has been stated that the expected loss without any data is $6.66; with data, the minimax expected loss becomes $6.26. Therefore, it does not pay to take a sample of two items unless the sampling cost is less than $0.40 or unless there is some value in collecting data, say, for making a future estimate of the a priori probabilities. In the case of $p(y_1) = \frac{3}{4}$ and $p(y_2) = \frac{1}{4}$, the expected loss is $5.00 without data and is $4.70 with data. Hence, with this a priori information, it pays to inspect two items only if the cost of observation is less than $0.30.

The use of a posteriori probabilities to arrive at an optimal strategy is illustrated with $p(y_1) = \frac{3}{4}$ and $p(y_2) = \frac{1}{4}$. Under these conditions S_4 turns out to be optimal.

TABLE 14.11 *Action Probabilities with Simple Strategies*

States of Nature	S_1		S_2		S_3		S_4		S_5		S_6		S_7		S_8	
	A_1	A_2	A_1	A_2	A_1	A_2	A_1	A_2	A_1	A_2	A_1	A_2	A_1	A_2	A_1	A_2
y_1	1.00	0	0.98	0.02	0.84	0.16	0.82	0.18	0.18	0.82	0.16	0.84	0.02	0.98	0	1.00
y_2	1.00	0	0.94	0.06	0.73	0.27	0.67	0.33	0.33	0.67	0.27	0.73	0.06	0.94	0	1.00

TABLE 14.12   *Average Economic Evaluation in Dollars*

States of Nature	S_1	S_2	S_3	S_4	S_5	S_6	S_7	S_8
y_1	0	0.20	1.60	1.80	8.20	8.40	9.80	10.00
y_2	20.00	18.80	14.60	13.40	6.60	5.40	1.20	0

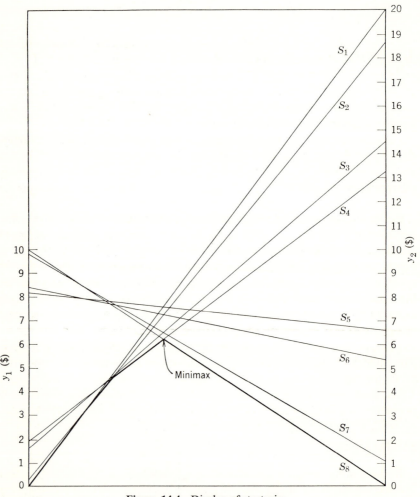

Figure 14.4   Display of strategies.

If y_1' is observed (the a posteriori probability),

$$p'(y_1) = \frac{\frac{3}{4} \times 0.82}{\frac{3}{4} \times 0.82 + \frac{1}{4} \times 0.67} = 0.79$$

$$p'(y_2) = 0.21.$$

On applying these probabilities to Table 14.8, A_1 is found to be optimal.

If y_2' is observed,

$$p'(y_1) = \frac{\frac{3}{4} \times 0.16}{\frac{3}{4} \times 0.16 + \frac{1}{4} \times 0.27} = 0.64$$

$$p'(y) = 0.36.$$

A_2 is optimal.

If y_3' is observed,

$$p'(y_1) = \frac{\frac{3}{4} \times 0.02}{\frac{3}{4} \times 0.02 + \frac{1}{4} \times 0.06} = 0.50$$

$$p'(y_2) = 0.50.$$

A_2 is optimal.

INVERTED SEARCH

There are situations in which the procedure of search is not under our control but the properties of that for which the search is being conducted are. In some circumstances of this type we wish to hide the truth and in others we wish it to be found. In evasive military tactics, for example, the problem is to avoid detection. In locating goods for sale in a retail store, on the other hand, the objective is to maximize the chance that things being looked for by customers will be found. The same holds true in designing filing systems and in systems of storage and retrieval of scientific information. In principle such problems present nothing that search theory cannot handle. The difficulty usually lies in obtaining a complete and accurate description of the procedure of search that is being used and of what is being sought. There have been relatively few applications of operations research to such problems outside of the military. Very little has been published on this subject.

SUMMARY

In this chapter we have considered the process of seeking information that is to be incorporated into a decision leading to action. Such a process is very general; for example, most research projects involve search in this sense. For this reason search and inference are very closely related processes; either may be considered as a special case of the other. Therefore, it is not surprising that statistical decision theory, which has been developed to improve inferential procedures, is applicable to most searches.

The term "search" has been used in OR mainly in military contexts to refer to inquiries directed toward locating something. We have used the concept in a much more general way: to refer to looking for any kind of information.

Two types of cost are involved in searches: the cost of obtaining information and the cost of error that results from its use. Errors are of two types: sampling and observational (observing what is not there or not observing what is there). The objective in designing a search is to find a procedure that minimizes the sum of these costs. This involves determining where to look or what to look at (sampling design), how many places to look or things to look at (sample size), and how to reach conclusions from what is observed (analysis of observations).

In this chapter we have considered several very simple search problems and illustrated how appropriate models can be constructed and (sometimes) solved. It is apparent from these examples that realistic searches are frequently difficult to represent and to design optimally. They can present a great challenge, however, to the modeling and model-solving ability of the researcher and considerable payoff to the searcher.

EXERCISES   (These exercises all require knowledge of calculus.)

1. Consider the distributive-qualitative problem in the special case in which there are only two classes. Let P be the fraction of class 1 in the population and $p_{ij}(r)$ the probability of classifying an i as a j when we spend r per item on classification. Let α_{ij} be the corresponding cost and suppose that our resources are fixed at R. Suppose we observe n out of N items and that the nonobserved items are classified as 1 or 2 according as $P\alpha_{11} + (1 - P)\alpha_{21}$ or $P\alpha_{12} + (1 - P)\alpha_{22}$ is smaller. Let θ be the value of the smaller. Show that the total cost will be:

$$n[p_{11}P(\alpha_{11} - \alpha_{12}) + p_{22}(1 - P)(\alpha_{22} - \alpha_{21}) + P\alpha_{12} + (1 - P)\alpha_{21}]$$
$$+ R + (N - n)\theta$$

and that this is minimized by solving

$$P(\alpha_{11} - \alpha_{12})\frac{d}{dn}(np_{11}) + (1 - P)(\alpha_{22} - \alpha_{21})\frac{d}{dn}(np_{22})$$

$$= \theta - P\alpha_{12} - (1 - P)\alpha_{21}$$

$$= \text{Min} \begin{cases} P(\alpha_{11} - \alpha_{12}) \\ (1 - P)(\alpha_{22} - \alpha_{21}) \end{cases}$$

Note:

(1) $p_{ij} = p_{ij}(r) = p_{ij}(R/n)$.

(2) $P\dfrac{d}{dn}(np_{11})$ is the marginal change in the correct number of classifications in class i when n is increased to $n + 1$. This concept is often helpful when the acuity functions are unknown.

2. Specialize the equation for n above in the following cases:

   (a) $p_{11}(r) = p_{22}(r)$.

   (b) $p_{11} = p_{22}$; $\alpha_{12} = -\alpha_{11}$; and $\alpha_{21} = -\alpha_{22}$.

3. Consider the situation of the previous problems when there are no constraints on the total resources. In this situation we wish to minimize the cost per item; that is, we wish to minimize

$$\bar{C}(r) = p_{11}P(\alpha_{11} - \alpha_{12}) + p_{22}(1 - P)(\alpha_{22} - \alpha_{21}) + P\alpha_{12} + (1 - P)\alpha_{21} + r.$$

Show that the best value of r satisfies

$$P(\alpha_{11} - \alpha_{12})\frac{dp_{11}}{dr} + (1 - P)(\alpha_{22} - \alpha_{21})\frac{dp_{22}}{dr} + 1 = 0.$$

4. Suppose that initially we have no information about P and we assume that it is uniformly distributed between zero and one; that is, the probability that P lies between $\pi + d\pi$ is $d\pi$ $(0 \leq \pi \leq 1)$ and 0 otherwise. If we ignore the possibilities of misclassification, show that the probability that $\pi \leq P \leq \pi + d\pi$ *and* that out of n observations we have seen m in class 1 is

$$\binom{n}{m}\pi^m(1 - \pi)^{n-m}\,d\pi.$$

By integration show that the probability of observing m in class 1 out of n observations is $1/(n + 1)$. Hence show that *after* our observations the density function for P is

$$(n + 1)\binom{n}{m}P^m(1 - P)^{n-m}$$

and the expected value of P, which we denote by $E(P)$, is $(m + 1)/(n + 2)$.

This leads to the following approximate scheme for classifying with limited resources R:

(1) Take the expected value of P when $m = n = 0$; that is $P = \frac{1}{2}$.

(2) Compute n_1 for resources R and $E(P) = \frac{1}{2}$.

(3) Make first observation with $r_1 = R/n_1$.

(4) Compute $E(P) = E(p_{11})$ using the result of the observation and the formula above.

(5) Compute n_2 for resources $R - r_1$ and probability $E(p_{11})$.

(6) Make second observation using $r_2 = (R - r_1)/n_2$.

(7) Continue until all resources are used.

5. Consider the following distributive-quantitative situation. The measured quantity y, is normally distributed with a mean equal to the design value y_0 and unit standard deviation. The actual measurement, y', is normally distributed about the true value y with standard deviation σ_r. The design tolerances call for rejection of parts for which the true value of y lies outside the range $y_0 \pm 2$, and in practice will be rejected if and only if the observed value y' lies outside this range. The costs associated with correct classification are zero, but accepting a part that should have been rejected costs $100 |y - y_0|$. Rejecting a part that should have been accepted costs $|y - y_0|$. Two measuring devices are available. The first costs 5 per item and has $\sigma_r = 0.2$, and the second costs 10 per item and has $\sigma_r = 0.1$.

Use numerical integration to find which device is preferable.

In view of the asymmetry of the cost function, can you suggest a better rule for accepting and rejecting items?

Suggested Readings

A good grounding is statistical decision theory is the best preparation for work on search problems. At the most elementary level, one can be introduced to the subject by Chernoff and Moses (1959). At a more advanced level, one can obtain much more detail from Raiffa and Schlaifer (1961) and Weiss (1961).

For some understanding of searches in the military context, the classical papers of Koopman (1956 and 1957) should be read.

Bibliography

Ackoff, R. L., *The Design of Social Research*, University of Chicago Press, Chicago, 1953.

——, *Scientific Method: Optimizing Applied Research Decisions*, John Wiley and Sons, New York, 1962.

Chambers, J. C., and D. F. Clark, *The Determination of Observational Errors Occurring in Information-Collection Processes*, Research Memorandum 4, Operations Research Group, Case Institute of Technology, Cleveland, Ohio, September 30, 1957.

Chernoff, Herman, and L. E. Moses, *Elementary Decision Theory*, John Wiley and Sons, New York, 1959.

Engel, J. H., "Use of Clustering in Mineralogical and Other Surveys," *Proceedings of the First International Conference on Operations Research*, The English Universities Press, London, 1957.

Houlden, B. T., *Some Techniques of Operations Research*, The English Universities Press, London, 1962.

Koopman, B. O., "Theory of Search," *Operations Research*, **4** (June 1956), 324–346; **4** (October 1956), 503–531; **5** (October 1957), 613–626.

MacQueen, J. B., "Optimal Policies for a Class of Search and Evaluation Problems," *Management Science*, **10** (July, 1964), 746–759.

Margenau, H., "Philosophical Problems Concerning the Meaning of Measurement in Physics," in C. W. Churchman and P. Ratoosh (eds.), Measurement: *Definitions and Theories*, John Wiley and Sons, New York, 1959, pp. 163–176.

McKnight, J. L., "The Quantum Theoretical Concept of Measurement," in Churchman and Ratoosh (1959), pp. 192–203.

Raiffa, Howard, and Robert Schlaifer, *Applied Statistical Decision Theory*, Division of Research, Graduate School of Business Administration, Harvard University, Boston, Mass., 1961.

Wagner, H. M., "Statistical Decision Theory as a Guide to Information Processing," The RAND Corp., p. 1160, August 26, 1957.

Weiss, Lionel, *Statistical Decision Theory*, McGraw-Hill Book Co., New York, 1961.

Yaspan, A. J., M. H. Halbert, and R. L. Ackoff, "An Exploratory Study on the Consideration of Observational Errors in the Design of Information-Collection Procedures," Research Memorandum 1, Operations Research Group, Case Institute of Technology, Cleveland, Ohio, November 15, 1956.

CHAPTER 15

Testing the Model and the Solution

INTRODUCTION

A model should be tested continuously while it is being constructed. If its testing is not carried on in parallel with its construction, the model tends to acquire a sanctity during its development that makes it difficult to evaluate the model objectively after its completion.

When the model is completed, it should be tested as a whole. If it fails such testing, the nature of its deficiency should be determined and corrected. The kinds of deficiencies from which a model can suffer are the following:

1. It may include irrelevant variables.
2. It may exclude relevant variables.
3. One or more relevant variables may be evaluated inaccurately.
4. Its structure (i.e., the function that relates performance to controlled and uncontrolled variables) may be in error.

The techniques that can be used in testing for these types of deficiencies are statistical in character. The more knowledge of statistical techniques is available to the OR team, the more adequate the testing procedure is likely to be.

In the discussion here we cannot provide the required statistical knowledge, but we shall identify that knowledge which is required and indicate where it should be used. Good basic coverage of the field can be found in Hoel (1954) and Mood and Graybill (1963).

RELEVANT AND IRRELEVANT VARIABLES

In most of the types of situations with which OR deals there are a very large number of variables that affect performance, but some have very large effects and others have little. Usually, only a few variables are important. These few are of principal interest to the researcher, because he should try to construct an adequate model with as few variables as possible. Management, on the other hand, generally wishes to include a large number of variables in order to make the model as "realistic" as possible. In one sense we can say that the objective of the researcher is to construct the simplest model that can reproduce reality with acceptable accuracy and precision.

The number of variables in a model is not as important as the way in which they are related to one another. A few variables correctly related may reproduce reality more accurately than a host of variables that are less correctly related.

Imagine a situation in which five variables affect performance. If Y_1 accounts for 50 per cent of performance, Y_2 for 20 per cent, Y_3 for 15 per cent, Y_4 for 10 per cent, and Y_5 for 5 per cent, a model with Y_1 alone may be as good as one that contains the other four, but not Y_1.

Even "obviously" relevant variables may not be relevant, or they may not be relevant in an "obvious way." For example, consider a problem that involved planning the production of parts for aircraft. It usually takes several years to complete an order for a particular type of aircraft. During this time many of the parts are redesigned. Hence, if all the parts that are required for producing, say, 200 planes are manufactured before the first plane is completed, many of these parts will be made obsolete by subsequent design changes that result from production difficulties and from ground and flight tests of the first planes produced. Therefore, in developing a production control system it is necessary to determine the probability that a part will be redesigned at various times after its initial production. Management pointed out that there was a predicting function widely used in the industry, which provided estimates of this probability as a function of the amount of time that has elapsed since initiation of production. The team decided to check the accuracy of the function. Recent data revealed that the number of engineering changes per period was constant over the life of the contract, because the number of engineers assigned to making such changes was usually constant over the life of the contract. Hence "time since initial production" turned out to be irrelevant.

To determine whether a variable has a significant effect on the measure of performance, various statistical techniques are available, of which the most commonly used are correlation and regression analysis and the analysis of variance and covariance. Knowledge of the differences between these statistical procedures and their capabilities and limitations should be at the disposal of the OR team. [See Ezekiel and Fox (1959) and Cochran and Cox (1950).] Here we can only touch on some of their more important characteristics.

Nearly all the statistical techniques that are available can be applied only to linear models, or to models that can be made linear by defining new variables. Thus $y = ax^2 + bx + c$ is a nonlinear model in x, but it is linear in x_1 and x, where $x_1 = x^2$. The usual methods of analysis throw light on how good a particular model happens to be, but there are virtually no recognized methods for deciding which model to test next if our first model fails. Choice of a model is often something of an art, where, like in all arts, the best teacher is experience. However, we are often able to start with some intuitively obvious assumptions, from which, with the aid of mathematics, we can then build what appears to be a reasonable model.

Correlation is a measure of the tendency of two variables, neither of which has been controlled, to vary together in accord with a linear relationship. It must be emphasized that a correlation coefficient is purely the result of a numerical calculation; it ranges from -1 to $+1$ in value, and linearly related variables produce values near either end of the range—toward $+1$ if they increase together and toward -1 if as one increases the other decreases. A value near zero indicates that no linear relationship exists; it does not, in itself, exclude the possibility of a nonlinear relationship. Usually we are interested in what happens to one variable if we succeed in controlling the other, and for this we require a *causal* relationship. Unfortunately, the existence of a linear relationship tells us nothing about causality. If we can rule out the possibility of a nonlinear relationship and obtain a correlation coefficient near zero, we can be fairly sure that no causal relationship exists, but the converse is not true.

There is an oft-repeated, if apocryphal, story that a correlation exists between beer sales, year by year, and parsons' incomes. The explanation, of course, is not that parsons drink enough beer to affect sales; rather, it lies in the relationship that both variables have with the general prosperity of the country.

Even where there is no obviously related intervening variable, correlations may be found because of chance factors alone. Tests have been designed to discover whether correlations observed in small samples might have arisen by chance, where no underlying relationship exists. The more common tests are valid only when both variables come from normal distributions, and the validity of this assumption must be carefully considered when interpreting results.

If two variables are causally connected and if the statistical assumptions involved in correlation analysis are valid, they will usually (but not always) show a significant correlation. Hence, when the statistical assumptions are valid and two variables are not found to be significantly correlated, we can conclude (subject to measurable error) that they are *not* causally connected by a linear relationship.[1] Therefore, at best, correlation analysis can only be

---

[1] In practice linearity requirements are not as restrictive as it would appear. A large class of nonlinear functions can be approximated by linear expressions, and all such functions are ruled out by near-zero correlation coefficients. Furthermore, as we have seen, redefining variables may convert nonlinear forms to linear forms in new variables.

used to tell us that a variable is *not* relevant. It is never sufficient to establish the relevance of a variable.

Correlation analysis can involve the interactions between more than two variables, and other than linear relationships.

Regression analysis can be applied where one of the variables is subject to control, say X; hence values of X can be set and subsequent values of Y can be observed. Therefore, if the statistical assumptions are justified and the regression of Y on X is significant, causal inferences can be drawn, subject to sampling error. But because this regression procedure involves controlling the variable whose relevance is being tested, and in testing OR models we are more likely to be concerned with the relevance of uncontrolled, rather than controlled variables, it has restricted usefulness.

The same is true for the use of modern experimental designs and the associated techniques of statistical analysis: the analysis of variance and covariance. These techniques make it possible for us to test the relevance of any number of controllable factors simultaneously and, furthermore, to determine if they *interact*. That is, we can determine if the *effect* on performance of one factor depends on the levels of others. It also provides an estimate of the variance in performance due to variables that are not controlled in the test. Hence, by comparing the total variance explained by the controlled variables with the "residual" variance, we obtain a notion of "how much" is explained by the variables being tested. If the "how much" is "little," we know that some relevant variables are excluded, but not which ones. We may have to go back to an analysis of the system to find out what is missing.

A variable, X, cannot be said to have a significant effect on performance, P, or on any other variable, Y, solely on the basis of a statistically significant regression coefficient or a favorable analysis of variance (or covariance). Even if we know that changes in X precede changes in P or Y, a regression equation at best tells us how one variable affects another *if* it affects it, not that it affects it. To establish relevance of X to P, we need to know either that the various X-values occur in situations that are otherwise the same with regard to all other relevant variables, or that the other variables are changing in the way assumed by the analysis.

No amount of observation alone can assure us on these matters. Hence assumptions are always involved in analyses of relevance, and these are part of the researcher's conception of the phenomenon under study. Strictly speaking, then, the relevance of a variable is assured by a causal model; it is not found in data. Observations may lead to acceptance, revision, or rejection of the model, but without some kind of causal model of the situation under study we cannot formulate a relevant experiment or data-collection procedure. Therefore, in order to establish the relevance of variables we must use both a model of the possible relationship between the variable and outcome and a

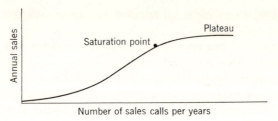

Figure 15.1 Assumed sales-call response function.

set of observations. This is illustrated in the following example, which also contains another important moral: changes in a variable may be relevant over a limited range of its possible values and irrelevant elsewhere.

In planning the expansion of the Lamp Division of the General Electric Company in 1953 to 1954, it was necessary to determine the number of additional salesmen required.[2] This in turn required knowledge of the number of accounts that should be assigned to a salesman, hence the number of calls that should be made on an account per year. To determine the latter, it was necessary to find the effect on dollar volume per account, of the number of sales calls.

It seemed reasonable to assume that the response of purchases to sales calls would take the form shown in Figure 15.1, and that the parameters of this response function would vary between types of accounts (e.g., wholesale versus retail and urban versus rural), if not between different accounts.

Accounts were classified and data were collected for each of a large sample of accounts on the number of sales calls and sales per year. A typical plot of the results for one class of accounts is shown in Figure 15.2. This plot

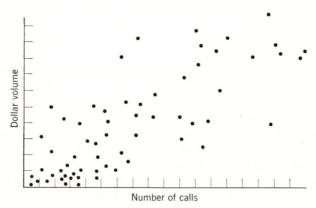

Figure 15.2 Example of plot of dollar volume versus number of calls.

[2] For a detailed account of this case, see Clark, Ackoff, and Waid (1956).

(and the others that were obtained) did not conform to the kind of response function expected. Increasingly complex ways of classifying accounts were used, but the results were no better. Multiple linear and curvilinear regression analyses were made with a large number of account characteristics and sales calls per year as the independent variables and the sales volume per year as the dependent variable. Sales volume appeared to be related to the number of sales calls, but the variance about any curve that was fitted to the data was very large. (See Figure 15.2.) The data did not prove that increases in number of calls produced increases in sales because many other explanations were possible; for example, salesmen may simply call more frequently on their larger accounts, whether or not this is necessary.

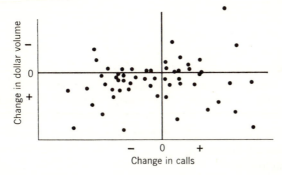

Figure 15.3   Example of plot of dollar volume change versus change in number of calls.

One possible explanation for the variability of the results obtained was that most accounts were being saturated with sales calls, hence most of the data represented random fluctuations about the plateau of the sales-response curves. If this were so, it would follow that changes in the number of sales calls per year (in the region beyond saturation) should not be accompanied by changes in amount sold.

The team set about to test this hypothesis. Changes in sales volume per account over two years were plotted against changes in number of sales calls per account over the same two years. A plot of typical results is shown in Figure 15.3.

These results were duplicated for several pairs of successive years and for two-year intervals as well. Analysis were made to determine if the quadrant location of an account (in plots such as that shown in Figure 15.3) could be explained by characteristics of the accounts. The results were negative. In a sense, then, the hypothesis of saturation had been confirmed, but another type of analysis was made to double-check this conclusion.

Accounts were classified by whether they had an increase or decrease in number of calls in 1953 as compared with 1952. They were then subclassified by whether they had an increase or decrease in 1954. This yielded the four classes of accounts shown in Table 15.1.

A statistical analysis was performed to determine whether or not there was a significant difference in average sales volume between any pair of these classes. No significant differences were found.

On the basis of these analyses the average number of calls per account was decreased and the number of accounts per salesman was increased by small increments over time until statistical analysis showed that the saturation point on the response curve was reached. Experimental probing to the left

TABLE 15.1

	Class			
	(1)	(2)	(3)	(4)
1952–1953	Increase	Increase	Decrease	Decrease
1953–1954	Increase	Decrease	Increase	Decrease

of the saturation point showed that there was a response curve of the character originally assumed, but that its slope in the "rising section" was much steeper than had been assumed.

In this example, we can see how causal assumptions, hypotheses, and data must interact in the search for the relevance of variables. Neither data nor theory alone is sufficient to do the job.

EVALUATION OF VARIABLES

The correct evaluation of a variable involves (1) the way in which it is defined, (2) the kinds of measurements of its value that are made, (3) the basis of the observations (the sample design), and (4) how estimates are derived from the observations. We shall consider each of these in turn.

Defining[3]

Before any operation of measurement can be performed, it is necessary to know what is to be measured. To avoid ambiguity we need a precise definition, and in formulating such a definition it is well to remember that the results of research must be communicated to others. In OR the *others* will seldom be scientists or engineers. Consequently, whenever possible, definitions should be consistent with everyday usage of language. It is ironic that the study of

[3] For a detailed discussion of this subject, see Ackoff (1962, Chapter 5).

communication itself has been confused by Shannon's use of the term *information* (Shannon and Weaver, 1949). Shannon regards a unit of information as the amount of ambiguity removed by a message that tells us which of two equally likely alternatives actually occurred. Thus to Shannon a message may contain information even when the receiver already knows its content or does not believe it. In everyday usage we would hardly consider a teacher to have *informed* his class unless the class believed him and acted accordingly. Shannon's concept would better be described as the amount of message, rather than the amount of information.[4]

The following steps can be taken to increase the effectiveness of definitions:

1. Examine as many past and current definitions of the concept as possible, keeping their chronology in mind.
2. Try to identify the "core of meaning" that runs through the different definitions.
3. Using this "core," formulate a tentative definition.
4. Determine if this definition serves the decision maker's objectives. If not, make necessary revisions.
5. Have the resulting definition reviewed as widely as possible and make any justifiable revisions suggested by the comments received.

To convert the definition obtained by the procedure just described into an operational form, it is necessary to specify explicitly the following factors:

1. The object or class of objects to be observed.
2. The conditions (environment) under which the observations should be made.
3. The operations, if any, that should be performed in that environment.
4. The instruments, if any, and the metric standards that are required to perform the specified operations.
5. The observation(s) that should be made.

These constitute *idealized* or *standard* procedures and conditions from which deviations can be measured. The effect of such deviations on the results obtained should be determinable. This requires the capability of measurement and adjustment of data. That is, we must be able to infer from the conditions obtaining and the procedures used what would have been observed under the standard conditions using standard procedures. Only by so doing can we compare observations made under different conditions and/or with different procedures.

---

[4] We do not wish to belittle Shannon's work, which has been of extreme value to electronic, communication, and control engineering. We merely point out that communication involves people as well as machines, and Shannon's definition of information does not include this concept.

Operational defining, in this sense, is well illustrated by the discussion in Darwin, Sears et al. (1946) of the measurement of length:

The International Prototype Metre is a bar of platinum iridium alloy (90% platinum, 10% iridium) of a special winged X-form section devised by G. Tresca to give maximum rigidity in relation to the weight of metal used; the neutral plane of the section is exposed throughout the length of the bar, and the metre is defined as the distance between two transverse graduations on the neutral plane, near the ends of the bar, when the latter is at the temperature of 0°C . . . .

It is necessary, of course, to maintain a close control and make accurate measurements of the temperature of the bars during comparison. For this reason the comparator is arranged so that the bars can be immersed, during measurement, in the inner compartment of a double water-bath, provided with stirring devices to maintain a uniform temperature . . . . Since different bars will have different coefficients of thermal expansion, it is necessary to determine these and make allowances for them in computing the results of comparisons actually made at other temperatures (pp. 152–154).

Measurement [5]

It is apparent from the preceding discussion that defining and measurement are very closely related. Measurement is the process of obtaining symbols to represent things, events, or their properties; the symbols are related to each other in the same way as that which they represent. For example, to know that a carton is 3′0″ wide and that a doorway is 3′6″ wide is to know that the carton will pass through the doorway. Measurements allow us to compare the same properties of different things, and the same property of the same thing at different times, and to describe how properties of the same or different things are related to one another.

Not every systematic procedure of assigning numbers to things or properties yields measurement; for example, assigning license numbers to automobiles is not measurement. Numbers are frequently used only for identification, as signs or names of things. A car with license plate 32 is not necessarily twice as large, heavy, costly, or anything else as a car with license plate 16. The things or properties represented by numbers do not necessarily have any or all the relationships between them that the numbers representing them have.

Measures are usually classified by how many of the properties of number the measures have. The principal classes are the following:

1. *Nominal scales:* numbers (or other symbols) are used to represent the class membership of things. All elements in the same class are assigned the same number and elements in different classes are assigned different numbers. The relationship on which such scales are based is *identity* or *difference*.

[5] For a more detailed discussion of this subject, see Ackoff (1962, Chapter 6), Churchman and Ratoosh (1959), and Stevens (1946).

2. *Ordinal scales:* numbers (or other symbols) are used to represent the order of elements of a set with respect to some relation(s) defined over the elements (e.g., *is larger than* and *is older than*). Ordered elements are said to be *ranked*. Not all orderings are the same. The research team should know the difference between at least the principal types of ordering (e.g., weak, partial, and complete).[6] The basic ordering relationships are "is greater than" and "is less than."

3. *Interval scales:* numbers are used to represent the magnitude of *differences* between the properties of the things represented. The Fahrenheit scale of temperature is such a scale. Hence the difference between 10° and 20°F is twice that between 10° and 15°, but we cannot say that something at 20°F is twice as warm as something at 10°F. Interval scales have arbitrary (not "natural") zero points (e.g., 0°F ≠ 0°C, but 32°F = 0°C).

Interval scales are unique up to a linear transformation. That is, a set of measurements $\{x_i\}$ can be transformed into other values x_i' by a linear transformation: $x_i' = ax_i + b$, where $a \neq 0$. The relative magnitudes for the differences between transformed values are the same as they were for the original values.

The basic relationship in interval scales is the equality of intervals or their differences.

4. *Ratio scales:* numbers are used to represent the ratio of magnitudes. This is measurement in the usual restricted sense. For example, an object that is 4′ long is twice as long as that which is 2′ long. These scales have "natural" (nonarbitrary) zero points and may be transformed by $x_i' = cx_i$, where $c > 0$ (e.g., transforming "feet" into "inches" or "yards").

Although numbers are used to represent measures obtained from each of the four types of scales, the mathematical and statistical operations that can be applied legitimately to these numbers differ. For example, we cannot add rankings or interval measurements meaningfully. The average rank of a set of items has no meaning, but the median rank does. Researchers should be familiar with the types of measures that he is using and with the arithmetical operations that can be performed on them. Models may fail if inappropriate operations are performed on the measures contained in them.

The difference between an index and a measure is also important. Suppose that we wish to measure a variable X but find it difficult to do so. If we can measure a variable Y that is highly correlated with X, measures of Y can be used as *indices* of X. Most scores on psychological tests are indices of the psychological properties of concern; the national level of machine-tool production is used as an index of general economic conditions, and so on. Indices are subject to a source of error to which direct measures are not

[6] For a detailed discussion of these types of ordering, see Ackoff (1962, Chapter 6).

subject: errors deriving from independent changes in X and Y. Unless the amount of correlation between measures of X and Y, and its variance, are known, there is no way of estimating the magnitude of this error. Furthermore, the index may be a measure on a kind of scale different from that on which direct measurements would be made. For example, we may think of an attitude toward something as measurable in principle on a ratio scale, but the test scores that serve as an index may be on an interval or ordinal scale.

The value and usefulness of a measure depends on its accuracy and precision. Accuracy and precision of measurement, however, are not ends in themselves. If we wish to move a table through a door, all that we need to know is whether the door opening is wider than the table. Before measuring, we need to know how much accuracy our task requires, and afterwards, how much we have. It is frequently costly to be either more or less accurate than necessary. (See the discussion of "observational error" in Chapter 14.)

Sampling[7]

It usually happens that if we repeat a measurement, the two results differ slightly. Thus even if we are measuring a specific object, we can imagine our procedure to consist of taking a sample of one or more elements out of the conceptually infinite population of measurements that we might have made. Alternatively, we may be aiming at a quantity which is, in some sense, representative of a class of elements, and our procedure may consist of selecting a subset from the class (or *population*) and performing measurements on each element of the subset. Such measurements themselves constitute a sample from all possible measurements that we might make on the subset. Furthermore, because properties may change over time, we may consider our procedure as a sample from the possible times at which measurements could have been made. Thus, in estimating a collective property, we start by specifying how we will sample one or more of the following:

1. The elements of the class of objects or events whose collective property is to be determined (e.g., a sample of machines, products, orders, or operators from a specified class).
2. The values of other properties that affect the property to be estimated (e.g., in experimentation, the values at which other variables are to be fixed).
3. The times at which observations are to be made (e.g., when traffic density at an intersection should be observed).

[7] For a more detailed discussion of this subject, see Ackoff (1962, Chapter 7), Cochran (1963), Deming (1960), and Hansen, Hurwitz, and Madow (1953).

The design of a sample involves determining how many observations should be made and what particular observations should be made. The accuracy and precision (bias and variance) of estimates derived from samples depend on both the size and kind of sample. The cost of observation also depends on these. Hence the researcher's objective should be to design a sample so that the sum of the cost of observations and the expected cost of error due to sampling and observation is as small as possible. This, of course, is a problem of the type that we identified as *search*.

To solve this type of problem even approximately, a familiarity with sampling theory is necessary. Here we merely identify the types of sampling design with which the OR team should be familiar, and we cite their principal advantages and disadvantages.

1. *Simple* (or *unrestricted*) *random sampling:* obtained by uniquely numbering each element of the population and using a table of random numbers to select the n numbers, hence the n elements to be observed. In such sampling every sample of size n has an equal chance of being selected, as does every element in the population.

2. *Systematic random sampling:* in principle we determine the fraction of the population to be observed (say, $1/k$) and then select every kth member from an ordered list of the entire population. In order to introduce randomness, we first select a random number between 1 and k (say, x), and the sample consists of population members whose numbers are $x, x + k, x + 2k, \ldots$. On this basis, *before we have chosen x*, every population member has an equal chance of being included in the sample, but of course every sample of size n does not.

When the population is or can be divided into subgroups, we can use the subgroups in our sample design. The most common designs are:

3. *Multistage random sampling:* obtained by first selecting a random sample of subgroups and drawing from each selected subgroup a random sample of its members.

4. *Stratified random sampling:* we try to make the sample representative of each subgroup by selecting random samples of prescribed sizes from each subgroup. The subgroup samples may be proportional in size to the number in the subgroups. If they are proportional to the size and standard deviation within subgroups, the sample is called *optimal*, because the estimate of the total population mean has the least possible sampling variance for a given sample size.

5. *Cluster sampling:* obtained by selecting all the elements from a random sample of subgroups.

6. *Stratified cluster sampling:* obtained by selecting a random sample from all subgroups at one stage and by selecting all elements in the subgroups selected at another stage. At least three stages are involved in this design. The more stages in a design, the more combinations of the various types of sampling are possible.

7. *Repetitive* (or *multiple*) *sampling:* obtained by selecting a random sample, analysis of which is used to design a second sample. This process may be continued. In the limit, one observation is made at a time and after each the decision is made as to whether or not to continue sampling. This is called *sequential sampling*.

These types of sampling involve either a complete count, a simple random sample, or a systematic random sample at each stage. If we repeated such sampling procedures, the estimates would vary but it is possible to determine the amount of variation from the data contained in a *single* sample. This is possible only because the sample design specifies (or implies) the probability that any given element of the population will be included in the sample. For this reason such designs are called *probability samples*.

In some cases the researcher may select a subgroup as representative of the population on the basis of a judgment to the effect that this subgroup is "typical." Such *judgment sampling* requires much stronger assumptions than probability sampling in order to justify it. The estimating errors derived from such samples can be computed only if there is available a record of estimates derived from such samples in the past together with knowledge of the true values that were being estimated in each case. This type of sampling may nevertheless be useful where the possible errors are not serious and probability sampling is not feasible. It is best used only for heuristic explorations, rather than for estimating values of a model's parameters. We might note in passing that human judgment is often quite good in choosing a sample to estimate a population mean, but it is usually unreliable when it comes to estimating ranges or other measures of dispersion.

The characteristics, advantages, and disadvantages of these types of samples are summarized in Table 15.2.

Estimation[8]

We have seen that measurement of a collective property of a class or population of objects results in a set of numbers obtained from a suitably chosen subset of the population, and that measurement of a single property of a specific object can also be considered in this light, provided that we imagine the population of all possible repetitions of the measurement. Once we have the observed values, say $y_1, y_2, \ldots, y_n$, we wish to use them to compute a

---

[8] For a more complete discussion of this subject, see Ackoff (1962, Chapter 8).

TABLE 15.2 *Sampling Chart*[a]

Type of Sampling	Brief Description	Advantages	Disadvantages
A. Simple random	Assign to each population member a unique number; select sample items by use of random numbers	1. Requires minimum knowledge of population in advance 2. Free of possible classification errors 3. Easy to analyze data and compute errors	1. Does not make use of knowledge of population which researcher may have 2. Larger errors for same sample size than in stratified sampling
B. Systematic	Use natural ordering or order population; select random starting point between 1 and the nearest integer to the sampling ratio (N/n); select items at interval of nearest integer to sampling ratio	1. If population is ordered with respect to pertinent property, gives stratification effect, and hence reduces variability compared to A 2. Simplicity of drawing sample; easy to check	1. If sampling interval is related to a periodic ordering of the population, increased variability may be introduced 2. Estimates of error likely to be high where there is stratification effect
C. Multistage random	Use a form of random sampling in each of the sampling stages where there are at least two stages	1. Sampling lists, identification, and numbering required only for members of sampling units selected in sample 2. If sampling units are geographically defined, cuts down field costs (i.e., travel)	1. Errors likely to be larger than in A or B for same sample size 2. Errors increase as number of sampling units selected decreases
1. With probability proportionate to size	Select sampling units with probability proportionate to their size	1. Reduces variability	1. Lack of knowledge of size of each sampling unit before selection increases variability
D. Stratified 1. Proportionate	Select from every sampling unit at other than last stage a random sample proportionate to size of sampling unit	1. Assures representativeness with respect to property which forms basis of classifying units; therefore yields less variability than A or C 2. Decreases chance of failing to include members of population because of classification process 3. Characteristics of each stratum can be estimated, and hence comparisons can be made	1. Requires accurate information on proportion of population in each stratum, otherwise increases error 2. If stratified lists are not available, may be costly to prepare them; possibility of faulty classification and hence increase in variability
2. Optimum allocation	Same as 1 except sample is proportionate to variability within strata as well as their size	1. Less variability for same sample size than 1	1. Requires knowledge of variability of pertinent characteristic within strata
3. Disproportionate	Same as 1 except that size of sample is not proportionate to size of sampling unit but is dictated by analytical considerations or convenience	1. More efficient than 1 for comparison of strata or where different errors are optimum for different strata	1. Less efficient than 1 for determining population characteristics; i.e., more variability for same sample size

397

TABLE 15.2 (*Continued*)

Type of Sampling	Brief Description	Advantages	Disadvantages
E. Cluster	Select sampling units by some form of random sampling; ultimate units are groups; select these at random and take a complete count of each	1. If clusters are geographically defined, yields lowest field costs 2. Requires listing only individuals in selected clusters 3. Characteristics of clusters as well as those of population can be estimated 4. Can be used for subsequent samples, since clusters, not individuals, are selected, and substitution of individuals may be permissible	1. Larger errors for comparable size than other probability samples 2. Requires ability to assign each member of population uniquely to a cluster; inability to do so may result in duplication or omission of individuals
F. Stratified cluster	Select clusters at random from every sampling unit	1. Reduces variability of plain cluster sampling	1. Disadvantages of stratified sampling added to those of cluster sampling 2. Since cluster properties may change, advantage of stratification may be reduced and make sample unusable for later research
G. Repetitive: multiple or sequential	Two or more samples of any of the above types are taken, using results from earlier samples to design later ones, or determine if they are necessary	1. Provides estimates of population characteristics which facilitate efficient planning of succeeding sample, therefore reduces error of final estimate 2. In the long run reduces number of observations required	1. Complicates administration of field work 2. More computation and analysis required than in nonrepetitive sampling 3. Sequential sampling can only be used where a very small sample can approximate representativeness and where the number of observations can be increased conveniently at any stage of the research
H. Judgment	Select a subgroup of the population which, on the basis of available information, can be judged to be representative of the total population; take a complete count or subsample of this group	1. Reduces cost of preparing sample and field work, since ultimate units can be selected so that they are close together	1. Variability and bias of estimates cannot be measured or controlled 2. Requires strong assumptions or considerable knowledge of population and subgroup selected
I. Quota	Classify population by pertinent properties; determine desired proportion of sample from each class; fix quotas for each observer	1. Same as above 2. Introduces some stratification effect	1. Introduces bias of observer's classification of subjects and nonrandom selection within classes

a Reproduced from R. L. Ackoff, *The Design of Social Research*, University of Chicago Press, Chicago, 1953, with permission of the publishers.

single number y, which is an estimate of the collective property Y in which we are interested. Of course, if we knew Y, the whole procedure would be unnecessary. Let us suppose, however, that we do know Y, but that we are permitted to use only an estimate of Y, y. In choosing our estimate we would clearly prefer one in which the cost due to the error $(y - Y)$ would, on the average, be as small as possible. Computation of such costs involves knowledge of the model in which y will be used and of the decision procedures that result. Historically, statisticians have had to develop methods of estimation in the context of "pure" science in which costs of error cannot be determined. Consequently, they defined formal criteria of good estimates in terms of consistency, efficiency, and sufficiency. Today it is often possible to estimate the costs of errors and to choose estimating procedures accordingly.

There are three general methods of obtaining estimates from samples, and we shall briefly describe each.

The Method of Moments. This method is due to Karl Pearson and is useful in estimating parameters of a distribution. Suppose we know that a sample comes from a population in which the density function for a single observation y is a function of x and of the parameters α, β, say $f(y, \alpha, \beta)$. We wish to estimate α and β from the sample. The first moment or mean of the population is defined as $\mu_1'(\alpha, \beta)$ where

$$\mu_1'(\alpha, \beta) = \int y\, f(y, \alpha, \beta)\, dy,$$

and the rth moment about the mean is $\mu_r(\alpha, \beta)$ where

$$\mu_r(\alpha, \beta) = \int [y - \mu_1'(\alpha, \beta)]^r f(y, \alpha, \beta)\, dy.$$

Pearson's method of estimating α, β is to calculate the corresponding moments from the sample and to equate them to the μ's. Thus we solve the equations[9]

$$\mu_1'(\alpha, \beta) = \frac{1}{n} \sum_{k=1}^{n} y_k = \bar{y},$$

$$\mu_2(\alpha, \beta) = \frac{1}{n-1} \sum_{k=1}^{n} (y_k - \bar{y})^2,$$

and in general if there are more than two parameters, we would use higher moments.

The Method of Maximum Likelihood. This method, due to R. A. Fisher, is of wider application than the previous method. However, in many cases it leads to the same results. Fisher argued that the probability of observing the

[9] For the second moment there are theoretical reasons why the divisor $(n - 1)$ is preferred to n.

sample actually seen, that is, n observations such that the kth observation lies between y_k and $y_k + dy_k$, is

$$f(y_1, \alpha, \beta)f(y_2, \alpha, \beta) \cdots f(y_n, \alpha, \beta) \, dy_1 \, dy_2 \cdots dy_n,$$

and that α, β should be chosen so as to make the actual observations more probable than any others. For convenience of maximization Fisher defined the likelihood function, $L(\alpha, \beta)$, as the logarithm of the multidimensional density function. Thus

$$L(\alpha, \beta) = \sum_{k=1}^{n} \log f(y_k, \alpha, \beta).$$

Maximization of L is equivalent to maximization of the probability, and we find α, β by solving the equations

$$\frac{\partial L}{\partial \alpha} = \sum_{k=1}^{n} \frac{1}{f(y_k, \alpha, \beta)} \frac{\partial f(y_k, \alpha, \beta)}{\partial \alpha} = 0$$

$$\frac{\partial L}{\partial \beta} = \sum_{k=1}^{n} \frac{1}{f(y_k, \alpha, \beta)} \frac{\partial f(y_k, \alpha, \beta)}{\partial \beta} = 0.$$

Bayesian Estimates.   In both of the previous methods the only information used, apart from that contained in the sample, was the form of the distribution. It often happens that we also know something about the distribution of the parameters. In any given population, of course, the parameters are fixed and do not have a distribution in the normal sense, but there are many occasions when we do not know the population from which the sample came. We only know the probability that it came from each of several populations. For example, suppose that we have adjusted a machine and that we use a go–no-go gauge on the first five items produced. This sample of five may have come from the output population of a correctly adjusted machine, or it may be from an incorrectly adjusted machine. We know from past experience that the machine is incorrectly set 25 per cent of the time and that when it is wrong it produces 30 per cent defectives. When it is right, it produces 5 per cent defectives. Assume that in our sample of five there was one defective. We now ask two questions:

1. What is the probability that the machine is correctly adjusted?
2. What is the expected fraction defective, if we do not readjust the machine?

Here we are asking what would happen, on the average, over all those occasions when a sample of five, following an adjustment, produced one defective. As we shall see, this is quite different from the average following *all* adjustments.

If the machine was correctly set, the probability of one defective in a sample of five is

$$5 \times (0.95)^4 \times 0.05 = 0.20363.$$

If the machine was wrongly adjusted, the probability of one defective is

$$5 \times (0.7)^4 \times 0.3 = 0.36015.$$

The probability that it was correctly set *and* produced one defective is

$$0.75 \times 0.20363 = 0.15272.$$

The probability that it was *in*correctly set and produced one defective is

$$0.25 \times 0.36015 = 0.09004.$$

Thus, of the occasions when it produces one defective, it is correctly set for a fraction of the time,

$$\frac{0.15272}{0.15272 + 0.09004} = 63 \text{ per cent.}$$

The fraction defective will be 5 per cent on 63 per cent of the occasions and 30 per cent on 37 per cent of the occasions. Thus our estimate of the average defective is

$$0.05 \times 0.63 + 0.3 \times 0.37 = 0.1425.$$

If we had used only the information in the sample, our estimate of the fraction defective would have been 1 in 5, or 0.20.

The Bayesian method has two apparent advantages over the other methods of estimation. First, it permits us to use *prior* information that we may have and, second, we can easily apply it directly to estimation of costs.

THE FORM OF FUNCTIONS AND THE MODEL

A model may be deficient because it contains incorrect functions or because it has an incorrect form as a whole. To find a function to express the relationship between variables is to find a curve, surface, or hypersurface (depending on the number of variables) that "fits" the data. Fitting a function, then, is a multidimensional estimation problem. Once the form of the function (e.g., normal, exponential, or gamma) has been selected, it remains to select the parameters of the function, itself a problem of estimation. There is no systematic way of selecting the best-fitting function for a set of data. Such a choice is usually made on the basis of a priori information about the relationship between the variables or by visually examining plots of the data. The larger the vocabulary of functional forms available to the researcher, the better his choice is likely to be. But although there is no limit to the number of functions that can be examined, in practice we require a "simple" function with as few variables as possible. If we have n observations, we can always obtain an exact fit by using a function with n parameters. If we have a single independent variable, we could use a curve of the $(n - 1)$th degree. Alternatively, we could use $(n - 1)$ different independent variables and a linear function; between these alternatives many other possibilities exist. However, none of them are of any value in a predictive sense. Thus some prior knowledge of the class of functions to be examined is essential. Within each class many functional forms exist and, because there is no available technique for making an optimal selection, the best that can be done is to examine different functional forms by comparing the distribution of estimating errors that they yield. Such a comparison involves testing the bias and variability of the estimates yielded by the function.

The goodness of a fit of a function should not be tested by use of the same data that are employed to obtain the fit. Therefore, part of the available data should be kept in reserve for testing the function. For example, in testing a function that is used to forecast demand, the function should be tested on data not used to develop the forecast, because the function is not likely to perform as well on previously unused data and it is this performance that is relevant.

In order to test a function (within, or of, the model), one must compare values of the dependent variable computed from the function with actual (observed) values of the variable. Let d_i represent the differences between the predicted and actual values. Then, to test the bias of the function, one tests the hypothesis $H_0 : E(d_i) = 0$; that is, the expected value of the differences is equal to zero. If the observed differences can be assumed to be normally distributed, the t-test can be used to test this hypothesis.

If the hypothesis, H_0, is rejected the model can be assumed to be biased. An explanation for the bias should be sought and, if found, the function should be modified appropriately. An unexplained "correction factor" should be added to the function only if no explanation can be found and if the data indicate that the bias is statistically stable, that is, if the d_i can be assumed to be a random sample from a well-defined probability density function.

Even if we have found an unbiased method of estimation, it may not be good enough for our purposes. We must also consider the reproducibility of our results. Thus in estimating a quantity whose true (but unknown) value is zero, we might have a procedure that always yields either plus or minus one thousand, with equal probabilities. Such a procedure is unbiased but it lacks precision. In fact we might prefer a second procedure which had a bias of, say, ten, but in which results always lie between plus and minus one hundred.

Statisticians usually measure precision by the standard deviation of the estimate. If we imagine the procedure (including drawing the sample, making measurements, and computing the estimate) repeated infinitely often, the estimates would have a standard deviation. If it is small, Chebychev's inequality shows that on any specific occasion when we use the procedure, the estimate will have a high probability of being close to the expected value. If the procedure is unbiased so that the expected value is zero, our estimate (made once!) will probably be close to the true value. Of course, we can only decide if the estimate is close enough when we know how it is to be used. For example, in a marketing experiment designed to find sales response to advertising expenditure, it was necessary to estimate sales in the absence of the experiment. Because the anticipated response to advertising was less than 5 per cent, it was essential to find estimates that were accurate within much less than 5 per cent. On the other hand, for many production scheduling problems, we can easily tolerate sales estimates that are subject to 5 per cent errors. Ultimately, an estimating procedure stands or falls on how well the model performs in the situation in which it is used.

⊀ TESTING THE SOLUTION

The OR solution to a problem is supposed to yield better performance than does some alternative procedure (usually the one currently in use). Acceptance of the solution by the decision maker depends more on the demonstration of such superiority than it does on appreciation of the research procedures.

A solution may be tested prospectively (against future performance). Where they are possible, prospective tests should be performed on as modest a scale as possible, that is, on as small a part of the system as can be used effectively for this purpose. Frequently it is possible to use the proposed solution on paper, alongside the existing system. This may permit a very realistic evaluation.

In a retrospective test it is necessary to reconstruct what actually did happen in the past. Values of the variables that appear in the model are seldom readily available. They usually have to be extracted from records that were not intended for this purpose. For example, one may want to know demand for a product per period, but the records may only show shipments. The effect of unfilled orders, canceled orders, and lag time in shipments must be taken into account in generating the estimate of demand.

When past data are used, it is important that the periods included cover the range of situations that are likely to appear in the future. Testing over an unusually good or bad time period may not be convincing to the decision maker.

The test, whether it uses past or future data, should be directed toward estimating the average improvement in performance that the proposed solution yields, and its variability. It is usually desirable to determine the probability that the proposed solution will not work as effectively as the alternative to it. Clearly, the smaller this probability is, the better.

The cost of putting the new solution into effect should be subtracted from the expected improvement in order to estimate *net* improvement.

In evaluating the solution, estimates of the performance of the system should be obtained without use of the model from which the solution is derived. If the solution is correctly derived from the model, and if the model is an exact representation of reality, the solution is necessarily better than any alternative decision procedure. But the question being asked involves the correspondence of the model to reality. We cannot assume the answer.

In some cases it is not possible to test the solution either retrospectively or prospectively. It may then be possible to evaluate the solution by "sensitivity analysis." Such an analysis consists of determining by how much the estimates used in the solution would have to be in error before the proposed solution performs less satisfactorily than the alternative decision procedure. As an example, let us turn to a "toy" decision model

$$U = XY + \frac{1}{X}$$

for which

$$X^0 = \frac{1}{\sqrt{Y}}$$

and

$$U^0 = 2\sqrt{Y}.$$

Suppose that in the past an alternative decision rule yielded a cost of 14.5 and that we have just obtained an estimate of Y, $y = 25$. Hence our estimate of the optimal value of X is $x^0 = 1/\sqrt{y} = \frac{1}{5}$. We now wish to determine whether the recommended procedure (i.e., estimation of Y as y plus the policy $x^0 = 1/\sqrt{y}$) will lower costs in the future.

One way of answering the question is to find how large Y would have to be before the policy $x^0 = \frac{1}{5}$ would result in costs in excess of past performance; that is, the values of Y for which

$$u^0 = \frac{Y}{5} + 5 \geq 14.5.$$

We obtain

$$Y \geq 47.5.$$

If we consider that our estimation procedure is unlikely to yield $y = 25$ when the true value exceeds 47.5, we decide that $x^0 = \frac{1}{5}$ will result in improvement. This line of reasoning implies that Y may change between our estimation of its value and the implementation of the policy. We are really asking, can Y nearly double in this time interval?

On the other hand, Y may be fixed, but our estimation procedure may be relatively inaccurate. In this case we might ask how much error in the estimate can be tolerated before $x^0 = 1/\sqrt{y}$ becomes worse than past performance. If the true value of Y is 25, then $x^0 = 1/\sqrt{y}$ would be worse if

$$\frac{25}{\sqrt{y}} + \sqrt{y} \geq 14.5.$$

This reduces to

$$y - 14.5y + 25 \geq 0,$$

the roots of which are $(\sqrt{y} - 2)$ and $(\sqrt{y} - 12.5)$. Hence, for x^0 to yield a cost greater than 14.5, either $y < 4$ or $y > 156.25$. If we judge that errors of this magnitude are unlikely, we consider our model to be insensitive to errors of estimation. If such errors are judged to be likely, the solution would not be reliable and would require modification.

It should be noted that the procedure just described does not test the validity of the model itself. It could tell us that Y is in fact equal to 25, but because the model is inadequate, the alleged optimal policy is incorrect. The only way to examine the validity of the model would be to use knowledge of the policy that yielded costs of 14.5. Suppose that the past policy were $x = \frac{1}{3}$; then in our model we require Y such that

$$\tfrac{1}{3}Y + 3 = 14.5$$

or

$$Y = 34.5.$$

If we consider it unlikely that an estimate of 25 would be obtained when the true value of Y is 34.5, we would have to reexamine the assumptions on which the model was built.

Usually, of course, several variables are involved and sensitivity to simultaneous errors should be determined. This can be done in most cases by an extension of the procedure just described.

Sensitivity analysis need not be restricted to situations in which retrospective and prospective tests cannot be conducted. It can also be used to determine whether the cost involved in such testing is justified.

Finally, it should be remembered that when a solution is put into operation improvements in performance may not be instantaneous. There may be a period of transition during which performance actually deteriorates. It is important to determine the magnitude and duration of this loss and to inform the decision maker of this. Otherwise he may authorize implementation but cancel it when he learns that expected improvements are not obtained at once. As we pointed out earlier (Chapter 4), simulation may be required to estimate the characteristics of the transition period.

CONCLUSION

We have considered the various ways in which a model may be defective and the steps that can be taken to minimize such deficiencies. The researcher should constantly evaluate his own decisions and procedures and take nothing for granted without examining the grounds on which they are accepted and without being aware of their consequences. Methodological self-conscious-ness, ability to define and measure, and command of a wide variety of statistical techniques are essential for producing effective solutions to real problems. The researcher who dedicates his efforts to improving the decision processes of others should be equally dedicated to improving his own research-decision processes.

The manager who is served by OR can seldom understand the technical details of the model and the process of deriving solutions from it. However, he can generally grasp the logic of the approach that has been used if the researcher effectively exposes it to him; but in most cases the acceptance of recommendations coming from research is based in part on faith and con-fidence in the methodological and technical competence of the researchers. This confidence is usually greatly affected by the way in which the researcher goes about testing his work and the conclusions drawn from it.

Managers are at least as sensitive to the quality of the research process as researchers are to the quality of the managers' decision processes. Managers will not normally act on research recommendation unless they understand how they were obtained and have some appreciation of the extent to which their interests have been safeguarded in the research process. The researcher should not make the mistake of assuming that the decision maker cannot distinguish between "good" and "bad" research because he is not a researcher himself. Keep in mind that one does not have to be able to lay an egg in order to tell the difference between a good and a bad one.

DISCUSSION TOPICS

1. Do you believe the following statement is true? Why? Can you find any relevant evidence?

The less we understand a phenomenon, the more variables we require to explain it.

2. Determine the correlation between the weights and heights of your class members. What does the result prove? Do the same for annual advertising (or R&D) expenditures and gross sales for a number of companies. Repeat the latter, using this year's expenditures on advertising (or R&D) and last year's sales. Compare the results and discuss their significance.

3. Provide operational definitions and appropriate measures for a few of the following: profit, overhead costs, employee morale, product leadership, competition, poverty, maintain-ability, reliability, bad drivers, and organization.

4. Identify some variables that are usually treated as intangibles or qualitative and try to find a way of treating them quantitatively.

5. Is gross national product (GNP) a measure of anything? If yes, what type of scale does it employ? Consider "I.Q." and "course grades" in the same way.

6. What sampling procedures would you use in the following and why?

   (*a*) To determine the distribution of annual income of full-time students at your school.

   (*b*) To determine the average percent of time classrooms are in use in your school during the semester between 9:00 a.m. and 5:00 p.m. on week days.

   (*c*) To determine the frequency of use in writing of words in the English language in the United States.

   (*d*) To determine whether there is a difference in pricing policies between supermarkets that give trading stamps and those that do not.

7. The "robustness" of an estimating procedure is its insensitivity to the assumptions on which it is based. How would you go about testing for such robustness of the various types of estimating procedure in a particular situation with which you are familiar and in which an estimate is required?

8. Find several case studies in the OR literature and evaluate the model-testing procedures used.

Suggested Readings

Here we repeat some of the suggestions for reading already made in the text of this chapter and add a few.

For general coverage of statistical methods: Hoel (1954) and Mood and Graybill (1963).

For correlation and regression analysis: Ezekial and Fox (1959).

For experimental design and analysis: Cochran and Cox (1950).

For definition and measurement: Ackoff (1962).

For sampling: a survey in Ackoff (1962), details in Cochran (1963).

For estimation: a survey in Ackoff (1962), details in Raiffa and Schlifer (1961).

Bibliography

Ackoff, R. L., *Scientific Method: Optimizing Applied Research Decisions*, John Wiley and Sons, New York, 1962.

Campbell, N. R., *An Account of the Principles of Measurement and Calculation*, Longmans, New York, 1928.

Chambers, J. C., and D. F. Clark, "The Determination of Observational Errors Occurring in Information Collection Processes," *Research Memorandum* 4, Operations Research Group, Case Institute of Technology, Cleveland, Ohio, September 30, 1957.

Chernoff, H., and L. E. Moses, *Elementary Decision Theory*, John Wiley and Sons, New York, 1959.

Churchman, C. W., and P. Ratoosh (eds.), *Measurement: Definitions and Theories*, John Wiley and Sons, New York, 1959.

Clark, D. F., R. L. Ackoff, and C. Waid, "Allocation of Sales Effort in the Lamp Division of the General Electric Company," *Operations Research*, 4 (December 1956), 629–647.

Cochran, W. G., *Sampling Techniques*, 2nd ed., John Wiley and Sons, New York, 1963.

———, and G. M. Cox, *Experimental Designs*, John Wiley and Sons, New York, 1950.

Darwin, C., E. Sears, et al., "A Discussion on Units and Standards," *Proceedings of the Royal Society of London*, 186A (1946), 149–217.

Deming, W. E., *Sample Design in Business Research*, John Wiley and Sons, New York, 1960.

Ezekiel, M. J. B., and K. A. Fox, *Methods of Correlation and Regression Analysis*, 3rd ed., John Wiley and Sons, New York, 1959.

Fisher, R. A., "Theory of Statistical Estimation," *Proceedings of the Cambridge Philosophical Society*, 22 (1925).

Gupta, S. K., *A Theory of Adjusting Parameter-Estimates in Decision Models*, Ph.D. Thesis in Operations Research, Case Institute of Technology, Cleveland Ohio, May 1960.

Hansen, M. H., W. N. Hurwitz, and W. G. Madow, *Sample Survey Methods and Theory*, Vol. 1, John Wiley and Sons, New York, 1953.

Hoel, P. G., *Introduction to Mathematical Statistics*, 2nd ed., John Wiley and Sons, New York, 1954.

Mood, A. L., and F. A. Graybill, *Introduction to the Theory of Statistics*, 2nd ed., McGraw-Hill Book Co., New York, 1963.

Raiffa, H., and R. Schlaifer, *Applied Statistical Decision Theory*, Division of Research, Graduate School of Business Administration, Harvard University, Boston, 1961.

Shannon, C. E., and W. Weaver, *The Mathematical Theory of Communication*, The University of Illinois Press, Urbana, 1949.

Stevens, S. S., "On the Theory of Scales of Measurements," *Science*, 103 (1946), 677–680.

CHAPTER **16**

Implementing and
Controlling the Solution

INTRODUCTION

There is a common tendency to think of the implementation of a problem's solution that is obtained by research as an activity that is initiated after the research is completed and for which the researchers have no major responsibility. In operations research, however, because the objective is to improve the performance of the system involved, the research is not completed until that improvement is obtained and unless it is maintained, that is, controlled.

In each phase of research discussed so far and in controlling the solution it is possible either to construct models of the research decisions or models of parts of them. This is not yet true of implementation. The problems in this essentially "artistic" phase of research are largely psychological and socio-logical in character; hence progress in solving them will probably have to await further developments in the behavioral sciences. In the meantime, dis-cussions of implementation are primarily based on experience and therefore are likely to contain more opinion than fact. The discussion of implementation in this chapter is no exception.

The opportunity to implement and control a solution comes only after the solution has been accepted by the responsible managers. Their acceptance depends not only on the quality of the research and the gains promised by the solution, but also on the nature and extent of their involvement in the research process and their identification with its results. We therefore first consider the relationship of managers to the research effort, then implementa-tion, and finally control.

PLANNING FOR ACCEPTABILITY AND
ACCEPTANCE OF THE SOLUTION

How little we know about obtaining acceptance of research results is illustrated by some experimental work by Churchman and Ratoosh (1960). They have developed a game for a four-man team, which involves managing a small simulated business. The underlying model of the market is a simple one, which can be explicitly formulated and solved. In the main the players have been graduate students in management who have had courses that equip them to construct the model and to derive the solution.

One member of the team is a "plant." He knows the solution to the game. After a number of plays of the game by a team—during which few teams have made an effort to construct a model and derive a solution—the "plant" pretends to discover the solution and suggests its adoption to the other team members. Only a very small portion of the teams have accepted the suggestion.

The experiments are directed toward finding the conditions under which a suggested solution to a problem will be accepted and implemented. Using what is "known" about these phenomena—most of which is obviously folklore—the experimenters have not yet been able to find a way to present the solution to teams so that it has a significant chance of being accepted.

Many professional OR men to whom these results have been presented have made suggestions intended to increase the likelihood of acceptance. These have been tested systematically in the experimental situation but have yielded no improvement in the results.

The moral of this extremely informative and provocative experiment is that at present we do not know enough to assure acceptance of research results under seemingly simple and favorable conditions over which the experimenters have considerable control. However, for reasons that we do not yet completely understand, the acceptance rate for solutions obtained in practice is greater than that obtained under the experimental conditions. This may indicate that the art of obtaining acceptance of solutions is more highly developed than the experimental results indicate, but we are not conscious of the reasons for the greater success in practice. Keeping this in mind let us examine this art as best as we can.

The OR team should begin to make the solution to the problem acceptable to managers before it is obtained. Ultimate acceptance of the solution by managers depends largely on their belief that the problem solved is the one they have and on their understanding of and trust in the process by which a solution was obtained. Hence their participation in the research is not only desirable but practically essential.

Each relevant manager should be met individually for consultation and discussion during the research. Such sessions should be supplemented by regularly scheduled meetings with the entire group of relevant managers organized as an advisory and review board. These sessions should occur every four to eight weeks, depending on the rate of progress and on the duration of the study. They should be held even if there is relatively little to report; hence they may be brief. Such meetings, however, can often result in removing the cause for delay; for example, sluggish collection of data by company personnel or too many diverting demands being made on the operations researchers' time.

During the early stages of the first project done in a company, some time should be spent in developing a general understanding of the nature of OR in management. This task is facilitated by the availability of at least two short books addressed to managers for this purpose: Duckworth (1962) and Ackoff and Rivett (1963). The use of outside speakers can often help in securing and maintaining managers' interest, particularly if cases from related organizations are frequently referred to. The equivalent of two to three days in an OR "appreciation course" can have a considerable payoff to managers and researchers as well. Many such courses are offered by universities and consulting groups. These are useful in convincing one or two key managers of the desirability of a course "at home and on sight" for a larger number of managers.

Continuous review of the work in progress by managers gives them assurance that all the significant aspects of the problem have been taken into account in a satisfactory way. It also enables them to absorb the research methods, techniques, tools, and results in small doses. This usually produces a better understanding of the research process than can be obtained from one large-scale confrontation in the form of a final report.

It may be difficult to induce managers to attend the first few formal meetings, but if these are well-run and fruitful, resistance dissipates rapidly. Participation of the managers who can benefit most from the research is more likely if they are being charged for the research. For this reason it is always desirable to have those managers for whom the research is being done pay for it. It is common, however, to have the corporation, for example, pay for research being done on a division's operations. Although it may seem that a manager should welcome research for which he does not have to pay, this is seldom the case. Only if he pays for it, can he be sure that the research is serving his, rather than someone else's, best interests. Therefore, wherever possible, he should at least share in the cost of the research.

Managers who are *not* directly involved in the research but occupy positions at the same level as those who are, should be included in the advisory and review group if possible. Their early participation is desirable because the project may eventually expand into their areas. Even if this is not so, it will make them more receptive to subsequent research in their own areas.

If a number of managers at the same level are involved in a study, the advisory group should also include one manager at a higher level who is in a position to coordinate the activities of the others.

It is not uncommon for one or more managers to believe that they know what the solution to the problem under study is before the study is started and to declare themselves accordingly. This may place them in a position of having to save face if the research produces unexpected results. If they participate in the research, they have the opportunity to modify their position slowly, so that the shift is almost imperceptible. It is important for the researcher to be aware of the potential opposition that an a priori position can generate. The researchers should take steps to assist the manager out of such a position without embarrassing him. On the other hand, the researchers should not set about to prove a position taken before the research had begun, however loyal they are to the manager involved. The reasons for this are too obvious to require discussion.

Because most OR studies extend over a number of months and because most organizations are periodically "reorganized," it is desirable to take steps to prevent the collapse of the project or the necessity to resell the problem if any one manager is moved from his position to another. This is best done by involving as many people in each relevant division or department of the organization as is possible, particularly those who are second in command.

Once confidence in the research team builds up in management, the problem of "unselling" may become more serious than that of selling. A few successes will incline managers to accept results that have not been thoroughly tested, particularly when they are under pressure.

The researchers frequently may not have as much time as they would like, but when they are so pressed it is important for them to point out what sacrifices in normal research procedures have been made, so that management is fully aware of the risks involved in accepting hastily obtained results.

No amount of formal arrangements between researchers and managers can be as important as warm and friendly personal relations based on mutual respect and understanding of common problems. An ounce of friendship is worth many pounds of care. Maintenance of good personal relationships with managers depends, to a large extent, on the ability of the OR team members to distinguish between their *findings* and their *opinions* when communicating with managers. Researchers should keep in mind that their expertise lies in their ability to find solutions to problems, not in *having* solutions to them.

Needless to say, the success of an OR team depends greatly on the effectiveness with which its members communicate *with* (not merely *to*) managers and others in the organization. Responsibility for reporting, therefore, should be given to the most effective communicator on the team, regardless of his rank. Most of us are quite *in*sensitive to our deficiencies in communication and are hypersensitive to criticism of our efforts along these lines. It is essential that we learn to face the facts about our speaking and writing, so that we can attempt to improve them.

Whenever possible, reports should be given orally rather than in writing. This permits feedback, that is, questions and answers. Questions are of no value, however, if they are not understood by the speaker. To promote such understanding, when the intent of a question is in doubt the speaker should restate it to the satisfaction of the questioner. This not only aids communication but indicates respect for the questioner and his remarks.

Oral presentations should not be read from a manuscript, because reports that are read tend to be dull and the need to pay attention to the manuscript makes the reader less responsive to the audience. Empathy with the audience is the most important attribute of an effective communicator; he must perceive and understand the response of the audience to what he is saying.

Presentations should be in the language of the audience, rather than in the jargon of OR. It is always difficult to present technical work nontechnically, but until this can be done, the material is not fully understood by the speaker or writer himself. Therefore, the need to present research results nontechnically should be treated not as a chore, but as a challenge to one's own understanding of the material to be presented.

Equations and derivations should not be presented to managers, except in emergencies or when specifically requested. Nevertheless, it should be made clear that technical paraphernalia lie behind what is being presented and are available on call.

Reports that must be written should not be modeled on O'Henry's short stories; that is, they should not have surprise endings. One can hardly do better than follow Aristotle's advice in organizing a written or an oral report: it should have three parts—a beginning, a middle, and an end. The beginning should state what is going to be done, the middle should do it, and the end should summarize what has been done.

Visual aids are usually required in oral presentations of OR. For small audiences flipcharts are best, because they can be used in a fully illuminated room and do not separate the speaker from his audience. The charts, or other visual aids, should be easy to read from the back of the room and *should be pretested to make certain that they are.* Individual charts or slides should contain only one idea simply stated, leaving much more of the surface blank than is covered with lettering.

Copies of the charts should be made on normal-size paper and distributed to the audience *after* the presentation as a record of it. The charts should therefore provide a self-sufficient digest of the oral report.

A report written to communicate results to management should be different from one prepared as a technical record that permits reproduction of the study. It is sometimes possible to combine these functions by use of technical appendices, but it should be made clear that only one part is intended for management. This can be done effectively by using paper of different colors in the two sections.

IMPLEMENTATION

Industrial and business managers who use OR usually expect the researchers to participate in implementing their results; hence they frequently select OR staff members for their ability to "follow through." To those who wish to do research on real problems but do not wish to be involved in implementing the results, this expectation of managers may not seem to be a good reason for becoming so involved. However, there is a good scientific justification for such involvement. It is only through implementation that many research results can be adequately tested. The larger and more complex the problem, the more likely this is to be the case. Hence implementation is always the "ultimate"—and sometimes the only—test of the value of a solution.

Implementation of a solution is very likely to raise problems that had not been anticipated during the research; hence it usually requires modification of the solution. If these modifications are not made by the researchers, the solution may either be maladjusted by those not equipped to make a proper adjustment or rejected by those who must carry it out and find it difficult to do so. If adjustments to a solution are required, it is clear that those who are responsible for having obtained the solution are in the best position to make the adjustments.

The operation researcher's attitiude toward implementation should be similar to that of an architect toward supervising the construction of a building that he has designed. To the architect, construction of his building is the ultimate consummation of his efforts. He cannot allow others to distort his design. He knows that problems will arise during construction that he has not anticipated and that, together with the contractors and clients, he can work out satisfactory solutions that do not change the essential characteristics of his design. Once the architect has obtained a design that satisfies him and his client, he prepares detailed working drawings and specifications that constitute a program for implementation. In this task he utilizes many persons with special skills, such as engineers and material experts.

The operations researcher, like the architect, should prepare detailed instructions for those who will carry out the solution; he must specify, program, and schedule their activities, and he must do so in their language. He must make sure that those who are to follow the instructions understand them and the reasons behind them. This may require a number of "briefings" of those who will put the solution into effect.

It is desirable to involve those who must participate in implementation at all levels of the organization in preparation for the implementation program. Their involvement prevents specifying the impossible and helps elicit a cooperative attitude from them. It also provides the decision makers with assurance of the "implementability" of the solution—an important consideration for them in deciding whether or not to accept the solution.

In preparing plans for a complex implementation it has often been found helpful to organize a formal advisory group consisting of those who will supervise aspects of the implementation. The more responsibility such a group can be given in preparing the plan, the better.

Those who are affected by the implementation, even though not involved in carrying it out, should also be taken into account. If so inclined, they can sabotage a solution in either apparent or subtle ways. Refusal to follow instructions, quitting, or even strikes may result, or they can make a system fail by other forms of noncollaboration that are difficult to detect. However, those who are affected should be taken into account not only because of possible hostility, but also because they can in many cases contribute positively to the solution and improve it. Some examples may clarify these possibilities.

The results of a study of a company's overall marketing strategy involved changing the salesmen's incentive plan. In consultation with management the researchers had previously agreed that the new plan must satisfy two conditions. First, it should be so designed that each salesman could calculate his own incentive earnings monthly and thus have no reason to distrust company calculations. In order to satisfy this condition, the best plan that the researchers could develop had to be modified, hence weakened so that it could be salesman-computable. In addition, separate tables had to be prepared for each of about a hundred salesmen, so that his computational task would be as simple as possible. Second, it was agreed that the plan should be such that if it had been in operation over the last two years, no more than 5 per cent of the salesmen would have had a lower total annual earning.

When the plan was developed, an extended meeting with all the salesmen was held. The researchers explained the reasoning behind the new plan and each of its characteristics, including those just mentioned. The salesmen asked many questions. Each question was answered in detail. Some of the answers required minor modifications in the procedures, most of which were made on the spot. When no further questions remained, the vice-president of marketing asked for a vote to learn whether the salesmen preferred the old plan or the new one. The vote was almost unanimously in favor of the new one.

In the second year improvements in the plan were proposed, which had grown out of the first year's experience. These were taken up with the salesmen in the same way and again received overwhelming support.

While still preparing the third plan, a group of the salesmen were called in for a discussion of the proposed changes before they were finalized. During the discussion they suggested certain modifications, which required violation of the computability requirement. When this was pointed out to them, they argued that there was no need for this requirement. They were willing to have the computations made for them centrally. It was then possible to introduce even greater improvements than had been anticipated.

In another case in which the management of an airline was hesitant to accept a new scheduling plan for stewardesses because it believed the results to be unacceptable to the young ladies, meetings were held with their union representatives. Management's apprehension turned out to be ill-founded because the stewardesses felt that the advantages to them of the new scheme far outweighed the disadvantages. In the process the managers learned something that they had not known before about a class of their employees.

In several cases it has been possible to enlist even the cooperation of customers who were under no compulsion to cooperate. For example, a study of inventories in one company revealed that if their wholesalers changed their ordering procedures in a certain way, both they and the company would benefit. Initial meetings were held with the wholesalers collectively, and then OR men visited each wholesaler separately and worked out a detailed operating procedure to suit his situation. Nevertheless, only a few wholesalers were willing to install the procedure. For these, the benefits were almost immediate, and they so reported to the others. Within a year more than 80 per cent of the wholesalers had converted to the new ordering procedures, and many suggested further changes that benefited both them and the company.

On the other hand, in a case in which a rigorous quantitative procedure was developed for making bids on construction jobs, those who had responsibility for preparing these bids felt that their task was being dehumanized and refused to adopt the new procedures. The possibility of such a response should have been taken into account in developing the procedure. It was taken into account in a second study done for another division of the same company, and the results were implemented there because the staff members participated in the development of new, more attractive, and more important tasks for themselves.

Planning for implementation, then, should involve the managers and all those who will be affected by it directly or indirectly. Once developed, the implementation plan should be pretested and "debugged." Actual performance of the solution after implementation should be compared with expectations and, where the divergence is significant, the reasons for it should be determined and appropriate adjustments should be made. Such evaluation and modification of implementation procedures are aspects of controlling the solution.

CONTROL

When the implementation of a solution extends over a significantly long period of time, the conditions under which the solution was obtained may change. For example, there may be an unexpected breakthrough in research or development, or a shift in the economy and demand for the goods or services, or a change in production technology, a competitor's strategy, interest rates on capital, or availability of skilled personnel. Such changes may significantly alter the nature of the problem, hence the effectiveness of the solution. The types of changes in the system that can occur can be classified as follows:

1. Changes in the utility of outcomes that affect the appropriateness of the measure of performance that was used; for example, if a major competitor significantly decreases its time to service customers, the value placed on service time in the company may change.

2. Changes in what is controllable; for example, a change in the law or its interpretation may permit a company to purchase another company that it could not acquire previously.

3. Changes in the constraints over control; for example, the acquisition of another company may change the amount of storage space available, hence increase an upper space limit imposed on inventories.

4. Changes in the values of parameters; for example, change in average demand per month for a product, which change affects its optimal purchase quantity.

5. Changes in the structure of the system, hence in the relationship between the measure of performance and the controlled variables and parameters; for example, sales may become more sensitive to price during a recession than they were during a prosperous period.

A solution may go out of control even when the system remains in control, either because the implementation plan is defective (e.g., a computer program is in error) or the plan is being executed incorrectly (e.g., the card-punch operators are making too many errors). Hence we distinguish between two aspects of controlling the solution: checking the system and checking the implementation.

The systems with which OR deals are almost certain to change in significant ways over time, and even the best-installed implementation procedures are bound to deteriorate over time. If preventive or corrective measures are not designed into the solution-procedure that is installed, the measures may be taken by someone who is not able to make the appropriate modifications of these procedures or, worse yet, the solution may be abandoned and replaced by the procedure that it had replaced. Hence it is essential to design controls into the implementation procedure and to make certain that these are exercised by qualified personnel.

For example, a manufacturer of industrial equipment recently had a study made of its parts-production and inventory-control system. The system that was developed involved using a reorder point (defined by a stock level) and a reorder quantity for each of several thousand parts. All the necessary information and the decision rules were put onto a computer, so that the total system was automated. Within six months it was apparent that inventories were increasing more rapidly than those who had designed the system had promised they would decrease. The responsible manager could get no satisfactory explanation of what was happening; hence he called on an external OR man to inspect the system and to advise him as to what he should do. After a few hours spent in learning about the system, the consultant drew a sample of thirty-five parts whose stock level was above the maximum allowed when the new system was installed. He then traced their history over the nine months since the system's installation. He found that more than one half of the parts had been reordered before their stock levels had been reduced to the appropriate maximum allowable quantity in the new system, and in some cases, had been reordered after this and again before reaching this quantity. The consultant also examined the history of about two dozen "mated parts," such as nuts and bolts, each of which was never used without the other. In every case he found that different quantities were recorded as having been consumed. The first discovery was contradictory to the rules by which the system was supposed to be operating, and the second was physically impossible. Clearly, the system was not operating as it was supposed to. A project was launched to set it right, and eventually it succeeded. Almost all the difficulties were found in the implementation program. This system had narrowly missed being completely discarded, together with the computers and men that were used to implement it.

Changes in the utility of outcomes can be determined either by periodically checking the measures of utility incorporated into the measure of performance or by reexamining the utility assumptions built into this measure. Such checks need only be performed when there is some indication that a change has taken place or is about to take place. Therefore, the solution controllers need access to those managers who are most likely to reflect changes in organizational utilities.

To check possible changes in controllable variables and in the constraints on them, regular contact with relevant management is also required. It is important to make these managers aware of this checking process, so that they will call potential or actual changes of these types to the solution controller's attention.

Implementation must be checked and controlled in the same way as production or clerical processes. Knowledge of statistical quality control and inspection procedures is therefore very relevant. For information of these procedures, see Duncan (1952), Grant (1952), Juran (1946), Littauer (1950), Shewhart (1939), and Tippett (1950).

Loss of control because of changes in structure is more difficult to guard against. Two essentially different approaches can be taken. These are illustrated in quality control of a production process. One may check the quality of the final product only, or one may also check the quality of parts or subassemblies of which the final product is composed. The second method increases the cost of control but reduces the costs that are due to defects. The same is true in controlling a solution. One can set a procedure for determining when a solution produces results that differ significantly from what was predicted and then look for the causes of this defect. On the other hand, one can set up controls on each aspect of the system and the implementation process. Because the second procedure may prevent a defective application of the solution, its greater cost must be weighed against the cost of error that it may prevent.

Controlling the Solution as a Whole

A solution is accepted by management on the basis of the promise that it appears to have. The promise may take one of two forms:

1. An improvement over the previous performance of a procedure which the solution is to replace. This promise may be in the form of an anticipated average difference in performance; for example, the solution will reduce monthly costs by an average of 10 per cent. Ideally, such a promise should be more precise and should show how the distributions of performances associated with the old and new procedures will differ. This would specify not only the mean difference but also the distribution about the means.

2. Where no relevant history is available, the promise must take the form of a level of performance, usually a mean. Here the distribution about the mean should also be indicated. Control of the solution as a whole, then, should consist of periodic tests to determine if the solution's actual performance meets the promise; that is, if it can be assumed to come from the promised distribution. Note that this is control over actual performance per period rather than the performance predicted from the model by using the solution's values of the controlled variables. It is desirable, therefore, to run simultaneously a control on the prediction errors. This can be used in two ways. First, if a systematic bias in the predictions appears, it can be corrected by adding an unbiased term to the model, or preferably the cause of the bias

can be determined and the model can be appropriately corrected. Improvement of the model is also required if the variance of the prediction errors is large. Modifications of the model to reduce variance may be required even if actual average performance meets the promises. Second, any nonrandom behavior of the errors of prediction may foreshadow difficulties with actual performance, hence initiate an inquiry that can prevent such difficulties.

If P_t represents the predicted performance for time period t and A_t represents the actual performance, the difference $P_t - A_t$ is a measure of the prediction error. However, because actual performance is likely to vary significantly from period to period, it is usually desirable to express the error of prediction as a fraction of actual performance; that is,

$$\frac{P_t - A_t}{A_t}.$$

Commonly used statistical control procedures and tests for randomness (e.g., sign and run tests and tests for serial correlation and cycling) can be used to analyze both prediction errors and differences between actual and promised performance. It is possible to formulate the design of a control procedure as a decision problem that is capable of being solved in principle. In practice, however, it is seldom possible to obtain an optimal solution to such a problem. Below we examine in more detail the corresponding problem that arises in connection with design of parameter controls.

In selecting or designing a control procedure it should be borne in mind that it may not be possible to determine actual performance without error. Such error may be due either to observation or to sampling. For example, complete counts of physical inventories cannot be taken each month and may have to be taken on a sampling basis. Furthermore, some of the counts may be in error. Appropriate statistical techniques are available for taking such errors into account.

Controlling Parameter Values

Some parameters are constant or are relatively constant over time; for example, the cost of raw material and labor or the price of a product. It is necessary in such cases to set up a procedure in which notice of changes in the values of such parameters comes "automatically" to the solution controllers. The controllers should periodically check the checking procedure itself to make certain that they are receiving the information that is needed as quickly as possible. It is important for the controllers not be become lax and assume that no news is good news; if they do, defective information sources are likely to assume that there no longer is a need for the information that they are supposed to supply.

Parameters that are either statistical in character (e.g., an average value, a percentage, or a probability) or whose value is estimated on the basis of a sample require a more carefully designed control procedure. Such a design involves the following steps:

1. Definition of a "significant" change in the value of the variable; that is, one that justifies a change in the solution.
2. Determination of
    (*a*) the frequency of control checks,
    (*b*) the size and type of sample of observations to be made, and
    (*c*) the type of analysis of the data that should be made (i.e., the test for significance of change and the significance level at which it should be conducted).

Ideally, these design decisions should be made in such a way as to minimize the sum of the following costs:

1. The cost of making the observations.
2. The cost of analyzing the observations.
3. The expected cost of error.

At present we can seldom design an optimal control procedure but must rely on judgment as well as on quantitative analysis. (For a detailed discussion of this design problem, see Ackoff, 1957.)

There is seldom, if ever, an advantage to testing a parameter more frequently than the solution containing it is applied. Because the cost of such a test is usually quite small compared to the expected cost of error, a check should be made before each application of the solution. This may require the collection of data between control checks, of course. Only if the parameter is known to be very stable over time or if the cost of the check is relatively high, should the test be made less frequently than the solution is applied.

Once the frequency of a control check on a parameter's value is determined, it is necessary to design the sampling procedure and to select a test of the hypothesis that a significant change has not occurred. A significant change is one that, if not adjusted for, will produce an expected cost of error that is greater than the cost of adjusting the solution. The cost of adjusting the solution varies from problem to problem, depending on the complexity of the implementation process. In some situations it may involve a modification of one individual's computation; in other situations it may involve costly reprogramming of a complex computerized data processing system. Once this cost of correction, whether large or small, is determined, the magnitude of a significant change of a parameter's value can be found by an appropriate analysis of the model and its solution.

For example, let us return to the "toy" model used in Chapter 14 and 15:

$$U = XY + \frac{1}{X}. \tag{16.1}$$

It will be recalled that the optimal value of X is

$$X^0 = \frac{1}{\sqrt{Y}}; \tag{16.2}$$

hence the optimal minimal value of U is

$$U^0 = 2\sqrt{Y}. \tag{16.3}$$

If an estimate of Y, y, is used, we obtain an estimate of X^0,

$$x^0 = \frac{1}{\sqrt{y}}, \tag{16.4}$$

and an actual performance whose value is

$$u^0 = \frac{1}{\sqrt{y}} Y + \sqrt{y}. \tag{16.5}$$

Therefore, the cost of the error $(y - Y)$ is

$$C(y - Y) = u^0 - U^0 = \frac{Y}{\sqrt{y}} + \sqrt{y} - 2\sqrt{Y}. \tag{16.6}$$

If, for example, Y was equal to 25 during the last period of application of the solution, the optimal value of X was $1/\sqrt{25} = \frac{1}{5}$ and the minimum value of U was $2\sqrt{25} = 10.0$.

Now suppose that we wish to find the range, Y_a to Y_b, within which changes of the value of Y produces expected costs of error that are less than the cost of adjusting the solution, say 0.2. Then we let $y = 25$ and substitute in equation (16.6),

$$C(25 - Y) = \frac{Y}{5} + 5 - 2\sqrt{Y} = 0.2.$$

Therefore,

$$Y - 10\sqrt{Y} + 24 = 0.$$

and

$$(\sqrt{Y} - 6)(\sqrt{Y} - 4) = 0$$

$$Y_b = 36$$

$$Y_a = 16.$$

If the value of Y lies between 16 and 36, the cost of changing the solution is greater than the improvement in performance. The asymmetry of the range is due to the asymmetry of U as a function X.

Now consider a model and its solution involving two parameters:

$$U = XY_1 + \frac{Y_2}{X}, \tag{16.7}$$

for which the solution is

$$X^0 = \frac{\sqrt{Y_2}}{\sqrt{Y_1}} \tag{16.8}$$

TABLE 16.1

Y_1	Y_{2a}	Y_{2b}
1	−2.25	0.25
4	0	4.00
9	0.25	6.25
16	1.00	9.00
25	2.25	12.25
36	4.00	16.00

and the optimal performance is

$$U^0 = \frac{Y_1\sqrt{Y_2}}{\sqrt{Y_1}} + \frac{Y_2}{\sqrt{Y_2/Y_1}} = 2\sqrt{Y_1 Y_2}. \tag{16.9}$$

Now suppose that the cost of changing the solution is 2.0 and that the values of Y_1 and Y_2 in the last period were 8 and 2, respectively. The cost of not changing the solution when these values actually do change is given by

$$Y_1\sqrt{\tfrac{2}{8}} + \frac{Y_2}{\sqrt{\tfrac{2}{8}}} - 2\sqrt{Y_1 Y_2} = 2.0.$$

Now we can set the value of Y_1 and solve for Y_2. There will be two solutions—an upper limit and a lower limit. An example is shown in Table 16.1. These results can be plotted as in Figure 16.1. The control check consists of determining whether the point (Y_1, Y_2) falls in the "Do not adjust" region.

If more than two parameters are involved, there are too many possibilities for precomputation to be feasible. Therefore, in such cases it is usually preferable to determine the effect of any apparent combination of changes when it occurs rather than try to set up criteria of significance in advance.

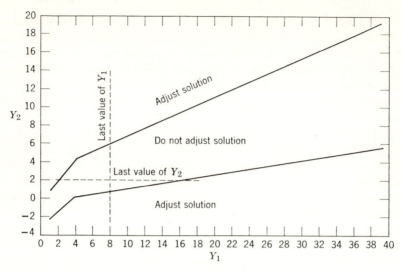

Figure 16.1   Bounds on simultaneous changes of two parameters.

Even if the range of insignificant changes cannot be determined, it is useful to construct statistical control charts—such as are used in quality control—for each parameter. These charts facilitate the perception of trends or other nonrandom fluctuations in a parameter's values.

For example, in a company whose market is divided into 250 areas a procedure was developed for providing monthly forecasts of sales for each area. This forecast was used as an input to a number of marketing decisions. The forecasting procedure was tested retrospectively, so that the distribution of its errors could be estimated. Using this distribution, a control chart was developed for each market area. As soon as monthly sales are known the forecasting errors are calculated and plotted. Whenever a forecasting error for a particular area turns out to be larger or smaller than one would expect to occur by chance, an inquiry is made into the corresponding month's activities in that area. In every such case over several years it has been possible to find an explanation; for example, a special promotion used by one of the company's wholesalers, the opening or closing of a store, or an unusual competitive action. By such analysis the company not only learns a great deal about what affects sales, but also learns the amount by which various changes in marketing effort affect sales; hence its managers can better evaluate alternatives available to them, particularly in the context of changes in competitive behavior. This knowledge has made it possible to enlarge the relevant marketing models and thereby take into account explicitly more controllable and uncontrollable variables.

When a significant change in a parameter's value appears to have occurred, an effort should be made to determine what caused it. Discovery of the cause enables one to determine if the change is permanent or temporary and frequently may reveal another variable that should be included in the model. For example, in a production-control problem involving a pharmaceutical, a control chart on sales per month was tested on past data before use. Three instances appeared in which sales increased abnormally in one month, decreased abnormally in the next month, and then returned to normal. On investigation this sequence turned out to be caused by the announcement of a price increase in one month that was to take place in the next month. Therefore, "price change" was introduced as a nonstatistical parameter in the model, because it could be determined in advance without error once appropriate communications were established.

If the cause of an apparently significant change in a parameter's value cannot be found, close observation of the parameter should be maintained over successive periods to determine whether the change was due to "chance variations" or not.

Most models involve a variety of assumptions. For example, demand may be assumed to be normally distributed or the amount of competitive advertising may be assumed to be relatively constant. Systematic procedures for checking such assumptions should be installed as part of the controls. This obviously requires an explicit formulation of the assumptions involved during the construction of the model.

SUMMARY

The objective of OR is to improve the performance of systems. This cannot be done unless (1) the responsible system managers accept the solution provided by the research, (2) the solution is implemented correctly, and (3) its effectiveness is maintained under changing conditions.

Acceptance of a proposed solution depends on how well the responsible manager understands it and the method by which it was obtained. Such understanding depends, in turn, on how much the manager has participated in the research process. As a minimum, he should review and criticize the work at frequent and regular intervals. The impact that such meetings have on managers is largely dependent on the effectiveness of the researchers' communication with them. Hence participation and effective communication are the keys to acquiring the acceptance of managers and the required cooperation of others who can affect the implementation of the solution.

Implementation should be carefully planned and scheduled. Detailed instructions should be prepared for all who are involved. The instructions must be capable of being understood and followed by those who are expected to do so. Implementation that is attained by use of authority without the presence of sympathetic understanding of why it is being carried out can easily be sabotaged. Cooperation yields better implementation than does compulsion. It should be sought as early in the research as possible, so that those who must implement results or are affected by them know that their interests have been taken into account and can feel partly responsible for, and identify with, the solution. Such awareness comes only from a deep understanding of the system and the model, and the ways in which the model's representation of the system is distorted or simplified. The significance of the distortion or simplification should be evaluated repeatedly. Repeated evaluation of these distortions and simplifications is an essential part of controlling the solution that is eventually attained.

Because the system and its environment usually change frequently, control of the solution is necessary to assure a continuing high level of performance. These changes should be detected and, when necessary, the solution should be appropriately adjusted for them. Effective controls not only make possible, but often lead to, better understanding of the dynamics of the system. This in turn can lead to improvements in the model and the solution derived from it. The design of effective controls requires a command of the techniques of mathematical statistics, but this is not enough. An awareness of the implicit (as well as explicit) assumptions underlying the solution is also necessary.

DISCUSSION TOPICS

1. In an OR project directed toward finding a best allocation of human and financial resources of your university or college, what type of advisory group would you set up and whom would you include in it?
2. What are the characteristics that distinguish good from bad class-room sessions and what is the relevance of these to the presentation of research results to a group of managers? Consider in particular the use of visual aids.
3. Consider a long-range transportation plan for a city. What possible technological developments might significantly affect the performance of the plan and how might controls over these be developed? Is there any way in which consumers' utilities for various characteristics of transportation might change over time and how might these affect the plan's performance? How can they be "controlled?"
4. How would you design an experiment to learn how to improve implementation of applied research results?
5. Consider an inventory control system of a supermarket chain. What aspects of this system itself should be controlled and how?
6. How can the measures of performance applied to managers affect their inclination to implement research results? How can such measures be used to encourage such implementation?

Bibliography

Ackoff, R. L., "The Concept and Exercise of Control in Operational Research," *Proceedings of the First International Conference on Operations Research,* 2nd ed., Operations Research Society of America, Baltimore, Md., 1957. 26–43.

———, "Unsuccessful Case Studies and Why," *Operations Research,* **8** (1960), 259–263.

———, and B. H. P. Rivett, *A Manager's Guide to Operations Research,* John Wiley and Sons, New York, 1963.

Churchman, C. W., and P. Ratoosh, "Innovation in Group Behavior," *Proceedings of the Second International Conference on Operational Research,* English Universities Press, London, 1960, pp. 122–128.

Duckworth, W. E., *A Guide to Operational Research,* Methuen and Co., London, 1962.

Duncan, A. J., *Quality Control and Industrial Statistics,* Richard D. Irwin, Chicago, 1952.

Grant, E. L., *Statistical Quality Control,* McGraw-Hill Book Co., New York, 1952.

Juran, J. M. (ed.), *Quality Control Handbook,* McGraw-Hill Book Co., New York, 1946.

Littauer, S. B., "Technological Stability in Industrial Operations," *Transaction of the New York Academy of Science,* Ser. II, 13, No. 2 (1950), 66–72.

Lynn, H. P., Jr., "How to be a Project Leader—Nine Helpful Hints," *Operations Research,* **1** (1954), 90–102.

Old, B. S., "On the Mathematics of Committees, Boards and Panels," *Scientific Monthly,* **63** (1946), 129–134.

Shewhart, W. A., *Statistical Methods from the Viewpoint of Quality Control,* U.S. Dept. of Agriculture, Washington, D.C., 1939.

Tippett, L. H. C., *Technological Applications of Statistics,* John Wiley and Sons, New York, 1950.

CHAPTER 17

Epilogue: Frontiers of Operations Research[1]

INTRODUCTION

In Chapter 1 we made a distinction between strategic and tactical problems and pointed out that most of OR and this book is devoted to the latter. It will be recalled that strategic problems are ones whose solutions (1) have a longer-range effect, (2) involve more of the organization, and (3) are more ends-oriented than are solutions to tactical problems.

Many strategic problems can be decomposed (at least in part) into a set of interacting tactical problems. Such sets, however, seldom consist only of prototype tactical problems. Therefore, in most strategic problems considerable work at the frontiers of OR is required.

Perhaps the most typically strategic problem in any organization is that of long-range planning. We examine this type of problem here and consider the role that OR can play in its solution.

THE NATURE OF PLANNING

Planning has four essential properties. First, *planning is anticipatory decision making:* it requires a time lapse between making decisions and carrying them out. This time lapse must be long enough to permit reconsideration of decisions previously made.

The need to reconsider decisions made in planning arises from its second essential characteristic: *planning involves a system of decisions.* That is, it involves a set of two or more decisions, each of which is dependent on at least one other decision. One decision depends on another if the effect of the first on the system's performance is itself affected by the second decision. Hence planning consists of a set of interacting decisions.

[1] This chapter borrows liberally from an article by R. L. Ackoff, "The Meaning of Strategic Planning," which appeared in *The McKinsey Quarterly*, Summer 1966, pp. 48–61.

Furthermore, the set of decisions required in planning is so large and so complex that it cannot be dealt with all at once. It must therefore be broken into interdependent subgroups of decisions. Hence the need to review previous decisions in light of subsequent ones.

Seen in these terms, budgeting—at least as it is customarily carried out—is not planning at all. This is because the budgeting of each component of the organization is done independently of the budgeting of the other components, all of which are then aggregated into an overall budget. This is not to say that budgeting cannot be a kind of planning, but that it seldom is.

The third essential characteristic of planning is the fact that *it takes place in a dynamic context.* By this we mean that the environment of the system for which planning is done is continuously changing in ways that will affect the very system being planned for, unless appropriate adjustments are made. Hence the system dynamically interacts with its environment.

The fourth and last characteristic of planning derives from the third: *the consequences of doing nothing to the system being planned for are more likely than not to be undesirable.* The reasons why many companies do not engage in long-range planning is that their managers do not really believe that the consequences of doing nothing are undesirable. Lacking long-range plans, managers are obliged to cope with so many short-run crises that they have no time left for the long-range planning that can prevent such crises in the future. Thus nonplanning provides its own rationale.

In short: Planning is anticipatory decision making. The decisions involved in it form a system of interdependent parts. Because this system is too large and complex to be handled all at once, planning must be done in parts, and each part must be evaluated and reevaluated in light of at least one other part. The system being planned for is part of a dynamic environment, which is such that organizational performance is likely to deteriorate unless management intervenes in the process that is taking place inside and outside the organization.

THE CONTENT OF A PLAN

Long-range organizational plans should, but seldom do, contain five parts:

1. Specification of organizational objectives and goals.
2. Specification of operating policies.
3. Determination of resource requirements, how they are to be generated, and how they should be allocated to components of the organization.
4. Design of the organizational structure that is required to carry out the plan.
5. Design of controls over the plan.

These parts cannot, of course, be prepared independently; because planning deals with a system of decisions, each part of a plan is necessarily dependent on at least one other. The order of discussion, therefore, is not the order in which the parts of a plan should be started or completed. Rather, all five parts should be developed simultaneously.

Objectives and Goals

Effective planning obviously requires that objectives and goals (which are objectives to which a desired time for attainment has been attached) be operationally defined, so that the degree of their attainment can be measured. For example, the assertion that the company seeks to attain "leadership in its industry" or "good public relations" means nothing without ways of measuring the degree to which these corporate objectives are attained. A statement of goals should not read like a sermon, as is commonly the case. It should be a set of instructions that provide the means for quantitative self-evaluation.

Among the operationally least-defined goals and objectives are those involving the concept of *profit*. Profit frequently appears to be a figment of the accountant's imagination. A change of accountant or the accounting system can easily create or destroy profits. Therefore, profit is not so much a matter of fact as a matter of policy. It is by *defining* profit, not merely proclaiming its sovereign importance, that a major corporate objective is set. To be "for profit" is no more meaningful than being "for virtue" without spelling out what virtue means. To create an ethic is not to come out for virtue, but to define it so that it can be used as a guide to behavior.

Moreover, if profit is not defined, the consequences can be serious. For example, one large corporation showed an annual operating loss over two decades. Once the shareholders became convinced that this was not a chance event, they installed a new president. In his inaugural address he promised that the company would show a profit in his first year of office, and it did. For that year, no equipment was replaced no matter how bad it was; no maintenance was done except the minimum required to keep the equipment running; telephone calls, travel, and the use of supplies and outside services were cut to the bone. During his second year of office the president began to negotiate a merger in order to avoid bankruptcy.

Obviously, most of us would say that the company's behavior was ridiculous; profits were not calculated correctly, because future costs incurred in that year were not taken into account.

OR can play a major role in avoiding such outcomes by assisting management in correctly formulating its objectives and goals. To see how it can do so, let us consider briefly how profit can be treated.

Profit must be conceptually explored to make explicit all that it embraces. By its nature profit occurs over time, and it is essential to make explicit the points of time at which profits are expected to arise. Unfortunately, there is no simple or universally accepted way of comparing two sets of profits that arise at different points of time. One method is to discount all profits to a fixed point in time; this requires specification of a discount rate. An OR team can help management find a rational basis for selecting a discount rate and can test the sensitivity of a plan to different values of this rate. A simpler method is to consider only those profits that arise over a specified period of time, called the "horizon." This is equivalent to a zero discount during the horizon and a 100 per cent discount thereafter. Still another method is to determine the discount rate at which the present value of income (gains) exactly equals the present value of outgoings (losses). Plans are then compared on the basis of the discount rates so found.

In its most general sense, profit is "gain minus loss." Each of these should be broken down into measurable components. Consider gain first. Gain can be equated to income. Income can be equated to the number of units of goods (or services) sold multiplied by the unit price. The volume can be broken down into various market-share components. For example, the volume of sales of a particular brand of coffee can be equated to

(*a*) total beverage consumption per capita, times
(*b*) the relevant population, times
(*c*) the fraction of total beverage sales that goes to beverages containing caffeine, times
(*d*) the fraction of total caffeine beverage sales that goes to coffee, times
(*e*) the fraction of coffee sales that goes to this brand.

This type of breakdown allows one to see how much growth will come from changes in population and to formulate goals for each of the various "market layers" enumerated. An increase in any of the fractions will produce an increase in this brand's sales. It is necessary, therefore, to be able to determine the impact on volume of this brand's sales of varying amounts of effort allocated to each layer of the market. OR can help to provide estimates of these important response functions.

Such a breakdown of volume should be made for each type of product (or service) that the company has or intends to make available. To do so requires a definition of product lines. Classification of products may not be the same for all functions of the business. For example, two products sold through the same type of retail store may be of the same type from a marketing point of view, but they may be completely different from a manufacturing point of view. Prepackaged cake frostings and cake mixes may be the same from marketing's point of view, because they are sold in the same places and

are related in consumption. They may be considered to be completely different, however, from manufacturing's point of view because of the differences
in their basic ingredients: sugar and flour. It is necessary, therefore, to develop
a classification of products into sets that can be combined to form the "lines"
relevant to each function of the business. How this may be done is shown
schematically in Figure 17.1. Such a procedure yields the smallest number of
sets that can be used for this purpose.

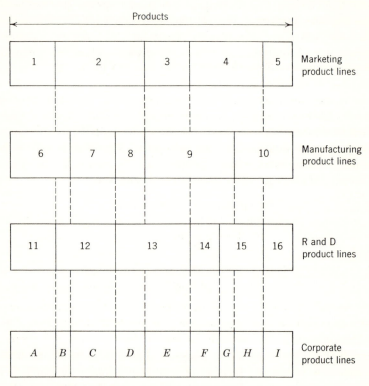

Figure 17.1   Procedure for constructing corporate product lines.

In addition to setting the volume objectives for each existing product line
and specifying from where the volume is to come, it is necessary to specify
how much volume is to come from new products (or services). In so doing,
objectives and goals are set for the research and development department or
for those responsible for acquiring new businesses. Hence "new" volume must
be broken down into that to be developed and that to be acquired. Note that
in so doing the objective "product leadership" is at least partially specified.

The price side of the income equation must also be specified, but to do so rationally requires estimates of how volume responds to price so that once costs are established, profits can be maximized. The dependence of costs on volume and of volume on price are relationships that OR can clarify.

The "loss" side of the profit equations must also be exploded into its various components by year and by product line. Such cost components as fixed labor costs, variable labor costs, costs of facilities, and costs of materials should be taken into account. In setting values of these cost components for the future, one essentially sets the organization's productivity goals. Furthermore, because at least some of the costs reflect turnover of personnel, the setting of them specifies in large part the organization's goals with respect to employee morale.

The cost equations should also contain the cost of money from various sources, hence establish goals for dividend payments to stockholders.

In looking at profit in this way, most, if not all, corporate objectives are taken into account. They are all expressed on a monetary scale, hence the problem of aggregation is eliminated. In effect, this procedure is very similar to that of "cost-benefit" analysis; it differs only in that it is applied to the organization as a whole.

It should be apparent why objectives and goals cannot be completely specified until at least policies have been set and resource requirements and capabilities have been determined.

Operating Policies

In a strategic plan, operating policies need not be established for each sub-unit of the organization; they are better formulated in tactical plans prepared by the subunits themselves. The strategic plan should be concerned only with those policies that involve interactions between the largest components of the organization. The nature of the policies that should be formulated will vary with the nature and structure of the organization.

To establish optimal policies of the sort involved, a model of the organization is required, in which each major subunit and its operations are adequately represented. Such general "planning" models of a firm have not yet been constructed. Models of various components of the firm have been constructed, and these can be bound together in an iterative procedure to approximate a model of the firm. For example, models of a firm's financial, production, and distribution functions have been constructed in many cases. Adequate models of research and development, marketing, and personnel are less common. But even where models of all the components are not available, linking together those that are available reduces the area of uncertainty to which judgment must be applied. The role of OR in developing and connecting these models should be apparent.

In addition to a model of the firm, a model of the firm's environment is also required. The environment can be subdivided into two parts: the consumer and the economy.

An adequate model of the consumer requires understanding of *why* he consumes, as well as where, with whom, when, and so on. Few companies have deep understanding of the nature of their products' consumption. OR can help to provide it. Recall the case of the petroleum company discussed in Chapter 3 in which a study was conducted to determine why drivers of automobiles and trucks select the service stations that they do. The study indicated that the principal reason for selecting a service station was to minimize the time required to obtain the product that was needed, rather than brand preference as is commonly supposed. The consumer cannot perceive the differences between brands of gasoline even where they exist. To assume that he selects on the basis of product characteristics, then, is to assume that he buys on the basis of preferences created by advertising. This gives him much less credit for rationality than he usually demonstrates. In general, in research directed toward understanding why the consumer does what he does, it is better to assume that he is rational (even if this involves assuming that the producer is not) than to assume that he is not.

If the producer understands the consumer's preoccupation with service time, he has a basis for effectively planning his distribution and sales, as well as his product.

Consider another example involving a British vending-machine company whose equipment was installed primarily in factories. It commissioned a study to determine why the English worker insisted on a tea break in the morning and afternoon. It was found that because of the carbohydrate-dominated diet of the British, the blood sugar level (which relates to the energy level) is at a low several hours after a meal. Hence the break provides the energy necessary for effective work. It was shown that productivity was higher and accidents fewer where such breaks were taken. Furthermore, this explained the high rate of sugar consumption during these breaks, usually in the form of "sweets."

Clearly, effective planning also requires a reasonably accurate picture of the future that includes information on all aspects of the economy and society that are relevant to the business. OR has an obvious role in the preparation of such forecasts, but it also has a less obvious role in this area. So much emphasis is placed on the uncertainties of the future that relatively little attention is paid to those aspects of the future that are virtually inevitable. Disclosure of these "inevitabilities" frequently provides a sounder basis for long-range plans than do forecasts of the uncertain aspects of the future.

For example, one analysis has shown that the amount of additional streets and throughways required in most urban areas to maintain the current level of congestion in the future exceeds the financial capabilities of urban governments. It was also shown that, because most urban vehicles carry less than two passengers, a small two-passenger vehicle would increase the capacity of city streets beyond anything that can be obtained by enlarging streets or increasing their number. It seems very likely, therefore, if not inevitable, that urban vehicles will ultimately be considerably reduced in size. Furthermore, analysis of the air-pollution problem in these urban areas indicates that the internal combustion engine will very likely be legislated against in the near-future.

Perception of these "inevitabilities" has led several companies to development projects for urban automobiles of the type implied in the analysis. To the extent that such vehicles become available, the conversion to them will be accelerated; hence such prophesies have a way of being self-fulfilling.

A similar analysis pointed to the inevitable demand for transmitting large amounts of data over wire. This, in turn, has led to major modifications and extensions in our national communication system.

Disclosure of the "inevitable" is not often a simple task; its results are usually obvious only retrospectively. OR can provide a major service to planners by performing the type of analysis required to disclose these relatively certain (relevant) aspects of the future.

Resources: Requirements and Provisions

There are four types of resources: men, machines and plant (i.e., equipment), materials, and money. Therefore financial planning—the only common type of resource planning—does not constitute comprehensive resource planning.

The questions to be answered in this part of the plan are the following. Given the objectives, goals, and operating policies, what resources of each type will be required when, and by whom? How can these resources best be generated, developed, or acquired? If investigation shows that the required resources cannot be made available, the goals or the policies will have to be revised until these parts of the plan balance. Thus there is continuous interaction between setting goals, specifying operating policies, and planning resources.

In resource planning it is obviously necessary to know how the productivity of an organizational unit is affected by the amount of resources made available to it. A continuing research effort is required to provide this kind of information. The type of model developed in the case discussed in Chapter 3 for budgeting R&D is required for each part of the business, and for each of the four types of resource for each function.

By use of a financial model of the firm, one can determine whether the necessary capital is likely to be available when needed. If not, decisions must be made whether to borrow and if so, how. If more capital is going to be generated than appears to be required, effective uses for it should be found. OR has developed and computerized the required type of financial model, so that the monetary implications of different plans and/or futures can be rapidly explored.

In previous chapters we have considered how OR can be used to determine the size or capacity of a facility, its location, when to replace it, and how often to maintain it. Therefore, OR has the required capabilities in this aspect of resource planning.

When materials are supplied by others, it is generally assumed that they will be available in the quantities required. If this future supply is considered to be uncertain or if the price too high, the organization should consider either acquiring or developing the capability of filling its own material requirements, or long-term contracts with external suppliers. OR can assist in evaluating such alternatives.

It is with respect to personnel (or manpower) that OR has been used least in resource planning. Modeling of acquisition, development, promotion, reassignment, and attrition of personnel have been discussed but, to our knowledge, not yet used in corporate planning.

Organizational Structure

By the structure of an organization we mean the way in which the members of an organization are divided into subgroups and assigned tasks; that is, the way in which labor (of all types, including managerial as well as manual) is functionally subdivided.

The importance of structure is illustrated by the following very much simplified example. Imagine a retail establishment whose purchasing department buys a particular product at the beginning of each month in a quantity Q, which this department determines. The purchased items are placed in stock until sold. The sales department sets the price P at which the item is to be sold. The lower the price that it sets, the more it can usually sell. The amount that is actually sold can be predicted within a certain range, but not exactly. Only items in stock can be sold; back orders are not possible.

Suppose that the purchasing department is assigned the objective of minimizing inventory-carrying cost. The sales department is assigned the objective of maximizing gross profit (i.e., the number sold multiplied by markup).

Now, the purchasing department will make pessimistic forecasts of sales and buy only an amount sufficient to meet this level, because if it buys too much inventory, carrying costs increase and the department suffers. The sales department, of course, wants the purchasing department to use an optimistic forecast, because its performance suffers if orders are not filled but not if items are left in stock. When the purchasing department selects an order quantity, Q_1, to meet a pessimistic forecast of sales based on price P_1, the sales department will raise its price to P_2, for which Q_1 is an optimistic purchase. If it does so, the purchasing department will revise Q_1 to a lower level, Q_2, which corresponds to a pessimistic estimate of sales for price P_2, and so on. The limit of this process is reached when nothing is purchased, hence nothing is sold.

This limit will not be reached, because both departments want to keep the company in business. They usually do so by severing communication with each other and predicting what the other will do. The point is that if an organization's structure is defective, it may be hurt if communications are good and the various departmental objectives are being attained.

The emergence in science of an ability to deal with the structural difficulties of organizations derives from recognition of a correspondence between this type of problem and a type of mathematical problem that recently has been receiving much attention. Even with large electronic computers it is frequently impossible to solve certain types of mathematical problems because they are too large or complex. Consequently, mathematicians have been studying ways of breaking such problems into parts, each of which can be solved and assembled in such a way as to give at least an approximate solution to the original problem. This process is called *decomposition*.

In very general terms, every organization's problem or objective is to maximize the difference between its gains and its losses (if we use the terms gain and loss in a very broad sense). The gains and losses of an organization depend on two kinds of things: first, the decisions that it makes which affect the variables that are subject to its *control* (e.g., price, amount produced, and advertising expenditures); and second, what happens to certain *uncontrolled* but relevant variables (e.g., competitive pricing, cost of materials, and general economic conditions). Consequently, if we can express an organization's gains and losses as functions of these variables—which is precisely what OR has developed a capability of doing[2]—we can express an organization's overall objective in mathematical form.

From then on the problem is to find the values of the controlled variables which, under certain conditions specified by the values of the uncontrolled variables, maximize the gains minus the losses. There are three aspects of this problem that merit attention. The first is the defects in the structure of the model itself. All models are at best approximations to reality, but in the models of entire organizations the differences with reality are frequently quite large. It is one thing to know that sales tend to increase as unit price decreases, and another to specify a mathematical expression for this relationship. However, mathematical methods of optimization can lead to a value for the optimal price only when we have a well-defined functional relationship. The

---

[2] See Sengupta and Ackoff (1965).

second aspect of the problem is that mathematical analysis can only handle specified values of the uncontrolled variables (or of the parameters of their distributions). As a consequence, an enormous amount of data must be obtained and processed in order for analysis to yield results of practical value. Finally, even if we have a "good" model and appropriate data, the sheer size of the optimization problem (the number of variables and constraints) may tax the capacity of available computers. To overcome the mathematical problem of computer capacity, the principle of *decomposition* has been developed. Large problems can be broken into parts, each of which contains at least one controlled variable, and when the parts (subproblems) are solved, their solutions can be reassembled. Often it is possible to think of these subproblems as the functional divisions of an organization, but this is not the only reason for functional divisions. If the problem were only one of mathematics and computer capacity, it would be solved by the development of better programming methods and computer technology.

There are three good reasons for functional divisions in organizations. First, despite modern communication systems, data transmission and analysis take time and money. The assembly of all relevant information at one central point may mean that it arrives too late to be of use. Second, we cannot yet reproduce the qualitative "feel" for a problem that the good manager brings to bear on it. No one person can have this "feel" for every aspect of the organization; hence we must permit individuals and divisions to become specialized. Finally, every manager who uses a computer to assist him in his decision making should understand how the computations are made. He neither needs nor should desire to understand the mathematical analysis, but he should insist on much more than a statement of results: an understanding of the logic of their derivation. A manager can have this kind of understanding only in the areas of his own experience and, because his experience is limited, he is much more likely to accept a model decomposed along functional lines.

The ability to obtain optimal decompositions—that is, the best organizational designs—is still restricted to fairly simple organizations, but it is being rapidly extended. For example, in the case of the simple retail establishment used illustratively above, it is possible to formulate the overall organizational objective (i.e., to maximize net profit) in mathematical terms and to break it into parts so that solutions of the parts can be aggregated into a solution of the whole problem. Such a decomposition involves assigning some responsibility for lost sales to the purchasing department and some responsibility for leftover stock to the sales department.

When real organizations are involved, it may not be feasible to restructure them, if such a process involves considerable reshuffling of responsibilities or if the groupings of tasks do not correspond to traditional groupings (e.g., if control of some "purchasing" variables and control of some "research-and-development" variables are placed together). Consequently, some alternative to restructuring an organization is required to solve many, if not most, structural problems. Two such approaches have been developed, each of which works within the existing structure of the organization.

One approach involves the executive's ability to direct each component to use specified values of at least some of the variables not under its control. It attempts to find those values that, if used by each unit in solving its problem, will yield solutions that can be assembled into at least a good approximation to the solution of the overall organizational problem. For example, to return to the retailing situation, what selling price should the executive tell the purchasing department to assume, and what available quantity of items should the sales department be instructed to assume? Again, the ability to answer such questions is rapidly increasing.

The concept of "shadow prices," which is becoming familiar to many managers, emerged from the use of such an approach to structural problems. Shadow prices are prices that one organizational unit is instructed to assume for goods or services received from another organizational unit. These prices may differ considerably from "true" prices.

The other approach involves the executive's ability to set limits on the values of variables within each component's control. It attempts to find those limits that, if used by each unit in solving its problem, will yield solutions that can be assembled into at least a good approximation to the solution of the overall organizational problem. For example, what upper and lower limits should be set on the quantity stocked by the purchasing department and the price set by the sales department? Here, too, ability to answer such questions is rapidly developing.

The three approaches to reduction of structural inefficiency that have been described have only begun to be explored, but they hold great promise of an important service that OR can offer to management in the near-future. But even when this is accomplished, much more will remain to be done.

Specification of the responsibility and measure of performance of each organizational unit is not enough. First, a plan should also provide a classification of the types of decisions required to carry out the organization's tasks. Second, it should indicate who, or what position, is to have authority for each type of decision. If more than one person is involved, the plan should specify how decisions are to be reached by the group—that is, whether any given participant's approval is necessary or sufficient (or both) for accepting or rejecting any proposal. Third, the plan should specify who is responsible for carrying out each type of decision. Fourth and last, it should contain the design of an information system that will enable these decisions to be made and implemented effectively. We shall return to this last requirement below.

Clearly, in many cases each decision cannot be considered separately; therefore, it is necessary to classify decisions in some way. In a five-year plan prepared for the Lamp Division of the General Electric Company, management decisions were classified as follows: (1) matters affecting the status and salaries of managers; (2) matters affecting the organization and operations of an operating unit; (3) matters affecting the organization and operations of a coordinating unit; (4) matters affecting the interaction of operating and coordinating units; and (5) matters affecting products in such a way as to involve more than one operating unit.

These decisions were further subclassified by (a) the amount of money involved, (b) the number of organizational units affected, (c) the duration of the effect, and (d) the reversibility of the decision.

In assigning authority and responsibility to individuals and groups, the optimal size of operating units in each function, the optimal number of units to be placed under one manager, and the optimal way to group units (geography, function, or product) all have to be determined. The information that is needed to perform this task is best provided in the analysis required for the design of the supporting management information system.

Management Information Systems.   Preoccupation with such systems has become widespread. It has approached the proportions of a fad. Much of it is misdirected by an overenthusiasm for the computer and new input and output devices. Some feel that if enough raw data are stored in a bank and if management can draw from it the answer to any question that it wants, "on line" and in "real time," the managerial millennium will have been reached. The claims to date far exceed the accomplishments.

Much of the current effort is misdirected, because it is based on three false assumptions. First, it assumes that management suffers more from lack of relevant information than from an excess of irrelevant information. Even a cursory examination of most manager's information load will show that this assumption is false; most managers suffer from an information overload. As a consequence, they cannot cope with all that is made available to them; hence they develop procedures that are less information-dependent. Adding more information to the already large pile will not help, but will only discourage further efforts to cope with it.

In order for management to use information more effectively, it must receive less than it does currently, and what it does receive must be relevant and timely. Hence the critical need is not so much to generate, store, and retrieve information not now available, but to *filter* (i.e., evaluate) useless information and *condense* what is useful. Therefore, filtration and condensation of information should be a major concern of information-system designers. As yet this has not been the case.

Second, current design practices are based on the assumption that if a manager has the information that he wants when he wants it, his decision making will necessarily be improved. Although this may be so in some cases, it clearly will not be in many, if not most, cases. In this book we have considered a number of relatively simple management problems in which, even if all the necessary information is available, it is still very difficult to find a good solution. For many decisions, then, information is not enough; *instruction* on how to make decisions is also required.

Finally, most information-system designers assume that if communication between managers were improved, organizational performance would also improve. In our discussion of organizational structure, and in the case of the department store in particular, we have already seen that good communication can produce bad performance if the structure of the organization is deficient.

These false assumptions arise not only from excessive enthusiasm for a new technology but also because of a failure to understand that an information system is only a subsystem; it must be imbedded in a *control* system. The one should not be developed without the other. The kinds of information systems required by management can only be designed by managers, systems analysts, and operations researchers working together.

The design of a management information system should be based on an understanding of the decision system that it must serve. Analysis should begin by identifying each type of decision that is required and the interdependence of these decisions. Such an analysis should produce a flow chart of decisions in which the interdependencies are clearly shown.

Next, each decision should be analyzed to determine what information is required to make the decision effectively. Such analysis requires the skills of operations researchers. Even decisions that cannot be optimized can usually be modeled well enough to indicate what their informational requirements are. One cannot find the answers by asking those who make the decisions. To do so is to run the risk of mechanizing many of the errors inherent in the current system, and frequently to add to them.

Only after these steps have been performed should the systems designers consider where the necessary information should be generated and how it should be transmitted, stored, treated, and retrieved. In current practice this step usually comes first, the first two steps being replaced by convenient assumptions wherever necessary.

Finally, it must be recognized that any information system, no matter how well designed, will have many deficiencies. Therefore, it is necessary to design into it a capability for evaluating its own performance and for correcting itself where necessary. This *control* of the information system may, and usually does, require the participation of managers and operations researchers. Managers should never be permitted to use an information system whose performance they are not capable of evaluating. If they do so, they have abdicated one of their major responsibilities to the information technician, who is not equipped to handle such responsibility effectively.

CONTROLS

The most essential assumption in any planning process is that much of the plan will turn out to be wrong. Therefore, provisions must be made for detecting errors and inefficiencies and for correcting the plan accordingly. A plan must provide for its own continuous improvement.

Recently one of the authors took part in a local television discussion, which dealt with the impact of technology on urban planning. In the course of the discussion the moderator displayed a sketch of a proposed city of tomorrow, in which only pedestrian traffic was on the surface, public transport and automobiles being restricted to two lower levels. The moderator was quite enthusiastic about this concept, but the discussants were not. We pointed out that every transportation plan is full of errors, many of which must be corrected after the plan is in operation. Most expressways, turnpikes, and so on, require constant modification once they are in operation. In the concept of a future city that the moderator showed us, the transportation network was structurally integrated with buildings, so that if any change in a road were required, buildings would have to be torn down or drastically modified. The cost of so doing, we pointed out, would reduce our ability to make changes, and force us to live with our planning errors rather than correct them.

A plan should provide a procedure for determining where it is failing and why, and provisions for correcting itself on the basis of this analysis. To accomplish this, a *control system* is required. Such a system in turn requires an organizational unit charged with the control responsibility and so placed in the organization's structure that it has access to the decision makers and the information required to carry out its function. Such a unit must be directly responsible to those managers who accept or reject the plan itself and therefore have the authority to modify it in operation.

A control system not only makes it possible to correct for errors, but also to respond to unforeseeable changes in conditions such as technological breakthroughs, international conflicts, shifts in the economy, or modification of the laws under which the organization must operate. It is always possible to predict with absolute certainty that the unpredictable will occur—and that this will require responsiveness of the organization if it is to pursue its objectives effectively under changing conditions. Lack of responsiveness to change is the best indicator of the need for planning in an organization.

PATTERNS OF PLANNING

Most plans, of course, do not contain all five of the elements that we have specified (i.e., objectives and goals, policies, resources, organizational structure, and controls). There is a wide divergence between the principles and practice of planning. By examining the patterns of planning that one can observe in practice and comparing them with the concept of planning developed here, it is possible to suggest some ways in which current planning practices can be improved, even with the underdeveloped technological capabilities available to us. We shall discuss three of these patterns: (1) *satisficing*, (2) *optimizing*, and (3)—if you will forgive an awkward attempt to fill a gap in our language—*adaptivizing*.

Satisficing

Most current planning is of this type. In it the planning process begins with the setting of goals that are believed (although seldom demonstrated) to be both feasible and desirable. Attribution of these properties to the goals is usually based on consensus among the planners. Once these goals are set— and they are usually set independently of other aspects of planning—operating policies are sought that are believed to be likely to attain the goals and are acceptable to management and to the people who must carry them out.

Feasibility in this context usually implies (1) no significant departure from current policies and practices, (2) at most, moderate increases in resource requirements, (3) no significant changes in the organization's structure (because this usually meets with opposition), and (4) little or no provision for possible errors or changes from expectations; hence little concern with controls.

Such planning concentrates almost exclusively on obtaining a feasible set of operating policies. It seldom formulates, let alone considers, alternative sets of such policies.

Satisficing is usually defended with the argument that it is better to produce a feasible plan that is not optimal than an optimal plan that is not feasible. This argument is only superficially compelling. Reflection reveals that it overlooks the possibility of obtaining the best feasible plan. Optimality can (and should) be defined so as to take feasibility into account,[3] and the effort to do so forces us to examine the criteria of feasibility that are seldom made explicit in the satisficing process. Furthermore, the approximate attainment of an optimal plan may be more desirable than exact attainment of an inferior one.

Not surprisingly, this type of planning seldom produces a significant break with the past. It usually produces a comfortable continuation of most current policies, practices, and aspects of the organization's structure, correcting only obvious deficiencies. Satisficing, because it often appears to be more concerned with justifying or correcting the past than with affecting the future, appeals to organizations that place great emphasis on survival and little on growth and development. It appeals to planners who are not willing to stick their necks out.

[3] See Anderson (1966) who has done so.

Optimizing

In this type of planning, the setting of goals and the selection of operating policies interact with one another; an effort is made *not* to do only well enough, but to do as well as possible. Resource requirements and means of generating and allocating resources are taken into account.

The optimizing approach to planning is largely a product of operations research. It calls for development of mathematical models of the system being planned for—models that can be analyzed or simulated to determine the effect of different policies and resource allocations on organizational performance.

As indicated above, however, we have not yet learned how to construct models of the firm that are both convenient to manipulate and sufficiently detailed to yield optimal overall plans. Hence multiple models, each representing a part of the system, are normally constructed and made to interact with one another so as to obtain approximately optimal solutions to planning problems.

Because the construction, validation, and use of these models usually require considerable research effort by experienced professional operations researchers, optimization planning is more time-consuming and costly than is the satisficing variety. This, together with the fright produced by the use of mathematical and scientific techniques, is enough to keep many managers away from such an approach to planning.

Efforts, even unsuccessful ones, to develop truly optimal plans almost always produce a valuable by-product out of the model building and model manipulation: the researchers gain a deeper understanding of the system being planned for. Unfortunately, they do not always succeed in communicating this understanding to the managers involved. This failure is often as much the fault of the managers as it is of the researchers; no amount of communication skills can bridge the gap of mutual distrust.

Now let us look at the negative side of the optimization pattern of planning. First, organizational structure is seldom explicitly treated in such planning, because the capability of doing so, as we saw, is only beginning to emerge. Therefore, attempts to optimize structure currently require extensive use of qualitative judgments. Too many optimization-oriented researchers prefer to avoid such judgments; hence they omit this essential part of planning.

Second, consider how optimization techniques are used to handle the problem of control. These techniques can take into account only those uncertainties concerning the future that can be identified beforehand. Through optimization, furthermore, we can develop a control unit or monitor to be *added to the system* to deal with these predictable uncertainties, but we cannot provide a control unit that is *built into the system*, leading to increased self-control of the units already in the system. This distinction and its significance is not easy to define or grasp. Let us try to clarify it by considering a third approach to planning, which attempts to correct this deficiency of the optimization approach to planning. The third approach is not prevalent in current practice. It is an aspiration that is yet to be realized.

Adaptivizing

The need for control arises not only out of our inability to forecast the future without error, or even our inability to conceive of all possible future states; it arises out of variations in the present. Demand for a product, for example, changes daily; so do the flow of money in and out of a company, delivery times of raw materials, and so on. To plan only for the "average" (or any other single value) of a variable activity is to invite crises, breakdowns, and poor use of facilities; imagine the performance of a highway that is designed only to accommodate its average load. Therefore, it is desirable to plan organizations and operations so that they can not only *adapt* to major changes in the future but also *adjust* themselves to short-run fluctuations in the demands that are made on them. Controls, as they are usually conceived in organizational planning, are directed toward adapting to large, permanent changes in the environment and the system involved, not to the short-range variations. Consider what is necessary to take care of such variations.

First, we obviously require flexibility of plant and equipment. For example, the direction of traffic flow in the third Lincoln Tunnel connecting New Jersey and New York City can be reversed depending on the change in demand from morning to evening. The same can be done on two center lanes of the expressway in Chicago. Such flexibility can be planned for, frequently with considerable economies to the organization. Three tunnels, one of which is reversible, can carry the same load as four, given the asymmetry of automobile traffic into New York from morning to night. Ideally, we would like to have facilities that expand or contract with use. This is possible to some extent. But because it is never completely possible, use of facilities should itself be subjected to some control.

There are two approaches to control. One attempts to stabilize demands made on a system over the long run, the other over the short run.

Consider the long-run orientation first. Recall the manufacturer of machine tools discussed in Chapter 3 whose demand was subject to large fluctuations in successive years. The company looked for another highly cyclical product line, involving the same technology, whose variations in demand ran counter to those of machine tools. It found such a class of products in highway construction equipment and entered the business. By so doing it reduced the variations of annual production loads to only a fraction of what they had been previously.

In another example used in Chapter 3 we showed how a company reduced the uncertainties arising from small orders that were often unprofitable by developing an incentive scheme for its sales force. It was profit-oriented rather than volume-oriented; it paid no commission on sales of unprofitable items and higher commissions than before on the profitable ones. This scheme drastically reduced the sale of unprofitable items and significantly increased those of profitable items.

The principle involved in this last type of control is one of the most important in adaptive planning, because it provides an effective way of handling short-range, as well as long-range, variations in the system. It involves motivating participants in the system to act in a way that is compatible with the interests of the organization as a whole, and it does this by providing incentives that make individual and organizational interests more compatible.

Consider this principle in the realm of traffic control and how it might be used to induce people to use transportation facilities in such a way as to serve their own and their community's interests more effectively. First, the tolls across bridges, tunnels, and turnpikes, at least during periods of heavy demand, could be made inversely proportional to the number of passengers in a car. More specifically, tolls would be based on the number of empty seats in an automobile. Thus a two-seat car with two passengers would have a lower toll than a six-seater with two, three, four, or five passengers. This would encourage use of smaller cars as well as better occupancy of all cars.

Second, tolls might be varied with demand. The heavier the demand for a facility, the higher the charges would be. Thus charges would be increased during peak hours and decreased during off-hours. The increasing use of helicopters to survey city street congestion and to provide reports of it on the radio is an effort to produce a better distribution of traffic over facilities, but it is relatively inefficient compared to what might be done.

Adaptive planning, then, should not only build into the system controls that protect against major and relatively stable changes in it and its environment; it should also build adaptiveness into the components of the system, so that short-run variations can be either more adequately handled or reduced.

If a completely adaptive system could be designed, it would require no planning. To the extent that adaptive planning succeeds, therefore, the need for planning is reduced. The ultimate ideal of the adaptive planner is a system for which planning is no longer necessary.

CONCLUSION

In this chapter we have considered what OR is not doing sufficiently, or not sufficiently well: contributing to strategic decision making, in particular to long-range organizational planning. We have indicated how it can contribute more effectively to such decision making even with its currently limited capabilities and where development of greater capabilities is needed.

When greater capabilities are developed, OR will be able to deal with organizations in their entirety, rather than merely with slices through them. Managers who currently have to treat the whole with only intuition and experience as their guides, will then have the methods of science at their disposal as well.

Bibliography

Anderson, Jacqueline, *Operations Research and Long-Range Planning*, Ph.D. Thesis in Operations Research, Case Institute of Technology, Cleveland, Ohio, 1966.

Ansoff, I. H., *Corporate Strategy: An Analytical Approach to Business Policy for Growth and Expansion*, McGraw-Hill Book Co., New York, 1965.

Branch, M. C., *Planning: Aspects and Applications*, John Wiley and Sons, New York, 1966.

Emery, J. C., *Organizational Planning and Control: Theory and Technology*, Ph.D. Thesis in Industrial Management, M.I.T., Cambridge, Mass., 1965.

Harris, Britton, "The City of the Future: The Problem of Optimal Design," paper presented at the 13th U.S. Annual Meeting, Regional Science Association, November 4–6, 1966, St. Louis, Mo.

———, "Inventing the Future Metropolis," Catherine Bauer Wurster Memorial Public Lecture Series, Harvard Graduate School of Design and M.I.T., Cambridge, Mass., May 12, 1966.

———, and R. L. Ackoff, "Strategies for Operations Research in Urban Metropolitan Planning," paper presented at the Fourth International Conference on Operational Research, International Federation of Operational Research Societies, Boston, Mass., 1966.

McDonough, A. M., *Information Economics and Management Systems*, Prentice-Hall, Englewood Cliffs, N.J., 1963.

Malcolm, D. G., and A. J. Rowe (eds.), *Management Control Systems*, John Wiley and Sons, New York, 1960.

Miller, S. S., *The Management of Diversification*, John Wiley and Sons, New York, 1963.

Optner, S. L., *Systems Analysis for Business Management*, Prentice-Hall, Englewood Cliffs, N.J., 1960.

Sengupta, S. S., and R. L. Ackoff, "Systems Theory from an Operations Research Point of View," *IREE Transactions on Systems Science and Cybernetics*, November (1965), 9–13.

Warren, E. K., *Long-Range Planning: The Executive Viewpoint*, Prentice-Hall, Englewood Cliffs, N.J., 1966.

Author Index

Ackoff, 20, 21, 51, 52, 53, 55, 56, 57, 58, 59, 93, 327, 355, 360, 382, 383, 388, 390, 392, 394, 396, 407, 408, 411, 421, 427, 428, 437, 447
Akers, S. B., 302
Alchian, A. A., 228
Anderson, Jacqueline, 443, 447
Anderson, R. L., 118
Ansoff, I. H., 447
Aris, R., 247
Arnoff, E. L., 21, 173
Arnold, H. J., 106
Arrow, K. J., 57, 203

Barlow, R. E., 228
Batchelor, J. H., 20
Bazovsky, J., 228
Beach, E. F., 93
Beer, Stafford, 18, 21, 93
Bellman, Richard, 230, 247, 278, 281, 302
Bennis, W. G., 18
Bentham, Jeremy, 49
Bevan, R. W., 21
Blake, K. R., 302
Bock, F., 322
Bohr, N., 60
Bowman, E. H., 203, 282
Box, G. E. P., 115, 118
Branch, M. C., 447
Brooks, S., 119
Brown, R. G., 194, 203
Buchan, J., 203
Bucher, B. D., 106
Burman, J. P., 119
Butler, J. W., 100

Camp, G. D., 21, 93

Campbell, N. R., 408
Chambers, J. C., 359, 382, 408
Chapanis, A., 21
Charnes, A., 173
Chernoff, H., 58, 86, 93, 355, 382, 408
Cherry, Colin, 18, 21
Chung, An-min, 173
Churchman, C. W., 21, 44, 51, 52, 55, 56, 58, 392, 408, 410, 427
Clark, C. E., 303
Clark, D. F., 359, 382, 388, 408
Cochran, W. G., 114, 118, 119, 385, 394, 407, 408
Cohen, K. S., 109, 110, 118, 119
Conway, R. W., 283
Coombs, C. H., 58
Cooper, W. W., 173
Coppinger, J. M., 22
Cox, D. R., 228, 274
Cox, G. M., 114, 118, 119, 385, 407, 408
Croes, G. A., 322
Crowther, J. G., 21

Dalleck, W. C., 203
Dantzig, G., 173, 322
Darwin, C., 392, 408
Davies, O. J., 119
Davis, R. L., 58, 59
Dean, B. V., 228
Dean, J., 228
Deemer, W. L., Jr., 109, 110, 111, 118, 120
Deming, W. E., 394, 408
Dorfman, Robert, 21, 173
Dresher, M., 350
Dreyfus, S., 247
Duckworth, W. E., 21, 411, 427
Duncan, A. J., 419, 427

449

Subject Index